T0207498

Lecture Notes in Computer Science 14044

Founding Editors

Gerhard Goos
Juris Hartmanis

The series Lecture Notes in Computer Science (LNCS), including its subseries Lecture Notes in Artificial Intelligence (LNAI) and Lecture Notes in Bioinformatics (LNBI), has established itself as a medium for the publication of new developments in computer science and information technology research, teaching, and education.

LNCS enjoys close cooperation with the computer science R & D community, the series counts many renowned academics among its volume editors and paper authors, and collaborates with prestigious societies. Its mission is to serve this international community by providing an invaluable service, mainly focused on the publication of conference and workshop proceedings and postproceedings. LNCS commenced publication in 1973.

Robert A. Sottilare · Jessica Schwarz
Editors

Adaptive Instructional Systems

5th International Conference, AIS 2023
Held as Part of the 25th HCI International Conference, HCII 2023
Copenhagen, Denmark, July 23–28, 2023
Proceedings

Editors
Robert A. Sottilare
Soar Technology, Inc.
Orlando, FL, USA

Jessica Schwarz
Fraunhofer FKIE
Wachtberg, Germany

ISSN 0302-9743   ISSN 1611-3349 (electronic)
Lecture Notes in Computer Science
ISBN 978-3-031-34734-4   ISBN 978-3-031-34735-1 (eBook)
https://doi.org/10.1007/978-3-031-34735-1

Foreword

Human-computer interaction (HCI) is acquiring an ever-increasing scientific and industrial importance, as well as having more impact on people's everyday lives, as an ever-growing number of human activities are progressively moving from the physical to the digital world. This process, which has been ongoing for some time now, was further accelerated during the acute period of the COVID-19 pandemic. The HCI International (HCII) conference series, held annually, aims to respond to the compelling need to advance the exchange of knowledge and research and development efforts on the human aspects of design and use of computing systems.

The 25th International Conference on Human-Computer Interaction, HCI International 2023 (HCII 2023), was held in the emerging post-pandemic era as a 'hybrid' event at the AC Bella Sky Hotel and Bella Center, Copenhagen, Denmark, during July 23–28, 2023. It incorporated the 21 thematic areas and affiliated conferences listed below.

A total of 7472 individuals from academia, research institutes, industry, and government agencies from 85 countries submitted contributions, and 1578 papers and 396 posters were included in the volumes of the proceedings that were published just before the start of the conference, these are listed below. The contributions thoroughly cover the entire field of human-computer interaction, addressing major advances in knowledge and effective use of computers in a variety of application areas. These papers provide academics, researchers, engineers, scientists, practitioners and students with state-of-the-art information on the most recent advances in HCI.

The HCI International (HCII) conference also offers the option of presenting 'Late Breaking Work', and this applies both for papers and posters, with corresponding volumes of proceedings that will be published after the conference. Full papers will be included in the 'HCII 2023 - Late Breaking Work - Papers' volumes of the proceedings to be published in the Springer LNCS series, while 'Poster Extended Abstracts' will be included as short research papers in the 'HCII 2023 - Late Breaking Work - Posters' volumes to be published in the Springer CCIS series.

I would like to thank the Program Board Chairs and the members of the Program Boards of all thematic areas and affiliated conferences for their contribution towards the high scientific quality and overall success of the HCI International 2023 conference. Their manifold support in terms of paper reviewing (single-blind review process, with a minimum of two reviews per submission), session organization and their willingness to act as goodwill ambassadors for the conference is most highly appreciated.

This conference would not have been possible without the continuous and unwavering support and advice of Gavriel Salvendy, founder, General Chair Emeritus, and Scientific Advisor. For his outstanding efforts, I would like to express my sincere appreciation to Abbas Moallem, Communications Chair and Editor of HCI International News.

July 2023   Constantine Stephanidis

HCI International 2023 Thematic Areas and Affiliated Conferences

Thematic Areas

- HCI: Human-Computer Interaction
- HIMI: Human Interface and the Management of Information

Affiliated Conferences

- EPCE: 20th International Conference on Engineering Psychology and Cognitive Ergonomics
- AC: 17th International Conference on Augmented Cognition
- UAHCI: 17th International Conference on Universal Access in Human-Computer Interaction
- CCD: 15th International Conference on Cross-Cultural Design
- SCSM: 15th International Conference on Social Computing and Social Media
- VAMR: 15th International Conference on Virtual, Augmented and Mixed Reality
- DHM: 14th International Conference on Digital Human Modeling and Applications in Health, Safety, Ergonomics and Risk Management
- DUXU: 12th International Conference on Design, User Experience and Usability
- C&C: 11th International Conference on Culture and Computing
- DAPI: 11th International Conference on Distributed, Ambient and Pervasive Interactions
- HCIBGO: 10th International Conference on HCI in Business, Government and Organizations
- LCT: 10th International Conference on Learning and Collaboration Technologies
- ITAP: 9th International Conference on Human Aspects of IT for the Aged Population
- AIS: 5th International Conference on Adaptive Instructional Systems
- HCI-CPT: 5th International Conference on HCI for Cybersecurity, Privacy and Trust
- HCI-Games: 5th International Conference on HCI in Games
- MobiTAS: 5th International Conference on HCI in Mobility, Transport and Automotive Systems
- AI-HCI: 4th International Conference on Artificial Intelligence in HCI
- MOBILE: 4th International Conference on Design, Operation and Evaluation of Mobile Communications

List of Conference Proceedings Volumes Appearing Before the Conference

1. LNCS 14011, Human-Computer Interaction: Part I, edited by Masaaki Kurosu and Ayako Hashizume
2. LNCS 14012, Human-Computer Interaction: Part II, edited by Masaaki Kurosu and Ayako Hashizume
3. LNCS 14013, Human-Computer Interaction: Part III, edited by Masaaki Kurosu and Ayako Hashizume
4. LNCS 14014, Human-Computer Interaction: Part IV, edited by Masaaki Kurosu and Ayako Hashizume
5. LNCS 14015, Human Interface and the Management of Information: Part I, edited by Hirohiko Mori and Yumi Asahi
6. LNCS 14016, Human Interface and the Management of Information: Part II, edited by Hirohiko Mori and Yumi Asahi
7. LNAI 14017, Engineering Psychology and Cognitive Ergonomics: Part I, edited by Don Harris and Wen-Chin Li
8. LNAI 14018, Engineering Psychology and Cognitive Ergonomics: Part II, edited by Don Harris and Wen-Chin Li
9. LNAI 14019, Augmented Cognition, edited by Dylan D. Schmorrow and Cali M. Fidopiastis
10. LNCS 14020, Universal Access in Human-Computer Interaction: Part I, edited by Margherita Antona and Constantine Stephanidis
11. LNCS 14021, Universal Access in Human-Computer Interaction: Part II, edited by Margherita Antona and Constantine Stephanidis
12. LNCS 14022, Cross-Cultural Design: Part I, edited by Pei-Luen Patrick Rau
13. LNCS 14023, Cross-Cultural Design: Part II, edited by Pei-Luen Patrick Rau
14. LNCS 14024, Cross-Cultural Design: Part III, edited by Pei-Luen Patrick Rau
15. LNCS 14025, Social Computing and Social Media: Part I, edited by Adela Coman and Simona Vasilache
16. LNCS 14026, Social Computing and Social Media: Part II, edited by Adela Coman and Simona Vasilache
17. LNCS 14027, Virtual, Augmented and Mixed Reality, edited by Jessie Y. C. Chen and Gino Fragomeni
18. LNCS 14028, Digital Human Modeling and Applications in Health, Safety, Ergonomics and Risk Management: Part I, edited by Vincent G. Duffy
19. LNCS 14029, Digital Human Modeling and Applications in Health, Safety, Ergonomics and Risk Management: Part II, edited by Vincent G. Duffy
20. LNCS 14030, Design, User Experience, and Usability: Part I, edited by Aaron Marcus, Elizabeth Rosenzweig and Marcelo Soares
21. LNCS 14031, Design, User Experience, and Usability: Part II, edited by Aaron Marcus, Elizabeth Rosenzweig and Marcelo Soares

47. CCIS 1836, HCI International 2023 Posters - Part V, edited by Constantine Stephanidis, Margherita Antona, Stavroula Ntoa and Gavriel Salvendy

https://2023.hci.international/proceedings

Preface

The goal of the Adaptive Instructional Systems (AIS) Conference, affiliated to the HCI International Conference, is to understand the theory and enhance the state of practice for a set of technologies (tools and methods) called adaptive instructional systems (AIS). AIS are defined as artificially intelligent, computer-based systems that guide learning experiences by tailoring instruction and recommendations based on the goals, needs, preferences, and interests of each individual learner or team in the context of domain learning objectives. The interaction between individual learners or teams of learners and AIS technologies is a central theme of this conference. AIS observe user behaviors to assess progress toward learning objectives and then act on learners and their learning environments (e.g., problem sets or scenario-based simulations) with the goal of optimizing learning, performance, retention, and transfer of learning to work environments.

The 5th International Conference on Adaptive Instructional Systems (AIS 2023) encouraged papers from academics, researchers, industry, and professionals, on a broad range of theoretical and applied issues related to AIS and their applications. The focus of this conference on instructional tailoring of learning experiences highlights the importance of accurately modeling learners to accelerate their learning, boost the effectiveness of AIS-based experiences, and to precisely reflect their long-term competence in a variety of domains of instruction.

The content for AIS 2023 centered on design processes and aspects, individual learner differences, and applications of AISs. More specifically, several works focused on Human-Centered Design, examining facets such as personality traits, improved self-awareness, human performance, learner engagement, trust and acceptance of AISs, as well as the establishment of communities of practice. In addition, a number of papers focused on design strategies and guidelines, discussing topics such as cognitive simulations, gamification, and design based on data intelligence and learner analytics. In the area of individual differences in adaptive learning, contributions elaborated on competency-based training, learner control, knowledge states of learners, stress and coping with task difficulty, as well as identifying individual differences as a predictor of usage of AISs. Finally, a selected number of papers focused on applications of AISs demonstrating issues of high practical value across different domains, such as math courses, architecture and design, simulation-based training, and content improvement services.

One volume of the HCII 2023 proceedings is dedicated to this year's edition of the AIS Conference and focuses on topics related to Human-Centered Design for learner acceptance, engagement, and performance; design strategies and guidelines for Adaptive Instructional Systems; individual differences in Adaptive Learning; and applications of Adaptive Instructional Systems.

Papers of this volume are included for publication after a minimum of two single–blind reviews from the members of the AIS Program Board or, in some cases, from members of the Program Boards of other affiliated conferences. We would like to thank all of them for their invaluable contribution, support and efforts.

July 2023

Robert A. Sottilare
Jessica Schwarz

5th International Conference on Adaptive Instructional Systems (AIS 2023)

Program Board Chairs: **Robert A. Sottilare,** *Soar Technology, Inc., USA* and **Jessica Schwarz,** *Fraunhofer FKIE, Germany*

Program Board:

- Benjamin Bell, *Eduworks Corporation, USA*
- Shelly Blake-Plock, *Yet Analytics, Inc., USA*
- Bruno Emond, *National Research Council Canada, Canada*
- Ani Grubišić, *University of Split, Croatia*
- Cheryl I. Johnson, *Quantum Improvements Consulting, USA*
- Maria Mercedes T. Rodrigo, *Ateneo de Manila University, The Philippines*
- Alexander Streicher, *Fraunhofer IOSB, Germany*
- Rachel Van Campenhout, *VitalSource, USA*
- Thomas Witte, *Fraunhofer FKIE, Germany*

The full list with the Program Board Chairs and the members of the Program Boards of all thematic areas and affiliated conferences of HCII2023 is available online at:

http://www.hci.international/board-members-2023.php

HCI International 2024 Conference

The 26th International Conference on Human-Computer Interaction, HCI International 2024, will be held jointly with the affiliated conferences at the Washington Hilton Hotel, Washington, DC, USA, June 29 – July 4, 2024. It will cover a broad spectrum of themes related to Human-Computer Interaction, including theoretical issues, methods, tools, processes, and case studies in HCI design, as well as novel interaction techniques, interfaces, and applications. The proceedings will be published by Springer. More information will be made available on the conference website: http://2024.hci.international/.

General Chair
Prof. Constantine Stephanidis
University of Crete and ICS-FORTH
Heraklion, Crete, Greece
Email: general_chair@hcii2024.org

https://2024.hci.international/

Contents

Individual Differences in Adaptive Learning

Human-Centered Design for Learner Acceptance, Engagement, and Performance

Improving Students' Self-awareness by Analyzing Course Discussion Forum Data

Arta Farahmand[1]([⊠]), M. Ali Akber Dewan[1], Fuhua Lin[1], and Wu-Yuin Hwang[2]

[1] School of Computing and Information Systems, Faculty of Science and Technology, Athabasca University, Calgary, Canada
afarahmand1@athabasca.edu, {adewan,oscarl}@athabascau.ca
[2] National Central University, Taoyuan City, Taiwan, Republic of China
wyhwang@cc.ncu.edu.tw

Abstract. The growing demand for self-paced online learning (SPOL) courses lead to post-secondary institutions exploring how information technology can be used to improve the quality of SPOL courses by evaluating teaching and learning strategies, methods, activities, and the way students engage with their studies. One of the main barriers in SPOL is that students may feel isolated as they learn in an individualized mode and collaborative learning could be difficult to realize. The isolation may be lessened when students interact in a course discussion forum. To improve students' self-awareness, it is needed to collect and analyze the forum data and visualize students' sentiments to provide feedback to the students. This paper presents a model for sentiment analysis using natural language processing techniques to visualize students' affective states towards the course as a strategy to enhance students' self-awareness. We used the Stanford MOOC Posts dataset, from Stanford University's eleven public online courses to test the proposed model. Finally, the paper presents a method to visualize the insights gained from the analysis in a student-facing intelligent learning dashboard (SF-iLDs) to support students' self-awareness of their sentiment towards the course to encourage adjustments to the level of engagement.

Keywords: Natural language processing · sentiment analysis · self-paced online learning · student engagement

1 Introduction

The growing demand for self-paced online learning (SPOL) in recent years has been largely attributed to the flexible and asynchronous nature of SPOL. However, this flexibility also creates several challenges for online learners. For example, students often lack direct student-student and student-instructor interactions, meaning students mostly learn in an individualized mode [1]. The isolation can be minimized by using technologies that enhance learners' interdependence and encourages individuals to collaborate with others during the learning process; however, these technologies have not been fully developed yet [2]. Learning distance and lack of fully developed technologies to encourage learner collaboration have caused SPOL students to feel isolated and disengaged

R. A. Sottilare and J. Schwarz (Eds.): HCII 2023, LNCS 14044, pp. 3–14, 2023.
https://doi.org/10.1007/978-3-031-34735-1_1

[1]. In addition to the solitude, students lack information on how they are performing compared to their peers. Without social interaction and formative feedback, students usually lack self-awareness (e.g., how they are performing, what are their learning gaps, and what they can do to improve?) [3].

To improve students' collaboration and active participation in an online learning environment, students need to have a satisfactory level of course engagement [2]. According to a study by McNamara et al. [4], language is a conduit for communicating and understanding information. Modern learning management systems (LMSs) collect an abundance of information about students, including information about students' interaction in the course forums with other students and the instructor [4]. This data can be mined using natural language processing (NLP) to better understand the depth of student's grasp of the course topics. Also, the analysis of discussion forum posts, using NLP, can provide insights into students' social interactions with other students and the instructor, which is a good indicator of their course engagement [4]. By studying students' social processes, researchers can discover patterns in students' cognition and behavior in SPOL courses, which otherwise could be ignored [5].

Therefore, a potential solution to decreasing students' sense of isolation in SPOL courses is to encourage students to engage with their peers in a meaningful way. This is because the course forums are continuously enriched with a large volume of posts that are generated daily and hides useful insights about the students [6]. By using NLP tools, these posts can be analyzed to better understand students' topic comprehension, high-order thinking, engagement, emotional state, and motivation. In other words, analysis of students' discussion board posts can provide insights into cognitive and metacognitive processes that underpin students' engagement, motivation, and learning gain [7]. For example, the feedback that is provided by students in discussion board posts can be used by an instructor to make improvements in teaching strategies [8]. Similarly, students can use the results of the analysis to better understand their emotional states in the course to increase their self-awareness. This allows students to adjust their high-order thinking and engagement, which could improve their course performance. In post-secondary institutions, NLP-based text analysis is also used to investigate the correlation between learners' feelings and drop-out rates in SPOL courses. For example, NLP is used to look at students' attitudes toward tuition fees and financial aid. Furthermore, NLP and text analysis are used to determine the effectiveness of courses based on students' reviews by examining the opinions about the course. Even though text analysis is used often in post-secondary institutions to better understand students' needs, researchers suggest that there is a wide gap in some areas concerning the analysis of student feedback that requires further investigation [6].

This study develops and tests a sentiment analysis model, analyzing course forum posts, using transformers and XLNet. This model can be used to detect and measure students' sentiment in SPOL courses to identify teaching or learning-related aspects of students' engagement to improve collaboration and decrease students' sense of isolation. Based on the above observations, the following hypotheses have been considered and tested in this research: *creating immediate visibility of students' sentiments can improve students' self-awareness in online learning.* The rest of the paper is organized as follows: Sect. 2 provides background information about the research; Sect. 3 describes the research methodology used to develop the proposed model; Sect. 4 describes experimental results to clarify the performance of the sentiment analysis model; and finally, Sect. 5 concludes the paper by summarizing the findings and the future research directions.

2 Background

Sentiment analysis (also known as opinion mining or emotion AI) is a sub-field of NLP that attempts to identify and extract opinions within a given text across blogs, reviews, social media, forums, and news [9]. Sentiment analysis is a task that focuses on the polarity detection and recognition of emotions towards an entity, which can be an individual, topic, and/or event [10]. In general, sentiment analysis aims to find users' opinions, identify the sentiment they express and then classify their polarity into positive, negative, and neutral categories [6].

Students' posts are affected by their emotions, and therefore the automatic detection of students' emotions from course forum posts can help to understand if the students are struggling in the course and what they dislike about the course [8]. Forum post analysis also gives clues to students about their cognition. Furthermore, visibility into these emotions can help students to gain awareness of their sentiment type (e.g., positive, negative, or neutral). When students gain self-awareness about the type of sentiment they feel, they can use this information to improve their learning experience and collaboration with their peers. For example, if negative sentiment is identified in a student's post, various adjustment strategies could be applied, such as suggesting to communicate with the instructor or other students; providing a positive reinforcement; sharing feedback related to struggling topics; or encouraging them to listen and learn from their mistakes [8]. The results of the sentiment analysis can encourage each student to collaborate with other students during their learning process, even when the instructor is not present. This may help to increase students' engagement. The term student engagement is described as a learning task and encourages students' cognitive process, active participation, and emotional involvement in their learning process [2]. Furthermore, cognitively, it will show students how their intellectual effort helps them acquire new knowledge. Finally, behaviorally, it encourages students to be active learners and participate positively in their learning process [2]. Several recent studies focused on NLP-based sentiment analysis of course discussion forums. Kastrati et al. [6] conducted a systematic literature review on deep learning-based methods for sentiment analysis in educational settings. This study highlighted the need for dealing with students' opinions and recognized its challenges due to the nature of the language used by the students and the large volume of information. Wen et al. [11] explored how the mining of forum posts can be used to monitor students' trending opinions toward the course. This study also identified a correlation between sentiment ratios, measured based on daily forum posts, and the number of students who dropped out each day. Li and Xing [12] found discussion boards as a valuable platform for students learning as they promote knowledge exchange. This study used recurrent neural networks (RNN) and generative pre-trained transformers (GPT) to provide students with emotional and community support using contextual replies. Chaplot et al. [13] performed sentiment analysis using an artificial neural network (ANN) to predict student attrition and showed how students' sentiment would affect their decision to dropout.

Moreno-Marcos et al. [14] analyzed students' sentiments in forum posts and detected patterns in students' behavior to identify complex emotions such as excitement, frustration, or boredom. This information can help students to better understand the emotions they exhibit in a course, which allows them to better engage with their peers through increased self-awareness. Hew et al. [15] developed a system using a supervised machine learning algorithm for sentiment analysis and hierarchical modeling to analyze course features that affected students' course satisfaction. The results showed that the course instructor, content, assessments, and course schedule had a positive impact on students' course satisfaction and completion. This study used both learner-level and course-level factors to predict student satisfaction. Estrada et al. [16] created a system that uses multiple sentiment analyses to identify learner-centered emotions (e.g., engaged, excited, or bored) through students' sentiments (i.e., positive or negative).

Although sentiment analysis research is growing in popularity, several research gaps have been identified in the existing sentiment analysis techniques that use students' forum posts in SPOL courses. The research gaps that we identified are the following: (1) most studies focused on identifying positive and negative sentiment, however, these studies did not go into deeper, such as identifying teaching and learning aspects and their associations with the students' sentiment [6]; (2) there is a lack of research which focuses on improving students' self-awareness using students' sentiment analysis results; (3) most sentiment analysis models did not deal with data bias, overfitting problem, and their explainability in the education domain; (4) most sentiment analysis models are unable to handle complex languages, such as double negatives, unknown proper nouns, abbreviations, and words with multiple meanings [6]; (5) There is a lack of benchmark datasets and an insufficient size for the existing datasets. It is also worth noting that there is a lack of resources, such as lexica, corpora, and dictionaries for low-resource languages (this is attributed to most studies being in Chinese or English language). Also, there are no standardized tools or approaches for sentiment analysis [6].

3 Methodology

The methodology for this study is using the NLP-based sentiment analysis model for the course discussion forum to identify student sentiment and visualize the sentiment in a student-facing intelligent dashboard (SF-iLD) proposed by Farahmand et al. [3] to help increase students' self-awareness. Researchers explored different sentiment analysis models and adopted XLNet, which is a generalized autoregressive pretraining language understanding model. XLNet was selected because its unsupervised representations of text sequences have shown great success in natural language processing applications [17]. Additionally, XLNet allows taking advantage of both autoregressive (AR) language modeling and autoencoding (AE). Using the XLNet model's autoregressive method to learn bidirectional context maximizes the expected log-likelihood of a sequence by writing all possible permutations of the factorization order. This gives the model the ability to utilize contextual information from all positions, providing better prediction. Furthermore, as a generalized AR language model, XLNet doesn't rely on data corruption. Therefore, XLNet doesn't suffer from the train-finetune discrepancy that other models like BERT are subject to [17].

The XLNet architecture for sentiment classification starts with the language model training. The first component of the language model is a word-embedding matrix where a fixed-length vector is assigned for each token (word) in the vocabulary and the sequence is converted to a set of vectors [18]. Next, researchers need to relate the embedded tokens in a sequence. In XLNet this is achieved with transformers [18]. A transformer is a deep learning model that adopts the mechanism of self-attention, differentially weighting the significance of each part of the input data [19]. In XLNet training, the objective of the model is to learn the conditional distribution of all permutations of the tokens in a sequence. XLNet accomplishes this by using samples from all possible permutations without needing to see every single relation [18]. A premutation is a language model that is trained to predict one token, given the preceding context; unlike the traditional model where tokens are predicted in sequential order, premutation predicts tokens in some random order [20]. The way this works is that given sequence X, an AR model calculates the probability $Pr(X_i|X_{<i})$. Here researchers calculate the probability of a token X_i in the sentence, conditioned on the tokens $X_{<i}$ preceding it. These conditioning words provide the context for the model. From this, the AR model learns the relationship between tokens [18]. Next, researchers use masking as a method to perform word prediction by intentionally hiding certain words in a sentence [19]. This process works by replacing certain tokens (words) with a generic mask token, then asking the model to recover the originals [18]. This allows the model to incorporate the context of the tokens both to the left and right of the word being predicted to get the best prediction [18].

The purpose of the XLNet-based sentiment analysis model for this study is to categorize students' discussion board posts as *negative, neutral, and positive* to discover insights about how students' sentiment affects their course engagement over time. Although the application of sentiment analysis in educational research is limited, its use is important to identify students' opinions over time and allows educators and students to reflect on teaching and studying strategies and make changes where required [21].

Sentiment classifiers are often used for binary classification (just positive or negative sentiment). In this study, the sentiment analysis focuses on the polarity of a text (positive, negative, neutral) and uses three discreet classes - between 1 to 7 – to categorize sentiment (refer to Fig. 1). As demonstrated, authors categorize students' sentiments as negative, neutral, or positive. The sentiment intensities often vary because of the subtleties of human language. In the model, if the polarity score is less than or equal to 3.5 then the sentiment is negative. If the polarity score is greater than 3.5 but less than 4.5 then the sentiment is neutral. If the polarity score is greater than or equal to 4.5 then the sentiment is positive [22].

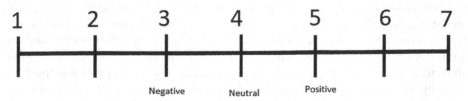

Fig. 1. The class labels for sentiment classification

4 Experiment and Results

4.1 Evaluation Metrics

We evaluated the training results to validate the accuracy of the model, using true positive against false positive predictions, and true negative against false negative predictions [23]. A true positive is an outcome where the model correctly predicts the positive class. Similarly, a true negative is an outcome where the model correctly predicts a negative class. A false positive is an outcome where the model incorrectly predicts the positive class and a false negative is an outcome where the model incorrectly predicts the negative class [24].

The model returns a score for a positive and negative label, which is used to determine the *negative, neutral, and positive* sentiment. Authors use the statistical value generated from the true and false positive, and true and false negative to calculate the model precision and recall, which are common measures to determine classification model performance [23]:

$$Percision = \frac{True\ Positive}{True\ Positive + False\ Positive} \tag{1}$$

$$Recall = \frac{True\ Positive}{Total\ Actual\ Positive} \tag{2}$$

The last measure used to evaluate the model is the F1-score, which is the harmonic mean of precision and recall values of a model:

$$F1score = 2 \times \frac{Precision \times Recall}{Precision + Recall} \tag{3}$$

4.2 Dataset

The sentiment analysis model for this study was developed using the Stanford MOOC posts dataset [25]. The dataset has 29,000 anonymized students' discussion board posts from eleven Stanford University public SPOL courses [25]. A bar plot was created to gain a better understanding of the distribution of sentiment of posts in the dataset as shown in Fig. 2. Of the 29,000 discussion posts, 8,830 discussion posts have a sentiment score of 4.5 or higher, which represents a positive sentiment, and 15,937 discussion posts have a sentiment score between 3.5 and 4.5, which represents a neutral sentiment. The remaining 4,233 discussion posts have a sentiment score of 3.5 or less, which represents a negative sentiment. Research has shown that student-to-student engagement and interactions through discussion board are important learning activity because it creates a venue for students to support each other [12]. As a result, providing students with information about their discussion post sentiment can create self-awareness, helping students to make a micro adjustment to their communication strategy with their peers. A study by Wen, Yang, and Rosé posit that making students aware of their course sentiment could give them a chance to engage in social learning in SPOL. It can be achieved by providing students with important information about their attitudes before and during the course [11].

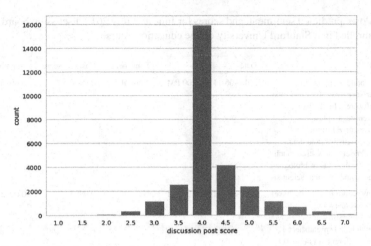

Fig. 2. Discussion board posts' sentiment score vs count for Stanford MOOC dataset

4.3   Results and Discussion

To motivate the students who generate stand-alone discussion board posts (i.e., no engagement or response from their peers), this study hypothesizes that the students' sentiment scores generated by the sentiment analysis model for their discussion board posts can act as a signal to create self-awareness about their sentiment and how it could affect their engagement (or lack of) with their peers. Such information can be meaningful to students because previous studies have shown a positive relationship between learning outcomes and social support. The studies found that information support in an online setting could help students achieve the intended course outcomes [12].

To present how the model works to create transparency in students' sentiments, the authors show the sentiment scores for one student in the Stanford MOOC posts dataset [25]. Table 1 presents the discussion posts with the positive and negative scores for one student enrolled in a SPOL course during June and July 2013. The results show that the students' sentiment in the discussion posts is neutral and positive. Figure 3 visualizes variation in this student's discussion board posts' sentiment score during the course.

Table 1. Posts, predicted sentiment, and scores for June and July 2013 discussion board posts for a student enrolled in a Stanford University online education course

Discussion Post	Date	Sentiment	Positive Score	Negative Score
Hello! In my opinion, I prefer to use Graph pad prism above SPSS and other statistical software. This software combines scientific graphing, comprehensive curve fitting, understandable statistics, and data organization. Prism is now used much more broadly by all kinds of biologists, as well as social and physical scientists	2013–06-11 6:24:00 PM	Neutral	0.9956	0.0010
I can't see any reason to exclude Excel for small datasets that wouldn't also apply to most other software let's say you send me an Excel spreadsheet 1) you and I have different versions 2) I may not have that software even installed 3) it costs too much for me to buy 4) it doesn't run on Linux (or possibly Mac) but like I said, those reasons apply to almost any software R of course if free, runs on windows, Linux and Mac but the learning curve may be more difficult than Excel	2013–06-11 7:15:00 PM	Neutral	0.9983	0.0012
I am not looking for an alternative to R. I am fine with R. I was wondering how statistics were going to be taught without any open-source software for commonality of use and explanation. Also, discussion of model answers to homework	2013–06-11 8:34:00 PM	Neutral	0.9962	0.0028
nonsense	2013–06-11 9:07:00 PM	Neutral	0.9974	0.0011
I seem to remember reading somewhere ages ago that Excel can introduce significant errors and shouldn't be used at all for what we could call serious analyses (i.e., for publications). Since there are so many much better free packages available, it makes sense *not* to use it in my opinion. Doing these simple calculations by hand also reinforces the concept - the mere fact of physically using your hands helps memory. I just finished a course on Special Relativity, lots of equations, and I can say it certainly did help using paper and pencil	2013–06-12 9:05:00 AM	Positive	0.0389	0.0007
Excel is great but it does not have built-in functions for nonparametric tests as well as anova, but I could be wrong. Examples include Wilcoxon rank-sum, spearman correlation, and testing for homogeneity to name a few	2013–07-24 4:47:00 AM	Neutral	0.9983	0.0010

Fig. 3. Discussion board posts' sentiment for a student enrolled in a Stanford University online education course during June and July 2013

Note that to accurately determine sentiment, two scores are calculated for each discussion post, a score for the negative sentiment and a score for the positive sentiment. For example, post 1 has a sentiment score of 0.9956 and a negative score of 0.0010 and is labeled as positive.

To verify the validity and accuracy of the predicted sentiment for each post, the authors calculated the Precision, Recall, and F1 score. Precision is the ratio of true positives to all items that the model has marked as positive (i.e., the number of true positives plus the number of false positives) [23]. The recall is the ratio of true positives for all the positive posts (i.e., the number of true positives plus the number of false negatives) [23]. F1-score is the harmonic mean of precision and recall values of a model [27]. Support is the number of actual occurrences of the class in the specified dataset [27]. Using these measurements, we can determine the overall accuracy of the prediction. The final Precision, Recall, F1-score, and Support for the model for the test dataset are presented in Table 2.

Table 2. Precision, Recall, and F1-score for sentiment predictions.

	Precision	Recall	F1 Score	Support
Negative	0.64	0.62	0.63	1084
Neutral	0.80	0.80	0.80	3981
Positive	0.78	0.80	0.79	2185
Model Accuracy (overall accuracy of prediction for test data): 0.77				**7250**

5   Conclusion and Future Work

We have presented our exploration of how information technology can be used to improve the quality of SPOL courses by evaluating teaching, learning strategies, methods, activities, and the way students engage with their studies. As part of the study, a state-of-the-art (XLNet) sentiment analysis natural language processing algorithm was used to create visibility for students' feelings towards the course as a strategy to enhance students' engagement through self-awareness. The insights gained from the analysis are visualized in a student-facing intelligent learning dashboard (SF-iLDs) to support students' self-awareness of their sentiment towards the course to encourage adjustments to the level of engagement.

A study by Shapiro et al. [28] found that motivation plays a key role in persistence, attitudes, and level of engagement; therefore, we can ascertain that the improvement in the students' sentiment indicates a change in their attitude toward the course and an increase in their engagement level. Accordingly, the authors suggest that creating visibility into students' sentiments in the discussion board can help students (by creating self-awareness) and instructors (by providing insight), leading to enhanced identification of the attitudes, which correlates with motivation and engagement.

This research contributes to knowledge by developing and testing a sentiment analysis model and analyzing course forum posts, using a convolutional neural network. This model can be used to detect and measure students' sentiment in SPOL courses to identify teaching or learning-related aspects of students' engagement to improve collaboration and decrease students' sense of isolation.

This study is limited by a lack of resources such as lexicon, corpora, dictionaries, and publicly available educational datasets to enable benchmarking. Also, there are no standardized solutions or approaches for performing sentiment analysis in education. This presents an opportunity for future research by adding lexicon, corpora, and dictionaries available to better predict students' sentiments to encourage collaboration and engagement in online courses.

References

1. Farahmand, A., Hongxin, Y., Dewan, A.A., Lin, F.: Removing barriers in self-paced online learning through designing intelligent learning dashboards, pp. 1–21 (2021)
2. Pellas, N.: The influence of computer self-efficacy, metacognitive self-regulation and self-esteem on student engagement in online learning programs: evidence from the virtual world of second Life. Comput. Hum. Behav. **35**, 157–170 (2014)
3. Farahmand, A., Dewan, M.A.A., Lin, F.: Constructing intelligent learning dashboard for online learners. In: IEEE CyberSciTech/ PICom/ DASC/ CBDCom 2021 (2021)
4. McNamara, D.S., Allen, L.K., Crossley, S.A., Dascalu, M., Perret, C.A.: Natural language processing and learning analytics. In: Handbook of Learning Analytics, pp. 93–100 (2017)
5. Chen, B., Chang, Y.-H., Ouyang, F., Zhou, W.: Fostering student engagement in online discussion through social learning analytics. Internet High. Educ. **37**, 1–10 (2018)
6. Kastrati, Z., Dalipi, F., Imran, A.S., Nuci, K.P., Wani, M.A.: Sentiment analysis of students' feedback with nlp and deep learning: a systematic mapping study. Appl. Sci. **11**(9), 1–23 (2021)
7. Elgort, I., Lundqvist, K., McDonald, J., Moskal, A.C.M.: Analysis of student discussion posts in a MOOC: Proof of concept. In: International Conference on Learning Analytics & Knowledge (LAK18) (2018)
8. Altrabsheh, N., Gaber, M.M., Cocea, M.: SA-E: sentiment analysis for education. Front. Artif. Intell. Appl. **255**, 353–362 (2013)
9. Genç, O.: The basics of NLP and real-time sentiment analysis with open source tools towards data science (2019). https://towardsdatascience.com/real-time-sentiment-analysis-on-social-media-with-open-source-tools-f864ca239afe. Accessed 12 Dec 2021
10. Kumar, A., Srinivasan, K., Cheng, W.-H., Zomaya, A.Y.: Hybrid context enriched deep learning model for fine-grained sentiment analysis in textual and visual semiotic modality social data. Inf. Process. Manage. **57**(1), 2–35 (2020)
11. Wen, M., Yang, D., Ros C.P.: Sentiment analysis in MOOC discussion forums: what does it tell us?, In: 7th International Conference on Educational Data Mining (2014)
12. Li, C., Xing, W.: Natural language generation using deep learning to support MOOC learners. Int. J. Artif. Intell. Educ. **31**(2), 186–214 (2021) https://doi.org/10.1007/s40593-020-00235-x
13. Chaplot, D.S., Rhim, E., Kim, J.: Predicting student attrition in MOOCs using sentiment analysis and neural networks. In: CEUR Workshop Proceedings (2015)
14. Moreno-Marcos, P.M., Alario-Hoyos, C., Munoz-Merino, P.J.: Sentiment analysis in MOOCs: a case study. In: IEEE Global Engineering Education Conference (EDUCON) (2018)
15. Hew, K.F., Hu, X., Qiao, C., Tang, Y.: What predicts student satisfaction with MOOCs: a gradient boosting trees supervised machine learning and sentiment analysis approach. Comput. Educ. **145**, 103724 (2020)
16. Estrada, M.L.B., Cabada, R.Z., Bustillos, R.O.: Opinion mining and emotion recognition applied to learning environments. Expert Syst. Appl. **150**, 1–12 (2020)
17. Yang, Z., Dai, Z., Yang, Y., Carbonell, J., Salakhutdinov, R., Le, Q.V.: XLNet: generalized autoregressive pretraining for language understanding. In: Advances in Neural Information Processing Systems, vol. 32, pp. 1–11 (2019)
18. McGoldrick, G., Cao, Y., Prince, S.: Understanding XLNet, Borealis (2019). https://www.borealisai.com/research-blogs/understanding-xlnet/. Accessed 21 Dec 2022
19. Verma, Y.: A complete tutorial on masked language modeling using BERT, Analyticsindiamag, (2022). https://analyticsindiamag.com/a-complete-tutorial-on-masked-language-modelling-using-bert/. Accessed 28 Dec 2022
20. Karan, P.: Understand how the XLNet outperforms BERT in Language Modelling, medium (2019). https://medium.com/saarthi-ai/xlnet-the-permutation-language-model-b30f5b4e3c1e. Accessed 28 Dec 2022

21. Nkomo, L.M., Daniel, B.K.: Sentiment analysis of student engagement with lecture recording. TechTrends **65**(2), 213–224 (2021). https://doi.org/10.1007/s11528-020-00563-8
22. Rao, P.: Fine-grained Sentiment Analysis in Python (Part 1). Towards Data Science (2019). https://towardsdatascience.com/fine-grained-sentiment-analysis-in-python-part-1-2697bb111ed4. Accessed 05 Jan 2023
23. Stratis, K.: Use Sentiment Analysis With Python to Classify Movie Reviews, Real Python (2020). https://realpython.com/sentiment-analysis-python/. Accessed 1 Jan 2022
24. Machine Learning Crash Course, Classification: True vs. False and Positive vs. Negative. https://developers.google.com/machine-learning/crash-course/classification/true-false-positive-negative. Accessed 29 Jan 2022
25. Agrawal A., Paepcke, A.: The Stanford MOOCPosts Data Set, datastage.stanford.edu. https://datastage.stanford.edu/StanfordMoocPosts/. Accessed 31 Jan 2022
26. J. Brownlee, "How to Choose Loss Functions When Training Deep Learning Neural Networks," Machine Learning Mastery, 2019. [Online]. Available: https://machinelearningmastery.com/how-to-choose-loss-functions-when-training-deep-learning-neural-networks/. [Accessed 2 February 2022]
27. Shung, K. P.: Accuracy, Precision, Recall or F1?", Towards Data Science (2018). https://towardsdatascience.com/accuracy-precision-recall-or-f1-331fb37c5cb9. Accessed 29 Jan 2022
28. Shapiro, H.B., Lee, C.H., Wyman Roth, N.E., Li, K., Cetinkaya-Rundel, M., Canelas, D.A.: Understanding the massive open online course (MOOC) student experience: an examination of attitudes, motivations, and barriers. Comput. Educ. **110**, 35–50 (2017)

Not All Pain Leads to Gain: The Role of Learner Engagement in Adaptive Flashcard Training

Maureen Namukasa[1]([🖂]), Meredith Carroll[1], Matthew D. Marraffino[2],
Cheryl I. Johnson[3], Daphne E. Whitmer[2], Whitney-Marie Igwe[1], and Morgan Nash[1]

[1] Florida Institute of Technology, Melbourne, FL 32901, USA
mnamukasa2020@my.fit.edu, mcarroll@fit.edu
[2] Naval Air Warfare Center Training Systems Division, Orlando, FL 32825, USA
matthew.d.marraffino.civ@us.navy.mil
[3] Quantum Improvements Consulting, LLC, Orlando, FL 32803, USA
cjohnson@quantumimprovements.net

Abstract. Adaptive training methods have been designed to enhance students' learning outcomes by tailoring the educational content based on the learner's performance during training. In the present study, we examined different adaptive sequencing methods for a flashcard-based trainer. One sequencing method, the Adaptive Response Time-based Sequencing (ARTS) algorithm presents cards based on an individual learner's accuracy and reaction time, such that incorrectly identified cards are prioritized over correctly identified cards. Although previous research has suggested that ARTS is more efficient and effective than other forms of flashcard sequencing, recent research was unable to replicate these findings. To that end, the current experiment compared ARTS to an adaptive control condition that reversed the ARTS algorithm and investigated if learner engagement plays a role in adaptive flashcard-based training. A sample of 50 college students learned to identify African countries in one of two adaptive flashcard sequencing conditions – ARTS and control. Engagement was measured using the flow state scale for occupational tasks and training effectiveness was determined by calculating immediate and delayed learning gains. Results revealed no statistically significant differences between ARTS and the control on immediate and delayed gains. Further, the ARTS group reported significantly lower engagement levels than the control group. A mediation analysis revealed that the relationship between the training and the learning gains was significantly mediated by engagement in an inverse format, suggesting that training reduced the levels of engagement which in turn canceled out the learning gains. Based on these findings, we present the theoretical and practical implications.

Keywords: Adaptive Training · Flashcards · Sequencing · Learner engagement

1 Introduction

Adaptive training methods have been designed to enhance students' learning outcomes by tailoring the educational content based on the learner's performance during training. Adaptive training proposes learner-centric models such that the training's difficulty and learning material are modified, adjusted, and finetuned to an individual learner's gradual progress and performance during the training [1]. Many scholars have endeavored to implement adaptive techniques into training technologies or platforms such as computer-based simulations [2], flashcard-based adaptive training [3]–[5], and virtual reality training [6]. Research examining the effectiveness of adaptive training approaches has reported a range of training benefits including enhanced learner outcomes [2, 7–9], improved learner experience [10], and increased training efficiency [3, 4, 10].

With regard to flashcard-based training specifically, one adaptive strategy to employ is to tailor the sequence, or order, that the flashcards are presented to the learner based on the learner's performance. One sequencing method called Adaptive Response Time-based Sequencing (ARTS) is an algorithm that utilizes reaction time and accuracy to prioritize the presentation of the flashcards and has been shown effective in the literature [1, 3, 4, 11]. Relying on consistent findings in learning and memory research, ARTS prioritizes flashcards based on learning strength such that flashcards that have low learning strength are prioritized over flashcards with high learning strength, which are spaced further back in the deck to make retrieval more challenging. However, recent research was unable to replicate the benefits of ARTS when applied to a vehicle identification task [1]. The findings of [1] may be due to learner engagement as it is theorized that the benefits of adaptive training stem at least partially from the impact that the adaptive training systems have on individual learning states. For example, as the material is adjusted to suit the learner's capabilities, adaptive training approaches allow the challenge level associated with materials and tasks to be optimized with the skill level of the learner. Challenge-skill match is a key component of engagement, during which an individual's perceived difficulty of the task and their skill level is optimized, leading to the psychological state of flow [12, 13]. Flow has been associated with high levels of engagement experienced during active involvement in a task or activity [14–16]. During the flow experience, the difficulty of the challenge increases the workload to a point where the highest level of engagement or concentration is reached resulting in high levels of performance [17]. Further, research suggests that learner outcomes can be profoundly impacted by even insignificant amounts of emotions [18, 19, 20]. Positive emotional states such as engagement can lead to positive effects on learning including, improved academic performance [21], improved course experience and skills development [22], improved learning experience [5], comprehension and commitment of material to memory [23, 24], and better information processing [25]. On the other hand, negative emotional states such as disengagement, frustration, boredom, and anxiety can have negative impacts on learning outcomes. For instance, disengagement can lead to disinterest in the subject matter demonstrated by hint abuse and cheating the system [26–28] and anxiety has been found to have a negative relationship with engagement [20, 29].

In an effort to understand the effectiveness of ARTS-based adaptive flashcard training, and the role of learner engagement, the current research effort was guided by two research questions. First, is the ARTS-based flashcard training more effective than an adaptive control condition that reverses the prioritization scheme in ARTS? Second, is there a difference in engagement experienced between the two training conditions?

2 Background

2.1 Adaptive Response Time-Based System

The ARTS algorithm is an adaptive sequencing system that orders flashcard presentations based on accuracy and response time. To summarize how ARTS works, cards that are answered correctly and quickly are presented after longer intervals (i.e., more trials) than cards that are answered correctly but slowly, or cards that are answered incorrectly [11, 30]. The ARTS system takes advantage of the *spacing effect*, a robust and consistent finding demonstrating that spacing out presentations during study results in better retention than massed presentations, which only aids in short-term memory [31–33]. One explanation for the spacing effect is the *retrieval effort hypothesis*, which suggests that more difficult, but successful retrievals during study support better long-term encoding [34]. Using accuracy and reaction time, ARTS assigns a priority score for an item that considers the most recent trial performance and the number of trials completed since the last presentation [30]. Flashcards that are recalled correctly and quickly are indications of higher learning strength and have lower calculated priority scores than flashcards that are recalled correctly but slowly. By dynamically sequencing the order of the cards in the deck based on priority, the spacing of cards is tailored to ensure well-learned items are presented after longer intervals to maximize learning efficiency (i.e., memory gain per unit time).

Several studies have used ARTS to test learning outcomes and efficiencies using primarily geography tasks [11, 30, 35], however, some research has explored ARTS with butterfly identification [4], and chemistry [3]. Although these studies have shown benefits for using ARTS, some recent research has not been able to replicate these findings. For instance, [1] were unable to find significant differences in efficiency or retention using a vehicle identification task. To follow up on the research conducted by [1] we were interested in comparing ARTS to a sequencing control algorithm that violates the assumptions of the spacing effect and retrieval effort hypothesis to test the effectiveness of adaptive spacing in flashcard-based study. In this control condition, the ARTS algorithm is used, but the presentation of the cards is reversed such that cards that are answered incorrectly are presented after longer intervals than cards that are recalled accurately and slowly, and accurately and quickly. By using this type of control condition, we attempted to maximize the adaptive spacing manipulation by comparing ARTS to a condition that presents cards in the theoretically least efficient manner possible. Therefore, we hypothesized that the ARTS condition would lead to higher learning gains than the control condition.

2.2 Learner Engagement

Engagement is defined as active involvement in a task that can be influenced by the learner's motivation [36]. Engaged learners may exhibit learner outcomes such as, interest in the material, concentration, knowledge acquisition, focused attention, loss of time consciousness, and enjoyment [13, 15]. For instance, [37] conducted a survey of 200 respondents aimed at understanding how learner engagement impacts learning in informal online contexts through value creation. They explored behavioral, cognitive, and emotional types of engagement with regard to instrumental and experiential learning outcomes. Results revealed that emotional engagement enhanced learner outcomes, by mediating the relationship between the training platform and learning outcomes. Another study conducted by [38] explored the relationships between learner engagement, learner outcomes (i.e., satisfaction, content learning, and generic competencies), academic ability, and epistemological beliefs in flipped learning. Undergraduate students ($N = 231$) were enrolled in the flipped learning model during which they studied learning material before class and completed a quiz, participated in group tasks, and then listened to a short lecture from an instructor. Learner engagement was measured by adapting the engagement scale by [39]. Results indicated that both pre-class and in-class engagement influenced content-related outcomes and satisfaction except for generic competencies which were only affected by in-class engagement. A two-stage longitudinal study by [28] explored the relationship between affects such as boredom and behavioral engagement with performance in a web-based tutoring system. They used archival data of two samples from a math tutoring system and developed automatic identifiers of students' affective states and engaged behaviors that were coded for analysis. Results of the correlational analysis revealed that concentrated engagement had the strongest association with high performance, and measures of affect and behavioral engagement can predict learning outcomes such as performance on standardized examinations.

Engagement can be attained at a micro or macro level [15, 40]. Micro engagement is derived from real-time involvement in a task, moment, or learning activity [40] experienced during participation in a class, course, or scenario [15]. Macro engagement extends for longer periods of time and can be in a myriad of contexts. For instance, students participating in learning-related activities pre- or post-lecture period, such as online searches about a topic or completing homework [15]. The state of flow by [41] has been purported to represent micro engagement of an individual at its peak [15], and flow is usually connected with engagement and learning [42–44]. Derived from the active interaction in a task/activity, flow is a psychological state during which an individual is fully immersed effortlessly in the task or activity and is characterized by enjoyment, enhanced focus, and feelings of success at the task at hand [16, 43, 45]. The flow theory posits several antecedents to flow, including (a) challenge skill balance when an individual's skills harmonize with the level of the challenge at hand, (b) goal clarity, in which there is knowledge of the task expectations, and (c) feedback, in which there is knowledge of task progress and the individual's performance [41]. The flow experience relies on challenge-skill balance such that individuals must perceive that they have the necessary skills required to succeed at the task, which culminates in performing tasks just for the experience of it rather than for external rewards [41].

Extant research has found positive influences of flow on learning outcomes. For instance, [46] conducted an experiment to understand the effect of the flow state on learning outcomes such as declarative knowledge and motivation in game-based learning. Undergraduate students were randomly assigned to two varying game versions in which they were trained, completed a game play, and their flow was measured using the flow state scale (FSS) by [47]. They found that flow had significant effects on declarative knowledge and motivation, and significantly mediated the relationship between declarative knowledge and motivation. Further, in a two-participant case study of occupational therapy patients by [48], the utility of flow was applied to an attention training task versus a regular occupational task. Flow was measured by the flow state scale for occupational tasks (FSSOT) by [49], and the results revealed enhanced improvements in neuropsychological performances and attention during and after the flow task but not in the control condition.

Despite the recognized utility of flow in learning, there have been limited interventions to investigate its value in flashcard-based adaptive training systems. In fact, sparse research has endeavored to experimentally investigate the role of engagement in learning pertaining to adaptive training systems, in general [50]. As flow is associated with high levels of engagement [42–44], we aimed to utilize a flow measure to capture micro-engagement during the training. Based on the knowledge of challenge-skill match, which is an important facet of flow, we hypothesized that ARTS, which adaptively spaced and presented the difficult cards based on the participant's performance (consistent with the retrieval effort hypothesis), would lead to higher engagement compared to the control condition, which adaptively spaced the cards contrary to theory.

3 Methods

3.1 Participants

A total of 51 individuals participated in the study. Participants were recruited from a university in the southeastern United States through the SONA system, which is an online tool used by psychologists to recruit research participants compensated with SONA credit, and college classes by which participants were compensated with extra course credit. All participants signed an informed consent form prior to the beginning of the experiment and the research was approved by the Naval Air Warfare Center Training Systems Division Institutional Review Board. One participant was excluded from the data analysis (see details in the preliminary analysis section), resulting in a final sample of 50 participants (13 females) with a mean age of 21.35 ($SD = 3.24$). Forty-four percent ($n = 22$) were Seniors, 34% ($n = 17$) were Juniors, 14% ($n = 7$) were Sophomores, 4% ($n = 2$) were Freshmen and 4% did not report their year of college. The majority of the participants (70%, $n = 35$) reported high school as the highest level of education attained, 12% had attained a bachelor's or associate degree, 4% attained a master's degree and 2% did not report their highest level of education. Twenty-four participants experienced the ARTS condition, and 26 participants experienced the control condition.

3.2 Experimental Design, Task, and Testbed

The study was a 2×3 between-within-groups repeated measures design, with a between-groups independent variable (IV) of training condition (ARTS vs. control) and a within-groups IV of trial (pretest vs. immediate posttest vs. delayed posttest). Participants were randomly assigned to either training conditions (ARTS or control) on the day of the experiment.

The ARTS condition was developed using an algorithm that utilized reaction time and accuracy to prioritize the presentation of flash cards to the participants. During the training, participants were tasked to select the correct name of the item on the screen as fast and accurately as possible. The ARTS system would then calculate a priority score. After each trial, priority scores were adjusted based on the number of trials since the last presentation and the highest priority card (lowest learning strength) was presented next. Cards continued to be presented to participants until they were mastered. ARTS works by prioritizing and presenting incorrect flashcards first, correct flashcards with slow reaction times second, and correct flashcards with fast reaction times third. Mastery of a card is established based on [34] concept of the *retrieval effort hypothesis* such that, shorter times required to identify a card correctly is an indication of higher learning strength. In this experiment, cards were mastered if the participant correctly answered a country four consecutive times in under six seconds.

The control condition was a reversed ARTS which flipped the algorithm such that the lowest priority card was selected for presentation. This algorithm was chosen because we wanted to test against an alternative adaptive algorithm and flipping the sequencing priority was theoretically the strongest manipulation. Prioritizing cards with high learning strength goes against the retrieval effort hypothesis by increasing the spacing for cards with low learning strength, thus decreasing the chances of a successful retrieval, and allowing cards with high learning strength to be easily retrieved.

Task. In the experimental task, the objective was to learn the names and locations of 38 countries on a map of Africa. Once the participant was placed in either training condition (ARTS vs. control), they were trained on the location and name of the African countries. Cards were presented as an image of the map of Africa with the target country on the map highlighted in blue and four answer options were presented below the card. During the training, participants were required to locate the country on the map and select its name as accurately and quickly as possible from the four-answer options provided. If the selected choice was correct, the answer choice was highlighted in green color and the participant would be prompted to click next to continue with the training (see Fig. 1). If the selected choice was incorrect, feedback was provided in the following way. Two cards were presented on the screen side by side with the left card showing the correct answer and the right card showing the participant's selected (incorrect) response (see Fig. 2). The location of the target country was highlighted in blue, the name was highlighted in green from the answer options, and text feedback informed the participant that this was the expected correct answer choice. The right hand-side card showed the location of the map that the participant had selected (wrong choice) highlighted in blue, the name from the list of options was highlighted in red color, and text feedback informed the participant that they had selected the wrong choice. After viewing the feedback, participants would click next to continue with the training. The order of the presentation of the cards was based on the training condition the participant was in.

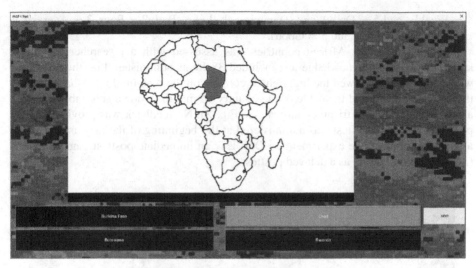

Fig. 1. Correct Response Feedback

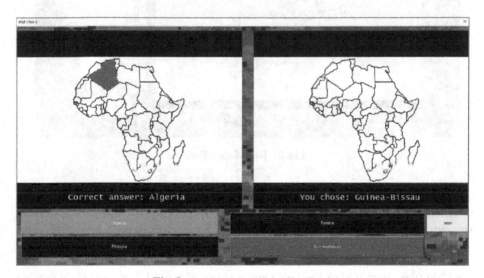

Fig. 2. Incorrect Response Feedback

3.3 Measures

Three types of measures were collected: (1) demographics, (2) knowledge, and (3) engagement. Demographic data were collected using researcher-developed items including (a) age, (b) biological sex (1 = male and 2 = female), (c) year of college (1 = Freshman, 2 = Sophomore, 3 = Junior, 4 = Senior, and 5 = Graduate), (d) education level (1 = High school, 2 = Associate's degree, 3 = Bachelor's, 4 = Master's, and 5 = Doctoral), (e) gaming frequency (1 = Never, 2 = Less than once a month, 3 = Monthly,

4 = Weekly, and 5 = Daily), and (f) gaming skill (1 = Bad, 2 = Poor, 3 = Average, 4 = Better than average, and 5 = Good).

Knowledge of the African countries was assessed with a researcher-developed knowledge test. The knowledge test included 38 items administered on the computer where participants viewed the highlighted country on the map on the left-hand side of the screen and selected the name of the country from a drop-down scrollable list with all the names of the African countries (see Fig. 3). No feedback was provided at this point. The knowledge test was administered at the beginning of the task as a pre-test, after completion of the experiment on Day 1 as an immediate posttest, and on Day 2 (5–9 days after Day 1) as a delayed posttest.

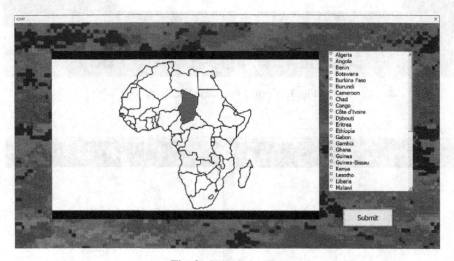

Fig. 3. Knowledge Test

Since the goal was to assess engagement at the micro level, and flow has been proposed to represent the highest level of micro engagement [15], learner engagement was measured using the FSSOT [49]. The FSSOT measures three factors of the flow experience, including (a) sense of control which has six items, (b) positive emotional experience with four items, and (c) absorption in the task which also has four items. The FSSOT is comprised of 14 items measured on a 7-point Likert-type scale ranging from strongly disagree (1) to strongly agree (7). Examples of questions from the FSSOT include: (1) I really enjoyed what I was doing, (2) My abilities matched the challenge of what I was doing, and (3) It felt like time passed quickly. Scores from the FSSOT can range from 14 (low) to 98 (high). The FSSOT was reported to have a reliability coefficient based on Cronbach's alpha of .918 [49]. It was reported to have content validity by an expert on flow theory and convergent validity as evidenced by the FSSOT total score being significantly negatively correlated with the total score of the State-Trait Anxiety Inventory (STAI; Spielberger, 1983; $r = -.537, p < .01$), and the score of STAI's anxiety absent items ($r = -.611, p < .01$), but not correlated with the score of SATI's anxiety-present items ($r = -.088, p = .175$) [49].

3.4 Procedure

The study was completed in two sessions on two different days. Participants were scheduled using the Acuity scheduling platform. When they arrived on Day 1, they signed an informed consent form and were randomly assigned to either one of the training conditions (ARTS vs. control). They then sat at a desk with a laptop computer. All the instructions for their tasks were embedded in the testbed, and they received minimal interruptions from the experimenter.

First, a pre-test was presented to determine their pre-training knowledge. After the pretest, participants were given a brief familiarization training using flashcards in the form of the African map with the target country highlighted in blue color and the name of the country provided below the map for five seconds. Each country appeared two times during the cycle and participants viewed the training until it was completed, which lasted five minutes. Next, participants completed the training phase during which the countries on the African map were presented using the flashcard trainer per their condition which lasted approximately 45 min, and they were prompted to take breaks periodically by the system (i.e., after every 50 cards). When the participant mastered a card (i.e., the participant got the card correct four times in a row in under six seconds), the system would inform the participant that they mastered that card and that card would be dropped from further study. That is, the participant was not tested on the dropped card for the remainder of the training. The training ended once the training time elapsed or once the participant mastered all the cards. Participants received a message when the training was complete.

Next, they rated their confidence in their ability to remember the items they had practiced during the training after a week had elapsed on a scale from 0% to 100% with a 20% interval. During the confidence rating, the country was presented on the map highlighted in a blue color on the left-hand side of the screen and the participant was required to select a rating from a list on the right-hand side of the screen.

Next, participants filled out the demographics and engagement surveys. After completing the surveys, participants were presented with a post-test similar to the pre-test but with the items presented in random order. Once participants completed the post-test, they were reminded to return for Day 2 one week later and dismissed. Day 1 lasted approximately 75 min.

On Day 2 (5–9 days After Day 1), participants returned to complete a delayed post-test which was similar to the one they had completed on Day 1 but with the items presented in a random order. Day 2 lasted approximately 15 min.

4   Results

4.1 Preliminary Analysis

Data were collected for 51 participants. One participant had an exceptionally high pretest score and scored nearly 100% on the post-test. This participant's data was omitted because it was an extreme outlier. Data from three other individuals were considered for removal, but they were ultimately retained. One participant experienced technical issues during the experiment on Day 1 and completed the immediate posttest on the following day. Examination of this participant's posttest scores revealed that they were consistent with others who experienced the same training condition. It appeared that this less than 24-h delay did not have tremendous negative impacts on the participant's performance and their data were retained. One participant paused the experiment to go and attend class and completed the posttest one hour later, it was decided that this data be retained due to the reasoning that an hour delay may not have impacted the results drastically. One participant had difficulty with understanding instructions because the participant had trouble understanding English. We examined this participant's scores on all the measures in the study and found that they were consistent with the scores of other participants who experienced the same training condition. Thus, it was decided that this participant's data be retained. The final sample resulted in 50 participants and the data were analyzed using SPSS (v. 27).

The effectiveness of the training was assessed as learning gains using participants' scores obtained from the pre-and post-tests. First, immediate gains were obtained based on the pretest scores and posttest scores obtained on Day 1. Second, delayed gains were computed from the pretest scores and posttest scores obtained on Day 2 (5–9 days after Day 1). Both the learning gains are expressed in the computational formulae below.

$$Immeddiate\ gain = \frac{Postscore - prescore}{100 - prescore} \tag{1}$$

$$Delayed\ gain = \frac{Delayed\ postscore - prescore}{100 - prescore} \tag{2}$$

4.2 Primary Analysis

To answer the research questions regarding whether the ARTS training condition was more effective than the control condition and whether there was a difference in engagement levels experienced between the two conditions, a Multivariate Analysis of Variance (MANOVA) was conducted. The training condition was the independent variable at two levels (ARTS vs. control) and immediate gains, delayed gains, and engagement scores were the dependent variables. The descriptive results indicated slightly higher immediate gains for ARTS ($M = .71$, $SD = .22$) compared to control ($M = .62$, $SD = .28$) and slightly higher delayed gains for ARTS ($M = .48$, $SD = .25$) compared to control ($M = .42$, $SD = .29$). Descriptive results also indicated that participants that received ARTS reported lower engagement levels ($M = 63.37$, $SD = 16.27$) compared to those in the control condition ($M = 71.08$, $SD = 10.03$). At the multivariate level, the results were significant, $F(3, 46) = 2.81$, $p = .05$, and did not violate Levene's test of equal variance. Since the results were significant at the multivariate level, we analyzed the univariate results. Univariate analyses indicated that the differences in immediate gains reported between ARTS and control were not significant, $F(1, 48) = 1.72$, $p = .19$, suggesting that the difference in immediate gains between the training conditions did not vary significantly. Likewise, the difference in delayed gains reported between the two training conditions was not statistically significant, $F(1, 48) = .68$, $p = .41$, implying that the delayed gains reported between ARTS and the control condition did not vary significantly. However, examination of the univariate results for engagement revealed that the differences in engagement levels experienced between the two training groups were significant, $F(1, 48) = 4.13$, $p = .048$, $\eta2 = .079$, suggesting that the differences in the levels of engagement perceived by the participants between ARTS and the control varied significantly, and 7.9% of the variance in engagement experienced can be attributed to the training condition (see Fig. 4).

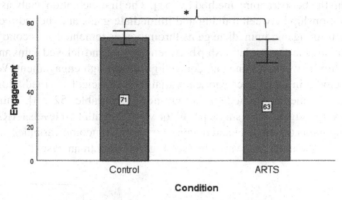

Fig. 4. Learner Engagement by Training

4.3 Secondary Analyses

The results above indicated that although the ARTS intervention had slightly higher learning gains compared to the control, it was not a statistically significant difference. The results further indicated that the engagement levels experienced were statistically different between the two training conditions, with participants in the control condition reporting higher engagement compared to ARTS. These results were unexpected and warranted further exploration of the data. Based on anecdotal evidence observed during the study, it was hypothesized that engagement was potentially influencing the relationship between the training and learning gains, and the possibility of interactions between participants' learner engagement and training conditions might have been impacting the effectiveness of the training. Specifically, throughout the study, it was observed that multiple participants in the ARTS condition complained about being presented with difficult items over and over again and seemed frustrated that they did not know the answers. This was not observed for participants in the control condition, which could potentially explain the higher engagement levels. This suggested that the ARTS condition might have been too difficult and frustrating, which disrupted the participants' flow experience. If this was the case, then despite the potential positive direct effect of the ARTS condition on learning gains, there may have been an indirect negative effect on engagement leading to negative effects on learning gains. Therefore, we explored these relationships by applying mediation analysis as described below.

Mediation Analyses. Mediation is achievable when the presence of a mediating variable significantly influences the relationship between the predictor and outcome variables that would otherwise be non-existent. The mediating variable thus helps to explain the underlying mechanism of the relationship between the independent variable and the dependent variable. Given that, we hypothesized that the training might be influencing engagement and in turn, the level of engagement experienced might be influencing the relationship between the training conditions and learning gains. Based on this, a mediation analysis was appropriate. To explore this relationship we conducted two mediation analyses using the bootstrapping method by [51]. The first mediation analysis examined the direct relationship between training and immediate gains and the indirect relationship between training and immediate gains through engagement. The second mediation analysis examined the direct relationship between training and delayed gains and the indirect relationship between training and delayed gains through engagement. We adopted a mediation model in which a categorical variable is sufficient for mediation analyses if entered into the mediation model as a multinomial variable [52, 53]. Thus, training condition was investigated as a single predictor variable with two levels (ARTS vs control). Learning gains (immediate and delayed) were the outcome variables, and learner engagement was the mediating variable. (see Fig. 5. For path analyses).

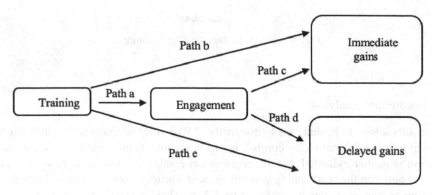

Fig. 5. Path Analysis of two Mediations

Results from the first mediation analyses indicated that training was a significant predictor of engagement (Path a: $b = -7.702$, SE $= 3.79$, p $= .047$). With engagement entered into the model, the total effect of training on immediate gains was not significant, (e.g., Path a + Path b + Path c: $b = .0938$, SE $= .0716$, $p = .1966$), the direct effect of training on immediate gains was significant (Path b: $b = .1429$, SE $= .0716$, $p = .05$) and indirect effect of training on immediate gains through engagement was significant (Path a + Path c) with indirect effects' 95% CI not including zero, (Path c: $b = -.0491$, BootSE $= .0284$, BootLLCI $= -.1162$ -and BootULCI $= -.0062$), suggesting that engagement partially mediated the relationship between training and immediate learning gains but in a negative way. Specifically, training had a significant positive direct effect on immediate learning gains, while having a significant negative indirect effect on immediate learning gains through engagement. As the direct effect of training on immediate gains was significant, this means that engagement had a partial mediating role, and accounting for engagement revealed a significant relationship between training and immediate gains.

Results from the second mediation analysis between training and delayed gains indicated that training was a significant predictor of engagement, (Path a: $b = -7.702$, $SE = 3.79$, p = .047). With engagement entered into the model, the total effect of training on delayed gains was not significant (Path a + Path d + Path e: $b = .0633$, SE = .0765, $p = .4121$), the direct effect of training on delayed gains was not significant, (Path e: $b = .1130$, SE = .0763, $p = .1453$), but the indirect effect of training on delayed gains through engagement (Path a + Path d) were significant with indirect effects' 95% CI not including zero (Path d: $b = -.0497$, BootSE = .0347, BootLLCI = $-.1405$ and BootULCI = $-.0033$), suggesting that engagement fully mediated the relationship between the training and delayed gains in a negative way. Specifically, although training had a positive, but non-significant direct relationship with delayed gains, it had a significant negative indirect effect on delayed learning gains through engagement. As the direct effect of training on delayed gains was not significant, this means that engagement had a fully mediating role between training and delayed gains. Based on these findings, we present the theoretical and practical implications.

5 Discussion

The purpose of this study was twofold. First, we endeavored to examine the effectiveness of an adaptive flashcard training algorithm (ARTS) by comparing it to a control condition. Second, we aimed to investigate whether ARTS, which leverages learner performance during the training and adapts the sequencing of learning material to the participants, would lead to higher engagement compared to a control condition. The results of the MANOVA revealed no significant differences in learning gains between the two conditions. Further, engagement levels experienced in ARTS were significantly lower than those experienced in reversed ARTS. As this was unpredicted, a follow-up mediation analysis was conducted to explore the reasons behind these results. Results from the mediation analyses indicated that the relationship between training and immediate learning gains was significantly, partially mediated by engagement, with training having a positive direct effect on immediate gains and a negative indirect effect on immediate gains through engagement. Further, engagement significantly fully mediated the relationship between training and delayed gains, with training having a positive, but non-significant direct relationship with delayed gains and a significant negative indirect effect on delayed learning gains through engagement. These findings should be interpreted with caution given several limitations of the study, including the self-report nature of the engagement measure and the small sample size.

5.1 Theoretical Implications

Our MANOVA findings with regards to the effectiveness of ARTS compared to the control condition did not align with other studies that have found positive effects of ARTS on learning gains [3, 4, 11]. This might be explained by the adaptive spacing algorithm in ARTS that prioritized the presentation of seemingly difficult cards more frequently than correctly scored cards, negatively impacting the participant's engagement and degrading learning gains. This is in line with the results of the mediation analyses that showed that the training had significant negative effects on engagement and that engagement significantly mediated the relationship between training and learning gains. This aligns with extant research that found engagement to mediate the relationship between training and learning outcomes such that when training reduces engagement, then engagement reduces learning effectiveness [43, 54, 55]. As such the inverse effects of the training on engagement might have cancelled out the benefits of the training.

Our findings with respect to ARTS reporting lower engagement compared to the control condition did not align with extant literature that has shown that effective training systems do have a positive relationship with learner engagement [56–58]. The MANOVA results indicated that participants in the ARTS condition reported significantly lower engagement than those in the control condition and we believe that the adaptive presentation of cards during ARTS might have bred a perceived challenge-skill mismatch among participants in ARTS. The ARTS condition utilizes spacing and mastery criteria to determine the adaptive presentation of cards to learners based on their accuracy and speed. ARTS was developed based on the science of learning findings, like the spacing effect to sequence the flashcards in a way that is more conducive to learning [4, 11, 34, 40]. That is, cards that participants incorrectly identified were presented more frequently than those correctly identified until mastery was achieved. There were a set of African countries in the training set that were particularly difficult to discriminate due to similarity in size, shape, name, and/or location. It is possible that this repetitive presentation of these difficult countries might have been perceived as a challenge-skill gap for participants, which bred negative emotions, disrupted the flow experience, and negatively affected their engagement scores. This is also supported by the mediation results that revealed a negative relationship between training and engagement. Challenge-skill match is a facet of the flow experience that can be attained when individuals perceive an optimization between the task demands and the skills they have [12, 41]. Extant research in learning supports that challenge-skill match positively influences learning outcomes [59, 60], and overall engagement [59, 61, 62], and challenge influences the variations in the flow experience [63]. However, when a challenge is perceived as negative, it breeds demotivation [64], and anxiety has a negative relationship with engagement [49, 65]. This was also consistent with comments from the participants in the ARTS condition as they expressed frustration pertaining to the repetitive presentation of the same difficult cards.

5.2 Practical Implications

Our findings also have implications for adaptive training system designers and educators to enhance the effectiveness of such training systems by accounting for learner engagement. This is because, when engagement was accounted for, the training had significant effects on learning gains. Designers should consider the design of systems that monitor engagement in real-time, detect times when the learner is disengaged or frustrated, and adapt material based on the combination of performance and state to foster learning. It appears that the repetitive display of difficult cards that were inaccurately identified may have created negative emotions as evidenced by the lower engagement scores for

ARTS compared to the control condition as well as the negative effect of the training on engagement. Perhaps there is a threshold for the number of times an individual gets an item wrong before getting frustrated and demotivated. Thus, future research should consider this and potential mitigation strategies.

Also, the difficulty of the flashcard content or learning material may have played a role in these results. There were some African countries that were very similar in location, name, size, and/or shape, and could have been difficult for participants to distinguish, which increased the perceived difficulty of the task itself, making it too demanding. Extant research in learning has found challenging tasks to engender higher learning outcomes [66, 67], however, caution is echoed with regard to ensuring that the tasks in adaptive training systems are not extremely challenging lest they stimulate frustration [68, 69, 70]. This means there is a tradeoff between task difficulty and its benefits and opens avenues for scholars to investigate the acceptable levels of difficulty to determine at what stage the challenge can become extremely difficult and detrimental to the effectiveness of the training and performance of the learner. Thus, designers of adaptive training systems might need to pay special attention to the difficulty of the material and how it impacts the effectiveness of the training.

6 Conclusions and Future Research

We presented novel findings regarding the influence of affective learning states, specifically engagement, in adaptive training interventions especially flashcard-based adaptive training, an underexplored area. We found that the effectiveness of the training with respect to learning gains was mediated by engagement such that training led to lower engagement which in turn canceled out the learning gains. When engagement levels were accounted for, we found that training had significant direct effects and indirect effects through engagement on immediate and delayed gains. Studying the impact of engagement in adaptive training is especially significant because adaptive training focuses on personalization of the training based on individual learners' strengths, experiences, and weaknesses during the training to adapt training material and content to their capabilities. Future research is needed that focuses on identifying other affective learning states and how they may impact the training effectiveness of adaptive training systems. Such research would inform future researchers and instructional designers on how to develop adaptive training systems that foster engagement and other positive affective states to optimize training outcomes.

References

1. Whitmer, D.E., Johnson, C.I., Marraffino, M.D.: Examining two adaptive sequencing approaches for flashcard learning: the Tradeoff between training efficiency and long-term retention. In: Sottilare, R.A., Schwarz, J. (eds.) Adaptive Instructional Systems. HCII 2022. Lecture Notes in Computer Science, vol. 13332, pp. 126–139. Springer, Cham (2022) https://doi.org/10.1007/978-3-031-05887-5_10
2. Landsberg, C.R., Astwood, R.S., Van Buskirk, W.L., Townsend, L.N., Steinhauser, N.B., Mercado, A.D.: Review of adaptive training system techniques. Mil. Psychol. 24(2), 96–113 (2012). https://doi.org/10.1080/08995605.2012.672903

3. Mettler, E., Burke, T., Massey, C.M., Kellman, P.J.: Comparing adaptive and random spacing schedules during learning to mastery criteria. In: *CogSci* Annual Conference of the Cognitive Science Society. Cognitive Science Society (US). Conference, vol. 2020, pp. 773–779 (2020)
4. Mettler, E., Kellman, P.J.: Adaptive response-time-based category sequencing in perceptual learning. Vision Res. **99**, 111–123 (2014). https://doi.org/10.1016/j.visres.2013.12.009
5. Whitmer, D.E., Johnson, C.I., Marraffino, M.D., Pharmer, R.L., Blalock, L.D.: A mastery approach to flashcard-based adaptive training. In: Sottilare, R.A., Schwarz, J. (eds.) HCII 2020. LNCS, vol. 12214, pp. 555–568. Springer, Cham (2020). https://doi.org/10.1007/978-3-030-50788-6_41
6. Zahabi, M., Abdul Razak, A.M.: Adaptive virtual reality-based training: a systematic literature review and framework. Virtual Reality **24**(4), 725–752 (2020). https://doi.org/10.1007/s10 055-020-00434-w
7. Durlach, P.J., Ray, J.M.: Designing Adaptive Instructional Environments: Insights from Empirical Evidence. Defense Technical Information Center, Fort Belvoir (2011). https://doi. org/10.21236/ADA552677
8. Graesser, A.C., D'Mello, S.: Chapter five - emotions during the learning of difficult material. Psychol. Learn. Motiv. **57**, 183–225 (2012). https://doi.org/10.1016/B978-0-12-394293-7. 00005-4
9. Holmes, J., Gathercole, S.E., Dunning, D.L.: Adaptive training leads to sustained enhancement of poor working memory in children. Dev. Sci. **12**(4), F9–F15 (2009). https://doi.org/ 10.1111/j.1467-7687.2009.00848.x
10. Landsberg, C.R., Mercado, A.D., Van Buskirk, W.L., Lineberry, M., Steinhauser, N.: Evaluation of an adaptive training system for submarine periscope operations. In: Proceedings of the Human Factors and Ergonomics Society annual meeting, vol. 56, no. 1, pp. 2422–2426 (2012)
11. Mettler, E., Massey, C.M., Kellman, P.J.: Improving adaptive learning technology through the use of response times (2011). https://eric.ed.gov/?id=ED549436. Accessed 28 Jan 2023
12. Engeser, S., Rheinberg, F.: Flow, performance and moderators of challenge-skill balance. Motiv. Emot. **32**(3), 158–172 (2008)
13. Shernoff, D.J., Csikszentmihalyi, M., Shneider, B., Shernoff, E.S.: Student engagement in high school classrooms from the perspective of flow theory. Sch. Psychol. Q. **18**, 158–176 (2003). https://doi.org/10.1521/scpq.18.2.158.21860
14. Alyüz, N., et al.: Towards an emotional engagement model: can affective states of a learner be automatically detected in a 1: 1 learning scenario?. In: UMAP (Extended Proceedings) (2016)
15. Carroll, M., Lindsey, S., Chaparro, M., Winslow, B.: An applied model of learner engagement and strategies for increasing learner engagement in the modern educational environment. Interact. Learn. Environ. **29**(5), 757–771 (2021)
16. de Manzano, Ö., Theorell, T., Harmat, L., Ullén, F.: The psychophysiology of flow during piano playing. Emotion **10**, 301–311 (2010). https://doi.org/10.1037/a0018432
17. Mark, G., Czerwinski, M., Iqbal, S.T.: Effects of individual differences in blocking workplace distractions. In: Proceedings of the 2018 CHI Conference on Human Factors in Computing Systems, Montreal, pp. 1–12 (2018). https://doi.org/10.1145/3173574.3173666
18. D'Mello, S.: A selective meta-analysis on the relative incidence of discrete affective states during learning with technology. J. Educ. Psychol. **105**(4), 1082 (2013)
19. Frenzel, A.C., Pekrun, R., Goetz, T.: Perceived learning environment and students' emotional experiences: a multilevel analysis of mathematics classrooms. Learn. Instr. **17**(5), 478–493 (2007)
20. Goetz, T., Hall, N.C.: Emotion and achievement in the classroom. In: International Guide to Student Achievement, Routledge, pp. 192–195 (2013)

21. Cronhjort, M., Filipsson, L., Weurlander, M.: Improved engagement and learning in flipped-classroom calculus. Teach. Math. Appl. Int. J. IMA **37**(3), 113–121 (2018). https://doi.org/10.1093/teamat/hrx007

22. Guo, Y.: The influence of academic autonomous motivation on learning engagement and life satisfaction in adolescents: the mediating role of basic psychological needs satisfaction. J. Educ. Learn. **7**(4), 254 (2018). https://doi.org/10.5539/jel.v7n4p254

23. Erhel, S., Jamet, E.: Improving instructions in educational computer games: exploring the relations between goal specificity, flow experience and learning outcomes. Comput. Hum. Behav. **91**, 106–114 (2019). https://doi.org/10.1016/j.chb.2018.09.020

24. Hou, H.-T.: Integrating cluster and sequential analysis to explore learners' flow and behavioral patterns in a simulation game with situated-learning context for science courses: a video-based process exploration. Comput. Hum. Behav. **48**, 424–435 (2015)

25. Leiker, A.M., Miller, M., Brewer, L., Nelson, M., Siow, M., Lohse, K.: The relationship between engagement and neurophysiological measures of attention in motion-controlled video games: a randomized controlled trial. JMIR Serious Games **4**(1), e5460 (2016). https://doi.org/10.2196/games.5460

26. Christenson, S., Reschly, A.L., Wylie, C.: Handbook of Research on Student Engagement, vol. 840. Springer, New York (2012) https://doi.org/10.1007/978-1-4614-2018-7

27. Finn, J.D., Zimmer, K.S.: Student Engagement: What is it? Why Does it Matter?. Handbook of Research on Student Engagement, pp. 97–131 (2012)

28. Pardos, Z.A., Baker, R.S., San Pedro, M.O., Gowda, S.M., Gowda, S.M.: Affective states and state tests: investigating how affect and engagement during the school year predict end-of-year learning outcomes. J. Learn. Anal. **1**(1), 107–128 (2014)

29. Loderer, K., Pekrun, R., Lester, J.C.: Beyond cold technology: a systematic review and meta-analysis on emotions in technology-based learning environments. Learn. Instr. **70**, 101162 (2020). https://doi.org/10.1016/j.learninstruc.2018.08.002

30. Mettler, E., Massey, C.M., Kellman, P.J.: A comparison of adaptive and fixed schedules of practice. J. Exp. Psychol. Gen. **145**(7), 897 (2016)

31. Bahrick, H.P., Bahrick, L.E., Bahrick, A.S., Bahrick, P.E.: Maintenance of foreign language vocabulary and the spacing effect. Psychol. Sci. **4**(5), 316–321 (1993)

32. Cepeda, N.J., Pashler, H., Vul, E., Wixted, J.T., Rohrer, D.: Distributed practice in verbal recall tasks: a review and quantitative synthesis. Psychol. Bull. **132**(3), 354 (2006)

33. Kornell, N.: Optimising learning using flashcards: spacing is more effective than cramming. Appl. Cogn. Psychol. Off. J. Soc. Appl. Res. Mem. Cogn. **23**(9), 1297–1317 (2009)

34. Pyc, M.A., Rawson, K.A.: Testing the retrieval effort hypothesis: does greater difficulty correctly recalling information lead to higher levels of memory? J. Mem. Lang. **60**(4), 437–447 (2009)

35. Mettler, E., Massey, C.M., Burke, T., Garrigan, P., Kellman, P.J.: 'Enhancing adaptive learning through strategic scheduling of passive and active learning modes. In: Proceedings of the 40th Annual Conference of the Cognitive Science Society (2018). https://par.nsf.gov/biblio/10087104-enhancing-adaptive-learning-through-strategic-scheduling-passive-active-learning-modes. Accessed 03 Feb 2023

36. Appleton, J.J., Christenson, S.L., Kim, D., Reschly, A.L.: Measuring cognitive and psychological engagement: validation of the student engagement instrument. J. Sch. Psychol. **44**(5), 427–445 (2006). https://doi.org/10.1016/j.jsp.2006.04.002

37. Wang, C., Mirzaei, T., Xu, T., Lin, H.: How learner engagement impacts non-formal online learning outcomes through value co-creation: an empirical analysis. Int. J. Educ. Technol. High. Educ. **19**(1), 1–26 (2022)

38. Lee, J., Park, T., Davis, R.O.: What affects learner engagement in flipped learning and what predicts its outcomes? Br. J. Educ. Technol. **53**(2), 211–228 (2022). https://doi.org/10.1111/bjet.12717

39. Moore, K.A., Lippman, L.H.: What do children need to flourish?: Conceptualizing and measuring indicators of positive development, vol. 3. Springer, New York (2006). https://doi.org/10.1007/b100487
40. Sinatra, G.M., Heddy, B.C., Lombardi, D.: The challenges of defining and measuring student engagement in science. Educ. Psychol. **50**(1), 1–13 (2015)
41. Nakamura, J., Csikszentmihalyi, M.: The Concept of Flow. Handbook of Positive Psychology, vol. 89, p. 105 (2002)
42. Whitson, C., Consoli, J.: Flow theory and student engagement. J. Cross-Discip. Perspect. Educ. **2**(1), 40–49 (2009)
43. Shernoff, D.J., Anderson, B.: Enacting Flow and Student Engagement in the College Classroom. *The Wiley* Blackwell Handbook of Positive Psychological Interventions, pp. 194–212 (2014)
44. Shernoff, D.J., Csikszentmihalyi, M.: Cultivating Engaged Learners and Optimal Learning Environments', Handbook of Positive Psychology in Schools, vol. 131, p. 145 (2009)
45. Csikszentmihalyi, M.: Flow and education. NAMTA J. **22**(2), 2–35 (1997)
46. Pavlas, D., Heyne, K., Bedwell, W., Lazzara, E., Salas, E.: Game-based learning: the impact of flow state and videogame self-efficacy. In: Proceedings of the Human Factors and Ergonomics Society Annual Meeting, vol. 54, no. 28, pp. 2398–2402 (2010)
47. Jackson, S.A., Marsh, H.W.: Development and validation of a scale to measure optimal experience: the flow state scale. J. Sport Exerc. Psychol. **18**(1), 17–35 (1996)
48. Yoshida, K., Sawamura, D., Inagaki, Y., Ogawa, K., Ikoma, K., Sakai, S.: Brain activity during the flow experience: a functional near-infrared spectroscopy study. Neurosci. Lett. **573**, 30–34 (2014)
49. Yoshida, K., et al.: The flow state scale for occupational tasks: development, reliability, and validity. Hong Kong J. Occup. Ther. **23**(2), 54–61 (2013)
50. Bell, B., Kelsey, E., Nye, B.: Monitoring engagement and motivation across learning environments, Los Angel (2019)
51. Hayes, A.F.: Beyond Baron and Kenny: statistical mediation analysis in the new millennium. Commun. Monogr. **76**(4), 408–420 (2009)
52. Hayes, A.F., Preacher, K.J., Myers, T.A.: Mediation and the estimation of indirect effects in political communication research. Sourceb. Polit. Commun. Res. Methods, Measures, Anal. Tech.**23**(1), 434–465 (2011)
53. Iacobucci, D.: Mediation analysis and categorical variables: the final frontier. J. Consum. Psychol. **22**(4), 582–594 (2012)
54. Hu, P.J.-H., Hui, W.: Examining the role of learning engagement in technology-mediated learning and its effects on learning effectiveness and satisfaction. Decis. Support Syst. **53**(4), 782–792 (2012). https://doi.org/10.1016/j.dss.2012.05.014
55. Nkhoma, M., Sriratanaviriyakul, N., Pham Cong, H., Khai Lam, T.: Examining the mediating role of learning engagement, learning process and learning experience on the learning outcomes through localized real case studies. Educ. Train. **56**(4), 287–302 (2014). https://doi.org/10.1108/ET-01-2013-0005
56. Ayçiçek, B., Yanpar Yelken, T.: The Effect of flipped classroom model on students' classroom engagement in teaching English. Int. J. Instr. **11**(2), 385–398 (2018)
57. Bond, M.: Facilitating student engagement through the flipped learning approach in K-12: a systematic review. Comput. Educ. **151**, 103819 (2020). https://doi.org/10.1016/j.compedu.2020.103819
58. Johnson, L.S.: Relationship of instructional methods to student engagement in two public high schools. Am. Second. Educ. **36**(2), 69–87 (2008)
59. Hamari, J., Koivisto, J.: Measuring flow in gamification: dispositional flow scale-2. Comput. Hum. Behav. **40**, 133–143 (2014). https://doi.org/10.1016/j.chb.2014.07.048

60. Shernoff, D.J.: Optimal Learning Environments to Promote Student Engagement (2013)
61. Procci, K., Singer, A.R., Levy, K.R., Bowers, C.: Measuring the flow experience of gamers: an evaluation of the DFS-2. Comput. Hum. Behav. **28**(6), 2306–2312 (2012)
62. Wang, L., Chen, M.: The effects of game strategy and preference-matching on flow experience and programming performance in game-based learning. Innov. Educ. Teach. Int. **47**(1), 39–52 (2010). https://doi.org/10.1080/14703290903525838
63. Ceja, L., Navarro, J.: "Suddenly I get into the zone": examining discontinuities and nonlinear changes in flow experiences at work. Hum. Relat. **65**(9), 1101–1127 (2012). https://doi.org/10.1177/0018726712447116
64. Oyama, Y., Manalo, E., Nakatani, Y.: The Hemingway effect: how failing to finish a task can have a positive effect on motivation. Think. Ski. Creat. **30**, 7–18 (2018). https://doi.org/10.1016/j.tsc.2018.01.001
65. Fullagar, C.J., Knight, P.A., Sovern, H.S.: Challenge/skill balance, flow, and performance anxiety. Appl. Psychol. **62**(2), 236–259 (2013). https://doi.org/10.1111/j.1464-0597.2012.00494.x
66. LePine, J.A., LePine, M.A., Jackson, C.L.: Challenge and hindrance stress: relationships with exhaustion, motivation to learn, and learning performance. J. Appl. Psychol. **89**, 883–891 (2004). https://doi.org/10.1037/0021-9010.89.5.883
67. Senko, C., Tropiano, K.L.: Comparing three models of achievement goals: goal orientations, goal standards, and goal complexes. J. Educ. Psychol. **108**, 1178–1192 (2016). https://doi.org/10.1037/edu0000114
68. Bloom, B.S.: Human characteristics and school learning. New York, NY, US: McGraw-Hill, pp. xii, 284 (1976)
69. Bloom, B.S.: The 2 sigma problem: the search for methods of group instruction as effective as one-to-one tutoring. Educ. Res. **13**(6), 4–16 (1984). https://doi.org/10.3102/0013189X013006004
70. Vygotsky, L.S., Cole, M.: Mind in Society: Development of Higher Psychological Processes. Harvard University Press, Cambridge (1978)

Trust Acceptance Mapping - Designing Intelligent Systems for Use in an Educational Context

Graham Parsonage[1,2(✉)], Matthew Horton[1], and Janet Read[1]

[1] University of Central Lancashire, Preston, UK
{gbparsonage1,mplhorton,jcread}@uclan.ac.uk
[2] University of the West of Scotland, Paisley, UK
graham.parsonage@uws.ac.uk
https://chici.org/

Abstract. Intelligent systems are not a new concept. It is generally accepted that the term 'artificial intelligence' or AI was first coined by Professor John McCarthy in 1956 and prior to that Alan Turing introduced what became known as the Turing Test in his 1950 paper, The Imitation Game. Given this relative longevity, it is perhaps surprising that the uptake of AI based systems in some sectors such as healthcare and education has been limited. This paper considers the deployment of an intelligent system in an educational context and proposes a model to inform the design of such based upon the relationship between trust and acceptance.

Keywords: Intelligent Systems · Education · Model

1 Introduction

Intelligent systems are not a new concept. It is generally accepted that the term 'artificial intelligence' or AI was first coined by Professor John McCarthy in 1956 [1] and prior to that Alan Turing introduced what became known as the Turing Test in his 1950 paper, The Imitation Game [18]. Given this relative longevity, it is perhaps surprising that the uptake of AI based systems in some sectors such as healthcare [5] and education [3] has been limited. This paper considers the deployment of an intelligent system in an educational context that monitors children's behaviour during interaction with a computer or other digital technology and potentially makes an intervention if it identifies activity that may not be in the child's best interest. A model is proposed called the Trust Acceptance Mapping Model to inform the design of such a system based upon the relationship between trust and acceptance.

1.1 Stakeholders, Trust and Acceptance

Designing any system for children is likely to require satisfying the requirements of at least three groups of stakeholders [11]:

© The Author(s), under exclusive license to Springer Nature Switzerland AG 2023
R. A. Sottilare and J. Schwarz (Eds.): HCII 2023, LNCS 14044, pp. 34–50, 2023.
https://doi.org/10.1007/978-3-031-34735-1_3

- The learner (child)
- Parents or carers
- The education establishment (teachers)

For the system to be effective the child should be accepting of the systems outputs whilst parents and teachers need to trust the system to make effective and appropriate judgments. Trust [10] and acceptance [19] are core components in the successful adoption of most systems but the potential for a stochastic intelligent system to change its output as it learns, potentially generating inconsistencies in its judgments, may make these goals harder to achieve [7]. Trust between humans is a complex and multifaceted concept supporting the belief that another will act with benevolence, integrity, predictability and competence [12]. When evaluating or testing intelligent systems for trustworthiness, studies often identify competence [20] and the transparency of the decision making process [16] as the primary exponents of trust. This study focuses primarily on the system's competence.

1.2 Intelligent Systems and Educational Context

The use of the term educational context as opposed to classroom is quite deliberate. Learning frequently takes place outside the classroom [2] and education is now delivered over diverse and often distributed platforms. Massive Open Online Courses (MOOCs) popularised mass online education in 2008 [9] and the Covid-19 lockdowns of 2020 and 2021 took education from all sectors out of the physical classroom and in to virtual spaces offered by environments such as MS Teams and Zoom [17]. This move online highlighted some key challenges, not least the issue of monitoring pupil and student engagement [13,14] and online behaviour [15].

Whilst mainstream school level education in the UK has largely returned to the physical classroom, the pandemic has fast-forwarded the development and adoption of hybrid and blended learning pedagogical approaches [21] highlighting the requirement for a tool that can aid parents and teachers to monitor and interpret children's interaction with content both online, remotely and in the classroom.

The context or location of the teaching and learning also informs the scope and nature of the interaction between the system and the child. Within the classroom, teachers are likely to have a higher degree of control over the content presented to the child than the parent or carer may have within the home. Consequently we concentrate on monitoring for engagement within the classroom whilst examining a wider set of use cases that may face parents and carers within the wider educational context.

1.3 Monitoring Engagement

Pupil engagement is widely considered to be a positive factor in, and an important driver of, pupil attainment [4]. Definitions of engagement range from a focus on interaction with a specific learning activity to a multidimensional approach requiring the pupil to engage at behavioural, affective and cognitive levels [8]. For the purpose of these studies, we consider engagement on task, namely a pupil's interaction with a computerised learning activity completed within an educational context. Furthermore, whereas some scholars conceptualise engagement and disengagement as related but separate phenomena [6], within this context engagement and disengagement are treated as the opposing ends of a single scale.

2   Studies

Three studies were conducted with the stakeholders to ascertain their trust and acceptance of a theoretical intelligent system to be deployed in an educational context. Children were surveyed on the level of their acceptance of interventions in their digital activity made by both adults and the technology. Parents and carers were asked whether they would trust a technology to either monitor or act if their child was exposed to a given set of use cases. Teachers were interviewed as to how they would feel if a system to monitor pupil engagement was deployed in their classroom, specifically their acceptance and trust in the system's outputs.

Study 1 surveyed children to assess their acceptance of intervention in a digital activity by either an adult or an intelligent system. Study 2 surveyed parents or carers to gain insight into their trust in an intelligent system to either monitor or intervene in a child's digital activity. For Study 3, teachers were interviewed to ascertain their attitudes towards the deployment in the classroom of a system that could monitor the pupils and make interventions if they showed signs of disengagement.

There were 4 research questions:

R1 Are children more accepting of an intervention from a responsible adult than an intelligent system? (Study 1)
R2 To what extent do parents and carers trust technology to monitor their child's digital activity? (Study 2)
R3 To what extent do parents and carers trust technology to intervene in their child's digital activity? (Study 2)
R4 Would teacher's trust an intelligent system to monitor children in their classroom for signs of disengagement and make appropriate interventions? (Study 3)

2.1   Participants

2.1.1   Study 1. One hundred and twenty-nine children were recruited from a secondary school located in the UK. There were seventy-six females and fifty-three males. Ages ranged from 11 to 17 years (mean = 13.27, SD = 1.462).

2.1.2   Study 2. Twenty-seven parents or carers were recruited through social media and word of mouth. There were fourteen females and eleven males, two participants did not disclose their gender. For the age ranges see Table 1. All participants participated voluntarily and no incentives were given.

Table 1. Adult Age Ranges

Age	Frequency	Percent
Age not Disclosed	1	3.7
25–34	2	7.4
35–44	15	55.6
45–54	6	22.2
55–64	3	11.1
Total	27	100.0

2.1.3   Study 3. Video interviews were conducted over two days with ten teachers, five male and five female from two UK secondary schools.

2.2   Apparatus

For the surveys carried out in Study 1 and Study 2, the data was collected remotely using a web-based interface. Paper versions of the survey were also made available. The survey software was developed using PHP and MySQL and hosted on an Apache web server. JQuery UI was used to implement the interactive user interface. The software was designed to be mobile responsive so that participants could complete the survey on smart phones and tablets as well as desktop PCs and laptops. Both studies combined questions using a Likert scale with values ranging from 1 to 10 where 1 indicated low consensus and 10 indicated high consensus.

Study 1 consisted of twenty-one questions. Twenty questions used the Likert scale and one question allowed the participant to enter free text. Study 2 consisted of thirty-two questions. Thirty questions used the Likert scale and two questions allowed the participant to enter free text.

2.3   Procedure

2.3.1   Study 1 was password protected and only made available to the participating school. The head teacher completed consent forms to allow the children to participate in the survey. Additionally, children were given the option to opt out individually before submitting their data. The surveys were completed in a supervised environment using either the web-based form or the paper survey.

The survey was made up of two groups of ten questions. The first group of questions asked how accepting a child would be if a parent/carer or other adult intervened in their use of a digital technology for a given (this being the variable under examination) use case. The second group of questions asked, if a technology existed that could monitor the child's actions and take some action, how accepting would the child be of the intervention. The use case for the intervention was the same for each group of questions. The use cases specified in the survey were:

1. Safety
2. Security
3. Curiosity
4. Control
5. Task completion
6. Appropriateness
7. Enjoyment
8. Productivity
9. Learning
10. Economic (e.g. in game purchases).

For the first group, the question related to safety read:

> How accepting would you be if an adult took some action which effected your use of a digital technology because they were concerned about your safety?

The corresponding question for the second group read:

> How accepting would you be if the technology took some action which effected your use of a digital technology because it was trying to keep you safe?

The labels on the Likert scale ranged from not accepting to very accepting. The children were also asked to provide their age and gender. One additional question asked the children to describe an occasion where an adult made an intervention related to their use of a digital technology and how they felt about it. The children were asked to complete all the questions and were able to navigate freely through the survey. The data was filtered prior to analysis so that only children who answered related questions across both groups of questions were included in the analysis for each pair of questions.

2.3.2   Study 2 was made up of a group of ten questions and a further group of 20 questions and used the same use cases as Study 1. Two additional questions allowed the participant to enter free text. The first group of questions asked whether the participant would personally intervene in their child's use of a digital technology. The second group of twenty questions asked whether participants would trust a technology to either monitor or to take action if the child was exposed to one of the use cases.

For the first group, the question related to safety read:

> How much would concern for your child's safety or wellbeing influence whether you would intervene in their use of a digital technology?

The corresponding questions for the second group read:

> To what extent would you trust the technology to monitor your child's safety?
> To what extent would you trust the technology to take appropriate action when monitoring your child's safety?

Participants were also asked to provide their age and gender and the age of their children.

The survey also contained two free text questions which asked:

Q13 Please describe any other factors which influence your decision to monitor and intervene in your child's use of digital technologies.

Q14 If applicable please describe any occasion when you have intervened in your child's use of a digital technology and the impact of that action.

The data was filtered prior to analysis so that only participants who answered related questions across both groups of questions were included in the analysis for each pair of questions.

2.3.3 Study 3 focussed on teachers' attitudes towards engagement in the classroom. The teachers interviewed were asked:

S3.1 What do you understand by disengagement?

S3.2 What strategies do you employ to identify disengagement in the classroom?

S3.3 Can you describe the interventions (or range of interventions) you employ in the classroom to address disengagement?

S3.4 How trusting would you be of the technology to monitor the children for signs of disengagement?

S3.5 How trusting would you be of the technology to intervene if it identified disengagement?

S3.6 What concerns do you have about the deployment of such a technology?

3 Results

3.1 Study 1

A comparison of the median scores recorded for the children's acceptance of an intervention by either an adult or a technology indicates that the children scored them both within a single point on the scale for all the given use cases (Table 2). With the exception of interventions for curiosity and control, all the use cases were ranked $\geq$ to the mid-point of the scale with participants indicating mid to high acceptance of an intervention whether it originated from an adult or a technology.

Mantel-Haenszel tests of trend[1] were conducted to understand whether there is an association between a child's level of acceptance of an intervention made by an adult and the level of acceptance of an intervention made by a technology for the same use case. The Mantel-Haenszel tests of trend showed a statistically significant linear association between the child's acceptance of intervention by an adult and their acceptance of intervention by a technology for all the use cases tested. Higher acceptance of an intervention by an adult was associated with higher acceptance of an intervention by the technology and vice versa.

---

[1] The Mantel-Haenszel test of trend is used to determine whether there is a linear trend (i.e., a linear relationship/association) between the two related ordinal variables that are represented in a crosstabulation table.

Table 2. Children's Acceptance of Intervention

Reason for Intervention	Median Score	
	Adult Acceptance	Technological Acceptance
Safety	6	6
Security	6	6
Curiosity	5	4
Control	4	4
Complete	7	7
Appropriate	6	5
Enjoyment	7	6
Productivity	6	6
Learning	8	7
Financial	5	5

Safety $\chi 2(1) = 50.595$, p < .01, r = .636
Security $\chi 2(1) = 71.045$, p < .01, r = .760
Curiosity $\chi 2(1) = 55.229$, p < .01, r = .673
Control $\chi 2(1) = 60.285$, p < .01, r = .697
Complete $\chi 2(1) = 29.188$, p < .01, r = .487
Appropriate $\chi 2(1) = 47.795$, p < .01, r = .618
Enjoyment $\chi 2(1) = 33.561$, p < .01, r = .520
Productivity $\chi 2(1) = 46.352$, p < .01, r = .614
Learning $\chi 2(1) = 37.725$, p < .01, r = .552
Financial $\chi 2(1) = 39.694$, p < .01, r = .573

A Pearson Partial Test of Correlation was used to establish the strength of the linear relationship between the variables and in all cases indicated a mid to strong positive correlation.[2]

---

[2] The Pearson test was recommended as the appropriate test to measure the strength of the correlation between the variable once a linear association had been established using a Mantel-Haenszel test of trend despite the data being ordinal and non-parametric. Spearman's rank-order correlation tests were also conducted and produced significant results in line with the results generated by the Pearson test.

3.2 Study 2

Question 2 (Q2) of Study 2 asked participants to rank how often they intervened in their child's use of digital technologies such as computers or mobile devices whilst Question 15 (Q15) asked to what extent would participants trust the technology to monitor their child's everyday use of a digital technology?

A scatter plot of Q15 by Q2 (Fig. 1) indicates that participants who ranked their frequency of intervention as low on the scale ranked their trust in the technology more highly than participants who indicated higher personal levels of intervention. A Mantel-Haenszel test of trend was conducted to understand whether there is an association between how often adults intervene in their child's use of digital technologies and to what extent they would trust an agent to monitor their child's everyday use of a digital technology. The Mantel-Haenszel test of trend showed a statistically significant linear association between frequency of intervention and trust, $\chi 2(1) = 4.999$, $p < .05$, $r = -.447$. Adults who indicated higher intervention rates were associated with a lower trust of the agent and vice-versa.

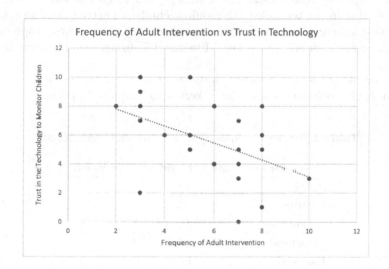

Fig. 1. Trust in Technology by Adult Intervention

Ranking the median scores for each of the use cases for personal intervention indicates that participants were more likely to intervene for reasons of safety, security, appropriate content and financial considerations (Table 3). These were also the use cases that participants indicated the highest trust in the technology to monitor or take action.

Questions 13 (Q13) and 14 (Q14) provided participants with the opportunity to elucidate further on the Likert responses. Q13 asked participants to; Describe any other factors which influence your decision to monitor and intervene in your

Table 3. Top 5 Intervention Categories Ranked by Median Score

Adult Intervention		Technology Intervention	
Safety	10	Monitor Financial	7
Security	9	Monitor Appropriate	6
Appropriate	9	Take Action Financial	6
Financial	9	Monitor Safety	5.5
Help	7	Monitor Security	5.5

child's use of digital technologies. Q14 asked; If applicable please describe any occasion when you have intervened in your child's use of a digital technology and the impact of that action. The answers provide a lens to further interpret the responses. Participants cite factors such as social media usage and online gaming where the child is interacting with a remote third party as reasons for intervention but also a desire to help and support the child in a digital activity. In all the use cases tested there was a strong positive correlation between participants' trust in the technology to monitor children's activity and to make an appropriate intervention. The tested cases were, Safety, Security, Appropriateness of Accessed Content, Enjoyment, Financial Transactions, Productivity and Learning.

An analysis of the median scores indicates that these two facets were scored within a single point on the 10-point Likert scale employed (Table 4).

Table 4. Trust in Technology to Monitor and Take Action

Reason for Intervention	Monitor	Take Action
Safety	5.5	5
Security	5.5	5
Appropriate	6	5
Enjoyment	2.5	3
Financial	7	6
Productivity	5	5
Learning	5	5

The Mantel-Haenszel test of trend showed a statically significant linear association between trust in the technology to monitor and trust in the technology to take action for all use cases.

Safety $\chi2(1) = 14.444$, p < .01, r = .811
Security $\chi2(1) = 3.383$, p < .01, r = .933
Appropriate $\chi2(1) = 7.730$, p < .01, r = .556

Enjoyment $\chi2(1) = 22.333$, p $< .01$, r $= .965$
Financial $\chi2(1) = 21.530$, p $< .01$, r $= .910$
Productivity $\chi2(1) = 18.562$, p $< .01$, r $= .862$
Learning $\chi2(1) = 17.096$, p $< .01$, r $= .844$

Participants indicated a higher level of trust in the technology's capability to monitor a use case (R2) than to take appropriate action (R3). In all cases except for Question 23 and Question 24, the technology's capability to monitor and improve the child's enjoyment of an activity, the median value recorded was $\geq$ to the midpoint of the scale indicating at least a mid-level of trust in the technology's capabilities to perform the described roles.

3.3   Study 3

In answer to the question, What do you understand by disengagement? (S3.1), nine out of the ten teachers interviewed identified it as task focussed manifested by the children not completing the work they had been set. Eight teachers also identified behavioural traits as an indicator of disengagement. Teacher's remarked that, 'Disengagement starts off with them not doing the work' and 'not completing the work they should be focussing on at that time'. Behavioural indicators described were 'gazing into space', 'clicking pens', and 'not partaking in discussions'.

When asked about the strategies they employed to identify disengagement in the classroom (S3.2), nine out of ten of the teachers stated that the most important factor was knowing the child. All of the teachers interviewed deployed a range of classroom management techniques to keep the children on track (S3.3). The teachers routinely patrolled the classroom during lessons as well as utilising questioning techniques and short task durations to maintain pupil engagement.

When asked about their feelings regarding the deployment of a system to monitor engagement (S3.4) and make interventions (S3.5) only one of the teachers interviewed indicated that they would not accept the technology in their classroom. The other teachers indicated their acceptance subject to criteria, the most common of which was that the system outputs must be accurate and support the children's learning. Teachers also expressed their concern that such a system may be used as a monitoring tool to report on their personal effectiveness rather than as a educational aid (S3.6).

4   Discussion

For the designers of intelligent systems for use in an educational context there is a requirement to balance the need of three or more stakeholders, the child, the carer or parent, and the teacher. The role of each of the parties depends to some extent on the context in which the system is deployed. Within the classroom the child is the subject of the observation and is likely to have little control over the technology and software they are interacting with whilst the intelligent system monitors them. The technology and software are selected by the school and teacher and safeguards are in place to minimise any risk to the child's wellbeing. The teacher is present in the classroom, available to receive feedback from the intelligent system and can act accordingly.

In a context outside the classroom, the child is likely to have far more freedom in what they choose to interact with. The same level of safeguards present in the classroom are unlikely to be in place and the responsible adult may not be present in the room or even at the same location. The child remains the subject of the systems observation but the system has a dual role of both monitoring the child and also intervening in the child's interaction with the digital world. This study examines a non-exhaustive set of use cases that may occur during these interactions.

The process of training the intelligent system to recognise these use cases is beyond the scope of this paper as is its implementation or embodiment. Rather, we concentrate on the interplay between the child's acceptance of the system's outputs and the adults trust in their accuracy. That the children surveyed indicated a level of acceptance of an intervention by the technology $\geq$ to the midpoint on the scale in all but two of the use cases is indicative that they are at least comfortable with the theoretical system concept. It is also interesting that the children drew little distinction between an intervention from an adult and an intervention from the technology (R1). The highest scoring use case across both categories was learning which may bode well for deployment within an educational context.

Parents and carers appear on the whole to be less trusting of the system than the children are accepting and draw a bigger distinction between their personal judgments and the systems judgments. Even so, a level of trust was indicated for all but one use case, enjoyment $\geq$ to the midpoint on the scale. This is important as they may not be physically present at the time their child is interacting with a digital device, particularly as the child gets older. It is interesting to note that of the adults surveyed those who felt more inclined to personally intervene indicated less trust in the intelligent system than those who made fewer personal interventions.

The teachers interviewed were broadly supportive of the deployment of the intelligent system in the classroom with only one teacher expressing complete opposition to its deployment (R4). The context is of course important and the system may have more of a monitoring role to identify disengagement and alert the teacher to make an appropriate intervention. This would appear to be the best supported use case with the children indicating a mid to high level of acceptance of the systems output and the teachers prepared to accept the technology within their classrooms.

4.1   Trust Acceptance Mapping Model

Within the wider educational context, we suggest that the system needs to balance the needs of both the children and the adult. The adult needs to feel sufficient trust in the system and the child needs to accept the systems interventions. This can be visualised by mapping levels of adult trust against levels of child acceptance for each of the use cases which we call the Trust Acceptance Framework (TAF). Placing trust along the x axis and acceptance on the y axis of a graph allows the data to be mapped as four quadrants (Fig. 2) with the characteristics summarised below. The top right quadrant can be regarded as the design goal where acceptance of system intervention and trust in the systems capability are both high.

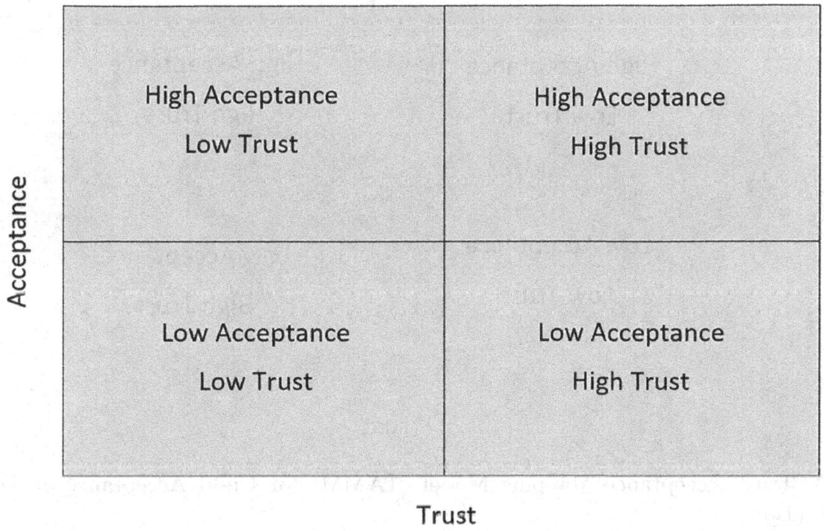

Fig. 2. Trust Acceptance Framework (TAF)

Top Left - High Acceptance and Low Trust

The child sees value in a systems capability
The adult has little or no confidence in the system capabilities or features

Bottom Left - Low Acceptance and Low Trust

The child sees little or no value in a systems capability
The adult has little or no confidence in the system capabilities or features

Top Right - High Acceptance and High Trust

The child sees value in a systems capability
The adult has confidence in the system capabilities or features

Bottom Right - Low Acceptance and High Trust

The child sees little or no value in a systems capability
The adult has confidence in the system capabilities or features

As a baseline the adults personal inclination to intervene in their child's digital activity is mapped against the child's acceptance of the intervention onto the TAF. This constitutes the Trust Acceptance Mapping Model (TAMM) (Fig. 3) which visualises the relationship between trust and acceptance for the given use cases for this configuration of the independent variables trust and acceptance.

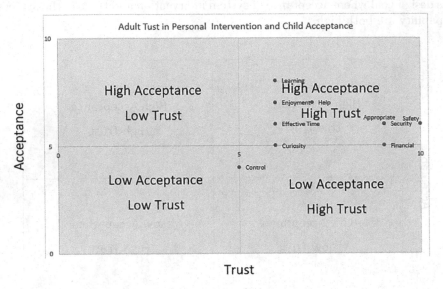

Fig. 3. Trust Acceptance Mapping Model (TAMM) for Child Acceptance of Adult Intervention

More formally the dependent variable *trust_acceptance* is a 2-tuple (couple) (x, y) where x is the trust value for the specified use case and y is the acceptance value for the specified use case and x and y are bounded such that $\{1..10\} \Rightarrow \{x \in \mathbb{Z} : 1 \le x \le 10\}$. The *trust_acceptance* values generated for each of the use cases are plotted onto the TAMM as Cartesian coordinates.

All the values for *trust_acceptance* except for the use case control fall within or on the border of the High Acceptance High Trust quadrant indicating that the adults are trusting in their own ability to intervene and the children are accepting of the interventions.

4.1.1 System as a Monitor. Figure 4 maps the data from Studies 1 and 2 onto the trust acceptance framework where the adult is expressing their level of trust in the systems monitoring of the child's behaviour and the child is expressing their level of acceptance of the systems output. The learning, productivity (effective time), appropriate content and financial use cases all sit on the edge of the High Acceptance and High Trust quadrant with adults placing greater trust in the monitoring of financial transactions and monitoring content whilst the children are more accepting of learning and productivity.

From a system designers perspective there is at least a consensus on the features on which a design can be based. The enjoyment use case sits in the High Acceptance and Low Trust quadrant indicating that whilst the children's acceptance of an intervention based on these grounds is high, the adult has little trust in the systems capabilities and it is unlikely to be accepted if implemented.

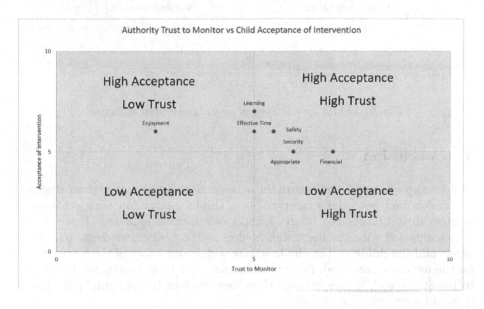

Fig. 4. TAMM for the System as a Monitor

4.1.2 System as an Interventional Agent. Where the system is required to intervene in the child's digital interaction as opposed to just monitor it, it is less trusted by the adults to execute interventions and none of the data points fall inside the High Acceptance High Trust quadrant (Fig. 5). Clearly this may have implications if there is no adult present to personally perform the intervention if the child is performing some action that may affect their wellbeing. This is an area for further work and one such path is to assess how the embodiment of the system affects stakeholders' trust and acceptance of its outputs.

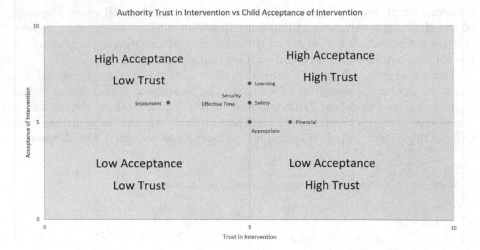

Fig. 5. TAMM for the System as an Interventional Agent

5   Conclusion

Child acceptance and adult trust in a theoretical intelligent system designed to monitor and potentially intervene in a child's interaction with a computer or other digital technology in an educational context is explored. Three studies were conducted with the main stakeholders in the system, teachers, parents or carers and the children. The children were widely accepting of the interventions for the use cases presented. Parents and carers were more trusting of the system to monitor the children's activity than they were of the system's potential to make an appropriate intervention.

It was identified that the system may have to play a different role dependent on the educational context it is deployed in. Within the school classroom, the teacher is present and the child's interaction with any technology is closely controlled. Under these circumstances it makes sense to deploy the system as a tool to monitor the children's behaviour and alert the teacher. The teachers interviewed were generally positive about the potential deployment of such a system in their classroom. In a wider educational context, there may be less control over the technology and software the child my encounter and the adult may not always be present. There is a conflict here between this increased risk to the children and the parents and carers decreased trust in the system to act as an interventional agent.

The Trust Acceptance Mapping Model is presented as a tool to indicate the likely success of the intelligent system design. Use cases which reside in the top right High Acceptance High Trust quadrant are likely to have a greater chance of adoption than those that fall in the other quadrants.

References

1. Andresen, S.L.: John McCarthy: father of AI. IEEE Intell. Syst. **17**, 84–85 (2002)
2. Brahimi, T., Sarirete, A.: Learning outside the classroom through MOOCs. Comput. Hum. Behav. **51**, 604–609 (2015). https://doi.org/10.1016/j.chb.2015.03.013
3. Celik, I., Dindar, M., Muukkonen, H., Järvelä, S.: The promises and challenges of artificial intelligence for teachers: a systematic review of research. TechTrends **66**, 616–630 (2022)
4. Christenson, S., Reschly, A.L., Wylie, C., et al.: Handbook of Research on Student Engagement, vol. 840. Springer, New York (2012)
5. Cornelissen, L., Egher, C., van Beek, V., Williamson, L., Hommes, D.: The drivers of acceptance of artificial intelligence-powered care pathways among medical professionals: web-based survey study. JMIR Formative Res. **6**, e33368 (2022)
6. Fredricks, J.A., Blumenfeld, P.C., Paris, A.H.: School engagement: potential of the concept, state of the evidence. Rev. Educ. Res. **74**, 59–109 (2004). https://doi.org/10.3102/00346543074001059
7. Glikson, E., Woolley, A.W.: Human trust in artificial intelligence: review of empirical research. Acad. Manage. Ann. **14**, 627–660 (2020)
8. Groccia, J.E.: What is student engagement? New directions for teaching and learning, pp. 11–20 (2018). https://doi.org/10.1002/tl.20287, https://onlinelibrary.wiley.com/doi/10.1002/tl.20287
9. Hidalgo, F.J.P., Abril, C.A.H., Parra, M.G.: MOOCs: origins, concept and didactic applications: a systematic review of the literature (2012–2019). Technol. Knowl. Learn. **25**, 853–879 (2020)
10. Holliday, D., Wilson, S., Stumpf, S.: User trust in intelligent systems: a journey over time. In: Proceedings of the 21st International Conference on Intelligent User Interfaces (2016). https://doi.org/10.1145/2856767
11. Hourcade, J.P.: Child-computer interaction. Self, Iowa City, Iowa (2015)
12. Mcknight, D.H., Chervany, N.L.: Trust and distrust definitions : one bite at a time. In: Proceedings of the workshop on Deception, Fraud, and Trust in Agent Societies held during the Autonomous Agents Conference: Trust in Cyber-societies, Integrating the Human and Artificial Perspectives, pp. 27–54 (2000)
13. Oyedotun, T.D.: Sudden change of pedagogy in education driven by COVID-19: perspectives and evaluation from a developing country. Res. Globalization **2**, 100029 (2020)
14. Pokhrel, S., Chhetri, R.: A literature review on impact of COVID-19 pandemic on teaching and learning. High. Educ. Future **8**, 133–141 (2021)
15. Prathish, S., Athi Narayanan, S., Bijlani, K.: An intelligent system for online exam monitoring. In: 2016 International Conference on Information Science (ICIS), pp. 138–143 (2016). https://doi.org/10.1109/INFOSCI.2016.7845315
16. Schmidt, P., Biessmann, F., Teubner, T.: Transparency and trust in artificial intelligence systems. J. Decis. Syst. **29**, 260–278 (2020). https://doi.org/10.1080/12460125.2020.1819094
17. Tandon, U.: Factors influencing adoption of online teaching by school teachers: a study during COVID-19 pandemic. J. Public Aff. **21**, e2503 (2021)
18. Turing, A.M.: Computing machinery and intelligence. In: Epstein, R., Roberts, G., Beber, G. (eds.) Parsing the Turing Test, pp. 23–65. Springer, Dordrecht (2009). https://doi.org/10.1007/978-1-4020-6710-5_3
19. Venkatesh, V.: Adoption and use of AI tools: a research agenda grounded in UTAUT. Ann. Oper. Res. **308**, 1–2 (2022)

20. Waytz, A., Heafner, J., Epley, N.: The mind in the machine: anthropomorphism increases trust in an autonomous vehicle. J. Exp. Soc. Psychol. **52**, 113–117 (2014). https://doi.org/10.1016/j.jesp.2014.01.005
21. Zhao, Y., Watterston, J.: The changes we need: education post COVID-19. J. Educ. Change **22**, 3–12 (2021)

Human Performance Data Lifecycle Management as a Foundation for Adaptive Training

Fritz Ray, Benjamin Bell[✉], and Elliot Robson

Eduworks Corporation, Corvallis, OR, USA
{fritz.ray,benjamin.bell,elliot.robson}@eduworks.com

Abstract. Despite much progress in adaptive training, the data driving adaptations are largely local and temporary. Significant enhancements to adaptive training are achievable given a more comprehensive picture of the competencies being trained and current and correct learner profiles. In this paper we present an approach to creating a human performance data layer that offers a foundation to enhance adaptive training. We describe multiple recent projects for the U.S. Navy that are converging on tools to support a lifecycle management approach for human performance data. By creating a digital thread of competencies and applying techniques that map performance data to corresponding competencies, these tools can provide a rich array of analytics to training managers, workforce planners, and line supervisors.

Keywords: Human Performance · Analytics · Competency-based Training

1 Introduction

1.1 Human Performance Data as a Touchstone for Adaptive Training

Adaptive training has enjoyed substantive advances as student modeling, intelligent tutoring, and discourse capabilities have accelerated. Adapting training using contemporary techniques (generally employing various AI approaches) leverages data generated during instructional interactions by the environment, user actions, entity behaviors, and outcomes [1, 2]. While much progress has been made, data used for adaptations are largely local and temporary. Broad enhancements to adaptive training efficacy are achievable given a more comprehensive and persistent learner profile and comprehensive picture of the competencies being trained [3, 4]. What is needed is a human performance data layer that offers a foundation to enhance adaptive training.

Throughout these three projects, we identified the need for a digital representation of Navy sailor capability throughout several identified sailor-centered phases: Education, Training, Certification, Qualification, Practice, and Mission Performance. These phases anchor what we term the human performance data lifecycle. Digitizing Navy authoritative source data, we laid out a dataset that included a number of these phases and linked

R. A. Sottilare and J. Schwarz (Eds.): HCII 2023, LNCS 14044, pp. 51–59, 2023.
https://doi.org/10.1007/978-3-031-34735-1_4

the data such that issues identified in practice could be analyzed to highlight training needs throughout the phases. This holistic approach to root cause analysis in the sailor domain supported training-based content remediation based on faults in practice, and enabled subsequent phases based on completion or experience in previous phases.

This digitization process overcomes the limitations of previous efforts to digitize written records, which were insufficient to render natural language free text into machine-actionable representations. Our approach blends document analysis and automation techniques that process PDFs, word documents, and spreadsheets to generate Linked Data that operates as an inventory of sailor capability data across the human performance data lifecycle. Once sufficiently digitized and linked, automation systems can augment human personnel management decision support capabilities by providing a structure upon which to record training or live performance, capture performance events using video, audio, or machine data as evidence, and remediate at a level of granularity specific to the issues identified while simultaneously being able to identify the impact of those faults.

In the next section we summarize how work performed for the U.S. Navy is converging to establish a lifecycle management approach for human performance data. By creating a digital thread of sailor competencies and applying techniques that map performance data to corresponding competencies, these tools can provide a rich array of analytics to training managers, workforce planners, and line supervisors.

1.2   Converging on an Approach: Three Separate but Related Navy Programs

Our expectations that adaptive learning can be enabled by effective human performance data management are informed by three recent projects for the U.S. Navy. In these projects, we applied human performance data lifecycle management techniques to 1) collect and report performance data that informs training gaps; 2) identify training based on these gaps and prescribe content germane to the sailor's current curriculum; and 3) update curricular pathways with training requirements detected using task-based training gap analysis.

Eduworks' support for the *Surface Training and Readiness Management System* (STRMS) included collecting and integrating performance data from multiple sources during on-ship exercises done as part of routine training and qualification procedures. This data will be sent shoreside and may be incorporated into training decisions to remediate performance gaps, support further training and qualification, and perform watch team staffing decisions.

In the *My Navy Learning* (MNL) project, we supported the use of data from STRMS, permitting ship systems, training officers, or the individual sailor to identify training goals and objectives and close training gaps.

For the *Rating and Career Domain Continuum Development* (RCDC) project, we applied tools to manage and update rating career flow maps outlining typical Sailor progressions through rating milestones using a task-based training gap analysis process, resulting in training development proposals used to address systemic training issues associated with new equipment or discontinued courses.

Each of these efforts developed new tools and techniques that contribute to our integrated, holistic approach to human performance data lifecycle management. In the following sections we discuss each program, and its resulting outcomes, in greater detail.

These three projects address different areas of the sailor-centered career long learning continuum (CLLC). As mentioned previously, these areas are Education, Training, Certification, Qualification, Practice, and Mission Performance, and are all contained with the Manpower, Personnel, Training, and Education (MPT&E) domain within the Navy under the Chief of Naval Personnel.

2   STRMS

The Surface Training and Readiness Management System (STRMS) is a program aimed at providing the Navy with a comprehensive tracking and training management system in support of unit readiness, individual Watch Stander qualification and proficiency, and tactical warfare competency. STRMS will also have the capability to track individual career progression, milestone accomplishment, and schoolhouse and shipboard data collection in support of Ready Relevant Learning (RRL).

Eduworks has been working with partners to create a comprehensive capability for managing competency frameworks and learner profiles to provide a human performance data layer for STRMS, with use cases centered in the Training, Qualification, and Practice areas of the CLLC. To the surface fleet, ensuring sailors are trained, qualified, able and ready to stand watch is a key MPT&E requirement for readiness, as manning directly affects operational availability of the ship and her specific capabilities. STRMS supports this requirement by providing new digital systems for training management, PQS qualification, and links these systems to watch team planning and performance evaluation. This cluster of connected systems provides decision support to ensure sailors are qualified before being required to stand watch, remediate issues found during evolutions, drills, and exercises, and monitor the pipeline to ensure sailors are on pace to be trained and qualified into the future.

To apply this level of adaptive qualification and manning information for a single ship, we digitized dozens of qualifications, evolutions, drills, and exercises into machine-actionable formats that were then shared with the appropriate systems and provided a data backbone for storing the representations, information about sailor experience against those representations, and computed comprehensive profiles for each sailor against each qualification. These representations were then exposed via web service for each system to consume, in order to provide a synthesized single picture of current sailor capabilities.

3   MNL

My Navy Learning (MNL) is an interoperable learning system supported by several technologies and proven learning techniques and AI/ML to provide blended and adaptive training capabilities. MNL uses AI/ML algorithms to tailor training to individual job and career path requirements, and to personalize training based on individual goals and skills.

Eduworks has been supporting MNL by incorporating CaSS to support a digital system that maps, tracks, and informs Sailor progress through career-long learning.

We performed competency mapping and framework development, Navy source data digitization, learner profile definition, and an advanced API to provide interoperability across Navy information sources and systems.

MNL supports the Education, Training, Certification and Qualification portion of the CLLC by providing the sailor with a dashboard tailored to their specific situation, accounting for their chosen profession, current job, ship type that they are on (if deployed), rank or rate, billet, and goals that have been set by the sailor, their detailer, or training officer. This rich applicability information is then used to identify courses, training, and qualifications in scope of their specific situation and highlight elements that are required in order to meet the sailor's goals.

To apply this level of adaptive training, we digitized numerous course structures, qualifications, and other linking frameworks that provided connections from course to certification, from course to qualification, and from qualification to exercise or drill. In addition, we created applicability information that was then used to orient this data to a sailor in a specific situation.

One way this data was used was to interpret signals from the STRMS project when sailors were not successful in performing an on-ship evolution or drill. This data was used to generate a goal for the sailor to remediate content associated with the particular step that was failed in order to address any training deficiencies within a very short window before the drill was attempted again.

4 RCDC

The Rating and Career Domain Continuum Development (RCDC) project supports the Sailor career progression process by providing tools for Navy personnel and manpower planners and managers.

RCDC supports the MPT&E continuum by coordinating and sustaining the Sailor CLLC through performing analysis of the CLLC, identifying and closing training gaps, and providing tools to support awareness of the CLLC, including tools that display and manage a career pathway called a Career Flow Map (CFM).

The CFM is a visual representation of an occupational career provided in a poster-sized form that is being digitized and made interactive. The CFM places all typical courses, qualification, and training along a 30 year career continuum, then augments that information with situational information by ship-type. This data was digitized into applicability information suitable for the CFM, but also MNL and STRMS. The CFM is being used to identify suitable points to place new training that is created via a rich task analysis process, and then validated and resourced through a front end training analysis process.

RCDC supports the skeletal structure of the sailor-centered CLLC by providing data management practices, tools, and a sustainment process.

5 Human Performance Data Lifecycle Management: A Synthesis

Across industries, many large organizations have successfully shifted from single-vendor vertical solutions for training to multi-component learning ecosystems. These learning ecosystems are a key component in meeting the increasing demand for detailed and fine-grained human performance, capability, and skills data. For example, HR and decision-making platforms (e.g. SAP success factors, Perform Smart, Cornerstone, etc.) are relying more and more on training data to make key decisions. Even outside of the training and HR verticals, new systems and software are emerging that provide deeper customization and personalization based on the needs and abilities of the user. For example, next-generation robotic exoskeletons in the Learning Environments with Augmentation and Robotics for Next-gen Emergency Responders (LEARNER) project funded by the NSF apply skills frameworks alongside robotic support systems to improve human-machine and machin-human understanding, making the exoskeletons more responsive to the user [5]. Applications of new embedding-based generative AI models in art (e.g. Midjourney, DALL-E 2, Stable Diffusion), text (e.g. GPT 3-4, ChatGPT, etc.), and audio (e.g. VALL-E AI) rely on input prompts, and the commercial use of these tools needs contextualization and localization. In all these examples, well-curated understanding of human users is key to their success. Human performance data lifecycle management covers a set of tools and practices that make use, transmission, reuse, and interpretation of data generated by individuals and teams possible.

Like many organizations, the US DoD is heavily invested in optimizing team compositions, maximizing readiness, and improving training. Navy projects like RCDC, MNL, and STRMS exemplify a broad human-centered learning continuum that is not centered on the classroom, degree, or on the job training, but pertains to every activity the person participates in. To support this holistic digital understanding of human performance, we propose three core elements of human performance data lifecycle management: digitization, definition, and interpretation, as shown in Fig. 1.

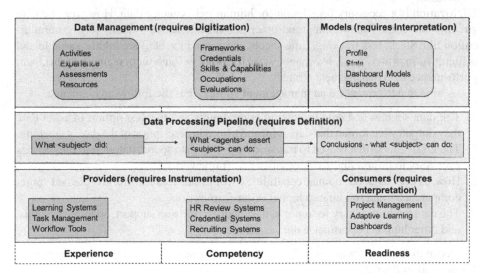

Fig. 1. Human Performance Data Lifecycle Management

Digitization

The digitization process refers to the creation of data streams and records of events, experiences, goals, and associated skills. It is the necessary first step towards realizing the full potential of new and emerging technology for human-machine interaction. Digitization consists of two steps.

First, the *digital encoding* of existing goals, business rules, doctrine, and other processes. This allows organizational objectives to be stated in terms of outcomes and related human factors. For example, a commercial organization might map sales targets to specific business sectors and skill sets for individual sales people; a commercial airline requires pilots and flight crew to maintain certifications, which have both skill and time components; and the DoD has doctrinal requirements that intersect with mission needs and local conditions. Representing doctrine, training goals, and target outcomes as interrelated frameworks has demonstrated significant improvements in training, process, and outcomes in the US Navy STRMS project. By digitizing existing Navy doctrine, policy, practice, requirements, and objectives, it has become possible to flow data from individual actions to mission outcomes.

Digital encoding is only the first step towards a digitized organization. Second, it is necessary to ensure that systems are able to produce human performance data streams. This *instrumentation* process is what ensures that digitally encoded frameworks can be linked to individual data streams in order to support downstream usage. Training is one of the first and most obvious places to implement instrumentation to report assessments and experiences at defined levels of granularity.

Definition

Digitization is a necessary foundation for human performance data. However, the data streams that come from training and other human-interactive systems (e.g. communication like Slack, task tracking, time sheets, work product, etc.) are highly variable and difficult to interpret, much less generalize. In order to implement a successful human performance data management strategy.

A human performance data management strategy has the following elements:

1. The data sources and data producing components and the description of what data they output, what format that data is in, and a human description of the data's meaning.
2. The ETL process that is used to transform existing data source output into the formats necessary to inform digitized activities and frameworks.
3. How assertions about human capabilities from data sources link to selected target competencies and roll up into higher order frameworks.
4. The data feeds necessary for reports, dashboards, decision support, adaptive systems, and other human performance data consumers.

As an example, we will break down the definition step for a fictional training system for new pilots (Fig. 2).

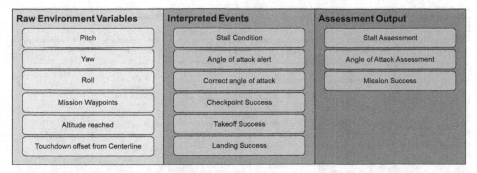

Raw Environment Variables	Interpreted Events	Assessment Output
Pitch	Stall Condition	Stall Assessment
Yaw	Angle of attack alert	Angle of Attack Assessment
Roll	Correct angle of attack	Mission Success
Mission Waypoints	Checkpoint Success	
Altitude reached	Takeoff Success	
Touchdown offset from Centerline	Landing Success	

Fig. 2. Human performance data elements for an example training system

This new pilot training system outputs three data feeds: Success or failure overall, instances where the angle of attack was too steep, and stall count. Each of these outputs is supported by internal variables used within the training environment to compute them. The human performance data management strategy will include each of these data elements, a human interpretable description, and relevant data format and standards. While it is possible to do this for raw environment events, it is not recommended. Best practices for human performance data management begin at the interpreted event level. An example of data fields used in this step are shown in Table 1.

Table 1. Data fields used for interpretation of human performance data

Data Element	Human Description	Data Description	Data Format/Standards
Stall Condition	Variable measures when aircraft stalls	A "1" and time stamp returned when stall occurs	Represented in IEEE P2881 and events are transmitted via xAPI
Stall Assessment	Variable assesses pilot against FAA frameworks	Pass determined by FAA regulations	Represented in IEEE P2881 and events are transmitted via xAPI

The diagram shown in Fig. 3 represents a high-level flow of human performance data as it moves through a hypothetical training sequence.

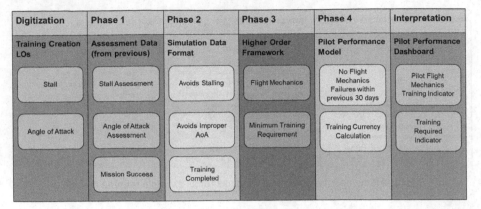

Fig. 3. Schematic flow of human performance data for example training system

Interpretation

A well-defined data stream linked to digitized objectives is a powerful foundation, but modern data consumers, ranging from personalized tutors to predictive analytics often require actionable inputs rather than raw data streams. For this reason, it is best practice to implement an interpretive layer between the raw data stream, digitized organization and end-user applications that act on human performance data. This interpretive layer defines how answers to questions about the human's estimated knowledge and skill and predicted performance are calculated. Different calculations, ranging from expert rules to statistical and AI approaches, can be implemented depending on the needs of the data ecosystem. The most successful architectures include easy ways to replace and compare calculation approaches. This provides the ecosystem with unbound scalability and flexibility as the state of the art continues to improve. To date, none of the early adopters of a complete front-to-back outcomes data-consuming end user.

6   Conclusions and Future Work

Contemporary approaches to adaptive learning are dependent on human performance data that are largely local and temporary. In this paper, we present a comprehensive approach to managing competency-based performance data that can achieve significant enhancements to adaptive training by calculating current and correct learner profiles. We describe a human performance data layer that has emerged from multiple recent projects for the U.S. Navy. From these efforts we have developed tools to support a lifecycle management approach for human performance data. Our results to-date offer strong preliminary support for achieving a digital thread of sailor competencies by applying techniques that map performance data to corresponding competencies.

In on-going work, we are maturing these tools to provide a rich array of analytics to training managers, workforce planners, and line supervisors. We are currently working with a large commercial airplane manufacturer to create a training needs analysis tool built using the technologies we describe in this paper. We are also working with the U.S. Air Force to apply competency-based tools to bringing more analytics and insights into the process of managing pilot training. And we have created a commercial platform, called Talent Cascade, that integrates these capabilities into a single interoperable suite of services.

References

1. Bell, B., Sottilare, R.: Adaptation vectors for instructional agents. In: Sottilare, R.A., Schwarz, J. (eds.) HCII 2019. LNCS, vol. 11597, pp. 3–14. Springer, Cham (2019). https://doi.org/10.1007/978-3-030-22341-0_1
2. Goldberg, B., Brawner, K., Sottilare, R., Tarr, R., Billings, D.R., Malone, N.: Use of evidence-based strategies to enhance the extensibility of adaptive tutoring technologies. In: Interservice/Industry Training, Simulation, and Education Conference (I/ITSEC) (2012)
3. Selmanagić, A., Simbeck, K.: Designing granular competency frameworks for adaptive learning on the example of Naïve Bayes classifiers. In: Proceedings of DELFI Workshops 2022, p. 137 (2022)
4. Goldberg, B., et al.: Forging competency and proficiency through the synthetic training environment with an experiential learning for readiness strategy. In: Interservice/Industry Training, Simulation, and Education Conference (I/ITSEC), Orlando, FL (2021)
5. Molnar, L., Mehta, R.K., Robson, R.: Artificial Intelligence (AI), the future of work, and the building of a national talent ecosystem. In: Rodrigo, M.M., Matsuda, N., Cristea, A.I., Dimitrova, V. (eds.) AIED 2022, pp. 99–103. Springer, Cham (2022). https://doi.org/10.1007/978-3-031-11647-6_17

Personality Traits
in the Emotion-Performance-Relationship
in Intelligent Tutoring Systems

Alina Schmitz-Hübsch[1,2]([✉]) [iD], Ron Becker[1] [iD], and Maria Wirzberger[2] [iD]

[1] Fraunhofer Institute for Communication, Information Processing and Ergonomics FKIE,
Wachtberg, Germany
{alina.schmitz-huebsch,ron.becker}@fkie.fraunhofer.de
[2] University of Stuttgart, Stuttgart, Germany
maria.wirzberger@iris.uni-stuttgart.de

Abstract. Affective Tutoring Systems (ATS) detect and mitigate critical emotional learner states with the aim of providing individualized support. In tutoring systems for safety-critical work environments, students are trained to achieve and maintain high performance, therefore an ATS should be capable of identifying critical emotional states hindering performance. Interindividual differences in the emotion-performance-relationship can be considered by using the ARC categorization system. The present contribution aims at developing a questionnaire-based method of classifying new learners to the categories. To that end, we investigated differences in personality traits between the different categories. In an airspace surveillance task, we measured performance, emotional valence, emotional arousal, and personality traits in $N = 50$ subjects. Results showed that a positive valence-performance-relationship, compared to a negative valence-performance-relationship, is associated with higher Neuroticism, lower Conscientiousness, and lower Openness to experience. There were no significant differences in the traits Agreeableness and Extraversion. Based on these results, a future ATS for safety-critical work environments could classify new learners in the ARCs using self-report data and thus dispense with physiological sensors. Thereby, user state diagnosis and evaluation for high performance is possible, setting the ground for an ATS adapting to critical emotional learner states.

Keywords: Emotional User State · Affect-Adaptive System · Safety-Critical Work Environment

"The extent to which emotional upsets can interfere with mental life is no news to teachers. Students who are anxious, angry, or depressed don't learn; people who are caught in these states do not take in information efficiently or deal with it well" [1].

1 Introduction

The opening quote by Goleman states concisely what many studies have suggested: Emotions influence learning success. This is not unexpected as emotions influence motivation, attention allocation, and memory formation, all constituting important determinants of

© The Author(s), under exclusive license to Springer Nature Switzerland AG 2023
R. A. Sottilare and J. Schwarz (Eds.): HCII 2023, LNCS 14044, pp. 60–75, 2023.
https://doi.org/10.1007/978-3-031-34735-1_5

learning success [2]. Affective states should therefore be considered in a learner state diagnosis [3]. *Intelligent Tutoring Systems* (ITSs) identify conditions hindering or promoting learning and adapt teaching material to a particular student and therefore allow for an individualized learning experience [3]. *Affective Tutoring Systems* (ATS) are ITS which specialize in detecting and mitigating critical emotional states. Vicente et al. [4] proposed that the learner's state in ITS should be diagnosed in order to induce cognitive and emotional arousal. Thereby, instructional material could be perceived as an interesting and engaging experience. D'Mello et al. [5] likewise suggested that learning environments that monitor and adapt to emotions in real-time are motivating and relevant to the learner. In their opinion, robust emotion recognition is essential for real-time affect-sensitive tutoring systems.

In our research, we aim at developing an ATS with a real-time diagnostic component of the emotional learner state for training systems in safety-critical work environments. These environments are characterized by time pressure, high complexity, risk bearing, and dependence on human reliability [6]. Failure leads to potentially serious consequences like loss of life, significant economic loss or property and environmental damage [7]. Avoiding errors and maintaining high performance is therefore crucial in safety-critical systems. Because of the severe consequences of failure, it is important to assist professionals in learning strategies to cope with and improve resilience [8] towards undesirable emotional states.

The first step towards creating an adaptive system is to determine the direction of adaptation [9]. It is essential to comprehend which emotional states should be fostered in order to develop an ATS for safety-critical work environments. Previous studies have discovered interindividual differences in the emotion-performance relationship which should be regarded in an ATS [10]. Schmitz-Hübsch et al. [11] therefore introduced a categorization system for these differences (*Affective Response Categories, ARC*). In the present paper, we propose to predict ARCs by users' personality traits enabling the system to categorize users correctly using self report data only. Thereby, ATS without physiological sensors detecting the emotional state as for example in Körner et al. [12] could nevertheless take the individual's emotion-performance-relationship into account. In perspective, an ATS could select appropriate adaptation strategies based on the learner's emotion-performance-relationship. To that end, we first investigate the differences in personality traits between the ARCs.

2 Background

Russell [13] provided a definition of emotion serving as a theoretical basis in the design of ATS [14]. The Circumplex Model of Affect [13] classifies emotions with two orthogonal dimensions: *Valence* describes how pleasant the emotion is and *arousal* defines its level of activation (see Fig. 1).

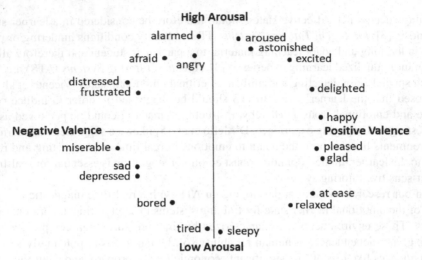

Fig. 1. Circumplex Model of Affect (adapted from Russell [13]).

2.1 Emotion and Learning

Emotional states have a direct or indirect influence on the learning process. For example, information is processed deeper and remembered better if it is emotionally touching and physiologically activating [15]. Furthermore, positive emotions such as joy facilitate creativity, self-regulation, and deeper information processing. However, they can also distract attention when not directed toward relevant learning material [3]. Negative emotions such as frustration can interfere with attention as well, because a learner's focus is shifted away from the task and toward unrelated situational distractions [16]. Motivational processes relevant for self- and action-regulation are also influenced by emotions. According to [17], positive emotions lead to higher motivation, more active engagement in learning activities, stronger interest, and stronger self-regulation skills. Negative emotions like frustration can on the one hand reduce motivation and on the other hand, fear of an exam can increase motivation and engagement in learning [18].

2.2 Affective Tutoring Systems (ATS)

Computer-based learning systems (ITS) enable virtual one-on-one interaction in teaching and learning. They analyze a student's responses and behaviors and adjust learning content accordingly [19]. ATS are ITS capable of adapting to a learner's emotional state, for example by reducing those emotional states with a negative impact on knowledge acquisition and learning outcomes [20]. Typically, an ATS consists of three components: the first one detects and classifies the learner's affective state. The second one utilizes emotional data and information about the current tutoring situation to create suitable responses and adaptations. A third component communicates with the student, often using a virtual tutor or pedagogical agent capable of expressing own emotions [20].

Arroyo et al. [21] developed an ATS for math training detecting the learner's affective state by various sensors and providing emotional support. Their recommendation for future work represents the development of models predicting desired and undesired emotional learning states. Woolf et al. [22] found that in an ITS, affective states comprising negative valence and high levels of arousal resulted in unproductive and therefore undesirable outcomes. In a literature review, Malekzadeh et al. [23] showed that in an ATS, positive emotional states have benefits for students for example by promoting cognitive flexibility. In contrast, negative states such as frustration and boredom were accompanied by unfocused and disruptive behavior and lower self-regulation. Picard [24] however argued that overcoming frustration or anxiety arising from increased task difficulty can serve as a rewarding eye-opener and increase in motivation.

The conflicting findings from literature regarding both, the emotion-learning-relationship and desirable emotional states for learning performance in ITS indicate the complexity emerging from ATS development. Especially in training systems for safety-critical environments, it is crucial to identify desired and undesired emotional states for high performance in a particular task.

2.3 Interindividual Differences in the Emotion-Performance-Relationship

Cai et al. [25] searched for emotional user states associated with high performance in a driving simulator study and showed an inverted U-shaped relationship with performance for both, valence and arousal. Moreover, there is evidence of low performance in human-machine systems, when users are angry or frustrated [26]. However, positive emotions can have distracting capabilities as well [27]. Schmitz-Hübsch et al. [11] simulated safety-critical work environments using an airspace surveillance task and explored the emotion-performance-relationship. Results showed that overall, high performance was associated with low arousal, independent if valence was positive or negative. They furthermore found interindividual differences regarding the valence dimension: Whereas for one group high performance was associated with positive valence, the other group achieved superior performance with negative valence. A third group did not show any relationship between valence and performance [11]. Vine et al. [28] observed similar interindividual differences in a flight simulator study with stress-inducing situational contexts. They examined the pilots' individual reaction and its influence on attentional control and performance. Results showed that subjects' evaluation of their personal relationship between situational demands and coping resources predicted both, attentional control and performance.

The observed interindividual differences in the relationship between emotion and performance present a challenge in the development of an ATS for safety-critical environments requiring rigorous training to avoid human error. In order to promote high performance for all learners individually, the system requires awareness of an individual's emotion-performance-relationship. Schmitz-Hübsch et al. [11] therefore proposed a concept for user classification considering these differences in three *Affective Response Categories (ARCs,* see Table 1). An ATS aware of a learner's ARC could implement suitable adaption strategies and thereby offer appropriate support for the individual. Therefore, it is necessary for a future ATS to understand the assignment of learners to categories.

Table 1. Affective Response Categories according to Schmitz-Hübsch et al. [11, 29]

ARC label	Description
0	No relationship between emotion and performance
+	High performance is associated with **positive** valence and low arousal
−	High performance is associated with **negative** valence and low arousal

2.4 Personality Traits in the Determination of ARCs

Enabling a future ATS to consider a learner's ARC, it first has to assign a new student to one of the three ARCs. In the present contribution, we investigate a possibility to facilitate this assignment based on questionnaires in contrast to physiological data as in Schmitz-Hübsch et al. [29]. This would allow a fast and straightforward classification, based on which the system's support in the learning process could be provided in a timely manner, even when the ATS does not employ physiological sensors as Körner et al. [12]. The omission of physiological data allows a cost-effective use of an ATS, which would thus be accessible to a larger community, and avoids ethical challenges concerning for example privacy. Trainees are in full control of emotional self-report data, while in an automatic diagnosis based on physiological data private emotional states might be revealed.

We assume personality traits to present a reliable predictor for the individual emotion-performance-relationship. Asendorpf [30] defined personality traits as all permanent individual characteristics in a person's experience and behavior, comprising a variety of competencies like intelligence and emotional capacities. Emotions can be regarded as personality traits if they are habitual emotions, presenting a persistent tendency to react with the same emotion in similar situations [31]. As both, cognitive and emotional competencies are part of personality, we assume that the emotion-performance-relationship is a related construct. Furthermore, this association is potentially mediated by coping styles in stress management that present a tendency towards particular coping strategies and are a part of personality as well [30]. A person's predisposition toward maladaptive coping styles like rumination could interfere with self-regulation and consequently impair performance [cf. 28].

The Big Five Personality theory describes personality using five orthogonal factors [32]. *Openness to experience* presents a general appreciation for art, adventure, unusual ideas and a variety of experience. *Conscientiousness* describes a tendency toward long-term planning and self-discipline, and *Extraversion* a tendency to gregariousness, dominance in social settings, and cheerfulness. *Agreeableness* presents a tendency toward kindness and harmony and *Neuroticism* a tendency to experience negative emotions, such as anxiety, anger, or depression [33].

Some of these traits are associated with certain coping strategies. For example, Neuroticism has been linked to low perceived coping capacities, suffering from negative emotions like anxiety, and coping strategies focusing on emotion as opposed to problem-focused strategies [34]. These findings provide an explanation for the results by Roslan et al. [35] who measured emotional arousal using physiological measures in a speaking task. Subjects scoring high on Neuroticism experienced a larger increase in skin conductance and heart rate than participants scoring low on Neuroticism. In contrast, Conscientiousness was found to be associated with high perceived coping ability and problem-focused coping [34]. Brouwer et al. [36] showed that in a stressful situation, low Conscientiousness scores were associated with a larger increase in heart rate compared to high Conscientiousness scores. Similarly, Openness to experience has been associated with greater stress resilience [37].

In the present contribution, we aim at exploring differences in personality traits between the three distinct ARCs. A prospective ATS could use these findings to assign new learners to one of the categories.

3 Methods

In a laboratory experiment, $N = 50$ student subjects (19–63 years, $M = 27.8$, $SD = 8.9$, 64% male, 34% female, 2% diverse) performed an airspace surveillance task. The experimental test environment is based on the *Rich and Adaptable Test Environment* [*RATE*; 38]. The simulation-based training environment comprises a Command and Control (C2) task mimicking cognitive requirements and situational awareness demands found in C2 as well as in air traffic control environments. This kind of simulation is commonly employed in training to enhance performance in safety-critical situations as recommended by Orasanu et al. [39]. The present gamified simulation allows for training of cognitive capabilities necessary in for example, drone defense, power plant or traffic control centers.

3.1 Experimental Task

In the experimental task, subjects pursued the goal of protecting their airport from approaching hostile drones (see Fig. 2). The overall task consisted of three subtasks: First, unknown drones had to be *identified* based on the Aeroscope signal sent by friendly drones. When there was no signal, the identity (bird or hostile drone) had to be assigned using the camera image (picture of a bird or a drone). Second, hostile drones approaching the airport had to be *warned*. Third, hostile drones proceeding to the inner parameter around the airport were *stopped* using a jammer.

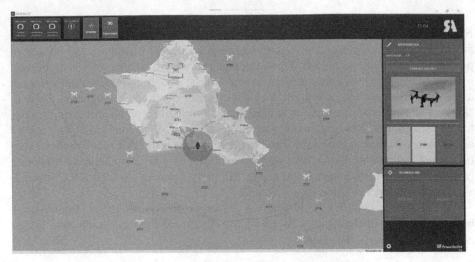

Fig. 2. Screenshot of the experimental testbed.

3.2 Operationalization of Variables

Figure 3 illustrates apparatus and experimental setup. To determine a trainee's ARC, continuous real-time diagnosis of emotional valence, emotional arousal, and performance is necessary. Emotional valence was operationalized through assessment of facial expressions using the Emotient FACET engine [40]. A Logitech C920 webcam recorded the subject's face with a frame rate of 25 Hz. A Tobii Pro Spectrum 300 Hz eye tracker captured pupil diameter to measure emotional arousal. Performance was assessed using the performance score described by Becker et al. [38] and considers task priority, accuracy and response time. The Big Five personality traits were assessed via the NEO-FFI-30, a validated German short version of the NEO-FFI with 30 questions [12]. Data was recorded and synchronized using the iMotions software [41].

3.3 Procedure

Before participating, all subjects were asked to sign a privacy statement and an informed consent according to the recommendations of the Declaration of Helsinki. The ethics committee of Fraunhofer FKIE reviewed and approved the study (ID: 22_002). Each trial began by calibrating the physiological sensors. Subsequently, subjects filled in a demographic questionnaire and the NEO-FFI-30 for personality trait assessment. They read the instruction of the experimental task and practiced it in a 15-min training scenario with increasing demands. The experimental scenario evaluated for the present contribution had continuously high demands and lasted for another 10 min. Every minute, there were on average 17 drones to be identified, five to be warned and four to be stopped. Three additional scenarios were presented in the experiment and finalized by all subjects to be analyzed in future work. Subjects left the laboratory after a debriefing and were compensated with 20€.

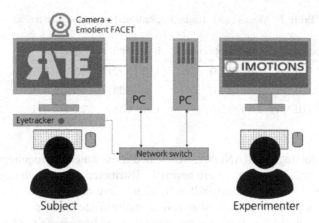

Fig. 3. Diagram of the experimental setup

3.4 Data Preparation and Analysis

The first step of data analysis was to determine the subject's ARC using emotional valence, emotional arousal and performance data. We defined all data points beyond 1.5 times interquartile range as outliers to be excluded [42]. Moreover, we normalized the data within each subject via the min-max method, which has been shown to be more effective than other methods in normalizing multimodal physiological data [43]. To account for varying sample rates of the different metrics, we averaged the measures across sequential time windows of 10 s. ARC determination followed Schmitz-Hübsch et al. [11], who calculated individual Pearson correlation coefficients of valence and performance as well as arousal and performance. We assumed that there is a relationship between emotion and performance present, when we found at least a small effect ($r < -0.1$ or $r > 0.1$, [44]). Tying in with evidence on performance benefits under low arousal [11], the first prerequisite for ARC + and ARC − is a negative correlation between arousal and performance. The second requirement is either a positive (ARC +) or a negative (ARC −) valence-performance-correlation. All other subjects are classified as ARC 0.

In the second step of data analysis, we determined differences in personality traits between the three ARC groups. As the analysis was exploratory, no hypotheses were defined. A subject's ARC was used as an independent variable with three levels and the Big Five personality traits as five dependent variables in a one-way multivariate analysis of variance (MANOVA). Data preparation and analysis was conducted in R studio and SPSS.

4 Results

The determination of the ARCs classified 38% of subjects as ARC +, 34% as ARC − and 28% as ARC 0. Table 2 shows the means and standard deviations of the three categories' personality traits.

Table 2. Means (and standard deviations) of personality traits.

ARC	N	Openness	Conscientiousness	Extraversion	Agreeableness	Neuroticism
0	14	2.51 (0.39)	2.07 (0.35)	1.92 (0.32)	1.86 (0.39)	2.04 (0.27)
+	17	2.32 (0.38)	2.08 (0.33)	1.84 (0.28)	1.91 (0.43)	2.33 (0.34)
−	19	2.65 (0.33)	2.30 (0.20)	1.88 (0.38)	2.02 (0.43)	1.94 (0.27)

Before conducting the MANOVA, we verified if the statistical requirements for this procedure were met. All groups were normally distributed across both dependent variables, as assessed by the Shapiro-Wilk test. There were no univariate outliers beyond 1.5 times interquartile range in the data and no multivariate outliers as assessed by the Mahalanobis distance ($p > .001$). Levene's test showed homogeneity of the error variances for all variables ($p > .05$) and Box's test indicated that there was homogeneity of covariances. Multicollinearity was not a confounding factor in the analysis, as correlations between dependent variables were low ($r < .3$). As all requirements were met, we proceeded with the statistical analysis.

A one-way MANOVA showed a statistically significant difference between the ARCs on the combined dependent variables, $F(10, 86) = 3.590$, $p < .01$, partial $\eta^2 = .294$, Wilk's $\Lambda = .498$. Post-hoc univariate ANOVAs were conducted for each dependent variable (see Table 3, significant results and statistical trends in bold). To account for the multiple comparisons problem, we corrected p-values using the false discovery rate method suggested by Benjamini et al. [45]. Results show a statistically significant difference between the ARCs for Neuroticism and a statistical trend for Consciousness and Openness to experience. Effect sizes were medium for Consciousness and Openness to experience and large for Neuroticism according to Cohen [44]. We found no differences for Extraversion or Agreeableness.

Table 3. Test statistics of post-hoc univariate ANOVAs.

Personality trait	F-value	p-value	partial η^2
Openness	$F(2, 47) = 3.752$	$p = .031$	.138
Conscientiousness	$F(2, 47) = 3.026$	$p = .058$	.114
Extraversion	$F(2, 47) = 0.235$	$p = .791$	.010
Agreeableness	$F(2, 47) = 0.657$	$p = .523$	.027
Neuroticism	$F(2, 47) = 8.273$	$p = .001$	.260

We finally calculated post-hoc Tukey-tests to identify which comparisons of the significant univariate ANOVAs show significant differences (see Table 3, significant results and statistical trends in bold). In Openness to experience, ARC + scored significantly lower than ARC −. There was only a statistical trend in Conscientiousness with ARC

+ scoring lower than ARC − as well. In Neuroticism, we found two significant effects. ARC + had higher scores than both ARC 0 and ARC −.

Table 4. Test statistics of post-hoc Tukey-tests for significant ANOVAs.

Personality trait	Comparison	M_{Diff}	95%-CI	p-value
Openness	+ vs. 0	−0.186	−0.497, 0.125	$p = .324$
	− vs. 0	0.146	−0.173, 0.464	$p = .514$
	+ vs. −	0.331	0.037, 0.626	**$p = .024$**
Conscientiousness	+ vs. 0	−0.013	−0.270, 0.244	$p = .992$
	− vs. 0	0.229	−0.035, 0.492	$p = .101$
	+ vs. −	0.216	−0.028, 0.459	$p = .092$
Neuroticism	**+ vs. 0**	0.288	0.034, 0.543	$p = .023$
	− vs. 0	−0.102	−0.363, 0.159	$p = .616$
	+ vs. −	0.390	0.149, 0.632	**$p = .001$**

5 Discussion

The present paper investigated if personality traits were capable of predicting interindividual differences in the emotion-performance-relationship in safety-critical work environments. To that end, participants were divided into the three ARCs accounting for individual differences. According to the three categories, users differ in their relationship of valence and performance. Mean differences in personality traits between the categories were tested for significance using a MANOVA. Results showed that a negative valence-performance correlation (ARC −) was associated with lower Neuroticism and a tendency toward higher Conscientiousness and Openness to experience. In contrast, a positive valence-performance correlation (ARC +) was associated with higher Neuroticism, lower Conscientiousness and lower Openness to experience. For the other traits, no differences were found.

5.1 Theoretical Implications

The present results are compatible with those by Schmitz-Hübsch et al. [10] and Vine et al. [28], who showed interindividual differences in the emotion-performance-relationship. Our findings thereby provide further evidence for the necessity of taking these differences into account when an ATS aims at promoting high performance individually. The distribution of ARCs within the inspected sample was similar to the one tested in Schmitz-Hübsch et al. [11], who observed an almost even split in thirds. Replicating this outcome provides first hints on a resembling distribution in the broader population.

Furthermore, our results show that the emotion-performance-relationship is associated with a subject's personality. One possible explanation for a positive valence-performance-correlation in individuals with higher Neuroticism and lower Conscientiousness scores lies in the association of coping styles and personality traits. Neuroticism was found to be correlated with low perceived coping capacities, higher anxiety and coping strategies focusing on emotion instead of problems [34], possibly leading to performance decrements in the presence of negative emotions that cannot be coped adequately. Conscientiousness, however, a personality trait associated with high perceived coping ability and problem-focused coping [34], might present a protective factor. In the presence of negative emotions, subjects with a higher Conscientiousness score classified in ARC − might have made a greater effort to perform well in the task than those with a lower Conscientiousness score classified in ARC +. Openness to experience, which is associated with stress-resilience [37] might have similar protective effects.

Another explanation for our findings can be based on the Appraisal Theory of Emotion [46]. According to this theory, emotions are caused by the evaluation of a stimulus and its correspondence to individual goals and expectations. Several processes such as bodily sensations and situational factors contribute to the emotional experience [47]. Possibly, the individual differences observed arise in the phase of appraisal. For example, if a person tends to exert an anger-prone appraisal style, events are often appraised in a way that leads to feelings of anger [48]. Previous research suggests that personality traits play an important role in this process [49]. The appraisal of one's low performance may have caused frustration in ARC + leading to lower engagement due to low Conscientiousness resulting in even lower performance. In ARC −, however, low performance could be associated with an anger-prone appraisal style resulting in a fierce determination to try harder.

For the traits Extraversion and Agreeableness, there were no significant differences present between the three categories. Extraversion describes a tendency toward gregariousness, while Agreeableness presents a proneness to kindness and harmony [30]. Both traits are associated with social interactions [50], which were not part of the present task. If performance was measured using a different task requiring social skills, Extraversion and Agreeableness might play a different role.

5.2 Practical Implications

Differences in personality traits between the three different ARCs indicate that a future ATS could determine a learner's ARC based on personality self-report only, without using physiological data. A higher score in Neuroticism and a lower score in Conscientious and Openness to experience would suggest a learner's affiliation with ARC +. In contrast, low Neuroticism, high Conscientious and high Openness points to ARC −. Assigning a new student based on self-report data only represents an advantage as not all ATS use physiological sensors to detect emotional state. For example, in Wu et al. [51], learners repeatedly selected words describing their emotions. Eliminating physiological sensors allows for low-cost user state detection facilitating accessibility of institutions and individuals to the ATS, allowing for more inclusive education.

Furthermore, ethical challenges arising from the employment of physiological sensors can be avoided. The European Commission proposes ethical guidelines on the use of AI and data in teaching and learning for educators [52] building on the seven key requirements for trustworthy AI specified in the Ethics Guidelines for Trustworthy AI and the Assessment List for Trustworthy AI (ALTAI) [55], developed by the High-Level Expert Group on AI. In an ATS, two key requirements are especially relevant: Human agency and oversight and Privacy and data governance. A person with agency is capable of determining choices regarding their life and can be responsible for their actions. Privacy and data governance include respect for a user's privacy, for quality and integrity of data, and access to data [55]. In an ATS, a learner should be, for example, able to opt-out if concerns have not been adequately addressed; and teachers and learners should be informed about what happens with their data, how it is used and for what purposes [52]. User state diagnosis via self-report vs. physiological data as proposed in the present paper, allows for high control by users, as they can decide for themselves what information they reveal, ensuring both, agency and privacy.

Based on the mapping of learner and ARC, an ATS could proceed with a diagnosis of favorable and unfavorable emotional states for learning. The diagnosis could then serve as indicator for the need of learning content adaptation as described in Petrovica et al. [20]. Thus, an ATS for safety-critical work environments could provide individualized support for optimal learning performance.

5.3 Limitations

Several limitations must be considered when interpreting the present results. Accurate classification of new learners based on personality traits is only likely to be successful if they match exactly the pattern observed (cf. Table 4). However, if a person simultaneously scores high on Neuroticism, Conscientiousness and Openness to experience, the classification is more ambiguous. Furthermore, confounding of ARC + and ARC − with ARC 0 is possible, since for this third category a significant difference was found only in the personality trait Neuroticism and only to one of the other two ARC categories.

The short version of the NEO-FFI used in the present contribution, with 30 instead of 60 questions, is also associated with restrictions. Correlations between the respective long and short scales are on average above $r = .90$ [12]. Nevertheless, the average German population loses on the short scale slightly in Neuroticism and gains in Agreeableness and Conscientiousness. These deviations affect some of the scales in which significant differences were found in the present data set. As the study was conducted in Germany and in German language, it may not be generalizable to other language areas or cultural groups.

Finally, the experimental task used represented a very specific type of task from the broader field of safety-critical work environments; however, there was no social interaction necessary. In a different task, for example, in a flight simulator or a learning environment for nuclear power plants, other personality traits such as Extraversion and Agreeableness could play a role as well.

5.4 Future Work

The NEO-FFI questionnaire is only one possible inventory to assess personality traits. Alternative questionnaires based on personality models other than the Big Five are, for example, the Freiburg Personality Inventory (FPI-R, 53) or the 16 Personality Factors Test [16PF, 54]. Further studies with these questionnaires could reveal additional differences in personality to obtain an accurate classification. Moreover, a combination of further questionnaire data such as age and gender and physiological data such as pupil width and emotional facial expression could be used to determine ARCs and achieve a richer data basis for multi-modal classification. Furthermore, results from this exploratory analysis should be replicated in a hypothesis-testing study for validation. Finally, other task types from the safety-critical task domain could be investigated to validate the generalization of both, the concept, and the classification. Conceivable task areas would be control centers of power stations, aircraft cockpits and many others.

6 Conclusions

The present paper investigates how personality trait differences relate to individual differences in the emotion-performance-relationship. We found a significant difference in the personality trait Neuroticism. A negative valence-performance-relationship was associated with lower Neuroticism as compared to a positive valence-performance-relationship. Furthermore, there was a tendency towards lower Conscientiousness and Openness to experience, when the relationship between valence and performance was positive. Based on these results, a future ATS for safety-critical work environments that classifies new learners in the ARCs using self-report data only could be regarded as promising direction.

Acknowledgments. The authors would like to thank Markus Vogt for implementing the experimental scenarios and preparing the questionnaire data. The reported research was supported by the Fraunhofer FKIE. We thank the Deutsche Forschungsgemeinschaft (DFG, German Research Foundation) for supporting this work by funding – EXC2075 – 390740016 under Germany's Excellence Strategy. We acknowledge the support by the Stuttgart Center for Simulation Science (SimTech). The reported research was supported by the Federal Ministry of Science, Research, and the Arts Baden-Württemberg and the University of Stuttgart as part of the Research Seed Capital funding scheme.

References

1. Goleman, D.: Emotional Intelligence: Why it Can Matter More Than IQ. Boomsbury, London (1995)
2. Tyng, C.M., Amin, H.U., Saad, M.N.M., Malik, A.S.: The influences of emotion on learning and memory. Front. Psychol. (2017). https://doi.org/10.3389/fpsyg.2017.01454
3. Petrovica, S.: Tutoring process in emotionally intelligent tutoring systems. Int. J. Technol. Educ. Mark. (IJTEM) **4**, 72–85 (2014)

4. de Vicente, A., Pain, H.: Motivation diagnosis in intelligent tutoring systems. In: Goettl, B.P., Halff, H.M., Redfield, C.L., Shute, V.J. (eds.) ITS 1998. LNCS, vol. 1452, pp. 86–95. Springer, Heidelberg (1998). https://doi.org/10.1007/3-540-68716-5_14

5. D'Mello, S.K., Craig, S.D., Witherspoon, A., McDaniel, B., Graesser, A.: Automatic detection of learner's affect from conversational cues. User Model. User-Adap. Inter. **18**, 45–80 (2008). https://doi.org/10.1007/s11257-007-9037-6

6. Boy, G.A.: Cognitive function analysis for human-centered automation of safety-critical systems. In: Proceedings of the SIGCHI Conference on Human Factors in Computing Systems, pp. 265–272 (1998). https://doi.org/10.1145/274644.274682

7. Knight, J.C.: Safety critical systems: challenges and directions. In: Proceedings of the 24th International Conference on Software Engineering, pp. 547–550 (2002). https://doi.org/10.1109/icse.2002.1007998

8. Talker, C.M.: Does attention training enhance stress resilience and performance in unforeseen safety-critical situations? In: 86th International Symposium on Aviation Psychology, pp. 268–273 (2021)

9. Hudlicka, E.: To feel or not to feel: the role of affect in human–computer interaction. Int. J. Hum Comput Stud. **59**, 1–32 (2003). https://doi.org/10.1016/S1071-5819(03)00047-8

10. Schmitz-Hübsch, A., Stasch, S.-M., Fuchs, S.: Individual differences in the relationship between emotion and performance in command-and-control environments. In: Sottilare, R.A., Schwarz, J. (eds.) HCII 2021. LNCS, vol. 12793, pp. 135–148. Springer, Cham (2021). https://doi.org/10.1007/978-3-030-77873-6_10

11. Schmitz-Hübsch, A., Stasch, S.-M., Becker, R., Fuchs, S., Wirzberger, M.: Affective response categories - toward personalized reactions in affect-adaptive tutoring systems. Front. Artif. Intell. (2022)

12. Körner, A., et al.: Persönlichkeitsdiagnostik mit dem NEO-Fünf-Faktoren-Inventar: Die 30-Item-Kurzversion (NEO-FFI-30). [Personality assessment with the NEO-Five-Factor Inventory: the 30-Item-Short-Version (NEO-FFI-30)]. Psychother Psychosom Med. Psychol. **58**, 238–245 (2008). https://doi.org/10.1055/s-2007-986199

13. Russell, J.A.: A circumplex model of affect. J. Pers. Soc. Psychol. **39**, 1161–1178 (1980). https://doi.org/10.1037/h0077714

14. Wang, C.-H., Koon-Lin, H.-C.: Constructing an affective tutoring system for designing course learning and evaluation. J. Educ. Comput. **55**, 1111–1128 (2018)

15. Vogel, S., Schwabe, L.: Learning and memory under stress: implications for the classroom. Sci. Learn. **1**, 1–10 (2016)

16. Hascher, T.: Learning and emotion: perspectives for theory and research. Eur. Educ. Res. J. **9**, 13–28 (2010)

17. Boekaerts, M.: Toward a model that integrates motivation, affect and learning. Br. J. Educ. Psychol. **2**, 173–189 (2002)

18. Méndez López, M., Peña Aguilar, A.: Emotions as learning enhancers of foreign language learning motivation. Profile Issues Teach. Prof. Dev. **15**, 109–124 (2013)

19. Nkambou, R.: A framework for affective intelligent tutoring systems. In: 7th International Conference on Information Technology Based Higher Education and Training (2006). https://doi.org/10.1109/ithet.2006.339720

20. Petrovica, S., Anohina-Naumeca, A., Ekenel, H.K.: Emotion recognition in affective tutoring systems: collection of ground-truth data. Procedia Comput. Sci. **104**, 437–444 (2017). https://doi.org/10.1016/j.procs.2017.01.157

21. Arroyo, I., Cooper, D., Burleson, W., Woolf, B.P., Muldner, K., Christopherson, R.: Emotion sensors go to school. In: Artificial Intelligence in Education, pp. 17–24. IOS Press (2009). https://doi.org/10.3233/978-1-60750-028-5-17

22. Woolf, B.P., Burleson, W., Arroyo, I., Dragon, T., Cooper, D., Picard, R.W.: Affect-aware tutors: recognising and responding to student affect. Int. J. Learn. Technol. **4**, 129–164 (2009)

23. Malekzadeh, M., Mustafa, M.B., Lahsasna, A.: A review of emotion regulation in intelligent tutoring systems. J. Educ. Technol. Soc. **18**, 435–445 (2015)
24. Picard, R.W.: Affective Computing. MIT Press, Cambridge (2000)
25. Cai, H., Lin, Y.: Modeling of operators' emotion and task performance in a virtual driving environment. Int. J. Hum Comput Stud. **69**, 571–586 (2011). https://doi.org/10.1016/j.ijhcs.2011.05.003
26. Kontogiannis, T.: Stress and operator decision making in coping with emergencies. Int. J. Hum. Comput. Stud. **45**, 75–104 (1996). https://doi.org/10.1006/ijhc.1996.0043
27. Gupta, R., Hur, Y.-J., Lavie, N.: Distracted by pleasure: effects of positive versus negative valence on emotional capture under load. Emotion **16**, 328–337 (2016). https://doi.org/10.1037/emo0000112
28. Vine, S.J., Uiga, L., Lavric, A., Moore, L.J., Krasimiraand, T.-A., Wilson, M.R.: Individual reactions to stress predict performance during a critical aviation incident. Anxiety Stress Coping **28**, 467–477 (2015)
29. Schmitz-Hübsch, A., Becker, R., Wirzberger, M.: Accounting for interindividual differences in affect-adaptive systems using deep learning techniques. Front. Psychol. (2023)
30. Asendorpf, J.: Persönlichkeit. In: Wirtz, M. (ed.) Dorsch - Lexikon der Psychologie, 20th edn. Hogrefe Verlag, Bern, Schweiz (2021)
31. Bergner-Köther, R.: Zur Differenzierung von Angst und Depression: Ein Beitrag zur Konstruktvalidierung des State-Trait-Angst-Depressions-Inventars. University of Bamberg Press, Bamberg (2014)
32. Goldberg, L.R.: An alternative "description of personality": the big-five factor structure. J. Pers. Soc. Psychol. **59**, 1216–1229 (1990)
33. Rauthmann, J.F.: Fünf-Faktoren-Modell. In: Wirtz, M. (ed.) Dorsch - Lexikon der Psychologie, 20th edn. Hogrefe Verlag, Bern, Schweiz (2021)
34. Penley, J., Tomaka, J.: Associations among the Big Five, emotional responses, and coping with acute stress. Pers. Individ. Differ. **32**, 1215–1228 (2002)
35. Roslan, N.S., Izhar, L.I., Feng, Y.X., Faye, I., Ho, E.T.W., Rahman, M.A.: An investigation of physiological correlates of neuroticism during speaking task. In: 2018 IEEE-EMBS Conference on Biomedical Engineering and Sciences (IECBES), pp. 515–519 (2018)
36. Brouwer, A., van Schaik, M., Korteling, J., van Erp, J., Toet, A.: Neuroticism, extraversion, conscientiousness and stress: physiological correlates. IEEE Trans. Affect. Comput. **6**, 109–117 (2014)
37. Williams, P.G., Rau, H.K., Cribbet, M.R., Gunn, H.E.: Openness to experience and stress regulation. J. Res. Pers. **43**, 777–784 (2009)
38. Becker, R., Stasch, S.-M., Schmitz-Hübsch, A., Fuchs, S.: Quantitative scoring system to assess performance in experimental environments, pp. 91–96 (2021)
39. Orasanu, J., Backer, P.: Stress and military performance. In: Driskell, J., Salas, E. (eds.) Stress and Human Performance. Lawrence Erlbaum Associates, Mahwah (1996)
40. Littlewort, G., et al.: The computer expression recognition toolbox (CERT). Face Gesture 298–305 (2011). https://doi.org/10.1109/FG.2011.5771414
41. iMotions Biometric Research Platform, 8th edn. iMotions, Copenhagen (2021)
42. Walfish, S.: A review of statistical outlier methods. Pharm. Technol. 1–5 (2006)
43. Jain, A., Nandakumar, K., Ross, A.: Score normalization in multimodal biometric systems. Pattern Recogn. **38**, 2270–2285 (2005)
44. Cohen, J.: Statistical Power Analysis for the Behavioral Sciences, 2nd edn. Lawrence Erlbaum Associates, Hillsdale (1988)
45. Benjamini, Y., Hochberg, Y.: Controlling the false discovery rate: a practical and powerful approach to multiple testing. J. Roy. Stat. Soc.: Ser. B (Methodol.) **57**, 289–300 (1995). https://doi.org/10.1111/j.2517-6161.1995.tb02031.x

46. Lazarus, R.S.: Emotion and Adaptation. Oxford University Press, New York (1991)
47. Moors, A.: Appraisal theory of emotion. In: Zeigler-Hill, V., Shackelford, T.K. (eds.) Encyclopedia of Personality and Individual Differences, pp. 232–240. Springer, Cham (2020). https://doi.org/10.1007/978-3-319-24612-3_493
48. Roseman, I.J.: A model of appraisal in the emotion system. Appraisal Processes in Emotion: Theory, Methods, Research, pp. 68–91 (2001)
49. Kuppens, P., Tong, E.M.W.: An appraisal account of individual differences in emotional experience: individual differences in emotional experience. Soc. Pers. Psychol. Compass 4(12), 1138–1150 (2010). https://doi.org/10.1111/j.1751-9004.2010.00324.x
50. Asendorpf, J.B., Wilpers, S.: Personality effects on social relationships. J. Pers. Soc. Psychol. 74(6), 1531–1544 (1998). https://doi.org/10.1037/0022-3514.74.6.1531
51. Wu, C., Lin, H., Wang, T., Huang, T., Huang, Y.: Affective mobile language tutoring system for supporting language learning. Front. Psychol. (2022)
52. European Commission, Directorate-General for Education, Youth, Sport and Culture. Ethical guidelines on the use of artificial intelligence (AI) and data in teaching and learning for educators: Publications Office of the European Union (2022)
53. Fahrenberg, J., Hampel, R., Selg, H.: Freiburger Persönlichkeitsinventar (FPI-R), 8th edn. Hogrefe Verlag, Göttingen (2010)
54. Schneewind, K., Schröder, G., Cattel, R.: Der 16-Persönlichkeits-Faktoren-Test (16PF). Huber, Bern (1994)
55. High-Level Expert Group on AI: The Assessment List for Trustworthy Artificial Intelligence (ALTAI). European Commission (2020)

Establishing an Effective Adaptive Instructional Systems Community of Practice

Robert A. Sottilare(✉)

Soar Technology, Inc., Orlando, FL 3281, USA
bob.sottilare@soartech.com

Abstract. This paper discusses the benefits and challenges associated with a path forward toward the establishment of an adaptive instructional system (AIS) community of practice (COP). At their simplest, AISs may be described as any form of instructional approach or strategy adopted to accommodate individual differences in learners to facilitate the effective and efficient acquisition of knowledge and skill. AISs use artificial intelligence and machine learning approaches to assess learner performance and proficiency, use learner information to select optimal interventions (e.g., feedback or direction) and recommendations for future instruction, and then observe the effect of their learner interactions to enable better decisions in the future. The goal of this paper is to demonstrate the importance of adaptive instruction and make the case for a global community of practice to develop standards, collaboratively develop capabilities, and share innovative solutions. Toward this goal, we identify significant challenges that require a large, multi-disciplinary community of experts to solve. Finally, we examine the potential impact of emerging AIS solutions that address some of the most difficult challenges in tailoring education and training for individuals and teams in the context of an AIS community of practice.

Keywords: adaptive instruction · adaptive instructional systems (AISs) · artificial intelligence · community of practice · individual differences · learner assessments · machine learning · tailoring instruction

1 Introduction

The saying "many hands make light work" is a proverb that suggests that a task or job becomes easier when many people work together to accomplish it. The origin of this saying is not clear, but it is believed to have originated from ancient times when people worked in agricultural societies and needed to work together to complete tasks such as planting, harvesting, or building. In English, the first recorded use of the phrase "many hands make light work" dates back to the 1300 s and this saying suggests the idea that it is easier to accomplish a task when many people work together.

Adaptive instruction systems (AISs) are computer-based systems that accommodate individual differences and tailor instruction to match learner needs, preferences, practices, and capabilities to acquire knowledge through a guided learning process [1–3].

R. A. Sottilare and J. Schwarz (Eds.): HCII 2023, LNCS 14044, pp. 76–93, 2023.
https://doi.org/10.1007/978-3-031-34735-1_6

They include complex education and training systems, tools and methods that require a diverse set of skills and expertise to design and develop solutions that are as effective as expert human tutors. Therefore, engaging many people in the AIS community to work together on a set of challenging problems will make AISs better for several reasons. First, different individuals bring different perspectives, ideas, and expertise to the development and improvement process. For example, instructional designers may bring expertise in learning theory, while software engineers may bring expertise in software design and development. By working together, they can create more effective and efficient AISs.

Second, collaboration can lead to more efficient and effective problem-solving. When different individuals work together, they can brainstorm ideas, identify potential issues, and develop solutions more efficiently than one person working alone. Third, involving multiple stakeholders in the development process can help ensure that the AIS being designed meets the needs of different users. For example, teachers, students, parents, and administrators may all have different needs and expectations for an AIS. By involving these stakeholders in the development process, developers can ensure that the system meets their needs (e.g., learning goals and skill or knowledge gaps) and is user-friendly.

Finally, working in teams or various sizes, up to a community, distributes the burden or workload, making the development process more manageable and efficient. With complex systems such as AIS, it can be challenging for one person to handle all aspects of the development process. By working collaboratively, developers can divide the workload and work more efficiently, bring diverse perspectives and expertise to bear on difficult challenges, and solve problems more efficiently.

2 Motivation for an AIS Community of Practice

Communities of practice (COPs) are a group of people who "share a concern or a passion for something they do and learn how to do it better as they interact regularly" [5].

They are important because they provide a platform for information and knowledge sharing, networking, personal and professional growth, support and encouragement, and advocacy [6]. By participating in communities of practice, individuals can learn, grow, and connect with others who share their practices and passions. Conferences are a forum for COPs to come together and provide a platform for individuals to share information and knowledge related to their practices. Members of the community can share their experiences, ideas, and best practices, which can help others learn and improve their skills. COPs provide opportunities for individuals to network and connect with others who share similar practices. This can lead to new collaborations, partnerships, and friendships, which can be beneficial both personally and professionally.

COPs also provide opportunities for individuals to learn and grow both person-ally and professionally. Members can participate in workshops, webinars, tutorials, and other events that enhance their skills and knowledge. COPs provide a sense of support and encouragement, especially for individuals who are pursuing their practices alone. Members can provide feedback, offer encouragement, and share their own struggles, which can help others stay motivated and on track. Finally, COPs provide a platform for advocacy and activism related to their practices. Members can work together to raise awareness, promote change, and advocate for their cause [7]. In 2011, representatives of the military services, the Advanced Distributed Learning (ADL) Initiative within the Department of Defense, the Defense Advanced Projects Research Agency (DARPA), and the Department of Education met under the auspices of the Human System COP to conduct an adaptive training workshop and discuss research projects conducted within government laboratories that furthered the state of practice in adaptive instruction [8]. Topics of discuss at this workshop included learner modeling, expert modeling, pedagogical models used to guide adaptive instruction, and the state of authoring tools for adaptive instruction.

Some of the skills and expertise represented in an AIS COP include learning theory and instructional design, software development, data science and analytics, user experience design (UX), educational policy, domain expertise, and project management. Members of the AIS COP with expertise in learning theory and instructional design can help ensure the reliability, validity, and effectiveness of AISs and alignment with best practices in education and training. Software developers contribute designs, and build and maintain the technology that powers AISs. Data science and analytics skills are critical for analyzing user data and identifying patterns and trends that can inform the development and improvement of learner models used to drive tailoring and interventions decisions in AISs. UX designers can help ensure that adaptive instruction systems are user-friendly, intuitive, and engaging for learners. Members with expertise in education policy can help ensure that AISs align with policy goals and promote equity and access for all learners. Depending on the specific AIS application, COP subject matter experts (SMEs) with domain proficiency in subjects such as math, science, engineering, computer programming, language arts, or social studies may be important for developing both content and assessments. Project managers can help ensure that the development and improvement of AIS technologies are efficient, organized, and meet the needs of stakeholders.

Finally, sales engineers can contribute to an AIS COP by providing insight into customer needs based on direct interaction. Sales engineering is a hybrid of sales and engineering that exists in highly complex industrial and commercial markets [9]. It is not mandatory that an AIS sales engineer have an engineering degree, as long as they have sufficient technical knowledge about AIS services or products in the marketplace. They can offer technical expertise, facilitate communication, promote the AIS value proposition, and provide feedback about product performance. Their unique perspective and expertise can help ensure that AIS systems are designed, developed, and improved to meet the needs of stakeholders (designers, developers, buyers, integrators, maintainers, and users).

3 Building an AIS Community of Practice

In this section, we discuss the process of building an AIS COP, its key elements, strategies for sustainment and growth, and general benefits to the community. Our goal would be to evolve A community of practice is an important theoretical construct that underlies a particular model of learning, namely, learning in which people, through a process of legitimate peripheral participation, take up membership in and identity with a community which serves as the home of these shared practices.

3.1 AIS COP Construction Process

Next, we discuss the steps and associated products from the AIS COP building process [10]. The first step is to define the scope and objectives of the AIS COP. This involves identifying the target audience, the specific topics or themes that the COP will focus on, and the goals that the COP seeks to achieve. The next step is to identify key stakeholders who will be part of the COP. This includes researchers, practitioners, educators, learners, policymakers, and other stakeholders who have an interest in AIS research and development.

Communication is critical for building a strong AIS COP. Leadership should develop a communication plan that outlines how the COP will communicate with its members, such as through email lists, social media, webinars, and conferences. To facilitate communication and collaboration, establish a virtual platform where COP members can share information, discuss topics, and collaborate on projects. This can be a website, a social media group, or a dedicated online forum.

Next, the AIS COP should organize events such as webinars, workshops, and conferences to provide opportunities for COP members to meet and collaborate in person. These events can be organized locally, regionally, nationally, or internationally depending on the scope of the COP. The leadership of the COP should identify resources and support for COP members to help them achieve their community goals. This can include access to research findings, training materials, and funding opportunities.

Next the COP should regularly evaluate the effectiveness of the COP and adapt it as needed. This includes seeking feedback from COP membership, and making changes to the COP's objectives, communication plan, and activities based on that feedback. Overall, building an AIS COP requires a strategic and systematic approach that involves identifying key stakeholders, establishing communication channels, providing resources and support, and regularly evaluating and adapting the COP. By following these steps, a strong and vibrant AIS COP can be constructed that contributes to the advancement of AIS research and development.

3.2 Key Elements of a Successful Community of Practice

In this section, we discuss the essential elements of a successful AIS COP. A successful AIS COP requires active and engaged members who are committed to the goals and objectives of the COP [11]. This includes researchers, practitioners, educators, learners, policymakers, and other stakeholders who have an interest in AIS research and development. Participation is an essential responsibility of the COP membership. A successful AIS COP should have clear and measurable goals and objectives that are aligned with the needs and practices of its members. This includes defining the scope of the COP, identifying the target audience, and setting achievable goals and objectives. We have outlined a set of goals in Sect. 4 of this paper. A successful AIS COP requires effective communication and collaboration among its members. This includes regular communication through email lists, social media, and other communication channels, as well as collaboration on research projects and other initiatives. The goals, activities and initiatives of the COP should be reviewed regularly by the membership and adapted as needed to meet their needs. There should be relentless pursuit of resources in order to fund the activities and initiatives. Last, but not least, a successful AIS COP has effective leadership and governance structures in place to ensure that the COP operates smoothly and achieves its goals. This includes establishing clear roles and responsibilities, providing leadership and guidance, and ensuring that the COP operates in a transparent and accountable manner.

3.3 Strategies for Sustainment and Growth of an AIS COP

In this section, we discuss strategies to sustain and even expand the AIS COP. One of the keys to the sustainment and growth of an AIS COP is recruiting [12]. This strategy involves identifying and engaging potential new members. This can be done through targeted outreach, such as through social media, email lists, and other communication channels. Current members should be incentivized to recruit new members. To attract and retain members, an AIS COP should offer valuable resources and support. This can include access to research findings, training materials, funding opportunities, and other resources that can help members achieve their goals. The AIS COP should encourage collaboration and knowledge sharing among its members. This can be done through online forums, webinars, conferences, and other events where members can connect with one another and share their experiences and insights.

Another strategy is to establish a culture of continuous learning. To remain relevant and effective, an AIS COP should establish a culture of continuous learning [13]. This can be done through ongoing training, professional development opportunities, and other initiatives that help members stay up-to-date with the latest trends and developments in AIS research and development. The AIS COP should also foster a sense of community and belonging among its members. This can be done through social events, recognition programs, and other initiatives that celebrate the achievements and contributions of members [14].

Last, but not least are strategies to foster participation by AIS COP members. Strategies such as developing a strong community culture [15] and a strong sense of ownership [16], and providing opportunities for professional development [17] should be actively and relentlessly pursued.

3.4 Benefits of a Strong Community of Practice

Developing a robust AIS COP may have several benefits for its members and the AIS marketplace including knowledge sharing and collaboration, professional development and networking, increased visibility and impact, access to resources and support, and innovation and continuous improvement.

A strong community of practice enables knowledge sharing and collaboration among researchers, educators, and practitioners. This collaboration can lead to the development of new ideas, approaches, and solutions, leading to more effective and efficient AISs. Being part of a community of practice also provides individuals with opportunities for professional development and networking with peers in different, but related disciplines. Benefits include workshops, conferences, and training sessions, shared experiences, and mentoring from experts in the field.

A strong community of practice can help to raise the visibility of AIS in the broader education community. This increased visibility can lead to more significant investment, more extensive adoption of AISs, and more significant impact on teaching and learning. Building a community of practice provides access to a broad range of resources and support, including technical expertise, funding opportunities, and mentoring. This access can help to overcome technical, social, and cultural barriers, leading to more effective and sustainable AIS solutions. Finally, a strong community of practice can drive innovation and continuous improvement in AIS tools and methods. Through sharing best practices, collaborating on research, and providing feedback on products and services, a community of practice can help to advance the state of the art in AIS technologies and keep pace with the rapidly changing landscape of education and technology.

4 Mission, Vision and Goals for an AIS COP

In thinking about an AIS COP as more than just an organization, the mission of a passionate group of like-minded experts could be stated as:

To promote the development, improvement, and adoption of adaptive instruction systems to personalize instruction and improve the way people learn.

This mission statement encapsulates several key elements that are central to the purpose of an AIS COP. First, it highlights the focus of AISs as tools to personalize instruction and improve learning methods. It underscores the goal of creating instructional systems that can adapt to the unique needs and abilities of each learner, rather than relying on a one-size-fits-all approach. The mission statement emphasizes the importance of development and improvement, indicating that the community is dedicated to advancing the state of the art in AISs. This suggests a commitment to ongoing research, development, and collaboration in order to continually improve the effectiveness of these systems. Finally, the mission statement infers the goal of improving instructional experiences for all learners. This reflects a broader commitment to equity and access in education, and suggests that the community is motivated by a desire to create systems that can benefit all learners, regardless of their backgrounds, abilities, or circumstances.

As we evaluated the mission space for an AIS COP, we should also seek inspiration from a vision statement that can provide the COP with long term goals. The vision statement below expresses a future state to be strived for by the COP.

To create a future in which all learners have access to effective personalized education and training experiences that accelerate their proficiency, enhance their retention, and optimize their transfer of skills for operational use.

The vision statement envisions a world in which all learners are able to receive education and training that are tailored to their individual needs and abilities, using technology and data to personalize each learner's needs. This statement emphasizes the transformative potential of AISs to revolutionize instruction and create a more effective, efficient, accessible, and usable learning environments for all. Based on the mission and vision statements, a set of five worthy AIS COP goals is proposed. Note these are not listed in any priority order or value ranking:

- **Goal #1 - Develop and improve AISs:** One of the main goals of an AIS COP should be to develop and improve adaptive instructional solutions. This includes leveraging data and technology to personalize learning experiences, improving educational outcomes, and creating more accessible instructional opportunities for all learners.
- **Goal #2 - Foster collaboration and knowledge sharing:** Another goal of an AIS COP should adopt is to foster collaboration and knowledge sharing among its community members. This can include sharing best practices, case studies, and research findings, but it can also include other relevant information to advance the state of the art in AIS or to identify resources to support goal #1 as well as communication methods for its membership (e.g., blogs, vlogs, podcasts).
- **Goal #3 - Advocate for adoption and implementation:** An important goal for an AIS COP is to advocate for the adoption and implementation of AISs in educational (e.g., schools) and training (e.g., military department of training) settings. This can involve partnering with institutions, policymakers, and other stakeholders to promote the value and benefits of AISs.
- **Goal #4 - Support professional development and training:** Another goal of an AIS COP should be to support the professional development and training of educators and others involved in the design and implementation of adaptive instruction systems. This can include offering training, workshops, and other learning opportunities to ensure that all stakeholders have the knowledge and skills necessary to effectively use and implement these systems. Feedback to doctoral students on the technical approaches in their dissertations might be another way to aid members of the AIS COP in their development.
- **Goal #5 -** Promote research and innovation: Finally, an important goal for an AIS community of practice is to promote ongoing research and innovation in the field of adaptive instruction systems. This can include funding research projects, offering research grants, and hosting conferences and other events to promote collaboration and idea sharing among researchers, practitioners, and other stakeholders.

5   Shared Technical Challenges in Adaptive Instruction

AISs can support education and training experiences in cognitive, psychomotor and collaborative learning domains and are typically composed of models of the learner (attributes of the recipient of instruction), the instruction (principles of how the instruction is delivered), a domain of instruction (knowledge about the topic of instruction), and a user interface [18].

Generally, there are three types of AISs which are categorized as intelligent tutoring systems (ITSs), intelligent mentoring systems (IMSs), and intelligent media [3]. ITSs are the most prevalent AISs and usually educate or trainer the learner without the need for a human instructor in the loop. IMSs are capabilities that brings together artificial intelligence and machine learning to help people with different aspects of life that could include recommendations for current or future learning experiences [19]. Intelligent media includes adaptive hypermedia that tailor instruction based on a model of the user's goals, preferences, and knowledge in contrast to linear media where all users are provided with a standard set of hyperlinks [20].

To be as effective and efficient as an expert human tutor or mentor, an AIS must be able to assess the learner's performance and make decisions about how to interact with the learner which involves the selection and execution of interventions (e.g., feedback, direction, guidance, reflective prompts, and questions). A self-improving AIS should also be able to evaluate past decisions to determine the effectiveness of interventions, and then use this information to adapt policies that drive intervention selection. With this in mind, we examine technical challenges related to optimizing learning using current AIS solutions and discuss technical challenges for future AISs.

5.1 Technical Challenges for AIS Research and Development

There are several technical challenges for AIS research and development that still need to be addressed to improve the effectiveness of these systems, and they include data availability, data quality, personalization, interoperability, scalability, and explainability. AISs usually rely on large amounts of data to make decisions about instruction. However, the quality and quantity of this data can vary widely, and collecting and processing data can be expensive and time-consuming. Improving data quality and finding ways to collect and process data more efficiently is an ongoing challenge. In the absence of higher data availability, research is needed to create methods to bootstrap AIS models based on lower data quantities to help alleviate this problem.

One of the primary goals of AISs is to provide personalized instruction, but achieving this goal is a complex technical challenge. Personalization requires understanding individual learners' needs, preferences, and practices, and creating instruction that meets those needs. Developing effective algorithms and techniques for personalization is an active area of research, but models of higher granularity with a larger number of dimensions will help provide a greater number of learner state indicators and a higher degree of confidence in the predictive accuracy of those models.

AISs need to be able to integrate with a wide range of systems, such as learning management systems, assessment tools, and educational content providers. Developing standards for interoperability and ensuring that AISs can work seamlessly with other systems is an ongoing technical challenge. Beyond data interoperability, the ability to make software calls to external services and use the results of those calls to enable flexibility in selecting instructional strategies is also desirable.

As the number of learners using AISs grows, there is a need for these systems to be scalable and able to handle large volumes of data and users efficiently. Developing scalable architectures and algorithms that can handle large numbers of learners in complex domains of instruction is a technical challenge that needs to be addressed. One design consideration to help scale AIS solutions is modularity. Modularity facilitates parallelization or parallel processing of different parts of the system, which can increase efficiency and reduce processing time. This is particularly important when dealing with large amounts of data from many learners. By designing an AIS with modular components, it becomes easier to upgrade or replace individual components as needed. This can be particularly important in complex domains of instruction where the components may need to be updated frequently to keep up with changes in the domain. Modularity also enables AISs to be customized and adapted to different instructional contexts, which can be particularly important in complex domains of instruction. For example, different modules could be added or removed depending on the needs of the learners or the specific learning goals. Modular AIS architectures make it easier to identify and isolate problems, which can simplify the maintenance and troubleshooting process.

AISs use complex algorithms and decision-making processes to provide instruction. However, these algorithms can be difficult to understand, and learners and educators may be hesitant to trust recommendations from a system they don't fully understand. Developing techniques for explaining how AISs make decisions and providing transparent and interpretable recommendations is a critical technical challenge. Explainable artificial intelligence (XAI) involves developing algorithms and techniques that can explain how an AIS makes decisions. This is becoming increasingly important as AISs become more complex and learners and educators want to understand how the system arrived at its recommendations. XAI techniques are being used to make AISs more transparent, interpretable, and trustworthy.

5.2 Emerging AIS Capabilities

There continue to be innovations in personalization of AIS solutions, but recent AIS development trends have been focused on gamification, natural language processing, and open learner modeling. Gamification involves incorporating game-like elements, such as badges, points, and leaderboards, into the learning experience. The goal of gamification is to increase learner engagement and motivation by making the learning experience more fun and interactive. AISs are using gamification techniques to create more engaging and effective learning experiences.

Natural language processing (NLP) involves analyzing and understanding human language. NLP techniques are being used in AISs to create more natural and conversational interactions between learners and the system. This includes developing conversational agents, chatbots, and other NLP-based tools to enhance the learning experience.

Open learner modeling is a trend in AIS research and development that involves providing learners with access to the system's model of their learning progress and performance. The goal of open learner modeling is to increase learner self-awareness, self-regulation, and metacognition by making the system's model of their knowledge and performance visible to them. Open learner model solutions offer transparency and customization. Open learner modeling involves making the system's model of the learner's knowledge, skills, and performance visible and accessible to the learner. This allows the learner to better understand their own learning progress and performance. It also enables learners to customize the way they view their learning progress and performance. This includes choosing the level of detail they want to see, selecting the metrics they care about most, and setting goals and targets for themselves. However, open learner modeling also raises concerns about privacy and security. It is important to ensure that learner data is protected and that learners have control over who can access their data.

6   Challenges and Opportunities for an AIS COP

Most of the challenges associated with the design, development, deployment and use of AISs fall into a few key categories: standards & recommended practices, content management, authoring tools, user interfaces and experiences, assessments, decision support, evaluation, accreditation, and social and cultural challenges. While many of these challenges are difficult to address, they serve as motivation to bring the community together. This is especially true for capability providers and developers of AIS solutions who seek to grow their market and market share.

6.1   Challenge: AIS Standards and Recommended Practices

Through the IEEE Learning Technologies Standards Committee (LTSC), AIS practitioners have sought to develop standard and recommended practices under Project 2247. Groups have met to debate and develop an AIS concept model, address interoperability to enable AIS component reuse, and debate and develop recommendations for the ethical use of AISs.

Also under the IEEE LTSC, a community of practice called the IEEE Industry Connections Industry Consortium on Learning Engineering (ICICLE) is an open forum and community-driven platform for defining the new profession of learning engineers and the educational experience required to be a proficient practitioner.

In 2020, there was a groundswell of support by the IEEE community to establish an AIS Consortium, a paid membership organization focused on impacting the educational technology marketplace and changing the way people learn. The AIS Consortium was created under the IEEE Industry Standards and Technology Organization (ISTO). The Consortium established committees and used its resources to engage in activities that included development of open source AIS solutions. Unfortunately, the AIS Consortium lost momentum and ceased operation in November 2022. This specific disappoint was a great motivation for the creation of this paper.

Finally, the AIS conference under the auspices of Human Computer Interaction International (HCII) was established in 2019 and this year is conducting its 5th annual conference. All of these efforts, whether directly or indirectly, are impacting the AIS standards development process and standards of related technologies/processes (e.g., IEEE 9274 Working Group's development of concepts, templates and patterns of learner experience data).

6.2   Challenge: Automating AIS Content Management

Adaptive Instructional Systems (AIS) content refers to the instructional materials, resources, and activities used within the AIS platform to facilitate personalized learning experiences. This content can include a wide range of media types, including text, images, videos, interactive simulations, and assessments. AISs are designed to be adaptive, meaning that content can be customized and personalized to match the learning needs, preferences, and goals of individual learners. To achieve this level of personalization, AIS platforms use a range of techniques, such as machine learning algorithms, data analytics, and natural language processing, to understand and analyze user data and interactions to develop a model of the learner.

One of the key features of AISs are their ability to customize and personalize learning content and experiences for individual learners. Managing this content requires an understanding of learner profiles, preferences, and performance, as well as the ability to create and deliver personalized learning experiences. By their nature, AIS provide tailored experiences, and this increases the demand for content over more traditional (non-adaptive) courses.

AIS content is usually organized into learning paths or courses, which learners can access through a variety of interfaces, such as web browsers, mobile devices, or virtual reality environments. Learners can interact with the content in different ways, depending on their learning styles and preferences, such as watching videos, reading text, answering questions, or engaging in interactive simulations. The quality and relevance of AIS content are critical factors in determining the effectiveness and success of any AIS platform. Therefore, creating and managing high-quality, engaging, and pedagogically sound content is a crucial aspect of building a successful AIS platform, and there are major challenges associated with content management.

AIS content must be of high quality and relevance to ensure effective learning outcomes. Managing and curating high-quality content requires a deep understanding of the subject matter, pedagogical principles, and best practices in instructional design. Content management challenges center on data complexity, scalability of content management solutions, and data security and privacy protection. AISs generate massive amounts of data, including user profiles, learning content, assessment data, and user feedback. Managing and analyzing this data requires advanced technical capabilities, including data integration, data mining, and data visualization processes. AISs are also designed to accommodate a large number of users, which means that the platform must be scalable and capable of handling a high volume of data, interactions, and content.

Scalability is also challenging, especially when dealing with resource-intensive tasks such as data processing, machine learning algorithms, and real-time feedback. AIS content is sensitive and may contain personally identifiable information (PII) about AIS users. Beyond PII, AIS content may also be proprietary, which means that it must be secured and protected against unauthorized access or misuse. Managing content security and privacy requires advanced technical capabilities, including data encryption, access controls, and compliance with relevant regulations. An AIS community of practice should be prepared to identify and enforce regulations governing the ethical use of AIS content.

The primary challenge for AIS content curation is to reduce the workload associated with curating very large caches of content for later application and use. Based on this challenge, research should be undertaken to automate part or all of the curation process. Additionally, we recommend the development of large, shared repositories would be a valuable community asset that enables members to leverage existing content that is available as either royalty free, open source, or licensed for a fee. Methods to automatically valid the quality and relevance of content objects would greatly enhance the efficiency of the curation process for AIS authors.

6.3 Challenge: Automating AIS Authoring Tools

Developing Adaptive Instructional Systems (AIS) authoring tools can provide several benefits, but it also presents some significant challenges. The first benefit is that AIS authoring tools enable educators and instructional designers to create customized and personalized learning content that meets the specific needs of learners. Authoring tools that enable the rapid creation of high-quality learning content, save time and effort for educators and instructional designers. Another benefit of AIS authoring tools is the ability to create content that is accessible to learners with disabilities (e.g., learners with low vision) or special needs. Collaboration between educators (who determine what to learn) and instructional designers (who determine what methods should be used to learn) can lead to the creation of high-quality, innovative, and engaging learning content. Finally, AIS authoring tools should include features that help ensure the quality and effectiveness of the learning content, such as analytics and feedback mechanisms.

AIS authoring tool design and development can also present significant challenges. The first challenge is the technical complexity of AIS authoring tools. They require advanced programming skills and knowledge of instructional design and learning theories to produce effect AISs. Another challenge tied to the first challenge is the high cost of development due to the knowledge and skill required to create AISs. AISs also require significant investments in software development, testing, and maintenance. The complexity of authoring tools can also influence user adoption and acceptance. AIS authoring tools may require educators and instructional designers to learn new tools and techniques, which can affect their willingness to adopt better technology solutions. AIS authoring tools should be compatible with other AIS platforms and systems, which can be challenging due to the lack of standardization in the field. At a minimum, AISs should be able to share performance assessment data to enable more expansive interventions (e.g., virtual characters providing feedback about their progress toward learning objectives). Finally, authoring tools should ensure that the content created is of high quality, engaging, and relevant to the learning goals of the AIS and its user. Based on this desirable outcome, a primary goal for the AIS COI should be to undertake research to automate part or all of the authoring processes such as defining learning objectives, sequencing content, and developing assessments.

Overall, developing AIS authoring tools can provide significant benefits that make it worth the investment to overcome some of these challenges. Adopting a user-centered design and a collaborative approach involving educators, instructional designers, and software developers will go a long way toward realizing the full impact of AIS benefits and overcoming significant challenges.

6.4 Challenge: AIS User Interface (UI) Design and Development

An effective UI design can provide an improved and more consistent user experience (UX), increased user engagement through personalization, and greater access to learning analytics through an open learner modeling concept. A well-designed AIS user interface can improve the user experience and make it easier for learners to access and interact with learning content. It can also increase learner engagement and motivation, which can lead to better learning outcomes. It can allow learners to customize and personalize their learning experience, such as selecting preferred content or activities. An AIS user interface can provide learners and educators with access to learning analytics, which can when combined with an open learner model can help visualize and track progress, identify areas of difficulty, and make data-driven decisions. Finally, a well-designed interface provides consistent branding and design language across the platform, which can enhance the platform's image and reputation.

The major challenges associated with AIS UI design include complexity, accommodations for user diversity, compatibility and interoperability with interdependent systems, visual design (look and feel), and implementation costs. Developing an AIS user interface can be technically complex, requiring advanced programming skills and knowledge of user experience design. An AIS user interface must be able to accommodate diverse learner needs, preferences, and abilities, which can be challenging to achieve. The UI might be required to exchange data with other AIS platforms and peripheral systems (e.g., learning management systems) which can be challenging due to the lack of standardization in the AIS field. The UI should be visually appealing and interactive and engaging, which can require significant effort and expertise in visual design. Finally, UI development can be costly based on both the complexity of the interface and the high level of skills required to design effective AIS interfaces. It is essential to adopt a user-centered design approach that involves learners, educators, and software developers when developing an AIS UI for broad use.

6.5 Challenge: Accurate, More Complete AIS Learner Assessments

Designing, developing and validating AIS learner assessments is complex and central to their effectiveness. AIS learner assessments that provide personalized examinations that are tailored to the individual learners' needs and abilities are more accurate and provide more relevant feedback. They can also provide learners with real-time feedback, enabling them to identify areas of weakness and adjust their learning strategies accordingly. Learner assessments can improve learning outcomes by providing learners with a deeper understanding of the material and promoting retention and providing context for the application of new knowledge. Effective assessments can reduce cognitive load by automating grading and providing instant feedback, enabling learners to focus on the material rather than on the assessment process. AIS learner assessments should be designed to provide a high degree of accessibility by accommodating learners with disabilities or special needs, such as providing audio or visual feedback.

Challenges associated with designing, developing and validating AIS learner assessment include technical complexity, evaluating validity and reliability of assessments, compatibility and interoperability, security, and cost. Developing AIS learner assessments can be technically complex, requiring advanced programming skills and knowledge of assessment design and learning theories. Learner assessments must be valid and reliable, meaning they must measure what they are intended to measure and provide consistent results across different learners and contexts. AIS learner assessments must also be secure to protect learners' privacy and sensitive data. In the context of a learning ecosystem, AIS assessments should be compatible with other AIS platforms and systems, which can be challenging due to the lack of standardization in the field. AIS assessments require significant investments to design, develop and validate them. Automation methods to mine assessment data from authoritative sources are being researched to reduce the workload associated with their design, development and validation.

6.6 Challenge: Optimizing AIS Decision Support

AISs use learner data along with artificial intelligence/machine learning (AIML) methods to determine the state of the learner (e.g., performance, emotions, proficiency level) and then select optimal interventions that are tailored to their needs and abilities. Personalized instruction is more engaging, effective and efficient that traditional instruction. AIS decision methods can make real-time decisions about the most appropriate interventions to provide, based on learners' current performance and progress toward assigned objectives. The tailoring of interventions can improve learning outcomes by addressing areas of weakness and building on learner strengths. Models of learner cognitive load can also influence AIS decision making by adapting the the difficulty level of the content aligned with the learner's capabilities per the Zone of Proximal Development (ZPD) [21]. Automating the selection of interventions can also influence AIS scalability by enabling the AIS to provide support to a larger number of simultaneous users.

The major challenges in providing an effective AIS decision support capability focuses on their technical complexity, but also the ability to reinforce valid decisions under a variety of learner and instructional conditions. Automated decision-making requires knowledge of advanced programming skills, knowledge of decision-making algorithms, and learning theories to create effective solutions, and these high level skills also drive costs. Again, all data-driven AIS processes must be secure and protect learners' privacy. To overcome these challenges, it is essential to adopt a user-centered and evidence-based approach that involves learners, educators, decision-making experts, and software developers in the design and development process. Additionally, the decision-making algorithms should be transparent, explainable, and auditable, enabling educators and learners to understand how decisions are made and why specific interventions are recommended.

6.7 Challenge: Transparent AIS Evaluation Methods

AIS evaluation methods should be focused to provide evidence-based insights into the effectiveness of the system, enabling developers to make data-driven improvements. AIS evaluation methods should be designed to measure the impact of the system on learning outcomes, providing objective evidence of its effectiveness. AIS evaluation methods can enable continuous improvement of the system, enabling developers to refine the system over time based on data from a growing number of user experiences over time. AIS evaluation methods should determine impact on learning outcomes, and ensuring that the system is meeting its intended goals. AIS evaluation methods should provide data on the system's effectiveness across a large number of learners and contexts.

The primary challenges for designing and implementing an AIS evaluation method include technical complexity which requires high level skills in advanced statistical analysis skills and knowledge of evaluation design and learning theories. Another challenge is bias and confounding variables which influence both the dependent variable and independent variable, and causing a spurious association. AIS evaluation methods must control for bias and confounding variables that could affect the results, such as differences in learner populations or instructional materials.

6.8 Challenge: Standards for Learner Accreditations Using AISs

Accreditation is a quality assurance process where the services and operations of AISs (and the organizations that create them) are evaluated and verified by an external body to determine whether applicable and recognized standards for education or training are met. The benefits of AIS accreditation is that learner achievements are recognized and documented which provides a tangible record of their progress and accomplishments. Formal accreditation can motivate and engage learners in the pursuit of a long term education or training goal that has clear objectives. Accreditation processes enhance the validity of learning experiences and provide tangible evidence that learners can use to compete in job markets and academic programs.

While AIS accreditation methods are intended to provide learners with a portable and transferable record of their achievements that can be shared across different contexts and platforms, this vision has not yet been achieved as evidenced by different accreditation standards across the globe. For example, the same experience may be perceived differently due to accreditation differences in the United States and other countries.

6.9 Challenge: Accounting for Social and Cultural Challenges in AIS Solutions

Establishing an AIS COP can provide significant social and cultural benefits, but it also presents some challenges. Benefits include knowledge sharing, collaboration opportunities, stimulation of innovative ideas, professional development, and networking. AIS COPs can facilitate the sharing of knowledge and expertise among members, enabling them to learn from one another and enhance their own state of practice. A COP can foster collaboration among its members, enabling them to work together on common goals and initiatives, or work together to solicit resources from third parties to achieve its goals. Innovation can be stimulated within the COP by encouraging members to share new ideas and approaches, and by providing a platform for experimentation and iteration. Another benefit of an AIS COP is the support for professional development by providing members with opportunities to learn and grow, and by enabling them to stay current with the latest trends, emerging technology, and common practices in the field.

Challenges can include cultural barriers, a lack of trust among the membership, the digital divide, resistance to change or resource constraints. Establishing an AIS COP might be challenging due to cultural barriers that may exist among members, such as differences in language, values, and norms. This the large or more global the organization, the more likely it is to encounter cultural barriers. AIS communities of practice can face challenges due to social fragmentation, such as lack of trust, communication breakdowns, and conflicting practices or goals among its members. Another barrier to success is the digital divide where some members have limited access to the technology needed to implement AIS solutions. In some countries, computer workstations are often shared, but smartphones are common. So, solutions should be designed to work on the available technology. AIS COPs may also encounter members who resist change due to significant investment or knowledge about existing solution. For example, reluctance to adopt new practices or technologies, or fear of losing control over the learning experience may be motivators to resist change. Finally, AIS COP participation may be time and resource-intensive, requiring significant investment in communication, coordination, and infrastructure. To overcome these challenges, it is essential to adopt a user-centered and evidence-based approach that involves members from diverse backgrounds and perspectives in the design and development process. Additionally, the community must be inclusive, transparent, and respectful, enabling members to share their ideas and collaborate effectively towards common goals. Finally, the community must be supported by robust communication, coordination, and infrastructure, enabling members to engage in meaningful dialogue and exchange of ideas.

7 Future Directions and Recommendations

There are many exciting research and development directions for an AIS COP, ranging from technical and pedagogical to ethical and social opportunities. By working collaboratively and sharing knowledge and expertise, an AIS COP can contribute to the advancement of adaptive instruction and help all learners achieve their full potential. Below are seven recommendations for community investments in research and development of new capabilities:

1. *Create new methods for personalized learning*: Our AIS COP should explore how to develop more sophisticated and effective personalized learning systems that adapt to learners' individual needs, practices, and goals.
2. *Integrate social and emotional learning*: Our AIS COP should investigate how to integrate social and emotional learning (SEL) into adaptive instruction, enabling learners to develop critical skills such as self-awareness, self-regulation, empathy, and collaboration.
3. *Enhance gamification*: Our AIS COP should explore how to leverage gamification techniques in new ways to enhance engagement, motivation, and learning outcomes in adaptive instruction.
4. *Apply Artificial intelligence to automate processes and reduce workload*: AIS COP can investigate how to integrate artificial intelligence (AI) and machine learning (ML) algorithms into adaptive instruction, enabling systems to analyze large data sets, detect patterns, rewarding successful adaptations (e.g., changes in instructional strategies) and optimize learning pathways in real-time.
5. *Enhance accessibility and inclusion*: Our AIS COP should also explore how to design adaptive instruction systems that are accessible and inclusive for learners with disabilities, enabling them to engage fully in the learning experience.
6. *Consider ethical and privacy issues:* Our AIS COP should investigate the ethical and privacy considerations associated with adaptive instruction, such as ensuring learners' data privacy and avoiding bias in algorithms and decision-making processes.
7. *Integrate AISs with other technologies:* AIS COP can explore how to integrate adaptive instruction systems with other technologies, such as virtual reality (VR), augmented reality (AR), and blockchain, enabling learners to engage in immersive and secure learning experiences.

8 Conclusion

This paper discussed the benefits and challenges associated with a path forward toward the establishment of an AIS COP. The goal of this paper was to demonstrate the importance of adaptive instruction and make the case for a global COP to develop standards, collaboratively develop capabilities, and share innovative solutions. We examined the process steps needed to establish a robust AIS COP, and discussed the importance of member participation. As a step forward, we crafted mission and vision statements along with a set of core goals for the AIS COP. While the challenges associated with adaptive instruction are significant, we made the case that a large, multi-disciplinary community of experts could address many of these challenges collaboratively, and that benefits associated with networking, innovation, and shared vision outweighed the challenges ahead. Finally, we made seven major recommendations for collaborative investment by the AIS COP.

References

1. Wang, M.C., Walberg, H.J.: Adaptive instruction and classroom time. Am. Educ. Res. J. **20**(4), 601–626 (1983)
2. Tsai, C.C., Hsu, C.Y.: Adaptive instruction systems and learning. In: Seel, N.M. (ed.) Encyclopedia of the Sciences of Learning. Springer, Boston (2012). https://doi.org/10.1007/978-1-4419-1428-6_1092
3. Sottilare, R., Brawner, K.: Component interaction within the Generalized Intelligent Framework for Tutoring (GIFT) as a model for adaptive instructional system standards. In: The Adaptive Instructional System (AIS) Standards Workshop of the 14th International Conference of the Intelligent Tutoring Systems (ITS) Conference, Montreal, Quebec, Canada (2018)
4. VanLehn, K.: The relative effectiveness of human tutoring, intelligent tutoring systems, and other tutoring systems. Educ. Psychol. **46**(4), 197–221 (2011)
5. Wenger-Trayner, E., Wenger-Trayner, B.: Introduction to communities of practice: a brief overview of the concept and its uses (2015)
6. Kilpatrick, S., Jones, T., Barrett, M.: Defining Learning Communities. Centre for Research and Learning in Regional Australia, Launceston, Tasmania (2003)
7. Antorini, Y.M., Muñiz, A.M.: The benefits and challenges of collaborating with user communities. Res. Technol. Manag. **56**(3), 21–28 (2013)
8. Goldberg, S., Sottilare, R.: Adaptive Training Workshop Summary. Human Systems Community of Practice (2011)
9. Reunanen, T., Röhr, T., Holopainen, T., Schneider-Störmann, L., Görne, J.: On the basis of the sales engineering competences and education. In: Kantola, J.I., Barath, T., Nazir, S. (eds.) Advances in Human Factors, Business Management and Leadership, pp. 160–172. Springer, Cham (2018). https://doi.org/10.1007/978-3-319-60372-8_16
10. Handley, K., Sturdy, A., Fincham, R., Clark, T.: Within and beyond communities of practice: making sense of learning through participation, identity and practice. J. Manag. Stud. **43**(3), 641–653 (2006)
11. Scarso, E., Bolisani, E., Salvador, L.: A systematic framework for analysing the critical success factors of communities of practice. J. Knowl. Manag. **13**(6), 431–447 (2009). https://doi.org/10.1108/13673270910997105

12. Wenger, E.C., Snyder, W.M.: Communities of practice: the organizational frontier. Harv. Bus. Rev. **78**(1), 139–146 (2000)

13. Wenger, E.: Communities of Practice: Learning, Meaning, and Identity. Cambridge University Press, Cambridge (1999)

14. Hollebeek, L.D., Juric, B., Tang, W.: Virtual brand community engagement practices: a refined typology and model. J. Serv. Mark. **31**(3), 204–217 (2017)

15. Cuddy, C.: Cultivating communities of practice: a guide to managing knowledge. Bottom Line **15**(2) (2002)

16. Wenger, E.C., McDermott, R., Snyder, W.C.: Communities of Practice: A Guide to Managing Knowledge, p. 304. Harvard Business School Press, Cambridge (2002). ISBN 1-5781-330-8

17. Wenger, E., Trayner, B., De Laat, M.: Promoting and assessing value creation in communities and networks: a conceptual framework (2011)

18. Sottilare, R.A.: A comprehensive review of design goals and emerging solutions for adaptive instructional systems. Technol. Instr. Cogn. Learn. **11**(1) (2018)

19. Dimitrova, V., Brna, P.: From interactive open learner modelling to intelligent mentoring: STyLE-OLM and beyond. Int. J. Artif. Intell. Educ. **26**, 332–349 (2016)

20. Brusilovsky, P.: Adaptive hypermedia. User Model. User-Adap. Inter. **11**(1–2), 87–110 (2001). https://doi.org/10.1023/A:1011143116306

21. Vygotsky, L.: Zone of proximal development. Mind in society: the development of higher psychological processes, 52-91, 157 (1987)

Design Strategies and Guidelines for Adaptive Instructional Systems

Directions for the Design of an Adaptive In-Game Re-engagement Dashboard for Teachers Using WHIMC

Jonathan DL. Casano(✉) , Mikael Fuentes , and Clark Joshua Paguio

Ateneo de Manila University, Quezon City, Philippines
jcasano@ateneo.edu

Abstract. This paper shows the ideation and development of an In-Game Dashboard within WHIMC that presents real-time statistics about player Re-engagement which teachers may utilize to support human-in-the-loop teaching. The attempt of converting the *delayed* analysis done from previous work (using Python and Pandas) to an instantaneous analysis within Minecraft (using Spigot API and JDBC) allowed the discovery of which elements in previous work are translatable into real-time statistics within WHIMC as well as how exactly these reports may be shown given the affordances and constraints of Spigot API and JDBC. It was found that showing frequencies such as the count of overlapping play times (Social Play), and showing which maps were visited within and outside testing hours (Free Exploration) may be implemented as real-time modules for the Dashboard. Other analyses, such as those that track data that happens over time, for instance, overlapping play times across days (Social Play), and presenting clustered archetypes or computations that are a result of clustering (Free Exploration) are not easily translatable. Since the Minecraft native API is not fully customizable, this paper demonstrated how the CommandExecutor API and HolographicDisplays API were utilized to provide the experience that approximates a working real-time Dashboard. The paper ends with a few suggested ideas for future work in terms of making the game adaptive as enabled by the frequencies and analyses being reported by the Dashboard.

Keywords: Minecraft · WHIMC · Human-in-the-loop teaching · Minecraft logs

1 Introduction

Re-engagement is defined as a learner's unprompted and voluntary re-interaction with a learning intervention [3]. It is last stage in the Process Model of Engagement composed of four stages namely, point of engagement, period of sustained engagement, disengagement and then (possibly) re-engagement [12]. Re-engagement is viewed to be important because this type of continuation desire as [13] calls it, is an indicator of intrinsic motivation and intrinsically motivated students have been shown to have better learning effectiveness [15].

© The Author(s), under exclusive license to Springer Nature Switzerland AG 2023
R. A. Sottilare and J. Schwarz (Eds.): HCII 2023, LNCS 14044, pp. 97–108, 2023.
https://doi.org/10.1007/978-3-031-34735-1_7

In a previous study [4], we tried quantifying re-engagement in an open-world, game-based learning environment called What-If Hypothetical Implementations using Minecraft (WHIMC; https://whimcproject.web.illinois.edu/), which are custom Minecraft worlds designed to show conditions of altered Earths [14], by looking at the in-game logs of students outside the prescribed hours of testing. These outside-of-testing-hours activities are understood to be done out of the student's own volition and hence were used to operationalize and understand re-engagement.

In this initial analysis we found that Social Play (*the affordance of being able to play with a classmate/s in real-time*), Free Exploration (*the ability to explore and visit different worlds*) and Interactive Learning Elements (*interacting with NPCs, observation making, and use of Science tools*) are the most-liked features of WHIMC and are therefore the potential triggers for re-engagement. Using logs of player positions, observation making behavior, and Science tools usage, we operationalized these re-engagement triggers and arrived at interesting insights such as (1) majority of the interactions with these triggers happened outside formal testing hours and (2) in terms of Social Play, an average of 8–16 concurrent players were observed during the first 6 nights outside testing hours and 75% of all nights registered concurrent users, among others.

The limitation of this first iteration lies in the speed of analysis; The *stats* reported in the preceding paragraph were generated using a 3rd-party software long after the data collection and testing with participating students and teachers were conducted. This meant that the cohort who could have benefitted from knowing these metrics namely, the teachers, weren't able to use them for the duration of the testing with WHIMC. Hence, teacher intervention as guided by the aggregated re-engagement metrics weren't possible.

This paper tries to address this limitation via a proposed dashboard for teachers usable within WHIMC. This dashboard was designed to show a real-time update of the status of the three Re-engagement triggers (Social Play, Free Exploration, and Interactivity) within the WHIMC worlds. Since an analysis done using a 3rd-party software is being ported into Minecraft itself, our formal research questions are as follows: **RQ1**: Which re-engagement elements identified in previous work are translatable into real-time statistics within the proposed WHIMC Dashboard? **RQ2**: How exactly can these real-time statistics be shown in the proposed WHIMC Dashboard?

2   Review of Related Literature

Recent research that utilized Minecraft logs extracted from gameplay aimed to investigate a diverse set of topics including STEM interest [7], student outcomes [1], and affect [6] among others. In these implementations, as well as in our previous work [4], the common approach was to do analysis on the collected logs at a later time, usually after the data collection step had been concluded. As these experiments typically involved teachers and their students, this implied that it wasn't feasible for teachers to use the insights generated from the analysis to influence their immediate instruction.

Hence, there is a missed opportunity to execute pedagogy that capitalizes on the availability of rich learner data combined with immediate teacher value judgment such as the human-in-the-loop teaching (HIL) [5]. In the context of computer-assisted education,

HIL is carried out by allowing the teacher to have access to the analysis and insights being generated by a computer-based learning intervention so additional interventions via the teacher's value judgment may be administered. It has been shown that HIL (1) helps teachers create better on-the-fly scaffolding activities for students [8], (2) leads to improved student outcomes and learning experience [2], and (3) facilitates engagement with scientific and mathematical concepts [5].

To the best of our knowledge, this work is one of the initiatory papers that attempt to report the analysis of in-game Minecraft student data back to an actual human instructor in real-time (HIL) as current attempts are more geared towards feeding in-game data back to an intelligent in-game agent that accompanies the player during actual gameplay [9]. In light of this, our proposed dashboard seeks to contribute to the ongoing literature on using Minecraft logs to inform teaching and learning practices [11] as well as contribute to the effort of previous researchers who are interested in creative ways by which human-in-the-loop teaching may be carried out in the classroom [10].

3   Methodology

To highlight how the design of the proposed dashboard is informed by previous work, the methodology is written in three parts. First, the context of the previous work, samples of the graphs that show our initial analysis of re-engagement triggers, and a summary of insights for each graph are presented. Second, how our proposed dashboard was designed to integrate these initial findings are shown with the help of wireframes and mock-ups. Finally, we describe the technical implementations of each part of the proposed re-engagement dashboard.

3.1   Context and Findings of Previous Work

Quantifying Re-engagement. A separate and earlier iteration of this work asked student respondents (*who played WHIMC in their classrooms for a span of several days*) to answer a Game Experience Questionnaire with open-ended questions meant to get an idea of which features in WHIMC were most liked and helpful [4]. Through a systematic coding process involving three (3) invited coders, the answers were thematically grouped into the categories of *Social Play*, *Free Exploration* and *Interactive Learning Elements*. [3] posits that since these elements are most favored, they are also the elements that have the potential to be re-engagement triggers. It was then time to operationalize these elements and see the extent to which they could be observed *outside testing hours*.

Using the position logs, observation making logs, and Science tools usage of the respondents who played WHIMC, these elements were operationalized as follows. *Social Play* referred to the number of concurrent gameplays recorded i.e. how many other students were playing while a student is playing? *Free Exploration* pertained to the number of maps visited by each of the players. *Interactive Learning Elements* presented an aggregate of observations made by the respondents, their recorded positions near NPCs which were regarded as approximations for NPC interaction, and the total number of times Science tools were used. As the goal was to quantify re-engagement, the analysis took note of which logs per re-engagement trigger happened within formal testing hours (*in the classroom*) and outside formal testing hours (*outside the classroom*). Those that happened outside testing hours were regarded as done out of the students' own volition and hence, are the results that were presented to make a case for quantified re-engagement.

Resulting Graphs from the Analysis of *Social Play.* The average number of concurrent players *outside testing hours* in the first 3 to 4 nights of the module implementations across the participating schools fell in the range of around 8 to 16 concurrent players per night (please see Fig. 1.a). 25 out of the 33 total night intervals for all Schools (~75%) recorded concurrent players.

Resulting Graphs from the Analysis of *Free Exploration.* Free Exploration was operationalized as the number of worlds visited over the students' play times. The analysis approach was to cluster the position logs via K-Means (with the optimal *k* being 6 as determined through the elbow method) then reduce the dimensions using Principal Component Analysis (PCA) for plotting. A cross-validation step was performed to determine what each of the clusters in the PCA plots were describing.

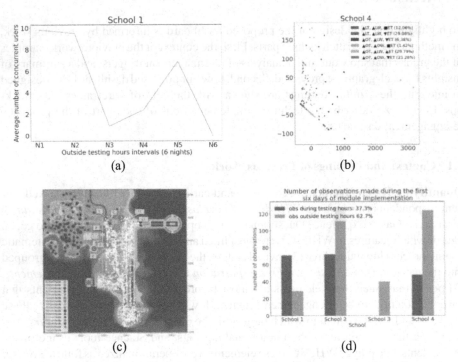

Fig. 1. (a) Quantified *Social Play*: Sample graph showing the average number of concurrent users outside testing hours for a school (b) Quantified *Free Exploration*: Sample graph showing the exploration archetypes of respondents who played WHIMC (c and d) Quantified *Interactivity*: Approximated NPC interactions and normalized tally of observations made within and outside testing hours.

Table 1.b shows the cluster attributes from the cross-validation step and Fig. 1.b shows the resulting PCA plots for each school which shows that about ¼ of respondents (regardless of the type of *free exploration* done) roamed around and visited the WHIMC worlds outside the prescribed testing hours.

Resulting Graphs from the Analysis of *Interactive Learning Elements*. The interactive learning elements that previous work attempted to quantify were (1) Interactions with NPCs (2) Number of observations made inside WHIMC (3) Science Tools usage. From these three, the number of observations and Science Tools usage were directly being recorded by the plugin within WHIMC. To quantify NPC Interactions, a proxy approach was developed by recording the distances and *fixations* of the recorded player positions from the NPCs in the WHIMC worlds (please see Fig. 1.c). Processing the observation and Science tools usage logs were also treated in a way that shows which among the recorded interactions happened *within* and *outside testing hours* (please see Fig. 1.d).

How these findings and graphs were integrated into the design of the proposed re-engagement dashboard are described in the succeeding subsections.

3.2 The Proposed Re-engagement Dashboard

Rationale. The dashboard idea was inspired by the work of [16] who created a dashboard for *Shadowspect*, a 3D geometry puzzle game, that allowed teachers to see a set of generated metrics from student interactions so teachers could properly analyze the effect of the activities within *Shadowspect* as well as guide the teachers towards creating additional lessons and activities to deepen learning (*human-in-the-loop teaching*).

Creating a dashboard for WHIMC seemed like an appropriate way to respond to the common feedback coming from teachers who participated in the study as well as teachers/audiences who attend the workshops organized by our laboratory where the findings of the previous papers are presented- *"How can we use this information in our classes?"* and *"Is there a way for me to know if my students are playing my created WHIMC learning modules outside class and if they are playing together?"* are a few repeated questions.

Design. The dashboard was envisioned as a heads-up display that can be shown or hidden by the teachers from within WHIMC either through a keyboard press or a special Minecraft command.

Since the intended users of the system are the teachers (who are interested in *what their students are doing*), in-game data was presented in the student level instead of showing the re-engagement stats per school similar to how the graphs in the previous work were presented. Hence, the dashboard's foreground highlights a scrollable list of students and their respective *Social Play*, *Maps Visited* and *Interactive Learning Elements* stats (please see Fig. 2). The technical implementations of these re-engagement stats as well as the details of how each stat was converted from being a part of an aggregate graph to its own student-level computation are discussed in the succeeding sections.

3.3 Technical Implementation of Dashboard Using Spigot API and JDBC

Spigot API + JDBC Affordances and Constraints. The front end of the dashboard was developed using Spigot API, a development framework for building native Minecraft plugins that is derived from a foundational codebase called Bukkit. To deploy the dashboard, PaperMC ver. 1.19.2 was utilized as the development server environment.

In terms of the backend, Java™ Database Connectivity (JDBC) was used to recreate the data analysis done in the previous work (which was written in Python + Pandas library) as well as break down the analysis to the student level.

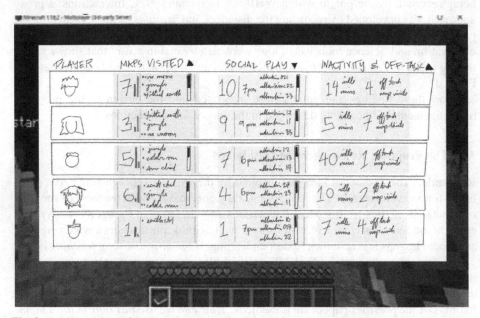

Fig. 2. Initial mockup of the Re-engagement Dashboard from the brainstorming session. Intention is for a Keyboard press or Minecraft command to toggle the display of the dashboard on top of the Minecraft main interface.

While the dashboard was envisioned to report the re-engagement stats in real-time (*updated as new data comes in*), one constraint of Spigot API that hindered this desired execution was the API's lack of server-side rendering (SSR). Hence, for now, to provide a pseudo-real-time feel when showing the stats, processing of all data to be shown in the dashboard happens at two checkpoints namely, (1) upon starting the server and (2) upon restarting WHIMC. This ensures almost zero delay when invoking the Dashboard stats in-game as the most updated statistics were already computed.

We also note that as part of Spigot API's security policy, creation of fully customized interfaces is not possible at the moment. Hence, as shown in the succeeding sections, the authors tried utilizing open-source libraries such as the HolographicDisplays API and CommandExecutor API to provide the desired Dashboard-like experience.

Social Play. To reflect Social Play on the dashboard, overlaps between the specific hours played by players, particularly outside of testing hours, were taken into account.

Initially, players were mapped to their respective schools. Play times that were recorded outside of testing hours were then separated from play times recorded during testing hours. The algorithm then takes the play times of each player and assigns it to each username. An initial value of zero (0) for the social play count is also assigned to each username. Afterwards, the algorithm goes through each username, takes their play times, and compares it with the play times of the other players. If the play times of two usernames are equal (i.e. *overlapping*), this counts as an instance of Social Play and is added to the Social Play count of the username being processed. Algorithm 1 shows this process formally.

Algorithm 1 Calculating for the social play for each player

initialize *unique_usernames*
initialize *play_times*
initialize *social_play_count*
for each *unique_username* **do**
　　unique_usernames.append(play_times)
　　unique_usernames.append(social_play_count)
for each element *e* in *unique_usernames* **do**
　for each element *i* in *unique_usernames* **do**
　　if *e.play_times* **equals** *i.play_times* **then**
　　　e.social_play_count++

Free Exploration. To reflect the Free Exploration component in the dashboard, an initial pass on the position logs was done to get all unique player usernames. These usernames were then mapped to the school they belonged to during testing. The username-to-school mapping was necessary to determine which of the logs happened during and outside testing hours as each school had its own schedule of testing that spanned several days.

Now that the usernames are mapped to the school and their respective testing hours, two sets of unique maps can be populated per player username namely, *unique maps visited during testing hours* and *unique maps visited outside testing hours*. The proper combination of these two sets (without repetition) is reported as the total number of maps visited by the player. The dashboard displays a scrollable list of all unique maps visited per player as well as colored markers to denote if the maps were visited during and/or outside testing hours. Algorithm 2 shows this process formally.

Interactivity. To reflect the interactivity component of the dashboard, the total number of observations made and science tools used per player are calculated. The unique player usernames and testing hours for each school had to be gathered first. An input file mapping the usernames to schools is used in order to more easily determine which of the logs happened during and outside testing hours.

Algorithm 2 Calculating for the total maps visited per unique player username
        initialize *unique_usernames* as new **Set**
        initialize *testing_hours* as new **Vector<pair>**
        initialize *unique_maps_outsidehours, unique_maps_withinhours* as new **Set**
        for each *row* in *position_logs* **do**
            set *unique_usernames.append(row.username)*
        for each element *e* in *unique_usernames* **do**
            if *e*.time is within testing hours **then**
                unique_maps_withinhours.append(usernames[e].append(e.map)
            else
                unique_maps_outsidehours.append(usernames[e].append(e.map)
        store all *sets* in global static variable *freeExploreStat* for display within WHIMC

To speed up the algorithm's search time, the observation logs are filtered such that only the logs between the first and last session of a particular school are present. Using the filtered logs, the total number of observations made as well as the number of observations made within testing hours is tallied per player. Subtracting the number of observations made within testing hours from the total results in the number of observations made outside of testing hours. The dashboard displays a scrollable list containing the number of observations made inside/outside of testing hours per player. Algorithm 3 shows this process formally.

Algorithm 3 Calculating for the total observations made per unique player username
        initialize *unique_usernames* as new **Set** // From input file
        initialize *testing_hours* as new **Vector<pair>** // From input file
        initialize *observations_outsidehours, observations_withinhours* as new **Set**
        for each *user* in *unique_usernames* **do**
            for each *row* in *observations_filtered* **do**
                if *row.username* **equals** *user* **then**
                    total++
                    if *row.time* is within *testing_hours* **then**
                        total_withinhours++
        total_outsidehours = total - total_withinhours
        observations_withinhours.append(total_withinhours)
        observations_outsidehours.append(total_outsidehours)
        store all *sets* in global static variable *interactivityStat* for display within WHIMC

---

4 Results and Discussion

Figure 3 shows screenshots of the prototype containing the different dashboard elements running on WHIMC version 1.19.2. Both Social Play and Interactivity components feature a report of the number of overlapping gameplay sessions of each student and the count of observations made within and outside testing hours respectively as heads-up displays that appear after typing a custom command. The Free Exploration component utilized the HolographicDisplaysAPI to embed the reported list of map visits within the Minecraft game space. Colors and special symbols are included in the representation of each map to denote whether the map was visited within and/or outside testing hours (e.g. ✳+ yellow text means visited within testing hours only, ☆+ aqua text means visited outside testing hours only, ✳☆+ white text means visited both within and outside testing hours).

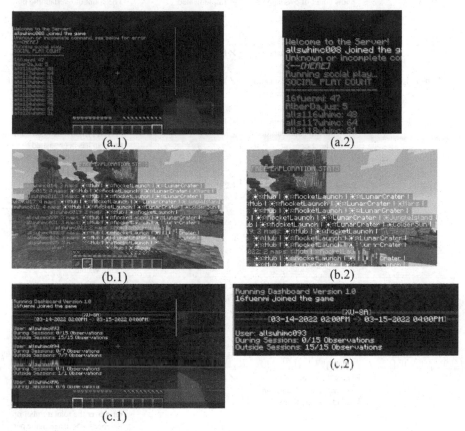

Fig. 3. The prototype of the Dashboard running in WHIMC version 1.19.2 (a.1) *Social Play* component (a.2) zoomed-in details of *Social Play* stats (b.1) *Free Exploration* component (b.2) zoomed-in details of *Free Exploration* stats (c.1) *Interactivity* component (c.2) zoomed-in details of *Interactivity* component.

To summarize, Table 1 shows the re-engagement elements that were analyzed and graphed in the previous work vis-à-vis the status of their re-implementation within the proposed Dashboard. We note that the resulting prototype did not exactly match the mock-up we had envisioned during the brainstorming session as per the discover of Spigot API's affordances and constraints as discussed in Sect. 3.3 but future work is set out to creatively build on top of this prototype so it is more aligned with the mockup envisioned.

Table 1. Matrix showing which of the elements in previous work were implemented in the proposed WHIMC dashboard.

Re-engagement Element	Specific feature present in previous work	Status of implementation within WHIMC dashboard	Specific details of re-implementation
Social Play	Show count of overlapping play times	✓ Implemented	The count of overlapping play times is reported as frequencies beside each player username
	Show count of overlapping play times over time	✗ Not implemented	N/A
Free Exploration	Show total number of maps visited	✓ Implemented	The count of total maps visited is reported as a frequency beside each player username
	Show which maps were visited within and outside testing hours	✓ Implemented	Beside each map visited per player, symbols that denote if the map has been visited *within* or outside testing hours are shown
	Show the username of students who have explored the map	1/2 Partially implemented	The HolographicDisplaysAPI used in showing the list of students who explored the WHIMC maps show up within the in-game world. Hence, showing too many (*more than 10*) leads to some rows not being visible
	Determine archetypes of exploration	✗ Not implemented	N/A
Interactivity	Show the observations made by the players within and outside testing hours	✓ Implemented	The observations that were made within and outside testing hours were listed as a ratio over the total number of observations made per player
	Show the Science tools use that happened within and outside testing hours	✓ Implemented	The Science tools usage that were made within and outside testing hours were listed as a ratio over the total number of Science tools usage made per player
	Show NPC interactions that happened within and outside testing hours	✗ Not Implemented	N/A

5 Conclusion and Future Work

This paper endeavored to answer two research questions namely, **RQ1**: Which re-engagement elements identified in previous work are translatable into real-time statistics within the proposed WHIMC Dashboard? **RQ2:** How exactly can these real-time statistics be shown in the proposed WHIMC Dashboard?

RQ1: As presented in Table 1, some components of each re-engagement trigger were successfully translated to real-time Statistics such as showing the count of overlapping play times (Social Play), showing which maps were visited within and outside testing hours (Free Exploration), and showing a running tally of observations created by each student while playing WHIMC (Interactivity). However, there are also some components of each re-engagement trigger that were not successfully implemented mostly because of the constraints posed by SpigotAPI such as showing any type of statistics that happens over time such as overlapping play times across days (Social Play), presenting clustered archetypes or any data that is a result of clustering (Free Exploration), and approximated NPC interactions using proximity of player positions with NPCs inside WHIMC (Interactivity).

RQ2: At this point, we have tested at least 2 ways of showing real-time statistics during WHIMC gameplay namely, (1) using Minecraft's CommandExecutor API to show a plain heads-up display containing the calculated re-engagement statistics (please see Fig. 3.a and Fig. 3.c), and (2) using the HolographicDisplays API to show the statistics as embedded in the Minecraft world itself (please see Fig. 3.b). The Holographic display approach is especially promising as there are ways to make the holograms clickable which may be an opportunity to implement functions such as filters (i.e. *show only students who are from class X*) and export (i.e. *save this information about my students in pdf*).

In addition to these intended future work, ideas for adaptivity for each Re-engagement element may also be explored as enabled by the prototype. Some ideas are as follows: (1) Students who visit maps outside class hours may be given access to additional quests (*Free Exploration*) (2) quests that would require collaboration among players may be activated based on the number of overlapping play times (*Social Play*), and (3) students who are detected to make more observations may receive additional prompts from NPCs about where to go in the world and what to observe (*Interactivity*).

Acknowledgments. The authors thank H Chad Lane and Jeff Ginger for their enthusiastic collaboration, Dominique Marie Antoinette Manahan, Maricel Esclamado, Ma. Rosario Madjos and Dr. Maria Mercedes T. Rodrigo for their support, the Ateneo Laboratory for the Learning Sciences, the Ateneo de Manila University, our funding agency Department of Science and Technology (DOST) for the grant entitled, *"Nurturing Interest in STEM among Filipino learners using Minecraft."*, and our Monitoring Agency the Philippine Council for Industry, Energy, and Emerging Technology Research and Development (DOST-PCIEERD).

References

1. Alawajee, O., Delafield-Butt, J.: Minecraft in education benefits learning and social engagement. Int. J. Game-Based Learn. (IJGBL) **11**(4), 19–56 (2021)

2. Bhutoria, A.: Personalized education and artificial intelligence in United States, China, and India: a systematic review using a human-in-the-loop model. Comput. Educ. Artif. Intell. **3**, 100068 (2022)

3. Cairns, P.: Engagement in digital games. In: O'Brien, H., Cairns, P. (eds.) Why Engagement Matters, pp. 81–104. Springer, Cham (2016). https://doi.org/10.1007/978-3-319-27446-1_4

4. Casano, J., Rodrigo, M.M.T.: Quantifying Re-Engagement in Minecraft submitted to 24th International Conference on Artificial Intelligence in Education, Tokyo Japan (2022)

5. Chen, F.: Human-AI cooperation in education: human in loop and teaching as leadership. J. Educ. Technol. Innov. 本刊已被维普网全文收录 **2**(01), 1381–1394 (2022)

6. Esclamado, M.A., Rodrigo, M.M.T.: Are all who wander lost? An exploratory analysis of learner traversals of Minecraft worlds. In: Rodrigo, M.M., Matsuda, N., Cristea, A.I., Dimitrova, V. (eds.) Artificial Intelligence in Education. Posters and Late Breaking Results, Workshops and Tutorials, Industry and Innovation Tracks, Practitioners' and Doctoral Consortium. AIED 2022. LNCS, vol. 13356, pp. 263–266. Springer, Cham (2022). https://doi.org/10.1007/978-3-031-11647-6_48

7. Gadbury, M., Lane, H.C.: Mining for STEM interest behaviors in Minecraft. In: Rodrigo, M.M., Matsuda, N., Cristea, A.I., Dimitrova, V. (eds.) Artificial Intelligence in Education. Posters and Late Breaking Results, Workshops and Tutorials, Industry and Innovation Tracks, Practitioners' and Doctoral Consortium. AIED 2022. LNCS, vol. 13356, pp. 236–239. Springer, Cham (2022). https://doi.org/10.1007/978-3-031-11647-6_42

8. Hobbs, L., et al.: Using Minecraft to engage children with science at public events. Res. All **3**(2), 142–160 (2019)

9. Hum, S., Stinar, F., Lee, H., Ginger, J., Lane, H.C.: Classification of natural language descriptions for Bayesian knowledge tracing in Minecraft. In: Rodrigo, M.M., Matsuda, N., Cristea, A.I., Dimitrova, V. (eds.) Artificial Intelligence in Education. Posters and Late Breaking Results, Workshops and Tutorials, Industry and Innovation Tracks, Practitioners' and Doctoral Consortium. AIED 2022. LNCS, vol. 13356, pp. 250–253. Springer, Cham (2022). https://doi.org/10.1007/978-3-031-11647-6_45

10. Howell, H., Mikeska, J.N.: Approximations of practice as a framework for understanding authenticity in simulations of teaching. J. Res. Technol. Educ. **53**(1), 8–20 (2021)

11. Nebel, S., Schneider, S., Rey, G.D.: Mining learning and crafting scientific experiments: a literature review on the use of Minecraft in education and research. J. Educ. Technol. Soc. **19**(2), 355–366 (2016)

12. O'Brien, H.L., Toms, E.G.: What is user engagement? A conceptual framework for defining user engagement with technology. J. Am. Soc. Inform. Sci. Technol. **59**(6), 938–955 (2008)

13. Schoenau-Fog, H.: The player engagement process-an exploration of continuation desire in digital games. In: Digra Conference, September 2011

14. WHIMC. (n.d.) What-If Hypothetical Implementations in Minecraft. Accessed from the WHIMC website: https://whimcproject.web.illinois.edu/

15. Zaccone, M.C., Pedrini, M.: The effects of intrinsic and extrinsic motivation on students learning effectiveness. Exploring the moderating role of gender. Int. J. Educ. Manag. **33**, 1381–1394 (2019)

16. Ruipérez-Valiente, J.A., Gomez, M.J., Martínez, P.A., Kim, Y.J.: Ideating and developing a visualization dashboard to support teachers using educational games in the classroom. IEEE Access **9**, 83467–83481 (2021)

Designing an Adaptive, Player-Centric Game on Animation Principles

Butch Adrian Castro, Jed Laszlo Jocson, and Jesus Alvaro Pato[✉]

Ateneo de Manila University, NCR, Quezon City, Philippines
{butch.castro,jed.jocson,jesus.pato}@obf.ateneo.edu

Abstract. The animation industry continues to grow in relevance due to the ubiquitous use of animation principles in multiple fields; with this growth resulting in many people taking an interest in the field. There are a multitude of entry points into the animation industry, from formal courses offered by respected institutions to free tutorials found in YouTube. Despite this, the researchers found that there is only a limited amount of media that teaches animation interactively, like video games. The researchers developed a modified 2D action adventure video game named *In-Between Frames: An Animation Adventure* that introduces its players to common principles used in animation. This paper aims on principles used in animation. This paper aims to present the Animation System, which is the core gameplay feature of the aforementioned video game. This Animation System, that allows the player to create and modify the animations of the player character whether it be the animations that allow for traversal or the attack animations used in combat, is used in the video game as a means to introducing certain animation principles found in the book Disney Animation: The Illusion of Life. This paper also describes what more can be added to the video game to make the experience more player-centric and adaptive. Concepts considered include dynamic difficulty adjustment (DDA), slow-motion and live feedback, and adaptive suggestions based on performance.

Keywords: Animation · Adaptability · Video Games

1 Game Analysis

In-Between Frames: An Animation Adventure is a modified 2D action adventure game about the principles of animation as its central mechanic. The player must organize and form animations out of keyframes and effects given to enable the actions necessary to progress in the game. Other resources on animation will also be used to build the story and the mechanics of the game. Through the Animation System and other various game mechanics, the game will introduce the player to the world of animation and how its fundamentals work.

R. A. Sottilare and J. Schwarz (Eds.): HCII 2023, LNCS 14044, pp. 109–122, 2023.
https://doi.org/10.1007/978-3-031-34735-1_8

2 Background

The main motivation for creating *In-Between Frames: An Animation Adventure*, is to educate its players about animation production. Animation has a major part in entertainment [1] ever since its industry boom in the last century, with uses that transcend its roles in movies and cartoons [2]. It is also heavily used in social media and marketing because of its flexibility and exposure. However, many studios still do not fund their artists and animators appropriately, leading to an unhealthy industry standard that underpays its animators [3]. Despite this, many new animators are still entering the industry, regardless of its production value growth issues [4]. Additionally, there are now more ways an individual could get into the art, whether it be through free animation software or online tutorials.

The video game should allow players to experience the process of animation in a simplistic but still informative manner. It should also teach the players a set of principles that are commonly used in the art of animation.

2.1 The 12 Principles of Animation

In-Between Frames: An Animation Adventure aims to teach its players principles that come from Chapter 3 of the book Disney Animation: The Illusion of Life [5]. Of course, these principles may not apply to all kinds of animation. Some of these principles may not be used for a number of reasons, such as comedic effect or closeness to reality. The researchers chose these principles as they are very prominent in most animations, and the book documents them very well.

1. Squash and Stretch. Squashing and stretching a character creates the illusion of elasticity, volume, and flexibility. It is commonly used to exaggerate movements and to make characters more dynamic.
2. Anticipation. Anticipation helps viewers discern what a character is going to do next with the use of preliminary actions in anticipation of another action.
3. Staging. This refers to the direction and focusing of the animation. The animation should have control over what, when, and where the focus of the viewer is on.
4. Straight Ahead Action and Pose to Pose. Straight Ahead Action means creating each frame chronologically. Pose to Pose means creating the keyframes or at least important frames first before creating the in-betweens. These two approaches are typically used in complement to each other.
5. Follow Through and Overlapping Action. These are the 'inertia' of animation. After actions are performed, succeeding animations will be performed in order to complete the effect of stopping the just finished animation.
6. Slow-in and Slow-out. In real life, nothing snaps to movement or to a halt instantly. There must be a transition from movement, to slowing, and to stopping and vice versa. Such is desired in standard animation, where no outrageous effects are expected.
7. Arcs. No things move in straight lines. Objects with a fixed length will always move in arcs. An example is a person swinging a stick with their arms. The stick and the arms of the person will not move in a straight line, rather they will revolve around the person in an arc.

8. Secondary Action. Secondary Action simply states that for a scene to be more attractive, the subject must be doing something else other than its primary action. This action should complement the primary action.
9. Timing. Timing of the number of drawings is important in animating actions. An action that has a high number of drawings will make the animation look smoother, but slower. On the other hand, the same animation with fewer frames will look snappy and quick.
10. Exaggeration. Animators commonly exaggerate movements and actions to make their animations more dynamic and appealing. Some of the usual exaggerations take place in the movement of the body and the expressions of the character.
11. Solid Drawing and Solid Posing. The subjects in the animation should be posed clearly and expressively. The subjects should still be understandable even if they were only silhouettes of themselves.
12. Appeal. The audience should be drawn to the animation and its characters in some way through design, simplicity, or significance.

During the first year of development, the principles: Squash and Stretch, Anticipation, Follow Through, Slow in - Slow out, Timing were implemented throughout the game's mechanics with their significance in the Animation System. For this year's development the researchers are focused on upgrading the Appeal, Staging, and Exaggeration to complement to the principles already present in the Animation System.

2.2 Traditional Animation

In Traditional Animation, there is the concept of keyframing. This refers to the drawing of individual images that depict movement. A key or an extreme is a key moment in an animated sequence. A single animation can have several keys depending on how complex that animation is. A keyframe is the drawing that corresponds to those keys. A breakdown is a frame between the keyframes that describes the motion between the keyframes. Finally, the inbetweens are all the frames between the keyframes that make the motion smoother.

2.3 3D Animation: Keys, Channels, Inbetweens

In 3D Animation, keys behave differently. Keys are also called events or time marks. These keys are associated with parameters such as vertex position, shaders, cameras, etc. Every key associated with an individual parameter is stored in a Channel. Inbetweens fill the gaps between the keyframes using several interpolation methods that compute the motion from one key to another.

3 Overview of the Game

3.1 Mission Statement

In-Between Frames: An Animation Adventure is a modified 2D action adventure game that introduces animation principles to its players by allowing them to arrange keyframes in order to create movement and combat animations that helps them progress through the game.

3.2 Target Audience

In-Between Frames: An Animation Adventure is a modified 2D action adventure game that is available on Windows 10/11 and Mac OS X operating systems. The targeted audience of the game are teenagers and young adults, more specifically, people aged 13 to 25. The game does not require any previous animation experience and can be enjoyed by anyone.

3.3 Storyline and Characters

The game takes place in The Marshlands, a once peaceful world that had been overrun by characters known as The Rejects. The player follows The Animus, after he had barely survived death from a surprise attack. No longer having access to his old keyframes, animations, and features, the player controls him throughout his journey in the Marshlands to take it back from its besiegers (Fig. 1).

Fig. 1. The Animus

The goal is to strengthen The Animus by collecting its keyframes in order to defeat the final boss and restore peace in The Marshlands.

3.4 Control Scheme

The game is fully keyboard controlled, mimicking a standard console controller. The W, A, S, and D keys are used for player movement and menu navigation. Keys U, I, J, and K simulate the face buttons of the controller and are used mostly as attack buttons. Q is used to perform the special attack. A and D are used for blocking/parrying. J and K are used to select and cancel from menus, respectively. The Spacebar and Left Control keys are used for jumping and crouching/crawling, respectively. The Escape and Tab keys are used to open and close respective menus.

4 Gameplay

4.1 The Animation System

The animation system is central to the entire gameplay experience. The way the player character moves around in the game world, how they fight in combat scenarios, and how they interact with NPCs and other objects of interest are reliant on the basic premise of the player being able to manipulate the animations of the player character. This system has to have enough depth that the players will be constantly interacting with it to see what more the system can offer, while accessible enough that the system can draw people who know nothing about animation.

The timeline is the method in which the player will be able to interact with the player character's animations. The game will feature a system wherein the player can arrange frames in a timeline, much like how it is done in animation software. However, the player will mostly only have to deal with the character layer. The background and effects layer will be used as well, however their application in gameplay will be different to the application of the character animation layer.

4.2 Keyframes, Breakdowns, and In Betweens

The game features a 2D character moving in 2D space. The backend of the animation system will be somewhat similar to how keyframes function in computer animation where each key represents positional data. However, the UI will emulate the way keyframes work in traditional animation where each keyframe is an image representing a singular frame in the animation. These keyframes will be placed on an animation timeline in order to create full animations (Fig. 2).

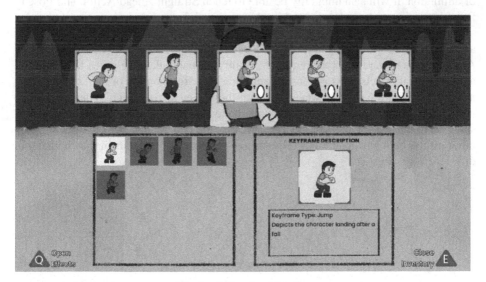

Fig. 2. Animation Timeline

Each image placed in the timeline represents keyframes. The player is able to place individual images in the timeline in order to represent the movement or attacks of the player character. However, the player cannot be expected to place every single inbetween between the keyframes, so the player is instead given keyframes and breakdowns to place in the timeline, and the inbetween frames are interpolated between each individual keyframe and breakdown much like how computer animation processes inbetweens. The keyframes are represented by images with the poses of the player character, like keyframes in traditional animation; but in the backend, those images contain data on the parameters of the player character's position.

With the ability to place keyframes and breakdowns, the player is able to change the stats of the player character dynamically. This applies to both exploration and combat as the player is able to manipulate the movement and attack animations of the player character. This has the potential to make each player's experience with the game different as they will make the animations they want with the tools given to them. With this system being as open as it is, it also gives the player the ability to make animations that will be detrimental to their movement and attack capabilities. The ability to make "bad" animations will allow for more experimentation to see which keyframes work in what order, or which breakdowns to put between keyframes to make the animation more cohesive.

4.3   Application of the 12 Principles of Animation in Game

While being able to place keyframes in an animation timeline could simulate the process of keyframing, another important aspect of animation are the principles that could make the animations look better. The keyframes on their own will only be able to do Anticipation, Follow Through and Overlapping Action, and Timing out of the principles of animation. It will also implicitly be able to teach Straight Ahead Action and Pose to Pose depending on how the player does their animations.

The Effects System is a means in which to apply most of the other principles of animation. More specifically, Squash and Stretch, Staging, Exaggeration, and Secondary Actions. This system gives the player the ability to manipulate the given keyframes to add additional effects. This is done by applying the effects on top of the keyframe it is modifying. Figure 6 shows a keyframe with the screen shake effect. When this frame plays during an animation, the screen will shake accordingly. Effects can also modify stats, so in this case, the effect greatly increases the attack power of the attack. Many other effects on many other kinds of keyframes will change the stats of the character in different ways (Fig. 3).

Fig. 3. Punch With "Screen Shake" Effect

4.4 Traversal by Animation

Throughout the game the player will get several new keyframes depicting movement and effects that could be applied to the animations to enhance the movement. Each of these movement options will be animated by the player using the timeline in the menu. Some examples of movement options that will be depicted by keyframes are walk and run animations, jump animations, crawl animations, swimming animations, etc. Without the necessary keyframes, the player character won't be able to do the simplest movements. For example, until they get the keyframes necessary to animate a jump animation, they won't be able to get past even short ledges.

The player could also get effects to modify their movement. For example, as seen in Fig. 7, a squash effect applied to the jump animation makes the jump go higher. In the case of a run animation, a motion blur applied to it will also make the player's movement speed much faster (Fig. 4).

Fig. 4. Jump Animation with and without Stretch effect

4.5 Background System

This game has a relatively small map compared to games like metroidvanias, but this small map can change drastically using the background system. In animation, there are several layers, and one of the layers is the background layer. The background layer essentially tells the viewer the location of the scene they are viewing in an animation. This game makes use of a similar concept with the background system.

The map of the game, while small, has several progression blocks. While most progression blocks can be overcome by having new animations, some progression blocks will require changing the background of the scene. Much like getting new keyframes, the player will also be able to unlock new backgrounds for the scene.

Changing the background does not change the layout of the overall map, but there are several things that are affected by changing the background of the scene. One such thing is the behavior of foreground elements. Consider an area with a large body of water and the player does not have an animation for swimming. Figure 8 shows that when the player changes the background to a winter scene, the water freezes over and the player will be able to traverse over it. This is one example of the way backgrounds can interact with foreground elements. Related to interaction with foreground elements are enemies. Certain enemies will only appear depending on the current background. The background can be changed freely in the menu, but there are some cases where changing the background could be detrimental. The player must be aware of their surroundings before changing the background. This system adds another layer of problem solving for the player (Fig. 5).

Fig. 5. Backgrond Effects with Body of Water

4.6 Combat

In combat scenarios, the inputs are different to that of the exploration scene. The directional buttons no longer move the character and there will be several attack buttons, each attack button corresponding to a limb on the player character.

Animating Attacks

In the menu, the player is able to animate four different attacks, each corresponding to an attack button. Each attack input has its own timelines that the player will animate. In general the attack animation will have three phases; the windup, the hit, and the followthrough. The player will be given the keyframes for all three of those phases and the breakdowns they can place in between each phase of the attack.

A set of keyframes can be animated differently depending on the breakdown placed in between two keyframes. Figure 6 shows the same windup and hit keyframes with different breakdowns in between them. This changes the property of the attack as seen on Fig. 7. The first breakdown which depicts the character raising his hand for a chop attack which gives the downward attack property. The second breakdown depicts the character pulling back for a gut punch gives a neutral attack property.

Fig. 6. Different Breakdowns

This mechanic of changing the animation between two keyframes entirely by using the breakdowns teaches the player the role of breakdowns in animation. That is to define the motion of the animation between two keyframes. Visually, this system teaches the concept of Arcs. The two different breakdowns depict a downward arc and an upward arc respectively. Of course, this won't be the only instance of changing breakdowns. There are more keyframes and breakdowns throughout the game that have this property.

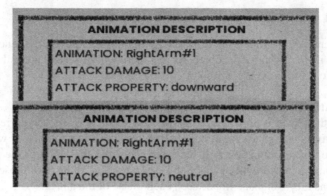

Fig. 7. Different Attack Properties Based on Breakdowns

The stats of the attack is dependent on how the player animates each attack. For example, if the player animates it in such a way that the windup is short, the attack will have low damage but high speed so they can keep using it. If the windup is long, the attack will deal a lot of damage, but the startup animation and the followthrough will be longer as well. The player can also opt to remove some keyframes from the attack, but it could be detrimental to gameplay. For example, the player makes a strong attack by having a long windup, but opts to remove the followthrough frame so that the attack has no end lag. Doing so will make a safe strong attack, but it will damage the player character because in reality, if a person tries to do any heavy attack without a follow through it will put tremendous amounts of stress on a person's muscles. There are many ways that animating the attacks could be detrimental, but that will be up to the player to explore. With this system, they are able to make their attacks how they want them with the given keyframes.

Attack Properties and Enemy Weaknesses
Another system that emphasizes the importance of breakdowns and effects in combat is the Attack Properties and Enemy Weaknesses. Each enemy type has specific resistances and weaknesses. Resistances greatly reduce damage taken and attacking the weaknesses deals more damage. These weaknesses can be targeted by using breakdowns to define the direction of the attack to change its attack property. These weaknesses will be somewhat obvious as to make identifying and targeting the weaknesses intuitive for the player. Hitting the enemy's weakness puts them in a stunned state where its resistances are negated making the enemy vulnerable to all attacks, not just its weakness. Figure 8 shows the difference between attacking an enemy with a resisted attack and an attack it is weak against.

Fig. 8. Attack Resisted vs Weakness

The enemy takes considerably less damage when it resists the attack and is stunned when hit with its weakness. To avoid spamming the enemy with attacks it is weak against, after an enemy is hit with an attack it is weak against, it will gain temporary resistance against that weakness.

4.7 Other Animation System Integrations

The Animation System is not just used to manipulate the animations of the player character. There are several situations wherein the player has to use the timeline to animate other objects or characters. These other interactions serve the main quest of the game and optional content.

NPCs
Much like the player character, the NPCs will also have their animations stolen by the villains of the story. As such a majority of them will be frozen in place or will have limited movements. The player will be able to find keyframes not only for themselves but also for these NPCs. These keyframes are also used in a timeline to reanimate these NPCs. Reanimating NPCs rewards the player in several ways. If the NPC plays a role in the main story, reanimating them rewards the player with progression. If the NPC doesn't play a role they could give optional keyframes, breakdowns, and backgrounds that give the player an advantage. Reanimating optional NPCs could also reward the player in additional lore for the world.

Puzzle Solving
There are some areas in the map where progression is blocked by an animation puzzle. These puzzles will test the player's knowledge of the principles that they learn throughout the game. These puzzles also bring up an animation timeline specific to the puzzle at hand.

One of the animation puzzles in the game is introduced when the player's path is blocked. Nearby is an NPC that lost their keyframes. The player must search for these keyframes, give them to the NPC, and arrange an animation to punch away the blockade.

This is an example of a puzzle that is necessary for progression. There will also be puzzles that are optional throughout the game's map.

Boss Fights

Boss fights are unique fights that the player has to go through to progress through the story. These fights won't necessarily only have the combat scene. Some boss fights will be similar to the animation puzzles wherein an animation principle will be tested when fighting a boss. These will be a combination of the exploration scene, combat scene, and other interactions with the animation system.

5 Adaptivity in In-Between Frames

Adaptivity in video games refers to the ability of the game's systems to adapt accordingly to the player's preferences, behaviors, and skills. *In-Between Frames: An Animation Adventure's* Animation System opens several avenues for developers to integrate adaptivity. Within this section, we will discuss some of the improvements that can be done to make the system more adaptive such as Dynamic Difficulty Adjustment, Slow Motion, and Live Feedback.

5.1 The Adaptiveness of the Animation System

The Animation System on its own lends itself well to be adaptive to an individual player's playstyle. Players arc given the option to animate the player character the way they want, which in turn affects the player character's stats differently. It can accommodate faster playstyles where the player deals less damage, but is able to attack more often, or slow but strong playstyles. The Animation System could also be used to solve a variety of traversal problems differently depending on what keyframes or effects the player has access to. While the current build of the game doesn't allow for much customization yet, building upon the base system could lead to a lot of unique customization options on the player's end. Just by adding more keyframes, breakdowns, and effects, the player has exponentially increased modes of play.

5.2 Dynamic Difficulty Adjustment

Dynamic Difficulty Adjustment (DDA) is a method that automatically adjusts the video game's features, behaviors, and scenarios depending on the player's performance. This is to ensure that the player does not feel bored or frustrated when the game is too easy or too difficult, respectively. In the game, DDA could be implemented by adjusting the enemy spawn points and attributes to fit the player's skill level. This way, players who have not mastered the Animation System can still enjoy the game, and more experienced players have more room for skill expression and challenge.

To determine the player's skill level, the game could consider several things, including:

- the player's keyframe ordering
- how much time the player spends creating animations
- how many times the player misplaces keyframes
- how much damage the player takes and deals in battle

5.3   Adaptive Additions to the Animation System

Slow Motion

A possible hurdle that inexperienced players may face while using the Animation System is identifying which parts of an animation are which. For example, the game's combat animations should follow a keyframe pattern of Breakdown → Hit → Follow Through to make them functional and deal damage. The Animation System could have an option to play the animation in slow-motion, so that players can easily identify each part of the animation and determine if the whole animation is usable.

Live Feedback

As order is very important in creating animations, the Animation System could also show suggestions on what keyframe to place after placing one. This could be implemented by highlighting the suggested keyframe/s so that the player will not have to think much about picking the correct keyframe to place and optimizing their animations. Another implementation of this is by showing tooltips and helpful messages about the animation itself, the keyframes, or the ways the player could create an animation.

6   Conclusion

The adaptiveness of *In-Between Frames: An Animation Adventure* is determined by the effectiveness and integration of the Animation System throughout all of its game mechanics. The Animation System is the game's unique and determining factor that sets it apart from the usual action adventure game. The system incentivizes players to study and learn the animation principles introduced in the game in order to progress through the game's challenges. The Animation System's design and integration into the game could be followed and improved upon by other game developers to fit in their respective games to increase their games' adaptiveness and heighten the uniqueness and overall player experience. Given the freedom that the Animation System grants its' players, there are numerous ways of improving the system for other games such as doubling down on the customization options and feedback quality of the system. Also, better integration of this system and other similar systems will ensure a more player-centric and adaptive experience.

Acknowledgements. We would like to thank Dr. Maria Mercedes T. Rodrigo and Mr. Walfrido David A. Diy for their guidance in the writing of this paper. With their expertise, we were able to expand on the topic of our study and carry out the necessary tasks with this project. We would also like to thank our subject matter expert and third panelist, Ma'am Molly Velasco-Wansom for helping us find resources and information on our topic and giving us advice on how to tackle the design elements of the game.

References

1. Arora, S.: broadcast2world. https://www.b2w.tv/blog/the-evolution-of-animation-a-brief-jou rney-through-time. Accessed 18 Mar 2021
2. Anime Motivation. https://animemotivation.com/anime-companies-bankrupt. Accessed 18 Mar 2021
3. Margolis, E.: Vox. https://www.vox.com/culture/2019/7/2/20677237/anime-industry-japan-art ists-pay-labor-abuse-neon-genesis-evangelion-netflix. Accessed 18 Mar 2021
4. Westcott, T.: An overview of the global animation industry. J. 3(3), 253–259 (2011)
5. Thomas, F., Johnston, O.: Disney Animation: The Illusion of Life. Abbeville Press, New York City (1981)

Cognitive Simulations for Adaptive Instructional Systems: Exploring Instruction Strategies with Simulated Tutors and Learners

Bruno Emond[3]([✉]) [ID], Reza Zeinali-Torbati[1] [ID], Jennifer Smith[1] [ID],
Randy Billard[2] [ID], Joshua Barnes[3] [ID], and Brian Veitch[1] [ID]

[1] Memorial University of Newfoundland, St. John's, Canada
{rzt313,jennifersmith,bveitch}@mun.ca
[2] Virtual Marine, Paradise, Canada
randy.billard@virtualmarine.ca
[3] National Research Council Canada, Ottawa, Canada
{bruno.emond,joshua.barnes}@nrc-cnrc.gc.ca

Abstract. Computational models of learners have been recognized to play various roles in training and learning environments. While optimized tutoring strategies should be determined through empirical investigation, the adaptive instructional system design space is too large to fully validate empirically. Synthetic data generated by simulated learners could be one approach to explore the interaction between learner behaviours and adaptive instructional system strategies. The current paper reports on a computer simulation design and results for modelling the effects of learning and training strategies on the learning and performance of simulated learners. The application domain is marine navigation. The computer simulation included a fairly autonomous learning agent with self assessment capabilities (reinforcement learning), and other means to acquire knowledge and skills including learning from instructions, and declarative memory base-level activation. Three instructional strategies were simulated: 1) a minimalist method leaving the simulated learner to proceed only by trial and error, 2) a discovery method where the simulated learners are left on their own but with an added capability to store a declarative representation of successful rules, and 3) a briefing then practice method, where all the declarative rules to execute tasks are in declarative memory prior to executing navigation tasks.

Keywords: Instructional strategies · Cognitive simulations · Adaptive instructional systems · Marine navigation · ACT-R

1 Introduction

Simulated learners are computational models of learners [27]. They have been recognized to play various roles in training and learning environments, such as

This project was supported in part by collaborative research funding from the National Research Council of Canada's Artificial Intelligence for Logistics Program.

R. A. Sottilare and J. Schwarz (Eds.): HCII 2023, LNCS 14044, pp. 123–136, 2023.
https://doi.org/10.1007/978-3-031-34735-1_9

to evaluate pedagogical effectiveness of instruction, test theories of how humans learn [13], support teachers' practice (teachable agents), embed simulated learners as part of a learning environment, and explore and test learning system design issues [16,26]. More recently, Wray has brought forward the use of simulated learners as a software verification method "to attempt to understand, prior to full-scale development, the potential benefits of adaptive algorithms and the requirements they impose on students and instructors" [27]. The Apprentice Learner Architecture [15] follows a similar approach where simulated learners can be combined with novel interaction designs to offer model transparency, input flexibility, and problem solving control to achieve greater model completeness in less time than existing authoring methods [24]. Other applications of simulated learners include modelling learning sequences [17], the role of time in learning [12], the design of AIS for self-directed longer-term learners [14], adaptive remediation in online training [20], and differential error types between human and simulated learners [25].

Even on a relatively simple task, the number of possible ways to design instructional intervention can grow very rapidly, presenting a challenge for evidence-based design if the only source of information is human performance and evaluation. It is not possible and often too costly to empirically determined which instruction strategy is the most effective and efficient. The lack of testing makes it difficult to ensure that lessons and guidance from design recommendations and prior studies in other domains have been effectively applied in the training application [26]. While optimized tutoring strategies should be determined through empirical investigation, the AIS design space is too large to fully validate empirically [5]. Synthetic data generated by simulated learners could be one approach to explore the interaction between learner behaviours and adaptive instructional system strategies.

Our objective is to improve maritime operations in Canadian waters using innovative scientific and engineering methods by enhancing operators' competencies using training simulators, such as adaptive instructional systems. The anticipated benefits of the efforts are: 1) an increase in knowledge of the cognitive demands and skill acquisition related to sea ice management in the context of freight transportation and small vessel emergency operations; 2) a cost reduction of training scenario development by testing alternative learning scenarios and instructional designs prior to empirical validation with human participants; and 3) an increase in training efficiency using optimized scenarios and adaptive instructions. Our approach consists of informing the design and implementation of adaptive instructional systems by conducting concurrent research activities using 1) Bayesian networks for modelling learning processes, 2) knowledge elicitation of expert instructors, and 3) simulated learners and tutors to explore AIS system design options [8]. The current paper falls under the third approach and builds on prior work in cognitive modelling [6,7,9–11], and training simulations [19,21,22].

The current paper reports on a computer simulation design and results for modelling the effects of learning and training strategies on the learning and performance of simulated learners. The computer simulation included a fairly autonomous learning agent with self-assessment capabilities (reinforcement learning), and other means to acquire knowledge and skills including learning from instructions, and declarative memory base-level activation. Three instructional strategies were simulated: 1) a minimalist method leaving the simulated learner to proceed only by trial and error, 2) a discovery method where the simulated learners are left on their own but with an added capability to store a declarative representation of successful rules, and 3) a briefing then practice method, where all the declarative rules to execute tasks are in declarative memory prior to executing navigation tasks. These conditions were modelled by enabling and disabling learning mechanisms of the ACT-R cognitive architectures. The paper is divided in a method section where the simulated learner, tutoring strategies and the simulation design are presented. A results and discussion section is followed by a conclusion.

2   Method

The method to explore the effects of instruction strategies on learning outcomes is based on executable cognitive models build with the ACT-R cognitive architecture [1]. A cognitive architecture consists of task independent cognitive resources such as declarative and procedural memories, and perceptual and motor capabilities. Figure 2 presents a high-level view of the ACT-R architecture modules and it is discussed in more details in the subsection on simulated learners. Cognitive models are constructed with cognitive architecture resources, but they are tasks specific. In the case of the current simulation, the cognitive models will include declarative and procedural knowledge relevant for a vessel navigation task.

2.1   Learning Task: Steering a Vessel Near an Object of Interest

The learning task consists of using a sequence of throttle and rudder operations to navigate a vessel near an object of interest on the water. The object of interest is not moving. The task starts with the vessel at a resting state with its head pointing towards one of eight cardinal directions (N, NE, E, SE, S, SW, W, NW). The object of interest, is located to the East of the vessel resting location. Figure 1 shows a vessel with an absolute bearing to the North, and the object of interest is a grey circle. This object of interest could be a ship or a person in water. However, this information is not relevant for the current simulation.

As the vessel travels, it needs to adjust its speed and approach to optimize its course. Some of these adjustments are directly dependent on the proximity to the object of interest, and are performed with throttle (speed) and rudder (direction) operations. The throttle actions available to the simulated learner are: stop, ahead-slow, ahead-half, and ahead-full. The rudder actions are midships (move the rudder straight from a port or starboard position), port (move the rudder to turn the vessel towards the port side), and starboard (move the rudder to turn the vessel towards the starboard side). At regular intervals, the simulated learner

	Start moving	Steer to course	Stay on course	Reduce speed	Adjust approach	Stop at OOI
Speed	Slow-speed	Moderate-speed	Fast-speed	Moderate-speed	Slow-speed	Stop
Approach	Any bearing	Ahead	Ahead	Ahead	Port-beam or Starboard-beam	Port-beam or Starboard-beam
Rudder	Any rudder	Midships	Midships	Midships	Port or Starboard	Midships

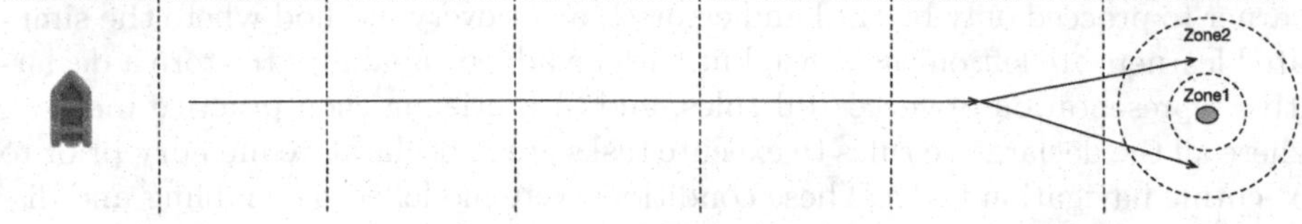

Fig. 1. The figure shows the intended path of a vessel navigating towards an object of interest (grey circle). During its course, the vessel has to change its speed and approach according to its proximity to the object, and its initial departure from a resting state. The table above the graphic represents the speed, approach, and rudder satisfaction conditions that are required to travel towards the object of interest. (Color figure online)

needs to apply one of these actions in order to meet the success conditions for each manoeuvre. The manoeuvres are (in order from departure to the arrival at destination): start moving, steer to course, stay on course, reduce speed, adjust approach, and stop at the object of interest (OOI). Steering to the course requires to orient the ship's head towards the distant object. During the learning task, the initial true bearing of the vessel is randomly set to one out of eight cardinal directions. The task ends by stopping the vessel either on the port-beam or starboard-beam side in relationship to the object of interest.

2.2 Simulated Learners

Simulated learners are based on the ACT-R cognitive architecture [1], which provides a range of empirically validated mechanisms to model human memory performance and learning. Figure 2 gives a system overview of the simulation components from the ACT-R cognitive architecture. The modules in light grey were included in the simulation. In addition, an extra module (dark grey) handles bidirectional communication with a tutor such as hint requests, hint responses, and unsolicited instructions from a tutor. The instructional module was first applied to a piano learning task [7], and is included here for a navigation task. The purpose of the instructional module is to integrate high-level means of communicating instructions leaving out the details of the communication medium (ex. visual, vocal, auditory).

Four ACT-R learning mechanisms are integrated to the simulated learners. These four mechanisms come essentially from the procedural and declarative modules. These learning mechanisms are: 1) applying production utility (reinforcement learning), 2) adding declarative information to its memory, 3) making declarative representation more accessible as a function of frequency and recency

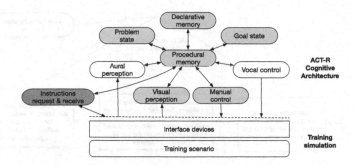

Fig. 2. ACT-R cognitive architecture for modelling human performance and learning. The modules in grey are used in the current simulation. The visual perception of the navigation states and manual control on the throttle and rudder are implemented at a level of abstraction that does not consider the true control physical locations and surrounding perceptual marine environment. The goal, declarative, procedural and imaginal (problem space) modules are used as provided by the architecture. In addition, an instructional module supports the communication between the simulated learner and a simulated tutor [7] (Color figure online).

of use (learning activation), and 4) creating new production by combining declarative retrievals to productions to reduce steps (production compilation).

Equations 1 and 2 define two learning mechanisms used by the ACT-R cognitive architecture. Equation 1 is the memory base-level learning equation and reflects the activation of declarative memory chunks as a function of the number of times a chunk is referred to and the time since it was last referenced. In addition, the equation takes two constant parameters for the decay rate and the basic initial activation level of memory chunks. The activation level is an important value for memory chunks which determines retrieval time and possible retrieval failure in case the activation level is not above some threshold.

$$B_i = ln(\sum_{j=1}^{n} t_j^{-d}) - \beta_i \tag{1}$$

where:

n = the number of presentation for chunk i;
t_j = time since the jth presentation;
d = decay parameter;
β_i = constant offset parameter.

Equation 2 specifies how the utility of a production is augmented or reduced as a function of receiving positive or negative reward values. The utility quantity of a production will determine which production is selected in the situation where two or more productions compete to fire. The production with the highest utility will be selected. The equation also has a learning rate parameter, and includes an initial utility value assigned to a production.

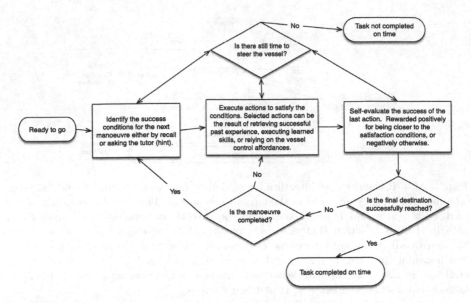

Fig. 3. The figure represents the simulated learners cycling process as they progress towards the destination. In general, the simulated learners go to an initial step of identifying what the success conditions are to complete a manoeuvre, then proceed to execute throttle and rudder actions, followed by a self-evaluating its performance. The figure also includes a simulation design which ends the work of the simulated learner if the task has reached a duration threshold. If this is the case, the task ends, and the simulated learning is presented with a new task, starting from the initial vessel at rest position.

$$U_i(n) = U_i(n-1) + \alpha[R_i(n) - U_i(n-1)] \tag{2}$$

where:

α = the learning rate;
$R_i(n)$ = effective reward value given to production i on its nth usage;
$U_i(0)$ = initial utility value of a production.

The simulated learners were developed to allow them to learn the task with only a minimal intervention from a tutor. Figure 3 shows the basic processing cycle of a simulated learner, starting from attending the navigation state, the simulated learner selects and applies a throttle or rudder action which might change the navigation state. Then, the simulated learner compares the previous state to the one resulting from the action to evaluate if this action produced progress towards the task goal (navigating towards the object of interest). Simulated learners could learn to use the throttle and rudder actions by adding new information to declarative memory, compile declarative to procedural knowledge (production compilation), and apply utility learning (reinforcement learning). Simulated learners were designed with self-evaluation capabilities to implement the fact that human learners can self-evaluate in similar driving task where actions to turn the wheels of a car can easily be assessed as meeting the intention to turn left or right, and generate internal positive or negative rewards for the action taken.

In addition to these two sub-symbolic learning mechanisms, the simulated learner makes use of production compilation. Production compilation works by attempting to compose two productions that fire in sequence into one new production. It allows a problem to be solved with fewer productions over time and therefore to be performed faster. By reducing the number of steps, production compilation can also model learning from instructions. Instructions get encoded initially as declarative knowledge which needs to be retrieved from memory to guide problem solving or psycho-motor actions. Through practice, production compilation can result in the drop-out of declarative retrieval as part of the task performance by transforming declarative knowledge (instructions) into procedural knowledge. The production compilation mechanism is built around sets of rules that are specific to buffer styles such as motor, perceptual, retrieval, goal and imaginal buffer styles.

2.3 Learning/Training Strategies

Table 1 gives an example of a tutor pedagogical choices. Effects of tutoring strategies and instructions can also be explored through the use of cognitive learner models during skill acquisition [2, 3, 18, 23]. The type of pedagogical interventions for the vessel manoeuvring learning is at the task level rather than the problem level. The tutor objective is to support task steps, rather than selecting the next navigation challenge given a learner skill mastery assessment.

Table 1. Properties related to pedagogical sequences. From Cockburn et al. [4].

Property types	Examples
Temporal	Feedback is provided either concurrently, immediately after, or delayed from a learner action
Aggregation	Feedback is provided independently for each discrete action or accumulated or a sequence of actions (after action review)
Modality	Instructions and feedback can be presented as text, speech synthesis, video, or statistics in tabular format
Performance	Feedback is provided in terms of deviation to an ideal sequence with no reference to its outcome or results
Results	Feedback is provided about the outcome of the action such as success or failure in relation to a desired outcome

Three configurations of simulated and tutor instructions are explored in the simulation for their effect on learning the navigation task. In all configurations, the simulated learners did not know what the success conditions were for each manoeuvre and what the next task to be performed was (see Fig. 1). Before each manoeuvre, if a simulated learner could not retrieve these conditions from declarative memory, it would ask for a hint to the tutor through the instructional module. Upon receiving this hint, the simulated learner would place it into declarative memory and proceed with the task execution. The following paragraphs describe the three learning/training strategies.

Trial and error: The simulated learner is on its own, trying throttle and rudder actions, self-rewarding itself as it gets closer to the manoeuvre satisfaction conditions.

Discovery: Same as trial and error, but with the additional capability to store in declarative memory a representation of successful actions to be retrieved in similar contexts, and eventually bypass memory retrieval through production compilation.

Briefing before practice: The simulated learner is provided with all the declarative knowledge required to execute the task before practice, and like discovery, during practice the model eventually bypass memory retrieval through production compilation.

Table 2. The table shows how the learning and performance capabilities of the simulated learners are distributed across the learning/training strategies.

	Learning / Training strategies		
Cognitive model capabilities	Trial and error	Discovery	Briefing and practice
Capability to assess the progress of navigation actions	X	X	X
Storage and retrieval of manœuvres satisfaction conditions provided by the tutor	X	X	X
Utility learning of navgation actions (Reinforcement learning)	X	X	X
Base level activation of declarative chunks	X	X	X
Production compilation		X	X
Storage and retrieval of declarative rule chunks		X	X
Prior knowledge of declarative rule chunks before practice			X

Table 2 shows in more details the presence (x) or absence (blank) of capabilities involved in the three learning/training strategies. For each of the three strategies, a total of 20 models performed 15 trials, over the eight navigation tasks defined by the initial vessel orientations. The cognitive models were reset before the sequence of trials making them new model, and kept learning until the end of the 15 trials of 8 initial cardinal orientation for a total of 120 tasks. Successes on task, number of events for each task, and number of actions per manoeuvres were collected during the simulation. The next section presents and discuss the results.

3   Results and Discussion

The current section describes and discuss the results of the simulation. The simulation included 20 simulated learners per learning strategies executing 15 trials over the 8 initial cardinal orientations of the vessel. Figure 4 presents the percent of successful completion of tasks during the course of the 15 trials. The figure indicates a common pattern where the performance is better at the beginning of the trial sequence. The sharper drop is with the trial and error strategy, overall the discovery strategy has the best performance. However, one would assume that if it were human subjects, the performance should be near perfect after a relatively small number of trials. One possible explanation for this pattern (not getting perfect performance) could be a consequence of the simulated learner lack of receiving correcting instructions in case of committing errors. Successful actions get self-rewarded and stored in declarative memory, but unsuccessful actions only get self-generated negative rewards. Given that the ACT-R conflict resolution mechanism applies a greedy selection algorithm (the production with the highest utility always wins), the simulated learner might be getting into a non-optimal state of action selection.

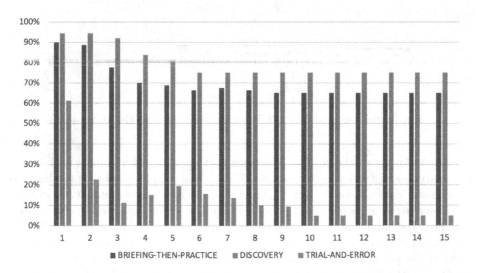

Fig. 4. Percent of successful task completion over the course of the 15 trials.

The Fig. 5 shows the total number of ACT-R events averaged over the 15 trials and 8 tasks. The whole data simulation generated 87,358,951 ACT-R events.

Events include all cognitive operations such as retrievals, visual processing steps to attend a visual location, gesture preparation, procedural conflict resolution, instructional module requests, etc. The figure clearly shows the large number of events associated with the trial and error strategy where the cognitive model exclusively relies on reinforcement to achieve tasks without consideration of the context in which a navigation operation is performed. The discovery and briefing-then-practice strategies exhibit similar pattern with the discovery strategy performing the tasks with fewer cognitive events. A smaller number of events indicates a higher performance efficiency.

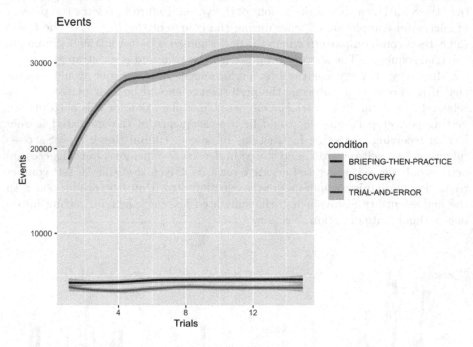

Fig. 5. Total number of ACT-R events averaged over the 15 trials.

Figure 6 presents the number of actions performed in order to meet each of the manoeuvres satisfaction conditions (see Fig. 1). The graphs show that the highest gain in efficiency is over the stay on course and reduce speed manoeuvres. These manoeuvres require a small number of actions to meet the satisfaction conditions. On the other hand, the steer to course and adjust approach manoeuvres requires many rudder operations in order to place the vessel on the correct course, which can only be performed by taking into account the navigation context.

Overall the discovery strategy has a better impact on learning than the other two strategies. This is not too surprising when it is compared to trial and error because of its lack of sensitivity to the navigation context, rudder and throttle operations varying in utility as a function of the type of manoeuvre to be performed. The higher performance of the discovery strategy when compared to the

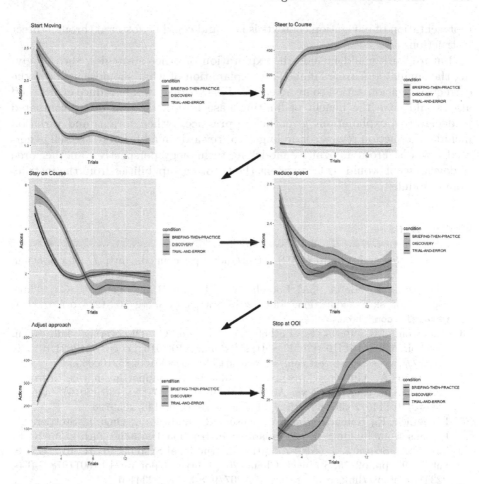

Fig. 6. Number of actions for each of the six manoeuvres to be performed by the simulated learners. See Fig. 1 for the details of the manoeuvre success conditions.

briefing-then-practice approach was not anticipated. In particular, all the correct navigation operations were encoded in declarative memory prior to engage in the navigation tasks. The benefits of the discovery strategy could be explained by the smaller decay of rule chunk activation compared to the debrief-then-practice strategy, given the recency of chunk encoding for the discovery strategy.

4 Conclusion

Computational models of learners offer the possibility of exploring how different learning conditions can impact learning and performance. The model specifications required by ACT-R, as well as the simulation data, offer a detailed level of cognitive analysis of the effect of instructional methods. Results from the simulation indicate that even in a relatively simple navigation task, the declarative representation of navigation contexts is key, and could be fostered through direct instructions.

Future work could include the exploration of other strategies, such as giving the simulated learners immediate explanation of what should have been the correct navigation action to avoid errors. This strategy would reduce errors, and also would have the benefit of limiting base level activation decay compared to declarative explanations given before practice. Other options and variation include after action review, or adding tutor rewards in addition to the self generated rewards. From a cognitive modelling technology perspective, another area of development would be to augment the tutoring capabilities from the instructional module.

References

1. ACT-R Research Group (2002). http://act-r.psy.cmu.edu, http://act-r.psy.cmu.edu

2. Anderson, J., Betts, S., Bothell, D., Hope, R.M., Lebiere, C.: Three aspects of skill acquisition, June 2018. https://doi.org/10.31234/osf.io/rh6zt, psyarxiv.com/rh6zt

3. Anderson, J.R., Betts, S., Bothell, D., Lebiere, C.: Discovering skill. Cogn. Psychol. **129**, 101410 (2021). https://doi.org/10.1016/j.cogpsych.2021.101410, https://www.sciencedirect.com/science/article/pii/S0010028521000335

4. Cockburn, A., Gutwin, C., Scarr, J., Malacria, S.: Supporting novice to expert transitions in user interfaces. ACM Comput. Surv. **47**(2), 1–36 (2015). https://doi.org/10.1145/2659796, https://dl.acm.org/doi/10.1145/2659796

5. Domeshek, E., Ramachandran, S., Jensen, R., Ludwig, J., Ong, J., Stottler, D.: Lessons from building diverse adaptive instructional systems (AIS). In: Sottilare, R.A., Schwarz, J. (eds.) Adaptive Instructional Systems. HCII 2019. LNCS, vol. 11597, pp. 62–75. Springer, Cham (2019). https://doi.org/10.1007/978-3-030-22341-0, http://link.springer.com/10.1007/978-3-030-22341-0

6. Emond, B.: WN-LEXICAL: an ACT-R module built from the WordNet lexical database. In: Seventh International Conference on Cognitive Modeling, pp. 359–360. Trieste, Italy (2006)

7. Emond, B., Comeau, G.: Cognitive modelling of early music reading skill acquisition for piano: a comparison of the Middle-C and Intervallic methods. Cogn. Syst. Res. **24**, 26–34 (2013). https://doi.org/10.1016/j.cogsys.2012.12.007, http://dx.doi.org/10.1016/j.cogsys.2012.12.007

8. Emond, B., et al.: Development of AIS Using simulated learners, Bayesian networks and knowledge elicitation methods. In: Sottilare, R.A., Schwarz, J. (eds.) Adaptive Instructional Systems. HCII 2022. LNCS, vol. 13332, pp. 143–158. Springer, Cham (2022). https://doi.org/10.1007/978-3-031-05887-5_11

9. Emond, B., Vinson, N.G.: Modelling simple ship conning tasks. In: 15th Meeting of the International Conference on Cognitive Modelling, pp. 42–44. Coventry, UK (2017)

10. Emond, B., West, R.R.L.: Cyberpsychology: a human-interaction perspective based on cognitive modeling. Cyberpsychol. Behav. **6**(5), 527–536 (2003). https://doi.org/10.1089/109493103769710550

11. Emond, B., West, R.L.: Using cognitive modelling simulations for user interface design decisions. In: Orchard, B., Yang, C., Ali, M. (eds.) IEA/AIE 2004. LNCS (LNAI), vol. 3029, pp. 305–314. Springer, Heidelberg (2004). https://doi.org/10.1007/978-3-540-24677-0_32

12. Essa, A., Mojarad, S.: Does time matter in learning? A computer simulation of Carroll's model of learning. In: Sottilare, R.A., Schwarz, J. (eds.) HCII 2020. LNCS, vol. 12214, pp. 458–474. Springer, Cham (2020). https://doi.org/10.1007/978-3-030-50788-6_34

13. Harpstead, E., MacLellan, C.J., Weitekamp, D., Koedinger, K.R.: The use simulated learners in adaptive education. In: AIAED-19: AI + Adaptive Education, pp. 1–3. Beijing, China (2019)

14. Lelei, D.E.K., McCalla, G.: How to use simulation in the design and evaluation of learning environments with self-directed longer-term learners. In: Penstein Rosé, C., et al. (eds.) AIED 2018. LNCS (LNAI), vol. 10947, pp. 253–266. Springer, Cham (2018). https://doi.org/10.1007/978-3-319-93843-1_19

15. MacLellan, C.J., Koedinger, K.R.: Domain-general tutor authoring with apprentice learner models. Int. J. Artif. Intell. Educ. (2020). https://doi.org/10.1007/s40593-020-00214-2, https://link.springer.com/10.1007/s40593-020-00214-2

16. McCalla, G., Champaign, J.: Simulated learners. IEEE Intell. Syst. 28(4), 67–71 (2013). https://doi.org/10.1109/MIS.2013.116

17. McEneaney, J.E.: Simulation-based evaluation of learning sequences for instructional technologies. Instruct. Sci. 44(1), 87–106 (2016). https://doi.org/10.1007/s11251-016-9369-x, http://link.springer.com/10.1007/s11251-016-9369-x

18. Ritter, F.E., Yeh, M.K.C., Yan, Y., Siu, K.C., Oleynikov, D.: Effects of varied surgical simulation training schedules on motor-skill acquisition. Surg. Innov. 27(1), 68–80 (2020). https://doi.org/10.1177/1553350619881591, http://journals.sagepub.com/doi/10.1177/1553350619881591

19. Smith, J., Yazdanpanah, F., Thistle, R., Musharraf, M., Veitch, B.: Capturing expert knowledge to inform decision support technology for marine operations. J. Marine Sci. Eng. 8(9) (2020). https://doi.org/10.3390/JMSE8090689

20. Spain, R., Rowe, J., Smith, A., Goldberg, B., Pokorny, R., Mott, B., Lester, J.: A reinforcement learning approach to adaptive remediation in online training. J. Defense Model. Simul. Appl. Methodol. Technol. (2021). https://doi.org/10.1177/15485129211028317, http://journals.sagepub.com/doi/10.1177/15485129211028317

21. Thistle, R., Veitch, B.: An evidence-based method of training to targeted levels of performance. In: SNAME Maritime Convention 2019, SMC 2019 (2019)

22. Veitch, E., Molyneux, D., Smith, J., Veitch, B.: Investigating the influence of bridge officer experience on ice management effectiveness using a marine simulator experiment. J. Offshore Mech. Arctic Eng. 141(4) (2019). https://doi.org/10.1115/1.4041761, https://asmedigitalcollection.asme.org/offshoremechanics/article/doi/10.1115/1.4041761/475585/Investigating-the-Influence-of-Bridge-Officer

23. Walsh, M.M., et al.: Mechanisms underlying the spacing effect in learning: a comparison of three computational models. J. Exp. Psychol. Gen. 147(9), 1325–1348 (2018). https://doi.org/10.1037/xge0000416, http://doi.apa.org/getdoi.cfm?doi=10.1037/xge0000416

24. Weitekamp, D., Harpstead, E., Koedinger, K.R.: An interaction design for machine teaching to develop AI tutors, pp. 1–11. Association for Computing Machinery, New York, NY, USA (2020). https://doi.org/10.1145/3313831.3376226

25. Weitekamp, D., Ye, Z., Rachatasumrit, N., Harpstead, E., Koedinger, K.: Investigating differential error types between human and simulated learners. In: Bittencourt, I.I., Cukurova, M., Muldner, K., Luckin, R., Millán, E. (eds.) AIED 2020. LNCS (LNAI), vol. 12163, pp. 586–597. Springer, Cham (2020). https://doi.org/10.1007/978-3-030-52237-7_47
26. Wray, R., Stowers, K.: Interactions between learner assessment and content requirement: a verification approach. Adv. Intell. Syst. Comput. **596**, 36–45 (2018). https://doi.org/10.1007/978-3-319-60018-5_4
27. Wray, R.E.: Enhancing simulated students with models of self-regulated learning. In: Schmorrow, D.D., Fidopiastis, C.M. (eds.) HCII 2019. LNCS (LNAI), vol. 11580, pp. 644–654. Springer, Cham (2019). https://doi.org/10.1007/978-3-030-22419-6_46

Learning Within Gameplay Loops: Considering Adaptive Educational Technology from a Game Design Lens

Erik Harpstead(✉) ⓘ

Carnegie Mellon University, Pittsburgh, PA 15213, USA
harpstead@cmu.edu

Abstract. Adaptivity has the potential to have a substantial impact on the field of Game-Based Learning. However, much of the existing work on adaptive strategies in games can be difficult to translate from the context of one game to another. I hypothesize that this is because existing work does not take into consideration how game designers think about games as dynamic systems. In this paper I will present the idea of Gameplay Loops as a game design lens for approaching adaptivity in games. I will illustrate this lens through a speculative case study envisioning how different forms of adaptivity might be implemented in an existing educational game.

Keywords: Adaptive Game-Based Learning · Game Design · Gameplay Loops

1 Introduction

Designing an instructional system for adaptivity is one of the most complex forms of instructional design. At a high-level, an adaptive instructional system moves through a loop of measuring some qualities of learners, processing those measurements through a pedagogical strategy intended to maximize a pedagogically relevant outcome, and finally executing the strategy by making changes to a learning environment. This loop can play out at a number of different time scales [1]. In step loop adaptivity, the system may react immediately to a learner as they take actions to solve a problem, in task loop adaptivity the system will consider how to alter the sequence or pacing of exercises for learners, and in design loop adaptivity systems can provide information to their designers who might then make decisions to adjust content to fit learners' needs.

Beyond this question of time scale, this simplistic model of adaption presents many questions that designers must answer. An obvious first question, which is highlighted by many perspectives in the field [1, 2], is what qualities of a learner should be adapted to? Often this will be some estimate of learners' cognitive knowledge or skills with intent of providing instruction tailored to their zone of proximal development. Alternatively, affective or motivational qualities could be used to support learners' engagement or persistence with a system.

© The Author(s), under exclusive license to Springer Nature Switzerland AG 2023
R. A. Sottilare and J. Schwarz (Eds.): HCII 2023, LNCS 14044, pp. 137–147, 2023.
https://doi.org/10.1007/978-3-031-34735-1_10

Another common question in the literature on adaptivity is how should the target qualities of learners be measured? The field of educational data mining has developed a large number of tools and techniques for measuring aspects of learning from their performance in interactive technologies [3]. Within work specific to game-based learning there are a number of examples of games used as assessments [4, 5] that employ a diverse array of techniques from stealth assessment [6] to co-design with target populations [7].

Beyond these two common questions however, a key consideration, and one underappreciated in the context of games, is how exactly should the game environment behave differently to enact a particular pedagogical strategy. While examples of such work certainly exist within the literature [8], it can be difficult for game designers to fully appreciate how the findings of this work can be applied to new game contexts. In this paper I will present a perspective on adaptivity using a lens of game design, with the goal of providing insight into how a game designer might think about these problems. I will further illustrate this lens in the context of speculating about how adaptive systems might be integrated into an existing educational game.

2   Adaptivity in Game-Based Learning

Our understanding of adaptivity within the context of game-based learning is still in its infancy. A promising initial framework within the space is provided by Plass and Panwar [2], in which they describe a number of examples of ways prior work has approached game adaptivity for learning. Within their taxonomy they highlight a number of types of game components that have been used adaptively in the past. These components can be understood in the context of the Adaptivity Grid provided by Aleven et al.'s [1], which organizes adaptive strategies into either the step loop (i.e. localized changes during problem solving), task loop (i.e. progression and sequencing of tasks) or design loop (i.e. data informed changes to a learning environment across populations or contexts).

Within the grain size of the step loop, Plass and Panwars' taxonomy includes Scaffolds and Cues, Feedback and Guidance, and Game Visuals. In each of these cases games make use of estimates of the learner to adjust local aspects of a game experience with the goal of maximizing learning. Some examples cited in the taxonomy include, *Prime Climb* [9], where an adaptive scaffolding strategy displayed tailored hint messages to players based on an estimate of their knowledge of prime numbers, or *ELEKTRA* [10], which used a character representing Galileo provided targeted feedback messages to players' based on estimates from a skill assessment engine.

At the grain size of the task loop, the taxonomy mentions Rehearsal Schedule, Difficulty Progression, and Conceptual Progression. Each of these components relates to the development of a learning experience across time and tasks with the goal of creating a smooth progression building up to more complex practice. Examples within these cases include *Fuzzy Chronicles* [11], which implemented an adaptive rehearsal schedule where players would be sent to a new game level of relatively equal difficulty when they failed rather than being forced to retry, and *Code Red Triage* [12], which automatically advanced players through its tiered content structure if they demonstrated sufficient mastery of target concepts.

More ambiguous within the context of the Adaptivity Grid is Plass and Panwar's discussion of adaptivity in a game's mechanical components. For example, the game

Tactical Combat Casualty Care [13] contains an AI director capable of completely reconfiguring or generating new scenarios based on players' demonstrated skill competency. With these kinds of complex generative techniques it is difficult to categorize where within the broader adaptive spectrum of adaptive loops.

While this taxonomy of adaptive gameplay components serves as a useful organization of the findings of prior work, it can at times be difficult to consider how one might apply any of these prior techniques to a new or existing game. Constructs such as "difficulty," "progression," or even "feedback" can have a highly contextualized character in a given game. Further, the dynamic nature of algorithmically adaptive systems can be difficult to anticipate within the context of the already highly dynamic nature of gameplay. While techniques such as simulations can help designers approach this problem somewhat [14], a gap will continue to exist between how adaptivity has been considered within the educational technology research community and how game designers actually think about the dynamic nature of their craft.

3   How Game Designers Think About Gameplay Loops

Within the field of game design the challenge of game creation is often described as a second-order design problem [15]. The goal of designing a game is to create a meaningful play experience for players. However, play is an ephemeral emergent state that arises out of players' interactions with game systems. Game designers can never directly design play; they can only create or make decisions about the rules and elements that give rise to it.

One of the ways that game designers work through this second order problem is by articulating *gameplay loops* [16, 17]. Gameplay loops involve players going through an iterative cycle of perceiving the game world, interpreting it with their current understandings and conceptions, making decisions and plans about what to do next, and then ultimately executing those actions and perceiving the consequences. These looping structures can be useful for thinking about implications of a game's mechanical structure in the presence of a player's own thought processes.

An additional consideration is that any individual game will often contain many different gameplay loops that exist at different grain sizes of interaction or hierarchies of time scale. This multiplicity of loops can present challenges to relating a particular game's design to the frameworks on adaptivity such as the Adaptivity Grid [1] as the distinction between what constitutes a "step" loop or a "task" loop can be ambiguous; potentially changing over the course of play.

As an illustration, consider the game *Minecraft* [18]. In *Minecraft* a low-level (short duration, high frequency, on the order of seconds) gameplay loop might look like a player navigating a cave, looking around their immediate environment to identify resources that they can mine, and then using a tool to collect them. At a more immediate level (medium duration and frequency, on the order of tens of minutes to hours), a gameplay loop might look like the process that the player goes through to lay out a design for a house, decide on the resources required to build it, and then plan individual delving missions to acquire those resources. Finally, a high-level loop (across multiple sessions with the game) might look like the steps a player must go through after deciding to take on the ender dragon (i.e. the "final boss" of the game), which requires them to find a portal hidden in a secret fortress somewhere on a large map, collect special resources used to open it in order to face the dragon, and craft powerful weapons and armor in order to survive the fight.

Each of these many gameplay loops exists simultaneously during an individual play session, and may come in or out of players' individual attention over the course of their play. To help focus design conversation game designers will often talk about the *core gameplay loop* as the one that players will spend the most active time thinking about, or alternatively, as the smallest unit of repeated gameplay decision-making cycles that players will find actively interesting. Prior work in game-based learning has shown that the core gameplay loop can be leveraged as a place to intrinsically integrate target learning content [19, 20] to positively affect learning outcomes.

Game designers have devised techniques for thinking about how to work with and compose these gameplay loops. Designers have created various diagramming approaches for notating dynamic game systems such as tension maps [21] or micro-machinations [22], which lay out explicitly how game elements relate and impact each other. These approaches can be used to tune and balance the relationships between key game elements to anticipate whether they are affecting intended outcomes or concepts [23].

Game designers also consider techniques for mapping out and designing for overall emotional or experiential arcs in games. Jesse Schell talks about mapping out an ideal interest curve [24], which often have an analogous character to traditional dramatic arcs with an initial hook followed by a period of rising action culminating in a climax and a dénouement. Relatedly, game designers often talk about the learning curve [25, 26] or progressive skill chain [27, 28] of their game and often attempt to have it take a similar shape to a traditional narrative progression. Beyond learning, Erin Hoffman-John advocates for considering not only the progression of expertise development in a game but also how the player goes through an emotional trajectory as part of the learning process [29].

4   A Game Design Lens on Adaptive Educational Games

I argue that we should think of adaptivity in games more in terms of dynamic gameplay loops rather than as manipulation of mechanical components. This is because I view educational game design as a third-order design problem (see Fig. 1). Inspired by Salen and Zimmerman's description where the playful goal of games can never be directly designed [17], educational games have a goal to affect some kind of knowledge change within players. However, this knowledge change can never be directly manipulated by the designer; it is a product of the experience a learner has in a particular environment. Following from the notion of second order game design, the designer cannot directly design that experience either; it arises out of the dynamic and active gameplay that is the result of the player interacting with the game's rules and systems. Ultimately, the designer can only make concrete decisions about those mechanics and systems. Thus, any kind of understanding of adaptivity within the context of educational games must not only attempt to account for how we might make changes at the mechanical level of a game but anticipate how those changes could propagate through an experience to impact knowledge change.

Fig. 1. A depiction of the Third-Order Design Problem of Educational Games.

Taking the third-order design perspective as a starting point allows us to highlight several questions about how adaptivity may live in such a system. For example, one can start to think about the individual steps of an adaptive loop (i.e. measuring learners, processing a pedagogical strategy, and taking actions to execute the strategy) as their own form of loop that would cross through and interact with the other gameplay loops. In some cases these adaptive loops may function in synchrony to gameplay, where manipulations would always correspond to a moment of assessment. However, this structure would also allow for the gameplay and adaptive loops to exist asynchronously or in cadence with each other, where the execution of a pedagogical strategy action might tune a parameter and thus indirectly impact the behavior of a gameplay loop.

Further recognizing how play experiences are built out of the dynamic interaction of several interlocking gameplay loops can highlight how seemingly singular concepts like "difficulty", which are often the focus of adaptive strategies, are actually compositional in nature. What makes a given moment difficult in a game could be a combination of complications encoding an interface, executing actions, anticipating consequences, or even poor planning in a macro loop that may not be apparent to the current context. Identifying the various systems that contribute to the composition of difficulty in a given game, and what "levers" can be pulled to manipulate them, would be essential to executing an adaptive difficulty approach in an educational game.

5 Speculative Case Studies: *Super Slime Battle*

In order to demonstrate the value of this game design lens on the design of adaptivity in game-based learning, in this section I will present a speculative case study about how adaptivity might be applied in the context of the existing educational game *Super Slime Battle*. To better illustrate how this lens can be applied, I have chosen a game that was not originally designed to be adaptive. Additionally, rather than presenting a single best option, I illustrate multiple different directions to present a picture of the larger design space of game-loop-focused adaptivity.

Super Slime Battle is an educational game developed by the Carnegie Mellon Robotics Academy as part of a series of cobot games, which teach players both about programming and about concepts in co-robotics [30, 31]. Players in a cobot game engage first in typical forms of gameplay such as jumping, driving, or exploring in order to accomplish typical gameplay objects such as traversing obstacles, collecting items, or defeating enemies. Coding is then introduced as a means to achieve existing objectives through the assistance of a co-robotic partner or "cobot", emphasizing the utility of collaborative interaction with partially controllable automated systems. Over time, players evolve complex strategies involving the cobot, self-motivating the need to design and implement program logic that is responsive to both player and world state. Ultimately, players in cobot games are positioned and tasked with *doing* human-robot teaming in both the operator and developer roles.

Super Slime Battle was the first in a series of games created using a co-design process with children in afterschool programs throughout the greater Pittsburgh area [31]. The goal of this co-design structure was to ensure the project was creating games that both dealt with target concepts and fit into children's existing interest in games.

In *Super Slime Battle* (see Fig. 2), players must defend their candy pile from waves of invading monsters by shooting them with slime. In addition to their slime weapon, players are also accompanied by a robotic companion who – through player-written block code (see Fig. 2) – can be programmed to attack, collect items, or even run into enemies, following logic that the player composes. Players are thus encouraged by the game's design to write computer code to implement strategies based around coordination of player and automated agent capabilities.

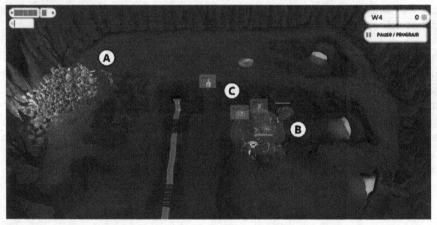

Fig. 2. A screenshot of *Super Slime Battle* showing the player character defending the candy pile (A), the cobotic partner fighting some monsters (B) and program event notifications (C).

From the perspective of the third-order design problem, *Super Slime Battle* has a number of gameplay loops that could be leveraged toward adaptivity. The game is structured as a series of levels, each containing a number of waves of enemies each occupying different lanes on the map. Each wave will appear after a set frequency delay, allowing a new wave to appear before the previous wave has been entirely dealt with. Further, monsters come in several types, each with different capabilities, including how fast they move, what routes they choose to navigate the map, how much health they have, and how large of a target they are. Each of these features of a level design can be used to compose difficulty for players and trigger changes in play strategy.

Players themselves also have a number of capabilities. Initially, players have the option of choosing from one of four characters that each have different types of slime launchers. Some are better suited for quick short range attacks while others are designed for precision long range interaction. In addition to making decisions about their own capabilities, players also have the ability to program different behaviors into their cobot partner (see Fig. 3). Programming is done through a custom block based language that exposes different event types and bot action commands to the player. While these programs often take the form of compositions of simple movement and action commends in response to events, they can also support a full suite of programming constructs such as loops and conditionals.

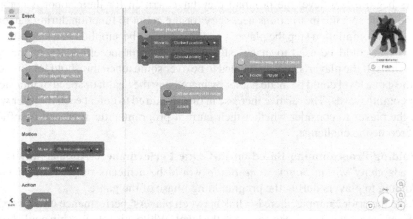

Fig. 3. A screenshot of the *Super Slime Battle* programming interface. Here the player has created three main cobot behaviors: (1) a behavior to move to the position of player's right click and then seek out the nearest enemy, (2) a behavior to attack when enemies are nearby, and (3) a behavior to return to the player when there are no longer enemies in the area.

The core gameplay loop of *Super Slime Battle* centers on clearing a single wave of enemies. During this process a player will take stock of where enemies are entering the scene, plan out how to engage them using either their own abilities or their cobot's, and then execute the plan. A macro-loop to the core loop would be the gameplay involved in a single level of waves. Before a level starts, the player has the opportunity to interact with their cobot and make changes to its underlying program. At this stage the player must consider how the prior series of waves went, as well as how their cobot behaved in making decisions about what changes to make. In order to facilitate the planning process in this macro-loop the game also provides visible event notifications (visible as C in Fig. 2) during the interactive micro-loop of combat with the monsters. This cross-loop design is intended to help players not just think about programming abstractly but also the value of programming in context of performance and cooperation with a cobot.

5.1 Adaptive Potential in *Super Slime Battle*

Within the broader game design of *Super Slime Battle*, there are a number of ways that the game design could be altered to provide hooks for adaptivity. With each of these cases I will highlight both what aspect of a learner might be adapted to, suggest how it might be measured, and finally describe what aspects of the game are manipulated to maximize the potential for learning the target content.

Manipulating Monster Stats to Emphasize Efficient Code. One category of learning goals that *Super Slime Battle* is designed to support is computational thinking and algorithmic problem solving through programing [32, 33]. Within this category, the game could further focus on skills related to efficiency and time complexity of code by manipulating the characteristics of the monsters in game.

This adaptive strategy could function within the gameplay loop of a level. When players begin a new level the program they have written for their cobot is compiled into the game specific instructions necessary for the cobot to function during gameplay. During this compilation step the player's code could also be supplied to a static analysis process that could be used to make estimates of the runtime efficiency of the cobot instructions. If the player's code is deemed to be over some tuned threshold for efficiency, then the game level could be made harder by increasing the health or speed of monsters in the upcoming waves. The relative increase in time required to defeat each monster would force the player to consider whether their current programmatic approach is sufficient to overcome the challenge.

Scaffolding Programming Based on In-Game Performance. Another way to consider adaptivity within *Super Slime Battle* would be a means of providing adaptive scaffolding to players during the programming phase of the game.

As in the prior example, there is a link between players' performance on a given level and the program that they use to approach the level. While this relationship could be used to adjust characteristics of monsters, it can also flow in the other direction, where level performance could provide insight into how a player might be misunderstanding their code. For example, the event system that is used to execute the cobot behaviors could track a frequency of events that are fired and result in no effect for the cobot, such as the number of times the player right-clicks without the bot reacting. Instances of players repeatedly firing events without effect may signal an attempt to execute a strategy during gameplay that is not properly implemented in their code. Such behaviors may arise from misconceptions with the logical of the programming interface where cobot behaviors must be connect to events in order to execute during gameplay. In such cases, the game could present a hint message guiding the player to consider adding an event block to their program, or even providing a full sample code event to demonstrate how the logic of events could be implemented.

Fostering Co-robotic Relationships through Wave Design. A final form of adaptive design that could be implemented in the context of *Super Slime Battle* would be related to one of the high-level learning goals of the game, that of fostering learners' understanding of co-robotics beyond merely programming.

A focus for this adaptive system could be the way in which players approach teamwork with their cobot partner [34] by splitting up tasks. While there is not necessarily a single "correct" form of cobot teaming intended within the *Super Slime Battle*, the game could be structured around fostering a player's exploration of alternative strategies and relationships by leveraging the way that monster waves are constructed. A potential measure of a players' teaming bias could be to count the number of monsters that are defeated by the player versus the cobot. Alternatively, an adaptive system could track the degree to which the player and cobot inhabit similar areas of the game map. In either case the game could make a quantitative judgment of the degree to which a player is acting independently, collaborative, or codependently with their partner. If over the course of gameplay the system detects that the player has a bias for one particular strategy over the others it could make strategic choices that could prompt the player to adjust.

For example, if the system decides that the player is acting too independently and not utilizing their cobot partner (e.g. nearly all monsters are defeated by the player) then it could construct a wave in which multiple monsters are sent simultaneously on separate lanes, requiring the player to make use of their partner to properly deal with the wave. Alternatively, if the player becomes overly reliant on remaining apart from their partner a similar strategy could be used in reverse to concentrate monsters in a single lane requiring strategic adaptation to pivot.

6 Conclusion

In this paper I have presented a perspective on adaptive educational games using a game design lens. Much like the field that it comments on, this perspective is still relatively new. My goal in articulating it here is to begin a conversation around how we might frame adaptive strategies from the learning sciences into the native language of games, i.e. dynamic gameplay loops. In order to further this conversation I plan on embarking on a more systematic review of the literature on adaptive educational games to catalog existing adaptive strategies and corresponding game design considerations that can continue to broaden our conception of the design space.

Acknowledgements. Thank you to Jessica Hammer who provided feedback on an earlier version of this work. This material is based upon work supported by the National Science Foundation under Grant No. 1906753.

References

1. Aleven, V., McLaughlin, E.A., Glenn, R.A., Koedinger, K.R.: Instruction based on adaptive learning technologies. In: Mayer, R.E. and Alexander, P.A. (eds.) Handbook of Research on Learning and Instruction. Routledge (2016). https://doi.org/10.4324/9781315736419.ch24
2. Plass, J.L., Pawar, S.: Toward a taxonomy of adaptivity for learning. J. Res. Technol. Educ. **52**, 275–300 (2020). https://doi.org/10.1080/15391523.2020.1719943
3. Baker, R.S.J. D, Siemens, G.: Learning analytics and educational data mining. In: Proceedings of the 2nd International Conference on Learning Analytics and Knowledge - LAK 2012, p. 252 (2012). https://doi.org/10.1145/2330601.2330661
4. Mislevy, R.J., et al.: Pyschometric Considerations in Game-Based Assessments (2014). https://www.envisionexperience.com/~/media/files/blog/glasslab-psychometrics.pdf.

5. Halverson, R., Owen, V.E.: Game-based assessment: an integrated model for capturing evidence of learning in play. Int. J. Learn. Technol. **9**, 111 (2014). https://doi.org/10.1504/IJLT.2014.064489

6. Shute, V.J.: Stealth assessment in computer-based games to support learning. In: Tobias, S., Fletcher, J.D. (eds.) Computer Games and Instruction, pp. 503–524. Information Age Publishers, Charlotte, NC (2011)

7. Kim, Y.J., Scianna, J., Knowles, M.A.: How Can We Co-Design Learning Analytics for Game-Based Assessment : ENA Analysis

8. Plass, J.L., Pawar, S.: Adaptivity and Personalization in Game-Based Learning. In: Plass, J.L., Mayer, R.E., Homer, B.D. (eds.) Handbook of Game-Based Learning. MIT Press, Cambridge (2020)

9. Conati, C., Jaques, N., Muir, M.: Understanding attention to adaptive hints in educational games: an eye-tracking study. Int. J. Artif. Intell. Educ. **23**(1–4), 136–161 (2013). https://doi.org/10.1007/s40593-013-0002-8

10. Kickmeier-Rust, M.D., Albert, D.: Micro-adaptivity: protecting immersion in didactically adaptive digital educational games. J. Comput. Assist. Learn. **26**, 95–105 (2010). https://doi.org/10.1111/j.1365-2729.2009.00332.x

11. Clark, D.B., Virk, S.S., Barnes, J., Adams, D.M.: Self-explanation and digital games: adaptively increasing abstraction. Comput. Educ. **103**, 28–43 (2016). https://doi.org/10.1016/j.compedu.2016.09.010

12. van Oostendorp, H., van der Spek, E.D., Linssen, J.: Adapting the complexity level of a serious game to the proficiency of players. EAI Endorsed Trans. Game-Based Learn. **1**, e5 (2014). https://doi.org/10.4108/sg.1.2.e5

13. Magerko, B., Stensrud, B.S., Holt, L.S.: Bringing the schoolhouse inside the box - a tool for engaging individualized training. In: 25th Army Sci. Conference (2006)

14. Holstein, K., Harpstead, E., Gulotta, R., Forlizzi, J.: Replay enactments: exploring possible futures through historical datareplay enactments. In: Proceedings of the 2020 ACM Designing Interactive Systems Conference, pp. 1607–1618. ACM, New York (2020). https://doi.org/10.1145/3357236.3395427

15. Salen, K., Zimmerman, E.: Rules of Play. MIT Press, Cambridge (2004)

16. Cook, D.: Loops and Arcs. https://lostgarden.home.blog/2012/04/30/loops-and-arcs/. Accessed 06 Feb 2023

17. Zubek, R.: Elements of Game Design. MIT Press, Boston (2020)

18. Mojang Studios: Minecraft (2011)

19. Habgood, M.P.J., Ainsworth, S.E.: Motivating children to learn effectively: exploring the value of intrinsic integration in educational games. J. Learn. Sci. **20**, 169–206 (2011). https://doi.org/10.1080/10508406.2010.508029

20. Cutting, J., Iacovides, I.: Learning by doing: intrinsic Integration directs attention to increase learning in games. Proc. ACM Hum. Comput. Interact. **6**, 240 (2022). https://doi.org/10.1145/336393

21. Strange, S.: Tension Maps: A porcess for identifying low-risk design opportunities. https://www.gamedeveloper.com/design/tension-maps-a-process-for-identifying-low-risk-design-opportunities. Accessed 08 Feb 2023

22. van Roze, R., Dormans, J.: Adapting game mechanics with micro-machinations. In: Foundations of Digital Games (2014)

23. Schreiber, I., Romero, B.: Game Balance. CRC Press, Boca Raton (2021)

24. Schell, J.: Experiences can be judged by their interest curves. In: The Art of Game Design: a Book of Lenses, pp. 279–294. CRC Press, Boca Raton (2015)

25. Linehan, C., Bellord, G., Kirman, B., Morford, Z.H., Roche, B.: Learning curves: analysing pace and challenge in four successful puzzle games. In: Proceedings of the 1st ACM SIGCHI

Annual Symposium on Computer-Human Interaction in Play - CHI PLAY 2014, pp. 181–190. ACM Press, New York (2014). https://doi.org/10.1145/2658537.2658695

26. Harpstead, E., Aleven, V.: Using empirical learning curve analysis to inform design in an educational game. In: Proceedings of the 2015 Annual Symposium on Computer-Human Interaction in Play, pp. 197–207. ACM, New York (2015). https://doi.org/10.1145/2793107.2793128

27. Miller, J.A., et al.: How do players and developers of citizen science games conceptualize skill chains? Proc. ACM Hum. Comput. Interact. **5**, 1–29 (2021). https://doi.org/10.1145/3474671

28. Horn, B., Cooper, S., Deterding, S.: Adapting cognitive task analysis to elicit the skill chain of a game. In: Proceedings of the Annual Symposium on Computer-Human Interaction in Play - CHI PLAY 2017, pp. 277–289. ACM Press, New York (2017). https://doi.org/10.1145/3116595.3116640

29. Hoffman-John, E.: Effective games: why we can't have nice things (Yet). In: Serious Play Conference (2016)

30. Rozo, L., Amor, H.B., Calinon, S., Dragan, A., Lee, D.: Special issue on learning for human–robot collaboration. Auton. Robot. **42**(5), 953–956 (2018). https://doi.org/10.1007/s10514-018-9756-z

31. Higashi, R., Harpstead, E., Solyst, J., Kemper, J., Odili Uchidiuno, J., Hammer, J.: The design of co-robotic games for computer science education. In: Extended Abstracts of the 2021 Annual Symposium on Computer-Human Interaction in Play, pp. 111–116. ACM, New York (2021). https://doi.org/10.1145/3450337.3483472

32. Wing, J.M.: Computational thinking. Commun. ACM. **49**, 33–35 (2006). https://doi.org/10.1145/1118178.1118215

33. Grover, S., Pea, R.: Computational thinking in K-12: a review of the state of the field. Educ. Res. **42**, 38–43 (2013). https://doi.org/10.3102/0013189X12463051

34. Stowers, K., Brady, L.L., MacLellan, C., Wohleber, R., Salas, E.: Improving teamwork competencies in human-machine teams: perspectives from team science. Front. Psychol. **12**, 1–6 (2021). https://doi.org/10.3389/fpsyg.2021.590290

Toward a New Paradigm: Learning Analytics 2.0

Thomas Penniston[✉]

University of Maryland, Baltimore County, Baltimore, MD 21217, USA
pthomas1@umbc.edu

Abstract. Innovation and advancements have led to the ability of higher education administrators and innovators to use machine learning (ML) to identify student academic risk behavior patterns at increasingly early points within a semester. These models bring with them the promise to help prioritize allocation of finite resources and inform scalable interventions to promote learner success. However, it may be more difficult to prioritize student needs when the measures for which a university is held accountable and use ML to predict are not specific to learning. How do we best navigate the ethical waters to emphasize and support student growth while simultaneously addressing business reporting needs? To begin this transformation, it's critical that we gather better, more meaningful direct measures to build the models we use to predict outcomes, even if it means sacrificing some level of predictive validity, and then use our intervention strategies to improve these specific behavioral inputs feeding the models.

Keywords: Learning Analytics · Nudging · Machine Learning · Ethics

1 Introduction

"I believe that education is the fundamental method of social progress and re-form."
~ John Dewey (1897).

"There's no such thing as neutral education. Education either functions as an instrument to bring about conformity or freedom."
~ Paulo Freire (2000).

I begin this essay with two quotes. One each from these pillars of modern educational philosophy, John Dewey and Paulo Freire. In the first, Dewey, the father of modern pragmatism, states in his early essay "My Pedagogic Creed" something we likely all take as benign and universally understood. And yet it would be difficult to articulate a more powerful sentiment. Education is simultaneously how we are and how we become, and the links between knowledge, experience, and social growth are inseparable. We and our destinies are shaped by education. Complementing and adding further context to Dewey's assertion, Freire's quote from *Pedagogy of the Oppressed* highlights the significance of making choices that liberate rather than shackle the learner. Liberating education, for Freire, is about individuals living up to their fullest potential, and it is contrasted by "banking constructs" of education, which lead to intergenerationally reproduced power dynamics and social injustices. Taken together, these quotes indicate a path toward a better tomorrow: Our past must inform but not dictate our future.

R. A. Sottilare and J. Schwarz (Eds.): HCII 2023, LNCS 14044, pp. 148–161, 2023.
https://doi.org/10.1007/978-3-031-34735-1_11

1.1 My Context

I grew up in Alaska in the 80s, and distinctly remember one winter afternoon in first grade, while my classmates were out building a fort and throwing snowballs, when I got into a fight with a classmate. We were both escorted to the office, and when we were brought before the principal, she produced a paddle and asked if we knew what it was. Of course, I'd heard stories about paddles. It's doubtful any kids in my school hadn't, but this was my first time actually seeing such a device in person. There were holes drilled through it, which I'd interpreted as a design enhancement to reduce air resistance and improve velocity. Someone had clearly put some considerable thought into engineering this apparatus to maximize its impact – both metaphorically and literally – on getting children to act differently. Ultimately, however, it was just a well-crafted stick.

I'm happy to report that I was not, in fact, paddled that day, and was released with a stern warning. (Many of my elders can attest to not getting off so easily with their school authorities in similar situations.) The incident, however, did have a long-lasting influence on how I think about the role of behaviorism in education, including punishments, as well as positive and negative incentives, particularly when juxtaposed with my later academic and research experiences. The overarching framing to consider for purposes of this discourse: How do we assure our modern intervention strategies, whether for behavioral or academic purposes, aren't similarly judged as unethical or even abusive in retrospect? How do we employ powerful new tools of educational analytics and intervention with intention and precision towards holistic student growth? These are complicated questions demanding nuanced solutions along with thoughtful consideration not only whether we *can* do something, but also if and when we *should* do it. Both intentions and impacts must be considered carefully.

1.2 A Brief History of Our University's Intervention Strategies

UMBC, a "mid-sized mid-Atlantic R1 institution" as I often refer to it at conferences, developed a data warehouse nearly two decades ago to address institutional reporting and accreditation needs, particularly related to student persistence, graduation rates, and time to graduate. This dynamic is of central importance to the eventual development of internal predictive models because it is typically much easier to work with the historic data that's already been ingested rather than to create new workflows to corral additional sources. In turn, our existing risk modeling is based on these scaled metrics, rather than upon direct measures of learning such as one might assess with a test or rubric (Harrison 2020) for which there is no state-level reporting mandate.

Over the past decade, various pilot projects have emerged to gain real-time insights into our student population and inform behavioral nudging campaigns.[1] Initially, these strategies were based on vendor-provided products. Using the outputs from these algorithms, we were able to identify some important gateway courses and hone strategies

---

[1] A curated list of these projects is available via the following address: https://analytics.umbc.edu/publications.

for student outreach, including use of messaging based on students' predicted chances of success. We found, however, that the black-box architecture of these solutions limited our ability to not only know exactly what measures were in the model, but also to gain insights through modifying feature inputs. In short, we were at the mercy of the party that designed the product, and if we don't know what's going into a model, how do we know we aren't unintentionally reproducing culturally biased outcomes (Cheuk 2021)? In the past several years, internal efforts have led to the development of our own set of predictive models and data visualizations. Building, testing, and deploying our own predictive models has led to greater opportunities for customization resulting in improved institutional fit along with a potential benefit for data-use transparency. However, the alignment between what is being predicted and the corresponding intervention strategies, as well as strategies for monitoring and evaluation, leave important questions unanswered.

1.3   The Status Quo: "The Right Message to the Right Person at the Right Time"

"Our records indicate that you are failing your Chemistry 101. You currently have a 59% in your class. There are only 3 weeks remaining in the semester and you will need 100% the remainder of the term to earn a C".

This slightly fictionalized message has a very punitive feel, doesn't it? My colleague Robert Carpenter has argued it's a bit like receiving a speeding ticket (Carpenter and Penniston 2019). Indeed, such a *nudge*, as the Nobel Prize winning economist Thaler and his partner Sunstein (2009) popularized, or intentionally designed intervention that can result in an individual or group behavioral modification, could have the unfortunate effect of pushing students away from class rather than redirecting them back to it. And who is this nameless, heartless harbinger from the void, and why couldn't this notification have been sent earlier in the term? Because the absolute last thing educators want to tell students at the end of the term is that all they need to do to pass their course is to suddenly become something they haven't been all semester: an A student.

Now let's consider this second message, a version of which was actually sent to students:

"I know this time of year can be busy and stressful, and while the end of the semester seems like it may take forever to get here, it will arrive before you know it. I am checking in with you to make sure that you are okay and to offer you some resources and support if you need them".

This second message attempts to articulate that the instructor cares and values the student as a human. Accompanied with some links to educational support services and sent early in the term with the course instructor's signature line at the bottom of the email and receiving this message may not be the kiss of death. There might – perhaps – be hope for the students who receive such a nudge?

2   Literature Review

Without digging into the diverse offerings from the humanities, there are three basic buckets of traditional scientific research: qualitative, quantitative, and mixed methods. Qualitative and quantitative methods will be described in further detail below, while the latter combines aspects of both, with the intention complementing meaningful statistical insights with rich contextual description (Johnson and Onwuegbuzie 2004).

2.1 Qualitative and Quantitative and Machine-Learning (Oh My!)

Qualitative research can take many forms, from focus groups to interviews and open-ended surveys, to content analysis, and so forth (Check and Schutt 2012). The resulting data from these analyses are descriptive and interpretive in nature and explain the context of and surrounding various constructs. These analyses typically tell us about what's going on with richer and more nuanced perspectives, but the scale of the data is too unwieldy to leverage for on-demand adjustments, or intervention strategies.

Quantitative research, on the other hand, can be broken out into two primary branches: Classical econometrics/statistics (Wooldridge 2009), and newer machine learning (ML) based methodologies (Hastie, Tibshirani and Friedman 2009). Of the former branch, there is a continuum of possibilities, included in a range from descriptive statistics to nonparametric and parametric inferential statistics, to causal and predictive modeling. These methods are helpful for considering the relationship between two or more variables and are particularly relevant for project monitoring and evaluation.

The key point here is in using classical statistics, one typically starts with representative data and then attempts to make population-level inferences through hypothesis testing. ML, however, does not work this way, and in many respects actually operates opposite to this orientation.

ML approaches fall into a range from supervised to unsupervised (Hastie, Tibshirani and Friedman 2009). An easy way to conceptualize them is deductive vs inductive. Supervised models start with an end point. You are using data to map, explain, or fit to an outcome. Predicting students' actual negative outcomes such as DFWs (i.e., a grade of D, F, or W), retention, or persistence, for example.

Unsupervised models operate in the opposite way. They take data and put them into digestible chunks, or buckets. So, we can start with a trove of attributes, and where human eyes may not see them, discern patterns and relationships. In educational terms, it might help to think about this as distilling learning management system (LMS) data (e.g., Canvas and Blackboard interactions, or clicks on content) and student information system (SIS) data, such as bio-demographic indicators and past academic performance variables, in order to determine different typologies of students' attributes and/or behaviors.

"Machine Learning" is a term that gets bandied about across traditional and social media quite frequently these days, but it may help some readers if we take a moment to demystify what the term actually means operationally as it is important to have a fundamental understanding of the methodologies to recognize the potential pitfalls discussed in this essay. Sharkey (2015) has suggested that ML is akin to dropping a bunch of Plinko chips down a peg board. In the supervised models, we would take a sample of the chips, dump them down, use the resulting outcomes to predict the pathway of the other chips, then map those results over to a wider population. And we can do this iteratively to improve a model's recall and precision moving forward. In an unsupervised model, we could establish a predetermined number of perhaps three or four groups and then look at how the chips cluster on the board to establish archetypes based on their proximity of the chips to one another.

In general, with ML approaches the more data the better the analyses. However, the quality of the data is also key; "garbage in, garbage out." as they say. (There's perhaps no better example of this dynamic than Microsoft spectacular failed release of its Twitter bot, "Tay."). If one uses ML to predict students' chances of earning a preferred outcome of an A, B, or C in a given course during their first term at a university, then they need to have some kind of data with which to develop and train a (supervised) mode. In this case, we can look back to our Plinko chips, which include various indicators that can be mapped to the successful outcome. Students standardized test scores and high school GPAs. I can also look at when folks registered for class (registering early is associated with positive outcomes, while registering late is associated with negative outcomes). Basically, anything that's been included in the student application that does not directly contribute to unethical modeling. So, although one should stay clear of including markers like race/ethnicity, gender, and nationality – three of the most studied algorithm bias inputs (Baker and Hawn 2021) – in predictive models of student success due to justifiable legal concerns and widely held (and socially constructed) attitudes, one could include Census data with median household income by zip code to control for socio economic status (SES). Note that one typically exercises no meaningful locus of control over their childhood household SES, but there is not the same degree of social concern for including this measure in a predictive model.

This dynamic begs the question of whether any attribute over which students have no direct control should be included in predictive modeling in education, which is a key argument of this paper. After all of the model inputs are determined, one would engineer features. Features are just operationally defined variables, which may, for example, require one to transform nominal variables into binaries, standardize numeric variables as z-scores, or apply other similar manipulations to create a functional data frame. One can include numerous features, but, as with traditional econometric, there is a risk of overfitting the model, which would reduce its plasticity when applying to a wider population (Hastie, Tibshirani and Friedman 2009). Given these features and subsequent model training, a probability of success is generated, ranging from 0 to 1, where 1 is 100% chance of achieving the given outcome.

3 The Analysis

As a particular example to illustrate the current challenges of traditional learning analytics, consider the following, recent UMBC findings. During the Spring 2022 15-week term, an ongoing ML-base nudging initiative included 2,421 students in 17 high-enrollment gateway STEM courses. Using historic data to initially train it, the model created a weekly predicted probability of students earning a DFW in the course participating in this pilot nudge project described earlier in this paper. ML modeling demonstrated .81 precision, meaning 81% of students identified as earning a DFW actually went on to earn one. Below is an illustration of the formula for calculating precision:

$$\frac{\text{Correctly IDed DFWs}}{\text{Correctly IDed DFWs} + \text{False Positives}}$$

The modeling also demonstrated .4 recall, or sensitivity. In turn, this 40% would represent all of the cases correctly identified as earning a DFW divided by the true positives and false negatives. Below is an illustration of the formula for calculating recall:

$$\frac{\text{Correctly IDed DFWs}}{\text{Correctly IDed DFWs} + \text{False Negatives}}$$

Predictions informed empathetic nudges that were sent to students with a $\geq 50\%$ predicted chance of earning a DFW for the term. Given the precedence of past UMBC projects, we know that by approximately Week 4 of the term, behaviors within a semester supplant pre-measures as most predictive features in our home-grown models. We see that 14.49% of students are predicted to earn this negative outcome according to the Week 4 values. That number drops down to 5.59% by Week 7, presumably because of student behavior in the given course and within their other courses. The actual DFW rate was 18.13%. Nudges were sent from an internal campus system during term weeks 4 and 7. A third alert based on a manual, instructor-referred rather than ML-informed message was also sent out. Only 6 of the participating courses made use of this legacy system, representing 286 nudges, or 11.8% of the total cases.

Notably, 34% of the students who received the first nudge went on to receive a DFW, while only 12% of the untreated students did. Of those students receiving both the Week 4 and Week 7 nudges, 66% earned a DFW. And 81.8% of students who received all three nudges earned a DFW. In other words, as students accumulate more nudges, their chances of success in their course greatly diminished. However, given the precision of the model described above, we see that almost exactly the same percentage of students would have likely earned a DFW independent of the intervention. In turn, given students appeared predisposed to earning a negative outcome, the relationship between nudging and observed DFWs appears corollary rather than causal. So, how do we determine whether this nudge was in any discernible way successful rather than a reification of the prediction – a self-fulfilling prophecy – and in turn help inform improved processes moving forward? Given that the chance of a negative outcome doubles between receiving the first and second nudge, this analysis focuses on the identifiable behavioral differences between the first and second nudge. From a classical econometrics/statistics perspective, the first question we must investigate is the extent to which the first nudge results in any measurable lift in terms of the dependent and independent predictive model inputs: DFWs and interactions, respectively.

There are a lot of individual constructs that get wrapped into a DFW. Instructors employ direct, observable behaviors as well as indirect measures. These data take the form of formative assessments, such as polling or quizzing, all the way up to the dreaded high-stakes test, which, in many people's minds, epitomizes summative assessments. Mixed into these measures might also be journals, blogs, portfolios, presentations, interpretive dances, and other means to infer learning along a qualitative to quantitative continuum (a blog, for example, could represent either qualitative or quantitative data depending on whether one developed a reliable and valid rubric for grading).

So, we have all these pieces which we typically roll up into an end of term percent based on the course grading schema and weighting. Assuming one is not auditing the given course, or has selected a P/F option, that percent is associated with an A-F letter grade, and only at this point can one create our institutionally meaningful binary, the DFW (Fig. 1).

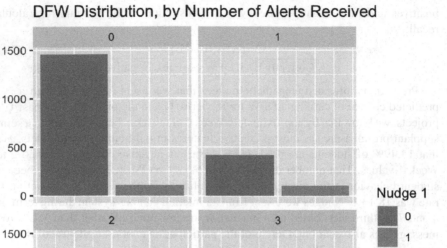

Fig. 1. The more nudges a student receives the more likely they are to earn a DFW.

The problem, as hopefully illustrated by the above description of the grading work-flow, is there are an incredible number of attributes and measures that must be distilled to arrive at this either/or outcome before we even begin to consider exogenous influences, or those external to the model (i.e., life). Only after boiling this sea of data might we begin to look at the relationship between our interventions and the given outcomes.

Since there are so many variables comprising the DFW, to change a student's state from a 1 to 0, or from a Yes to a No – i.e., redirect a student from failing to succeeding – the impact of any intervention must be great enough to overcome the initial trajectory in much the same way one must overcome a physical object's inertia to redirect it. In turn, the more at-risk students are, or the later in a semester they are identified, the more impactful the intervention must be to benefit them.

What does this all mean for our present conversation? Well, it is exceptionally difficult to measure the efficacy of an intervention strategy using DFWs alone. There's typically too much inertia to overcome to help students as we'd like without something more dramatic than a nudge. At the same time, from a pragmatic perspective, measuring student awareness of resources is only consequential to the extent such recognition leads to action with measurable lift in an observable behavior associated with learning (i.e., a direct measure of learning). Also, given sample size and environmental factors, it's impossible to state X caused Y *ceteris paribus*, mostly because we don't know what all things being equal actually means under the best of circumstances, let alone amidst a pandemic and its associated trailing effects. In this particular analysis, determining a causal relationship between a treatment and a state change $(1 \rightarrow 0)$ is exceptionally difficult. Using propensity score matching based on the initial ML-generated predictions, for example, results in collinearity since all students achieving a certain threshold received a nudge.

Early identification of at-risk students helps but does not fully mitigate this dynamic. Particularly regarding the behavioral nudge campaign, it perhaps makes sense to look at other behavioral measures, such as interactions and time spent in the LMS because those are the variables that we have available to us, and because they have over the course of multiple projects proven reasonable proxies for engagement.

As Fig. 2 above below, students identified for messaging not only start off below their peers in LMS engagement, but they fall even further behind following the initial notification. Part of the problem is that even as our insights are enhanced and we merge our data silos, there remain gaps in what we know about our learning ecosystem. It's reasonable, for example, to assume that if a student receives a nudge from the system, then they may seek out resources that are not LMS specific. That student could chat with their professor or visit the Student Success Center, for example. Doing so wouldn't be captured in our existing data and this self-efficacy might benefit students in their other classes (also unmeasured in the current analysis). These outcomes could perhaps indicate the nudging was successful, and we simply aren't yet fully aware of the complex picture to evaluate it. However, any academically successful connection with a human advocate would result in students being redirected to do their class work, which would in turn (if the advice were followed), result in greater interactions within and signal from the LMS. Key here is how we operationally define, measure, and track these successes. We would hope these interactions would amount to more than just clicking on *stuff* to improve one's grade, but who knows? In any event, we are unfortunately not seeing this outcome with our current data.

Bb Interactions Pre/Post Nudge 1, by Nudge/No Nudge

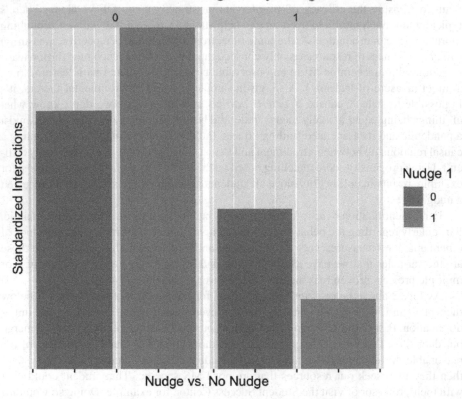

Fig. 2. Nudging is not associated with increased LMS engagement.

3.1 Why's the Status Quo Problematic?

Reich (2022) succinctly summarized the tendency of using big data in learning analytics as revealing the Truth that "students who do stuff do other stuff, and students who do stuff, do better than students who don't do stuff" (p. 192). Yes, one can use interactions within an LMS as proxies for engagement but acting to increase these measures can be perceived by some students as Orwellian and potentially contribute to increased stress for students who are already identified as at-risk (Brown, Basson., Axelsen, Redmond, and Lawrence, 2023). And although we believe more engagement is better than less, the link between *interactions* and *learning* isn't yet substantiated. The question that arises, therefore, is how do practitioners move beyond using clicks to predict and increase clicks into a new paradigm of leveraging meaningful insights to support direct measures of students' success? And just as consequential: How would we know if any of our data-informed interventions have a positive impact?

These questions help establish an ethical operational starting point. If one uses ML to predict students' chances of earning a preferred outcome of an A, B, or C in a given course during their first term at a university, we begin with some kind of data to develop and train a (supervised) model. In this case, I might create features with various indicators that can be mapped to the successful outcome. Students standardized test scores and high school GPAs. I can look at when they registered for class (registering early is associated with positive outcomes, while registering late is associated with negative outcomes). Basically, anything that's been included in the student application that does not directly contribute to unethical modeling. But what do we do if a student has a sufficiently high probability of an undesirable outcome? In other words, given *learning analytics is analysis* in action, the $64,000 question is: What ethical action should we take?

3.2   First, Do no Harm!

The first concern in moving forward is doing so ethically. Would it be acceptable, for example, to use predicted values to advise students? Our university Provost has justifiably said "no." Afterall, if we include premeasures that may be closely correlated with SES into that model and then advise based on these values, aren't we simply promoting social reproduction, and perhaps using this "unbiased" tool to sort students based on historically unjust dynamics? In turn, if a student grows up in a poorer neighborhood associated with poorer outcomes, do we accept it would be OK to suggest to them to take a lower-level math course based on the probability of their success, which would ultimately lead them to a different major, different, lower paying job, reduced lifetime earning potential, and a perpetuation of the cycle? Does doing so, as Freire argued, leads us toward elevating freedom over conformity? On the other hand, if we have data and we know of risk, aren't we compelled, ethically, to act if we have a valid treatment (Fritz and Whitmer 2019)?

In general, students' chances of success in a course can follow a simple x, y plot, whereby the weeks of the semester are along the x axis while their cumulative engagement relative to their peers is plotted along the y axis. Students' use of the university's LMS, for example, or their interactions with various digital tools can be included as model inputs. Perhaps attendance, or network pings, can be included. All of these proxies for engagement are included in the models, and over the course of a few weeks, replace these pre-measures as most consequential in determining student success. It's important, however, to emphasize that these behaviors are not available at Week Zero to act upon models informed by them.

That's not to say that proxies aren't valuable or that we shouldn't use descriptive and predictive analysis to close the gap between access, success, and upward mobility. Nor is it problematic to use adaptive learning based on ML in a closed model, such as through use of courseware that reinforces probability and statistics skills (Van Campenhout, Jerome, and Johnson 2020). Our institution is piloting use of these types of platforms to scaffold student content acquisition in high-enrollment gateway STEM courses (Carpenter, Fritz, and Penniston, in press). Indeed, leveraging ML to triage students into buckets to address allocation of finite resources is a reasonable, scalable, and widely accepted business proposition (Prinsloo and Slade 2017). It makes sense from an economic standpoint to address persistence and graduation rates. The ethical difficulties, rather, arise when we think in terms of *data driven* instead of *data informed* practice, particularly when the outcomes we predict are tied to institutional reporting outcomes that don't necessarily align with students' best interests, including learning.

Higher education often tries to thread a semantic needle by differentiating between *learner* vs *learning* analytics (Bishop 2017), but this is largely a distinction without difference if we're focusing first on our students' needs. They are, after all, our business. It's incumbent, therefore, upon higher education pedagogues and administrators alike to look for collaborative ways to flip the existing paradigm by measuring success as student learning (which may subsequently contribute to improved persistence and graduation rates) rather than trying to improve institutional measures in the hope of student learning as a byproduct. Reflecting back on our opening quotes from Dewey and Freire, highlighting the interconnection of knowledge, experience, and social growth, we must vigilantly re-evaluate our business practices to assure students' learning needs are prioritized. So, what do we do?

The overarching flaw in having a *general* predictive model is it directs us to *general* rather than targeted intervention strategies. We send all too easily ignored behavioral nudge notifications, which despite all our best intentions to encourage self-efficacy, can be interpreted by the recipient as thinly veiled threats. "Come to office hours". "Go to class". We refer them to case managers who may direct them to one-on-one tutoring. They, in turn, must spend additional time on content remediation without additional benefit, such as micro-credentialing, which is easily interpretable as a negative outcome. A stick, for some. Thus, the status quo would be greatly improved if the intervention were designed to affect marginal gains for direct measures of students' learning rather than increases in proxies for engagement, or indirect measures such as reduced DFW rates. We use ML as a tool to triage students into buckets, informed by models that, depending on when the runes are read, can be reliant on pre-measures closely tied to features over which students have no locus of control, such as where they were born and raised. The institution might use these approaches to move the needle on 6-year graduation rates, but is that inherently a win for our students, or is it a win for the university, and then only secondarily, and hopefully by extension, the students?

4 Conclusion

And so, I return to my opening question: How do we assure our modern intervention strategies aren't similarly judged as misguided, callous, or even abusive in the future? It would be ironic, given the quotations I started this paper with, to now provide a prescriptive cookie-cutter framework that could possibly fit all schools' needs, let alone the needs of their students. Practices evolve over time through democratic dialogue at individual institutions, and throughout the preceding essay I've attempted to remain descriptive in discussing existing considerations, albeit not entirely neutral. I don't shy away from my positionality. Education, to channel my inner Freire, is inherently political. So, in what ways might we shift our existing practices to better scaffold students' growth to help them live up to their fullest potential? As I've alluded to throughout this paper, there are certain areas that all schools might consider—my own included—in moving toward an improved version of their own unique learning analytics practices.

4.1 Authentic Experiences: Measure What's Needed, not Merely What's Available to Us and We Can Get Away With

To begin with, we should be intervening in alignment with our learning outcomes.

Well-designed courses, such as those that meet the best-practice framework of Quality Matters standards, should explicitly articulate a direct link between what is being taught during any given class, back to unit-level objectives, continuing up the hierarchy to course-level goals, and ultimately on to institutional functional competencies. Such alignment is a hallmark of best practices and an institutionally scalable intervention (Fritz, Hawken and Shin 2021) while more holistically designed courses can help improve the insights instructors and administrators gain within a term (Fritz, Penniston, Sharkey, and Whitmer 2021). Surely in our new reality in higher education ushered in by the pandemic, we can, and indeed are duty bound, to better instrument all courses to achieve these ends? Evidence of learning must be directly measurable rather than only available in aggregate form through indirect constructs like letter grades, and easily discernible and available grading may ultimately prove more meaningful than institution-level nudging. Yes, although there was not an increase in student interactions subsequent to their receiving a nudge in the current analysis, intervention strategies may be associated with such gains (Brown, Basson, Axelsen, Redmond, and Lawrence 2023). However, we should be careful not to conflate the signal, in the form of clicks, for example, with what we're really in the business of supporting: learning.

To that end, whenever possible, intervention strategies will be most effective and ethical when aligned with well-defined learning goals and achievable functional competencies, rather than based on institutional reporting metrics (such as persistence rates) to assure we don't inadvertently introduce perverse incentives that benefit the university at the expense of the learner. It wouldn't be, perhaps, the first-time higher education was steered astray by prestige, market forces, and self-preservation in the ongoing quest for improved institutional rankings (O'Neil 2017). To this end, if our students need to demonstrate written and oral communication, then we need to work toward directly measuring them doing so at scale and provide interventions accordingly. And these measures must be taken in advance of or at the beginning of a semester to provide a baseline to assure we don't find ourselves late in the term telling students they suddenly need to become an A student to pass their class and graduate on time.

It is possible and entirely reasonable to make a substantive paradigm shift in terms of policy beginning institutionally from the top down. If our digital ecosystem is to live up to its yet-to-be-realized potential, then we need improved model inputs, which requires both strategy and significant outlay of resources in terms of money, time, wherewithal, and to achieve these ends, training. Authentic experiences and direct measures will contribute to content salience. What does that mean in layman's terms? Simply that if university's hope to address students' math, science, or reading deficiencies, we must work with faculty to design courses to align with institutional learning goals and functional competencies and then measure these constructs as observable behaviors early and throughout each term. Tag relevant assessment items as evidence of learning in not only online and hybrid, but also face-to-face courses to support real time measurement of progress toward outcomes.

In this way, we might identify students as being at risk by indicators including standardized placement tests, ALEKS scores, or lexical complexity on written work relative to peers, and thereby not only track growth, but also connect tailored interventions to address students' specific learning needs. If our ML identified students with a low Flesch-Kinkaid score on an institutionally mandated first year reflection, for example, that marker might be useful for automatically connecting those individuals to some form of asynchronous, self-directed learning modules, or, depending on the severity of the need, perhaps mandating tutoring. To address this need, our institution has been developing both a learning record store (LRS), which will include more disaggregated measures than our current data warehouse provides to identify student learning, along with a comprehensive learner record (CLR) system to capture the full picture of learners' experiences (Braxton, Sullivan, Wyatt, and Monroe 2022). We must also consider incentivizing the work students put into their own content remediation along their customized pathways. Yes, students should take responsibility for their own learning (Tinto 1993); doing so is both virtuous and a reward unto itself. At the same time, we also have a broader system that incentives one to possess a degree, but not necessarily to learn. It stands to reason, therefore, that if we nudge to support self-directed learning (Fritz 2017), and there is no subsequent demonstrated positive lift in learning, then surely we need to re-evaluate not only our methods, but also our incentive model? Offering carrots rather than just sticks is one option to encourage self-regulated growth. Again, our institution is already moving in this direction with a nascent program of micro-credentialing (Braxton, Sullivan, Wyatt, and Monroe 2022). Perhaps there might even be a valid argument made for piloting a program to pay students who participate in certain forms of remediation.

Taken together, these are neither impossible, nor easy things to accomplish. Shifting our orientation will require strong will and collaboration, creative problem-solving skills, leadership from all directions along with capital of every conceivable type, and more than just a little bit of patience, humility, and dare I say *moxie*. In the long run, however, we will best assure our collective social growth and the fulfillment of our core mission when we prioritize course design and interventions that align with student learning.

References

Baker, R.S., Hawn, A.: Algorithmic bias in education. Int. J. Artif. Intell. Educ. 1–41 (2021). https://doi.org/10.1007/s40593-021-00285-9

Bishop, M.: Splitting hairs: Exploring learning vs learner analytics (and why we should care). The EvoLLLution (2017). https://evolllution.com/technology/metrics/splitting-hairs-exploring-learn-ing-vs-learn-er-analytics-and-why-we-should-care/. Accessed 6 Feb 2023

Braxton, S.N., Sullivan, C., Wyatt, L.A., Monroe, J.: Capturing student achievement and learning pathways at the university of Maryland, Baltimore county: digital badging and the comprehensive learner record. In: Huang, Y. (Ed.), Handbook of Research on Credential Innovations for Inclusive Pathways to Professions, pp. 396–417. IGI Global (2022). https://doi.org/10.4018/978-1-7998-3820-3.ch020

Brown, A., Basson, B., Axelsen, M., Redmond, P., Lawrence, J.: Empirical evidence to support a nudge intervention for increasing online engagement in higher education. Educ. Sci. **13**, 145 (2023). https://doi.org/10.3390/educsci13020145

Carpenter, B., Penniston, T.: Leveraging Predictive Analytics to Support Student Success [Conference presentation]. OLC Innovate, Denver, CO, United States, 2–5 April 2019

Carpenter, T., Fritz, J., Penniston, T.: Banking on adaptive questions to nudge student responsibility for learning in general chemistry. In: Data Analytics and Adaptive Learning: Research Perspectives (in press)

Check, J. Schutt, R.: Research in Education. Thousand Oaks. SAGE, CA (2012). ISBN: 978–1412940092

Cheuk, T.: Can AI be racist? Color-evasiveness in the application of machine learning to science assessments. Sci. Educ. **105**(5), 825–836 (2021)

Dewey, J.: My pedagogic creed. Sch. J. **54**, 77–80 (1897)

Freire, P.: Pedagogy of the Oppressed (30th anniversary ed.). Continuum (2000)

Fritz, J. (2017). "Using Analytics to Nudge Student Responsibility for Learning," Ch. 6 in New Directions for Higher Education, 2017 (179), pp. 65–75. https://doi.org/10.1002/he.20244

Fritz, J., Hawken, M., Shin, S.: Using learning analytics and instructional design to inform, find, and scale quality online learning. In: Online Learning Analytics, pp. 95–114. Auerbach Publications (2021)

Fritz, J., Penniston, T., Sharkey, M. Whitmer, J.: Scaling course design as learning analytics variable. In: Blended Learning Research Practices, vol. 3 (2021). Ch. 5. https://doi.org/10.4324/9781003037736-7

Fritz, J., Whitmer, J.: Ethical learning analytics: do no harm versus do nothing. New Dir. Inst. Res. **2019**(183), 27–38 (2019). https://doi.org/10.1002/ir.20310

Harrison, J.: Bridging Student Learning Outcomes Student Success Analytics. UMBC Faculty Development Center (2020). https://calt.umbc.edu/wp-content/uploads/sites/50/2020/01/Bridging-SLOs-and-Success-2-pp-pamphlet.pdf. Accessed 6 Feb 2023

Hastie, T., Tibshirani, R., Friedman, J.H.: The Elements of Statistical Learning : Data Mining, Inference, and Prediction (Second edition). Springer, Cham (2009).

Johnson, R., Onwuegbuzie, A.J.: Mixed methods research: a research paradigm whose time has come. Educ. Res. **33**(7), 14–26 (2004)

O'Neil, C.: Weapons of Math Destruction. Penguin Books (2017)

Prinsloo, P., Slade, S.: Ethics and learning analytics: Charting the (un) charted. SoLAR (2017)

Reich, J.: Learning Analytics and Learning at Scale. by Charles Lang, Alyssa Friend Wise, Agathe Merceron, Dragan Gašević, and George Siemens, 2nd edn. SOLAR, Vancouver, Canada (2022)

Sharkey, M.: Predicting Attrition: It's Math, Not Magic [Conference presentation]. Online Learning Consortium (OLC) Conference, Orlando, FL, United States 14–16 October 2015

Thaler, R.H., Sunstein, C.R.: Nudge. Penguin (2009)

Tinto, V.: Leaving College, Rethinking the Causes and Cures of Student Attrition, 2nd edn. The University of Chicago Press, Chicago (1993)

Van Campenhout, R., Jerome, B., Johnson, B.G.: The impact of adaptive activities in acrobatiq courseware - investigating the efficacy of formative adaptive activities on learning estimates and summative assessment scores. In: Sottilare, R.A., Schwarz, J. (eds.) HCII 2020. LNCS, vol. 12214, pp. 543–554. Springer, Cham (2020). https://doi.org/10.1007/978-3-030-50788-6_40

Wooldridge, J.: Introductory Econometrics: A Modern Approach (4th Ed.). Cengage Learning, USA (2009)

Considerations for Developing a Generalized Gradebook for an Open-Source Intelligent Tutoring System Framework

Anne M. Sinatra[✉]

US Army Combat Capabilities Development Command (DEVCOM) Soldier Center, Orlando, FL 32826, USA
anne.m.sinatra.civ@army.mil

Abstract. The current paper describes a use case of an open-source intelligent tutoring system (ITS) framework, the Generalized Intelligent Framework for Tutoring (GIFT). GIFT has been primarily used by researchers, and it is a highly flexible system that allows for tutoring to be created in the topic area of the author's choice. While there are tools to output data from GIFT, there is not a traditional standardized gradebook tool that can be easily used by a non-researcher. Due to the generalizable design of GIFT, and the unique characteristics of intelligent tutoring performance, this is an interesting design challenge. The current paper discusses the current state of data export in GIFT, describes the adaptive courseflow approach to tutoring in GIFT, and discusses potential approaches to visualizing adaptive tutoring data in a way that instructors can easily understand and gain the maximum knowledge from.

Keywords: Intelligent Tutoring Systems · Gradebook · Generalized Intelligent Framework for Tutoring · GIFT

1 Introduction

Adaptive instructional systems (AISs) and intelligent tutoring systems (ITSs) can collect large amounts of data about learner performance, however, there also needs to be careful consideration into how to display that data. Further, the approach to displaying the data may differ based on the intended end-user of the data. The Generalized Intelligent Framework for Tutoring (GIFT; [7]) is an open-source framework that can be used to create ITSs. GIFT has been designed to be flexible, and tutors can be created in the domain topic area of the tutor author's choice. GIFT can utilize a wide variety of instructional materials ranging from static PowerPoint presentations to interactive computer-based simulations. As open-source software, GIFT's flexibility also provides additional opportunities for researchers with many different technical backgrounds and expertise in different topic areas to utilize the system for their unique needs.

Thus far, GIFT has primarily been used by researchers. However, there have been some initial pilot implementations utilizing course materials (e.g., [6]). One potential

R. A. Sottilare and J. Schwarz (Eds.): HCII 2023, LNCS 14044, pp. 162–173, 2023.
https://doi.org/10.1007/978-3-031-34735-1_12

challenge that has been identified for the use of GIFT in a classroom setting is the current approach for extracting data from GIFT [5]. GIFT does not currently have a traditional gradebook feature. In terms of current visualizations, there has been work on after action review and playback capabilities in GIFT in the form of the Game Master Dashboard [2], as well as work on the STEEL-R (Synthetic Training Environment Experiential Learning for Readiness) competency dashboard [4]. Additionally, GIFT has an existing ability to extract learner data into spreadsheets. However, there is not currently a built-in traditional interface to view the grade of the student and the questions/answers that led to that specific score.

While there are learner management systems, including open-source ones that could be integrated with GIFT, there is a unique design consideration regarding a gradebook for GIFT. GIFT is highly flexible in what topic is being taught and how the lessons are being constructed. Therefore, the output for different tutors may look drastically different. Additionally, there are multiple ways that GIFT can adapt.

2 Adaptive Tutoring Performance in GIFT

As a flexible framework, there are multiple approaches to adaptive tutoring in GIFT. If using an external training environment such as Virtual Battlespace or Unity then real-time assessment is configured by the author in a Domain Knowledge File (DKF). The DKF contains information about what the learner will be assessed on during a simulation or their interaction with the system, and how to evaluate them on it. The performance output can currently be seen in the Game Master visualization tool. However, there is a simpler type of adaptation in GIFT that does not require the use of an external training application: the adaptive courseflow object. The adaptive courseflow approach is fairly straightforward and can be authored in the GIFT Authoring Tool. The data from performance in the adaptive courseflow can currently be exported as a.csv file and opened in Excel.

2.1 Adaptive Courseflow

In a traditional class that is primarily utilizing GIFT for tutoring and remediation without an external training application, the adaptive courseflow object would be the preferred method of adapting content. The adaptive courseflow object in GIFT is based on Merrill's Component Display theory [3] and has 4 quadrants: rules, examples, recall and practice [1]. The rules phase and the examples phase, which is optional to author, present instructional materials associated with specific author defined concepts to the learners; the recall phase, which is required, provides quizzes on the concepts; and the practice phase, which is optional to author, can include an interaction with a training application that tests the concepts. In the recall phase, if the learner does not meet the author defined threshold for number of questions correct for proficiency in each defined concept, then GIFT will provide remediation materials on the specific concept(s) that were not passed. This remediation is in the form of content that was either previously presented or new to the learner. The remediation can either be more passive (e.g., slide show, PDF, image, webpage, video) or active (e.g., highlight passage, conversation tree, summarize passage). After remediation, the learner is navigated back to the recall phase and receives another quiz. If the learner misses the same or different concepts, they go through remediation again. The learner may receive the same or different remediation materials based on the amount of content available, and what they have previously received. This will continue until the learner either passes all concepts, or until the system stops them if the author has requested a maximum number of times the remediation can occur (e.g., 3 times). See Fig. 1 for a visual representation of the adaptive courseflow process.

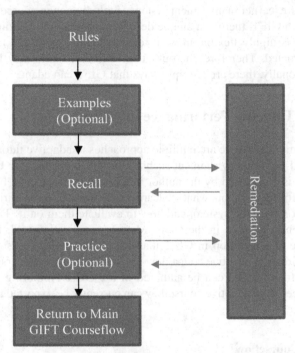

Fig. 1. The adaptive courseflow process in GIFT. The rules and examples phases present material to the learner on the identified concepts in the form of slides, images, webpages, etc., and then the recall phase presents multiple choice questions on the concepts. If the learner does not meet the proficiency defined by the course author on specific concepts, they will receive remediation based on the available course materials. The type of remediation material may also vary based on what the system knows about the learner. Once they pass the recall phase for all concepts they can move onto practice. Practice is associated with an external training application and has assessments of the concepts as well. Based on the concepts missed, there will be remediation, and once performance goals are met the learner moves back into the main GIFT courseflow.

2.2   GIFT Data Output and the Adaptive Courseflow

In the current state of GIFT, examining the data output which represent the adaptive tutoring and remediation provided by the adaptive courseflow object is challenging. The data can be extracted into a.csv file which can be opened in Excel. There is a checkbox that allows for the data to be represented in a manner that is similar to a traditional gradebook with each learner on a separate line, however, it will not include all of the same nuance of extracting the data individually. Further, the questions that are provided to the students are not always the same, and sometimes based on the names the questions are given by the author or the system, the columns can be in a scrambled order.

To fully see the adaptivity, it is necessary to extract the data without merging it; this results in multiple lines for each learner with different time stamps. To fully understand the information that is being provided it is necessary to both reorder the columns so that they can be compared side by side to understand what questions were provided, and to examine the performance for each concept. After remediation is received and the recall phase occurs again, another line is created in the file, and a new score is provided for each concept. This can be a difficult process to understand for a researcher, and due to the many different approaches that can be taken to defining concepts and adaptive courseflows in a GIFT course it may not be the same exact process each time the data is extracted and examined.

While a researcher may be able to devote the time to look at and organize the data spreadsheets to get a general understanding of the performance of the learner on each concept and how much remediation they received, this would likely be challenging for an instructor who might have limited time to interact with the system. It is important to consider what the most frequent generalized measures and items of interest may be to an instructor, and to extract that data into a summarized gradebook that can easily be viewed and interpreted. Also of note is the added complexity, as each time that the individual goes through the recall phase, they need to answer questions about all of the concepts again. This creates an additional metric that tracks how many times the learner failed or passed a specific concept.

General information of interest to the instructor may include, but is not limited to, the following.

- How many times was remediation presented to the learner overall?
- Did the learner pass all of the concepts?
- If the learner goes through the recall phase more than once did they miss a concept that they previous got correct?
- How many times did the learner get remediation on a specific concept?
- What remediation materials did the learner receive?
- What specific questions did the learner receive during the recall phase?

Additionally, due to the generalized approach used in GIFT, the concepts, topics, and ways that the adaptive courseflow object are structured can vary for each and every tutor.

2.3   Addressing the Challenge of a Standardized Gradebook for GIFT

In order to create a standardized gradebook output for GIFT that reflects adaptive courseflow performance, it needs to be designed in such a way that it makes sense regardless of the way that the adaptive courseflow was configured. It is important to determine what the most important metrics are for an ITS, and perhaps even to provide configurable options to an instructor who wants to examine the performance of the individual learners within their class.

The general metrics mentioned in the section above may be helpful to an instructor, but they may also want to be able to look deeper into the question-by-question performance and if specific questions are being missed more than others. Additionally, careful consideration should be put into designing an approach that will allow for individual adaptive learner behavior and remediation to be examined in more depth if the instructor wishes. The next section of the paper further describes the current process in GIFT, and discusses potential approaches that could be utilized to design a generalized gradebook output.

3   Potential Approaches to Designing a Generalized Gradebook Output in GIFT

For the purposes and scope of this paper, only performance in the recall and related remediation phases will be discussed, not the optional practice phase. Further, for the purposes of the discussion in this paper, an example course structure with associated concepts is described below. This example will help to contextualize the discussion.

3.1   Example Course and Adaptive Courseflow Setup

The example to be used in this paper is of a course that has four different concepts, and 2 different adaptive courseflows. The breakdown is described below.

- Overall GIFT Course Title: Memory
- GIFT Course Concepts (four total):

  - Sensory Memory
  - Short Term Memory
  - Long Term Memory
  - Working Memory

- The Adaptive Courseflows are as follows (two total, with two concepts each):

  - Adaptive Courseflow 1 (AC1; Concepts: Sensory Memory and Short Term Memory)
  - Adaptive Courseflow 2 (AC2; Concepts: Long Term Memory and Working Memory)

The overall GIFT course topic is "Memory" and there are two adaptive courseflows: AC1 (Sensory Memory and Short Term Memory) and AC2 (Long-Term Memory and Working Memory). Each of these adaptive courseflows are made up of two concepts. See Fig. 2 for a visual representation of the GIFT Course in the GIFT Course Authoring Tool.

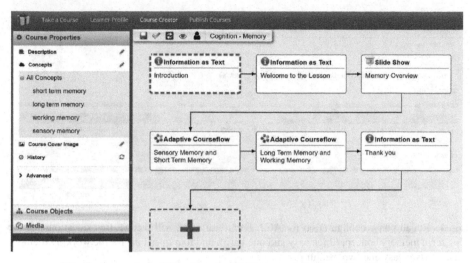

Fig. 2. Screenshot of the example GIFT course being used for this paper.

For AC1 there are a total of six possible questions that can be received during recall (two for short term memory, and four for sensory memory). For AC2 there are a total of eight possible questions that can be received during recall (four for long term memory and four for working memory). The configuration of the recall phase of AC1 can be seen in Fig. 3, and AC2 can be seen in Fig. 4.

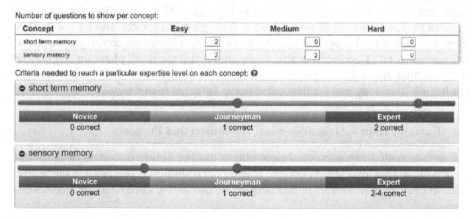

Fig. 3. Recall phase configuration for AC1. Each individual will receive two questions for the short term memory concept (easy), and four questions for the sensory memory concept (two easy and two medium).

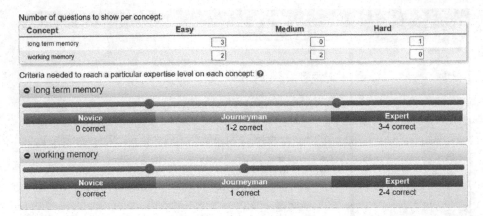

Fig. 4. Recall phase configuration for AC2. Each individual will receive four questions for the long term memory concept (three easy and one hard), and four questions for the working memory concept (two easy and two medium).

The way that both Adaptive Courseflows are configured will result in all the available questions being asked each time. However, in GIFT it can be authored such that less than the available number of questions will be requested (e.g., seven out of eight), in which case different questions may be asked each time. In order to "pass" a course concept and move forward the learner will need to perform at the expert level. Therefore, as shown in Fig. 3, for AC1, for the short term memory concept the learner will need to get two questions correct, and for sensory memory the learner will need to get two to four questions correct. Additionally, as shown in Fig. 4, for AC2, for the long term memory concept the learner will need to get three to four questions correct, and for the working memory concept the learner will need to get two to four questions correct. In the case of this particular GIFT course, it is also configured that if the recall phase on any concept is failed three times the course ends. This is a reconfigurable number; however, any gradebook should account for the course being authored in this way.

3.2 Example Data for Discussion and Demonstration Purposes

For demonstration purposes, the below output has been created to show what performance might look like (this is not real learner data). In Fig. 5 you can see the merged version of the example learner data. In Fig. 6 you can see the same data exported without merging.

User_Id	short_term_memory_Correct	sensory_memory_Correct	long_term_memory_Correct	working_memory_Correct
1	1	2	0	1
2	1	0	3	0
3	2	4	0	1
4	1	2	3	2
5	2	3	3	3
6	1	2	2	2

Fig. 5. Example learner data for six different run through of the Memory GIFT Course. In this version each line is a different learner. There is a column for the number correct for each of the concepts (short term memory, sensory memory, long term memory, and working memory).

User_Id	short_term_memory_Correct	sensory_memory_Correct	long_term_memory_Correct	working_memory_Correct
1	1	2		
1	2	3		
1			0	1
1			1	0
1			3	4
2	1	0		
2	2	2		
2			3	0
2			0	4
2			3	4
3	2	4		
3			0	1
3			0	2
3			3	1
4	1	2		
4	2	4		
4			3	2
5	2	3		
5			3	3
6	1	2		
6	1	2		
6	2	4		
6			2	2
6			0	1
6			3	4

Fig. 6. The same example learner data as in the previous figure, but not merged by learner. Performance of the same learner is represented on multiple lines, which are aligned with their User_Id and vary based on how many times they went through the recall phase/received remediation.

3.3 Interpreting the Example Data Output

As can be seen in Fig. 5, simply merging the data by learner does not give a full story, as the only score provided for each concept is the first time that specific learner answered questions in the recall phase. The non-merged version is required to see the performance during the adaptive tutoring and multiple recall phases, however, due to the adaptive nature of the tutoring the meaning of each line may not be entirely clear to a reader.

Figure 7 shows a highlighted version of the same output that can help the reader understand the performance of the learner for the concepts, and in the overall adaptive courseflows. Multiple line entries indicate that remediation occurred, and that the learner answered questions in the recall phase an additional time.

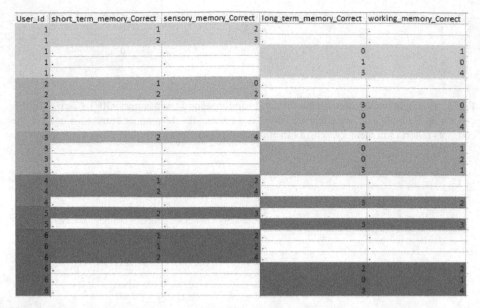

User_Id	short_term_memory_Correct	sensory_memory_Correct	long_term_memory_Correct	working_memory_Correct
1	1	2		
1	2	3		
1			0	1
1			1	0
1			3	4
2	1	0		
2	2	2		
2			3	0
2			0	4
2			3	4
3	2	4		
3			0	1
3			0	2
3			3	1
4	1	2		
4	2	4		
4			3	2
5	2	3		
5			3	3
6	1	2		
6	1	2		
6	2	4		
6			2	2
6			0	1
6			3	4

Fig. 7. The same example data as in Fig. 6 but highlighted to visually separate each learner and each adaptive courseflow output. Each learner is a different color. The two columns on the left represent AC1 (short term memory and sensory memory), and the two columns on the right represent AC2 (long term memory and working memory).

Learner 1's performance can be interpreted as follows from Fig. 7: AC1 was passed after going through the recall phase twice (there are two lines of scores), which means that they received remediation once; AC2 was passed after going through the recall phase 3 times (there are three lines of score), which means that they received remediation twice. In order to know which concepts were passed and failed it is required to cross reference with how the course was set up. Which in this case was that for short term, sensory and working memory at least 2 questions had to be correct, and for long term memory at least 3 questions had to be correct to pass. Therefore, in AC1, learner 1 passed the sensory memory concept, and failed the short term memory concept during the first recall phase. They then received remediation on short term memory, and passed both concepts in the second recall phase. For AC2, they failed both long term memory and working memory the first time, then they received remediation on both, and failed a second time, then they passed them both the third time. In the case of learner 3, they never passed the second adaptive courseflow, as you can see that the working memory number was lower than 2 on the third recall, which means they received remediation twice, then the course ended after the third failed recall.

It takes effort, time, and understanding for an individual to export, arrange, and then interpret the current output from GIFT in regard to adaptive courseflows and remediation, as demonstrated in Figs. 5 through 7. However, the information that is available from the adaptive courseflow is important and would be helpful to an instructor.

If the system could track and output information in an approach that is similar to a gradebook which includes some of the most helpful general information it would be preferred, and then in the future there could be potential options to click on an item and see more details about it. At minimum some generalized questions that could easily be answered by the system that were mentioned earlier in the paper are as follows:

- How many times was remediation presented to the learner overall?
- Did the learner pass all of the concepts?
- How many times did the learner get remediation on a specific concept?

Figures 8 and 9 provides a potential approach that could be used to displaying this information in spreadsheet/gradebook form. This may be a good first approach to implementing a gradebook as it leverages the existing spreadsheets produced by GIFT, and it is conceptually similar to a traditional gradebook an instructor might create. Figures 8 and 9 are a summary of the example data in Fig. 7. This information could be a first step to summarizing the adaptive courseflow, and then in the future it could be used as a basis for building a visualization interface that is interactive and allows for clicking on the item to learn more about it or to see a different view of the data.

User	Passed AC1?	Passed AC2?	Passed All Concepts?	Total Times Remediated Overall	Times Remediated on AC1	Times Remediated on AC2
1	Yes	Yes	Yes	3	1	2
2	Yes	Yes	Yes	3	1	2
3	Yes	No	No	2	0	2
4	Yes	Yes	Yes	1	1	0
5	Yes	Yes	Yes	0	0	0
6	Yes	Yes	Yes	4	2	2

Fig. 8. Example of potential updated data extraction gradebook output which shows each user on each line and includes summary information of if the learner passed the overall adaptive courseflows, how many times they were remediated overall, and how many times they were remediated in each individual adaptive courseflow. AC1 represents adaptive courseflow 1.

User	Times Remediated on Short Term Memory (AC1 Con1)	Times Remediated on Sensory Memory (AC1 Con2)	Times Remediated on Long Term Memory (AC2 Con1)	Times Remediated on Working Memory (AC2 Con2)
1		1	1	1
2	1	1	1	1
3	0	0	1	1
4	1	0	0	0
5	0	0	0	0
6	2	2	2	1

Fig. 9. Continued example of potential updated data extraction gradebook output. This is additional data that would be visualized as the instructor scrolled to the right. It represents the individual concepts that make up the adaptive courseflows.

The summary data presented in Figs. 8 and 9 would help an instructor understand the performance of the learner, how much remediation they were receiving, and which concepts they were not passing. This could be continued for each adaptive courseflow in the gradebook, and each concept. There could also be overall summaries for the number of times remediated throughout the entire tutoring experience. In order for this to be implemented in GIFT, logic would need to be added to the export tool to both chunk together the concepts that are part of an authored adaptive courseflow overall in order to check to see if the courseflow was passed, and also to compare it to what has been authored in the adaptive courseflow to confirm if an individual concept was passed or failed. It would be greatly helpful to the instructor if the threshold for passing the concept was visible to them as well, potentially in the header of the column. The gradebook output would look slightly different based on how the GIFT course was authored, with more or less columns based on how many adaptive courseflows there were, and how many concepts they were made up of. Abbreviations such as AC1 (Adaptive Courseflow 1), AC2, AC3, Con1 (Concept 1), and Con2 could be used in addition to the title to help the instructor understand how the header is linked to the structure of the GIFT course.

Columns that could be included are as follows:

- Passed Adaptive Courseflow 1 (AC1), 2, 3, etc.
- Number of Adaptive Courseflows passed
- Times Remediated on AC1, 2, 3, etc.
- Times Remediated on each individual concept of AC1, 2, 3, etc.
- Total Times Remediated in all Adaptive Courseflows

Future research can examine different ways to visualize the adaptive courseflows and to add additional details that an instructor may be interested in, such as what questions were asked during the recall phase, what questions were missed during the recall phase, and what remediation was provided during the remediation phases. This information is more difficult to discern from the current GIFT outputs, and could be considered as parts of a future gradebook interface. Starting with an approach of summarizing the information and including each learner on individual lines in a spreadsheet will assist an instructor in understanding the performance of the individual learners.

4 Conclusions

While the focus of this paper has primarily been on how GIFT currently operates, and how a gradebook could be created for GIFT, the discussion and lessons learned are highly applicable to other tutoring software that need to take multiple domains and reconfiguration into account. Remediation is particularly difficult to represent in the gradebook due to the sequential nature of the event in GIFT. One of the particular challenges of creating a gradebook interface for GIFT is that it is very flexible – the domain of the tutoring can vary, the number of adaptive courseflows can vary, the number of the concepts in the adaptive courseflows can vary, and the thresholds for passing a course concept can vary. The tool and outputs that are created need to be able to account for the different configurations as well as output information that is understandable by the individual who will be reviewing the outputs. An initial approach and way forward is to identify items that are relevant to instructors and independent of domains (which has begun to be done in this paper), and to include them in an exportable file in gradebook form with each line separated by individual learner. This would be a good starting point for providing context to an instructor on performance in the tutor, and additional features and easy to use interfaces can be built in the future to further demonstrate learner performance.

Acknowledgement. The research described herein has been sponsored by the U.S Army Combat Capabilities Development Command – Soldier Center – Simulation and Training Technology Center. The statements and opinions expressed in this paper do not necessarily reflect the position or the policy of the United States Government, and no official endorsement should be inferred.

References

1. Goldberg, B.S., Hoffman, M.: Adaptive course flow and sequencing through the engine for management of adaptive pedagogy (EMAP). In: AIED Workshops (2015)
2. Goldberg, B., Brawner, K., Hoffman, M.: The GIFT architecture and features update: 2020 edition. In: Proceedings of the 8th Annual Generalized Intelligent Framework for Tutoring (GIFT) Users Symposium (GIFTSym8), p. 11. US Army Combat Capabilities Development Command–Soldier Center (2020)
3. Merrill, M. D.: Component display theory. Instr. Des. Theories Models: An overview of their current status 1, 282-333 (1983)
4. Owens, K., et al.: Synthetic training environment experiential learning for readiness (STEEL-R) demonstration. In: Generalized Intelligent Framework for Tutoring (GIFT) Users Symposium (GIFTSym10), p. 71 (2022)
5. Sinatra, A.M.: The 2022 instructor's guide to the generalized intelligent framework for tutoring (GIFT). In: Generalized Intelligent Framework for Tutoring (GIFT) Users Symposium (GIFTSym10), p. 21 (2022)
6. Sinatra, A.M., Robinson, R.L., Goldberg, B., Goodwin, G.: Generalized intelligent framework for tutoring (GIFT) master gunner course pilot study. In: Virtual Poster Presented at the 2022 Army University Learning Symposium (2022)
7. Sottilare, R.A., Brawner, K.W., Sinatra, A.M., Johnston, J.H.: An updated concept for a Generalized Intelligent Framework for Tutoring (GIFT). *GIFTtutoring. org*, 1–19 (2017)

Precision Learning Through Data Intelligence

Eric Watz[1]([⊠]) [iD], Peter Neubauer[2] [iD], Ramona Shires[3] [iD], and Jeremy May[1] [iD]

[1] Aptima, Inc., Fairborn, OH 45342, USA
{ewatz,jmay}@aptima.com
[2] Aptima, Inc., Bend, OR 97709, USA
pneubauer@aptima.com
[3] Aptima, Inc., Orlando, FL 32034, USA
rshires@aptima.com

Abstract. Simulations and learning environments often generate massive amounts of human performance data, which can be a challenge to manage and interpret in a meaningful manner. Lacking a context that provides meaning to data, it exists as information stored on computers, data centers, and cloud infrastructure. With the ever-increasing need to understand and act on learner performance data, there is a growing interest in tools and techniques that can help organizations transform performance data into actionable insights.

The assessment of human performance is critical to providing efficient and effective training. Modern training environments, especially live and virtual distributed environments, are rich with data representing multiple modalities and formats. One foundational challenge involves storing this wealth of data in a common format with metadata to support queries and analyses such as predictive models and proficiency tracking necessary to support managed learning over time.

This paper presents use cases behind a scalable data lake architecture and considerations for a common human performance assessment data storage method. In addition, lessons learned in storing, managing, and cleaning longitudinal data are presented. These methods provide insights into a data-centric solution that offers scalability, flexibility, maintainability, and usability.

Within a precision learning ecosystem, interoperability between applications can be achieved through proper application of software design methods and architectures, as well as information exchange based on established standards for data exchange. To effectively realize a precision approach to learning and training competency-based assessments, organizations need to be able to collect, integrate, and share performance data in a way that is both efficient and effective. This includes the use of enterprise-level tools and systems that can handle the scale and complexity of the data while also providing the necessary analytics and reporting capabilities. These solutions must be able to convert and present performance data in ways that are meaningful and actionable, such as by visualizing data in charts and graphs, or using advanced analytics techniques to uncover deeper insights into learner performance. This paper explores software architectures that enable rich data exchange and interoperability in a learning and training ecosystem and paper includes lessons learned from integrating modeling and simulation applications with cloud-native, big data handling tools.

Precision learning and training systems that fuse multiple data sources to predict current proficiency and future training needs are essential to managing

R. A. Sottilare and J. Schwarz (Eds.): HCII 2023, LNCS 14044, pp. 174–187, 2023.
https://doi.org/10.1007/978-3-031-34735-1_13

localized and longitudinal learning goals for individuals, teams, and teams of team. This is the foundation for adaptive proficiency-based training that improves training efficiency and effectiveness. One approach to leveraging performance data to inform proficiency-based training is through the use of competency-based assessments. The process of defining competencies is known as knowledge engineering and involves defining the specific skills and knowledge required for a particular role or task, then measuring an individual's performance against these defined competencies. By capturing and analyzing data on competency-based performance, organizations gain valuable insights into the strengths and weaknesses of their workforce, which can be used to inform training and development initiatives. This paper addresses the needs and data tagging requirements that enable robust capture and processing of learner performance. These metadata are shown as key enablers to unlocking actionable insights from information that began as purely data.

Keywords: Precision Learning · Microservices · Knowledge Engineering · Analytics · Data Lake · Event-based Architecture

1 A Need for Precision Learning

Training organizations, both commercial and military, face many challenges in today's fast-paced training environment. Training efforts are shifting away from a focus on training completion to one focused on performance-based outcomes. As a result, the need to measure and verify student performance and proficiency has never been more important. Even with this shift to a performance-based model, most training still focuses on "teaching to the class"; progressing an entire group of students through the schedule using a one-size-fits-all approach that that cannot fully consider each student's individual learning experiences or outcomes, nor the wide variation in student knowledge and skill levels [1]. Therefore, the challenge is to provide optimized experiences for development of an individual's knowledge, performance, and proficiency.

Precision learning has emerged as the convergence of 1) personalizing and tailoring training at scale, 2) adapting and optimizing a student's learning path, 3) emulating rich human feedback, and 4) transforming the student from a passive recipient of information to an active participant in their learning process. It leverages AI and other precision technologies to allow training to be exact and accurate, using a "surgical focus to deliver exactly the right content in the right way in order to create learning flow for each student" [4].

During one-on-one human tutoring, instructors offer hints and guidance in response to the students' verbal and nonverbal cues. They also modify the sequence of training content and direct the student to additional practice time or skill remediation activities, as required. In distributed and virtual learning environments, advanced learners can waste precious time reviewing material that they have already mastered, whereas marginal learners do not receive the additional remediation that they need to meet the course proficiency standards. Precision learning seeks to address this need [1].

Precision learning is data driven and deeply rooted in the science of learning. It is enabled through human performance measurement and providing high-quality feedback to students during blended learning activities. In the context of this paper, blended learning can mean any combination of computer-/web-based training, classroom training, and other training delivery mechanisms such as simulations, simulators, and or part-task trainers. Importantly, it aims to emulate, not replace, live instructor/mentor guidance. Although conventional learning theory states that it takes 10,000 h (or roughly 10 years) to achieve domain expertise, providing tailored, deliberate practice with relevant feed-back can greatly accelerate the time it takes novices to perform at a high level of proficiency [2, 3].

Although technology enables collection of large volumes of training data, more work is needed to leverage the data generated for truly assessing human performance and proficiency. Precise assessment of human performance is critical to providing efficient and effective training. Measures and assessments linked with performance constructs known as competencies can provide analysts with intelligent data to inform the tracking and management of learner state.

Competency-based assessments are a critical component of a precision learning and training system. The process of defining competencies is known as knowledge engineering and involves defining the specific skills and knowledge required for a particular role or task. These competencies are elicited from experts in the field by trained facilitators. Once the competencies are defined, an individual's performance can be measured against these defined competencies and can be linked to measures of performance and assessments. These competency-based assessments are an effective approach to leveraging performance data to inform proficiency-based training. Competency-based assessments also provide valuable insights into the strengths and weaknesses of the workforce, which can be used to inform training and development initiatives. For example, if a competency-based assessment reveals that a significant portion of the workforce lacks a particular skill, an organization can prioritize training and development activities to address this gap. In addition, competency-based assessments can be used to evaluate the effectiveness of training programs by comparing pre- and post-training assessments to measure improvements in competency levels.

To effectively leverage competency-based assessments, it is important to properly define and tag the data used in the assessments. Time spent developing the data tag classification structure is critical to properly analyzing the training data. By employing a well thought-out data tagging construct, data on the competencies being measured, the individual's performance against these competencies, and any additional context that may be relevant, such as the training program or development initiative that the individual participated in, can be robust and precise.

Another important aspect of using competency-based assessments is the ability to aggregate and analyze data on a larger scale. For example, organizations can compare competency levels across different departments or teams, or track changes in competency levels over time. By capturing and analyzing this data, organizations can identify trends and patterns in their workforce's performance, which can be used to inform strategic workforce planning and development activities. Instructors and decision makers can gain valuable insights into the strengths and weaknesses of their learners, which can be used to inform training and development initiatives and improve the overall efficiency and effectiveness of training programs. Therefore, proper data tagging and data management practices are essential to effectively leveraging competency-based assessments and realizing the full benefits of precision learning and training systems.

2 Storage and Tagging of Training Data

Data is essential to a precision learning ecosystem and is a requirement to understanding the efficiencies and effectiveness of training. Without data, instructors and individual learners rely on educated guesses and general-purpose curriculum, which leads to both under and over training. In the defense industry, it is imperative that warfighters receive the right training at the right time, improving readiness while also reducing costs. With actionable and intelligent training data, informed decisions can be made leading to better training and increased learner preparedness.

The area of computer-aided data-driven learning has existed since the late 1950s [9]. Today, the field faces increasing new challenges handling with the volumes of data collected from distributed heterogenous systems and complex requirements. It is imperative that data-driven learning systems be capable of transforming data from their initial representation as binary 0's and 1's into actionable information at the syntactic level. This would be the equivalent of decoding computer network packets exchanged between interoperable distributed training simulators. At the semantic level, these learning systems must begin to correlate the syntactic information into knowledge. In the final stage of the data transformation cycle, as shown in Fig. 1, the pragmatic level sees 1's and 0's that were received as a message or network packet being translated into intelligence [10]. For the purpose of this paper, this end state is labeled as "training intelligence". At the pragmatic level, we reach a thorough understanding of the data's origins, its structure, its applicability to particular training domains, and its meaning to learner performance.

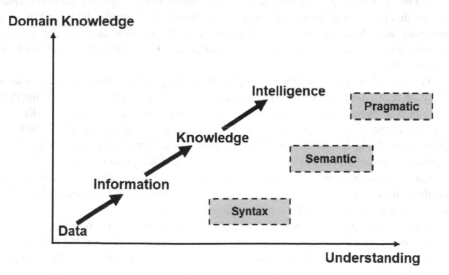

Fig. 1. From Data to Intelligence (adapted from Weigand and Paschke, 2012)

A data-driven learning system must represent data at these levels to properly measure, track, and report learner proficiencies over time.

The U.S. Department of Defense's Digital Modernization Strategy [11] identifies data as a strategic asset and prioritizes "data being visible, accessible, understandable, trusted, and interoperable" to "generate insights that answer critical operational and business questions" [11]. While the document places a significant emphasis on cyber security and operations, the overall recognition that data has value and the associated Big Data Platform approach applies to human performance data, too [11]. It is noteworthy that human performance and training data is one facet of larger force-wide data management and analytics challenges.

Shifting training approaches from what has been the traditional focus on rigid, syllabus driven training to focus on data-driven decisions, known as proficiency-based training (PBT), demands technical and organizational advancements. On the technical side, increasingly sophisticated distributed training environments offer a wealth of data, such as radio communications, electronic chat, data links, video, network data between interoperable simulators, expert observers, and self-report surveys. Live aircraft may also be rich sources of data [12]. Managing, analyzing, and producing actionable results from the data is an area of active work both within the U.S. Air Force (USAF) and across the DoD enterprise [13]. On the organizational side, shifting from continuation training approaches, such as the Ready Aircrew Program (RAP), to proficiency-based approaches is underway within the USAF and other organizations. The process is incremental as the organizations explore the options and drive technical requirements [14]. The USAF Air Combat Command's (ACC) "Future Training Concepts – 2020" vision identifies the need to "[integrate] live and virtual training outcomes … [to] take full advantage of all training to produce combat-ready warfighters and accurate pictures of unit readiness" [15]. Training outcomes data integrated across live and virtual environments is pivotal to maximizing force readiness with limited budgets. The 2021 Deputy Secretary of Defense's "Creating Data Advantage" [16] memorandum outlines the unsurprising path to this integration through open specifications for automated data interfaces. An enterprise-wide learning system architecture must permit rapid analysis and retrieval of multi-format multi-modal data across traditional silos of human performance and training data.

This data-driven approach to training requires integrating performance assessment, data collection, data storage, and proficiency prediction into a robust system that combines best of breed features from data analytics platforms and provides feedback to trainees, instructors, and decision makers. The overall system, generally known as a Knowledge Management System (KMS), "helps instructors provide their students with learning materials and activities while tracking participation and progress through data systems and assessments" [17]. The implementations and capabilities vary considerably, but data storage is a common requirement. Other literature and commercial products address needs and benefits of the overarching KMS [18].

The transformation of data into actionable training intelligence requires a different foundation of data collection, storage, and processing than traditional big data applications. Building on related work from the big data field as it relates to capturing human performance information from operational and training environments, we focused on defining the challenges, requirements, and guiding principles for the data storage aspect.

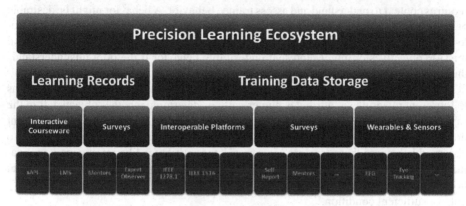

Fig. 2. Hierarchy of Data Storage to Enable Precision Learning

The training data storage suggested in Fig. 2 has multiple users with distinct needs. These needs are expressed in the form of "user stories", a technique commonly used within Agile software development practices [19]. We define user stories related to data storage and analytics of human performance data as follows:

- *Researcher*: As a researcher, I want to explore all the data with familiar analytics tools so that I may advance the state-of-the-art for proficiency-based training.
- *Learner*: As a learner, I want to promptly view my data following training events and visualize insights into specific nuances of my performance. The data should help me understand what went right and identify areas for improvement.
- *Instructors and Decision Makers*: As an Instructor or Decision Maker, I want action-able, trust-worthy data for planning and execution so that I may be safe and effective with limited resources and best understand the ready state of my forces.
- *Engineer*: As an engineer, I want a maintainable, secure, scalable, and extensible system so that may be used to rapidly deliver actionable results to operational users and research teams.

While it is arguably possible to define additional user categories and user stories, these broad categorizations are sufficient for developing data storage requirements. Given these users, a training data storage solution must meet several requirements. First, the solution must support proficiency-based adaptive training in operational and research contexts. Additionally, the solution must store multi-modal, multi-format, multi-source opera-tional and training data and provide for forward-looking analytic capabilities. Finally, the solution must provide an extensible platform to solve current and future storage, retrieval, and analysis problems.

3   Adding Context to Data

Beyond the technical aspects of data collection, storage and processing, training data requires context to understand and assess trainee behavior. A behavior might be desirable or undesirable depending on circumstances. For example, an aircraft entering a surface-to-air threat's engagement zone might represent desirable behavior to achieve critical mission objectives or might represent undesirable behavior if the pilot misunderstands the threat's capabilities.

Measurement in science refers to rules for assigning values to object attributes so as to represent quantities of attributes numerically or determine whether objects fall in the same or different category with respect to a given attribute. Performance measurement differs slightly. Performance measurement is a process of assigning numerical values to observed behaviors that represent aspects of latent attributes like intelligence, motivation, knowledge, etc. We can measure observed behaviors that represent performance; however, in a learning and training environment measurement by itself is a necessary but not sufficient condition.

To understand human performance, we also require the concept of assessments. Assessment is a process of evaluating a learner's current state against a desired state (e.g., goal, objective, standard). In an educational setting, students and teachers may be interested in assessing how much have the students learned compared to other students in the region, state, nation, etc. In a military setting, trainees and instructors may be interested in assessing trainees' proficiency against established norms or qualifications. Examples of this assessment are military fitness training exercises such as pushups, pull ups, and a timed run over a specified distance. In the United States, middle-school and high-schools leverage educational assessments to determine where students are on their learning journey, how much they've learned, their strengths, and opportunity areas for additional growth [5]. Stacy et al. formalizes these concepts [20] and indicates that training produces raw data, both system-based data collected directly from training devices and subjective-data like evaluations or surveys. Measurements, such as range to the nearest threat or G-load on an airframe, are derived from raw data but do not directly indicate acceptable or poor performance. Assessments add context-sensitive interpretations of measurements, like releasing a weapon inside or outside accepted ranges. Context includes the events and other information surrounding the behavior stream, such as adding new assessments based on risk of injury to civilians. Multiple contexts may apply simultaneously. Context may be static throughout the training event or dynamically changing.

A training event is created to allow learners to demonstrate their mastery of learning objectives. When learning objectives are linked with learning events, precision learning systems have the necessary context for understanding and evaluating human performance data. Absent an understanding of the learning objectives for the event, precision learning solutions are unable to assess the learner's performance in that event in more detail than a level of course completed or mission success.

4 Enabling Precision Learning Through Systems Design

A precision learning and training approach requires integrating performance assessment, data collection, data storage, proficiency prediction into a robust system that combines best of breed features from data analytics platforms and provides feedback to trainees, instructors, and decision makers. The overall system, generally known as a Precision Learning Ecosystem (PLE), can assist instructors in providing their students with learning materials and activities while tracking participation and progress through data systems and assessments [17]. PLEs are a collection of technologies linked together through a common systems design, and intended to enable robust data capture, processing, storage, and retrieval capabilities for human performance data. PLEs integrate with Knowledge Management Systems and provide additional services that deliver recommendations to maintain the learner's range of skill state at a high state of readiness. The PLE system architecture is a key consideration when implementing a solution capable of tracking and managing learner states over time.

Effective PLE systems designs can promote data intelligence through robust and extensible storage, query, and analytics options. One approach is to build outwards from a scalable data lake architecture. This type of architecture consists of a data management system that has been developed to handle the massive amounts of performance data generated in simulations and learning environments. It is designed to store the data in a common format with metadata to support queries and analyses. This architecture is scalable, flexible, maintainable, and usable. A scalable data lake architecture is based on the data lake concept, in which a flexible data repository stores multiple types of data in its raw or common data format. These raw formats may include structured, semi-structured, and unstructured data. The data lake design provides a means for multiple applications and software services to query and access its data. For instance, features as documenting APIs, defining the data contracts, and providing examples further ease the burden of data querying and data access. When an example application is provided, other applications can more seamlessly request, trust, and view available data.

A data lake is an improvement over data warehouse models, structured data schemas and the 'single source of truth' concept, because it stores relational data from domain specific applications, and non-relational data from other sources including mobile apps, IoT devices, text-based feeds, and sensors. In a data lake you can store all of your data without up-front design or the need to know what questions you might need answers for in the future. Using the data lake's backend storage capabilities, novel types of analytics such as SQL queries, big data analytics, full text search, and machine learning can be used to turn captured information into intelligent data [7].

Organizations store data in a variety of formats, from human readable text-based formats such as JSON, to well established Big Data formats like Avro and Parquet, to binary simulation data that complies with the Distributed Interactive Simulation (DIS) [21] standard, without having to convert the data to a specific format. We often observe that multiple interwoven communications and data formats standards are employed in operational and training environments. For example, the Experience API (xAPI) is widely used across industry and government for storing and exchanging learning records [6, 23]. The High Level Architecture (HLA) and the DIS protocols are two examples of network protocols enabling interoperable distributed training simulations [22]. In addition to DoD modeling and simulation standards, information can be collected from Internet Relay Communication (IRC) systems in the form of chat data. Chat data is represented in IEEE-standardized formats and is communicated via XMPP (Extensible Messaging and Presence Protocol) or IRC. Comma-separated value (CSV) data are exported from collaboration tools such as Microsoft Excel. Data captured from survey tools often contains highly variable content. This content is often text-based in nature and may require knowledge of the specific survey tool to understand the data; however, a precision learning architecture that supports Extract – Transform – Load (ETL) data processing pipelines can be easily adapted to ingest and store this new information. The precision learning ecosystem's architecture should abstract the details of data formats and may leverage indexer technologies to aggregate disparate data and enable searches over multiple data formats.

Additionally, the precision learning ecosystem system design offers significant scalability. It can handle the massive amounts of data generated by simulations and learning environments without sacrificing performance. The system architecture achieves this using horizontally scalable technologies, which means that PLE services can be easily extended by adding more nodes to a database cluster or additional compute resources. This horizontal scalability allows the system to grow as the volume of data increases over time. Software designed for and deployed in containers can also be scaled through the use of container orchestration software.

Systems that process human performance and training data must maintain a flexible design. This concept manifests itself as the system deferring understanding and modeling data until a point in time when the data is relevant to current questions and analytics. In contrast, traditional relational data storage requires substantial up-front effort to store and model the data. Given the volume of data available in a typical training environment, much of that up-front effort would be wasted; therefore, a flexible systems design approach to data facilitates relevant analytics faster and with less effort. Using an event-based architecture and microservices, new services are seamlessly added into the precision learning ecosystem. As new services come online, they operate on existing data and events produced from the PLE and generate new events that are stored in the data lake backend and consumed by other downstream services.

A microservices architecture provides benefits that can improve the overall performance and reliability of an application. One of the key benefits is improved scalability. Microservices allow for independent scaling of specific services, which can lead to better resource utilization and improved performance. This means that if one microservice experiences a higher demand, it can be scaled up independently of other microservices, allowing the rest of the application to continue functioning as normal. New microservices are added and deployed without requiring a full rebuild of the entire system, thereby saving developer time and delivering higher value to the end user.

Microservice architectures deliver additional resilience over monolith architectures. By decomposing a monolithic application into smaller, independent services, the failure of one service is isolated and does not affect the entire system. This results in improved resilience and fault tolerance, making the application more robust and less likely to experience downtime. These improvements are particularly important for mission-critical applications where availability is a key concern.

Faster deployment cycles are another benefit of microservices architecture. Since microservices are smaller and less complex than monolithic systems, individual microservices can be developed, tested, and deployed faster and more reliably than larger monoliths. This enables teams to innovate and deliver new features to customers more quickly. In addition, because microservices can be developed and maintained by smaller teams, collaboration is improved which leads to faster problem resolution and higher code quality. These factors combined can help organizations reduce engineering costs and increase the value proposition to their customers.

In addition to microservices, event-driven software architectures can enable a precision learning ecosystem to deliver data intelligence to the end user. Event-driven software architectures provide several benefits that can improve the overall performance and reliability of an application. These architectures consider data as 'streams of immutable facts'. Systems built around event-driven architectures offer persistent storage of event streams, which allows for the decoupling of time from the processing of the event. One benefit being, historic data is stored and made available to microservices that need it. Data entering such a system is placed into a stream, and the various microservices within the system operate on these data streams, performing computations, analytics, and calculations, and in turn these services generate (or emit) new events. Thus providing reliable, repeatable computations at any given time. These new events become part of the shared source of truth in the event-driven software architecture and are available for consumption by downstream services.

Another benefit is that of decoupled systems. Event-driven architecture allows for the decoupling of systems, which allows for greater flexibility and improved maintainability. This means that changes made to one part of the system will not impact other parts, reducing the risk of unintended consequences.

Event-driven architectures positively contribute to the system's scalability. By handling events asynchronously, systems that consume this information can be horizontally scaled, adding more consumers to handle increased loads as needed. This makes event-driven systems well-suited for applications that experience fluctuations in demand, as they can scale to meet the needs of the system in real-time. Compared to monolithic solutions, systems designed around an event-driven architecture can scale according to the data needs, whether it be the amount of data or the number of events that need to be processed [8].

4.1 Importance of Correct Time Keeping

Events during training, especially training simulations, are often time sensitive. Correctly keeping time in a training event is important to assessing the learner, measurement computation, and synchronizing distributed simulations and systems. When assessing a pilot's performance, a pilot may perform a maneuver correctly, but at the wrong time, likely indicating poor performance. Incorrect time keeping in measurement computation may yield inaccurate results. For example, calculating an aircraft's acceleration requires position/orientation data combined with elapsed time. If the system does not keep the correct elapsed time, the measurement will produce incorrect results. Time is critical in distributed training where the experiences of multiple learners must be synchronized. For example, a learner in the role of an air traffic controller must observe the same activities at the same time as another learner in the role of a pilot. If the pilot is receiving directions based on an event that happened ten minutes ago, the training will be frustrating and unreliable to the learner. Many types of learning and training, like watching pre-recorded videos, are not time sensitive as they rely on the learner to study at their own pace. However, time-sensitive interactive simulations are increasingly common with the emergence of affordable virtual reality and augmented reality technologies.

To correctly process time-sensitive training data, the system must distinguish between event and processing times. The event time is the moment when something occurs within the training, such as the timestamp when a pilot achieves a particular airspeed. Processing time is the moment when the system applies algorithms or criteria to the data and arrives at a measurement or assessment. Given that data may move through a multi-step processing pipeline, a single event may have multiple related processing times. However, event and processing times are always different. Any real system has latency and inter-dependencies between data elements. The difference between processing time and event time (the lag or skew) varies depending on overall system workload, system availability, data volume, and complexity of the computations. If the time difference is small, the system appears real-time to human observers and delivers results almost as the learning events occur.

Oftentimes, real-time processing is unnecessary to achieve learning objectives. For example, students and instructors often do not have time to review outcomes until after the training concludes. Instructional designers must consider the data processing requirements and deliver the time constraints to system engineers. It is, however, critical to distinguish and track event and processing time. Should developers blur this distinction, it will be difficult to deliver reliable, reproducible, and trustworthy measurements and assessments necessary for precision learning.

Decoupling an event-driven system from event time to rely on processing time allows certain components to operate independently of real-time. Why is this architecture decision important to a precision learning ecosystem? It enables measurements that require additional compute resources can operate slower than the measurement system's internal clock. Examples of this are highly complex algorithms requiring iteration over multiple large lists, and performing mathematical operations on the pairs. Such an example would be a pairwise-comparison algorithm, wherein every friendly entity is compared against every non-friendly entity and the algorithm then runs an iterative calculation to determine the precise maneuver parameters at which the friendly must maneuver to avoid an incoming weapon. Algorithms of this complexity are capable of running real-time when the number of players in the event is low. With a 4 vs. 4 event and assuming 8 iterations of the maneuver parameters inner algorithm, each 'tick' of the pairwise comparison measurement would generate (4 x 4 x 8) 128 comparisons. In today's training and operational environments, the number of players can exceed 100; assuming at any given time there are 30 vs 30 players active and with the same number of inner algorithm iterations, we now require 7,200 comparisons per 'tick' of the measurement algorithm. For a system-based measurement tool that operates on an internal clock of 10 Hz, this measurement algorithm alone requires 72,000 calculations per second along with 900 list iterations. As exercises become ever larger, the challenges of running advanced performance algorithms increase significantly. Advanced computing techniques such as cloud-native lambda functions may be used to mitigate some of these challenges but are often unavailable in the secure training environments where these algorithms operate. Using an event-based architecture where the measurement can operate on event time would allow the measurement to effectively run slower than other parts of the system and perform its calculations using available compute resources. This architecture results in an ability for the measure to process data when it has completed the previous calculations and is ready for the next iteration.

Event- driven measurements also enable computations to occur faster than real-time if the data are available, such as during a post mission review session where the replay is occurring at 5x normal speed it may be possible to calculate certain measures using this data stream. Another example for above-real time measurement calculations is for post mission analytics that may rely on multiple sources of information which may not be available during a mission. Many live systems such as aircraft contain data cartridges or "pucks" that capture system information during flight. After the training event concludes and the aircraft has landed, technicians remove the data cartridge and the puck data must are downloaded, parsed, and stored in a precision learning ecosystem's data lake. Once the data have been stored, measures that require this information can now be run and their results added to the system's backend for additional analytics.

The use of events, and by extension, data-driven APIs allows for loose coupling between components, reducing the impact of changes in one part of the system on other parts. This loose coupling makes event-driven systems more flexible and adaptable to change. It also makes it easier to integrate new components into the system, as they do not need to be tightly coupled to the rest of the system.

Through employment of event-based architectures and microservices, we have illustrated how these systems design concepts apply to a precision learning ecosystem, and how data are captured, processed, stored, and transformed to deliver data intelligence to users. The PLE provides a robust data backend that is accessed by multiple applications and microservices and event based architectures allow organizations to easily access and use their performance data. These architectures also support the expert and exploratory analytics and reporting capabilities, which enable organizations to convert and present performance data in ways that are meaningful and actionable.

5 Conclusion

Efficient and effective training relies on assessment of learner performance. When learning objectives are defined and linked to training events, this makes it possible to assess learners based on their demonstrated mastery of proficiencies. Training environments produce volumes of information in the form of data. These volumes of data can be captured, processed, and transformed into training intelligence to enable proficiency-based training and assessment. This paper describes several methods that, when applied to a precision learning ecosystem, can reduce the gap between data and training intelligence.

Central to this data transformation is the need to store and manage the information generated from learning and training environments. A robust data backend that supports rapid onboarding and integration of novel data formats is paramount in the data to training intelligence transformation process. Precision learning ecosystems must account of multi-modal, multi-format data capture, processing, storage, and management pipelines and must align that information with data generated by internal services. In addition to data storage another method of transforming data into training intelligence is through knowledge engineering. Knowledge engineering methods and processes generate the learning constructs, or competencies, that are required to provide essential context to date. Context provides meaning to data; with meaning, the data become drivers of proficiency-based assessments.

The transformation of data into training intelligence is positively impacted through effective systems design. Precision learning ecosystems are complex systems of systems and leverage knowledge management, knowledge engineering, measure and assessment technologies and recommendation engines. This paper describes lessons learned in processing large volumes of information at the system level and illustrates system design concepts such as microservices and event-driven architectures as a means to effective design principles that drive precision learning ecosystems. Microservices provide a means for complex systems to be designed for resilience and scalability. Event-based architectures were introduced as another method key to the transformation of data into training intelligence. These architectures pair well with microservices and focus on the data within the system as concurrent streams of truth; the system's data are added into topics which can be queried, replayed, and operated on as individual microservices support.

This paper illustrates the value of data and software systems architecture in transforming data into actionable insights to enable effective and efficient precision training. Precision learning is driven by data intelligence which arises from sophisticated training environments linked to learning objectives, data capture and transformation using contextual driven algorithms, and building resilient systems architectures. These methods and engineering designs enable transformation data into actionable insights and which provide a foundation for precision learning.

References

1. Spruill, J., Beaubien, J., Kleinman, L: Precision learning at CSCS: teaching to the student, not just the class. In: Interservice Industry Training, Simulation and Education Conference (2020)
2. Ericsson, K.A., Charness, N.: Expert performance: its structure and acquisition. Am. Psychol. **49**(8), 725–747 (1994)
3. Ericsson, K.A., Krampe, R.T., Tesch-Romer, C.: The role of deliberate practice in the acquisition of expert performance. Psychol. Rev. **100**(3), 363–406 (1993)
4. Serfaty, D.: "Human Performance in the Age of AI", Plenary Address, 2019 Naturalistic Decision Making Conference, San Francisco (2019)
5. MAP Suite. https://www.nwea.org/the-map-suite. Accessed 06 Feb 2023
6. Rustici Software. xAPI Adopters. xAPI.com (2020).https://xapi.com/adopters/. Accessed 01 May 2020
7. What is a Data Lake? https://aws.amazon.com/big-data/datalakes-and-analytics/what-is-a-data-lake/?nc=sn&loc=2. Accessed 07 Feb 2023
8. THE FOUR ADVANTAGES OF AN EVENT-DRIVEN ARCHITECTURE. https://www.voltactivedata.com/blog/2021/03/event-driven-architecture/#:~:text=3.-,Scalability,that%20need%20to%20be%20processed. Accessed 07 Feb 2023

9. Dear, B.: The Friendly Orange Glow: The Untold Story of the PLATO System and the Dawn of Cyberculture. Pantheon Books, New York, USA (2017)
10. Weigand, H., Paschke, A.: The Pragmatic Web: Putting Rules in Context (2012). RuleML
11. Department of Defense. "DoD Digital Modernization Strategy" (2019). https://media. defense.gov/2019/Jul/12/2002156622/-1/-1/1/DOD-DIGITAL-MODERNIZATION-STR ATEGY-2019.PDF. Accessed 09 Feb 2023
12. Noah, D., Bennett, W.: Secure live virtual and constructive advanced training environment (SLATE). In: Simulation Interoperability Workshop, 2019-SIW-036 (2019)
13. Watz, E., Neubauer, P., Kegley, J., Bennett, W.: Managing learning and tracking performance across multiple mission sets. In: Interservice/Industry Training, Simulation, and Education Conference (I/ITSEC), Paper No. 18304 (2018)
14. United States Government Accountability Office, "Air Force Training: Further Analysis and Planning Needed to Improve Effectiveness", GAO-16–684, (2016)
15. Future Training Concepts – 2020. Air Combat Command, U.S. Air Force (2019)
16. Department of Defense, "Creating Data Advantage" (2021). https://media.defense.gov/ 2021/May/10/2002638551/-1/-1/0/DEPUTY-SECRETARY-OF-DEFENSE-MEMORA NDUM.PDF
17. Falvo, D.A., Johnson, B.F.: The use of learning management systems in the United States. TechTrends: Link. Res. Pract. Impr. Learn. **51**(2), 40–45 (2007)
18. Bennett, W., Berlingo, M., Tripp, L., Watz, E.: Creating systems to actually manage learning: creation of a service oriented architecture. In: Simulation Interoperability Workshop – Fall 2016, 16F-SIW-043 (2016)
19. Scott, A.: User Stories: An Agile Introduction (2003). http://www.agilemodeling.com/artifa cts/userStory.htm#InitialFormal. Accessed 02 June 2020
20. Stacy, W., Merket, D., Puglisi, M., Haimson, C.: Representing context in simulator-based human performance measurement. In: Interservice/Industry Training, Simulation, and Education Conference (I/ITSEC), Orlando, FL (2006)
21. IEEE 1278.1–2012: Standard for Distributed Interactive Simulation – Application Protocols. Institute of Electrical and Electronics Engineers, Computer Society (2012)
22. IEEE 1516–2010: Standard for Modeling and Simulation (M&S) High Level Architecture (HLA) – Framework and Rules. Institute of Electrical and Electronics Engineers, Computer Society (2010)
23. Advanced Distributed Learning Initiative, U.S. Department of Defense. "xAPI Specification". https://github.com/adlnet/xAPI-Spec. Accessed 01 May 2020 (2017)

Individual Differences in Adaptive Learning

Learning to Take the Right Turn – Which Learning Media is Best Suited to Learn a Sequence of Actions to Solve a Rubik's Cube?

Daniela Altun[1]([✉]) and Daniel Schulz[2]

[1] Fraunhofer FKIE, Bonn, Germany
Daniela.altun@fkie.fraunhofer.de
[2] Universität zu Köln, Cologne, Germany
Daniel.schulz@uni-koeln.de

Abstract. The present study compares the three learning tools paper instructions, video instructions and virtual reality when learning a sequence of actions. 60 participants are divided into those three learning tool groups and are given the task of learning a certain solution sequence of eight steps for the Rubik's Cube with the assigned learning tool. Participants in the video instructions and paper instructions groups also receive a real Rubik's Cube for practice. In order to rule out inter-individual differences between the subjects, we recorded the ability to rotate mentally. Subjects had unlimited learning time until they can reproduce what they have learned without access to the learning tool.

We assessed the retention performance one week later - without renewed contact with the learning tool. A transfer task followed in which the participants had to transfer their ability to perform the newly learned 8-step-sequence to a similar solution sequence. We measured performance using a developed scoring system. This study examines whether the learning tools differ in terms of retention performance, transfer performance and usability. A correlation between the mental rotation ability and the learning success can provide information about the adaptation of learning materials.

Keywords: Learning tools · media · VR · Virtual Reality · Video · Paper · Transfer · Retention · Usability

1 Introduction

Learning is an important factor in all our lives. We learn how to walk, how to ride a bicycle, how to drive a car and how to do basic math. We train in order to improve, learn a new set of skills and as we keep learning, we might not always be aware which learning tool is actually best suited for a given learning context or even to us as an individual.

Various factors influence learning success. On the one hand the individual learner type and depth of processing impact the individual retention [1, 2] on the other hand the learning situation or the learning tool used [3]. Hasselhorn and Gold (2013) summarize that the type of learning, which can be determined by the depth of processing, the given

R. A. Sottilare and J. Schwarz (Eds.): HCII 2023, LNCS 14044, pp. 191–205, 2023.
https://doi.org/10.1007/978-3-031-34735-1_14

structure and the guidance provided by a person or a program, has a major effect on learning success [4]. This raises the question of how we can use training resources to improve learning success [4]. Various approaches are possible to clarify this question. On the one hand, we can discuss the didactics, that determine how the training material is embedded in the transfer of knowledge; on the other hand, different implementations within a training material can be compared. Another starting point is to compare the suitability of different training aids on an identical learning object. Some studies chose this approach to compare a learning outcome based on the training tools used [3, 5, 6]. Since the comparison usually refers to specific application contexts in which one medium/training tool proves to be more advantageous than the other, there are still many areas and comparisons that have received little attention so far [7]. These comparisons often take place to evaluate further development of a specific training area, from the results of which general implications can rarely be derived. In addition, previous comparisons or studies on the effect of training tools often have the limitation that either only one training tool was tested against a control group that had no access to a training tool (e.g. [8]), or by adding the tested learning tool without having a comparison condition (e.g. [9]). This type of study is criticized by Clark and Feldon (2014), since in this form it is almost impossible to make any statement about the quality of a tool [10]. Studies that directly compare training tools with each other often do so by comparing only two training tools: one that is currently used in training and a new one that is evaluated on the basis of the comparison [3, 11, 12].

Other factors that are only rarely examined are the effect of the training tool on retention at a later point in time and the application of what has been learned to demonstrate the learned competence in a transfer task. In order to be able to make a broader comparison, we compare three training tools (instructions on paper, via video and in virtual reality (VR)) in this study. We chose a task that is as neutral as possible. Participants had to learn a sequence of steps on the Rubik's Cube and a transfer task. This is allows us to draw conclusions for a broad variety of training areas. We selected the learning materials in such a way that they are either currently relevant in education/training (paper and video) or in future education (VR). This study aims at shedding some light on which learning tool (paper, video, VR) is opportune to achieve the highest learning success and learning transfer as well as the highest usability scores when it comes to learning an action sequence.

1.1 Paper Instructions

Paper instructions in the form of written text are a well-known learning material. Mayer, Hegarty, Mayer and Campbell (2005) show that paper instructions also have their advantages using written and statically illustrated instructions [13]. They presented the subjects with explanations for complex relationships in their study. The result shows that these were learned better or at least equally well with static images compared to an animated representation [13]. Which, in the author's opinion, speaks against an unrestricted advantage of moving images and thus shows advantages to the classic knowledge transfer via paper in this area. Al Madi and Khan (2015) also found partial benefits for written text in their analysis of their study [5]. They found that subjects who received information in text form were better able to integrate it into existing knowledge. However, when it came to concept recognition, they found an advantage using video.

1.2 Video Instructions

Videos are well suited as a learning material in many cases. Moving pictures can explain complex issues, changes over time or connections between things in an easy perceivable way. In the field of e-learning, the use of videos is becoming increasingly popular and is considered to be very relevant for the future [14, 15]. Herzog and Sieck (2011) perceive a growing proportion and increasing use of video instructions, referring to the highly frequented learning channels on YouTube [16].

Choi and Johnson (2007) found advantages in using videos compared to texts for problem-based instructions [17]. The benefit of the videos was greater learner satisfaction and better understanding. In addition, the participants of the video-based instruction performed better on a test one month later than those instructed by text. Therefore, Choi and Johnson (2007) argue that video-based instructions lead to better retention than text-based instructions [17]. The result confirms one of their earlier studies, in which - without measuring retention performance - they asked participants about the subjective perception with regard to retention [18]. In the field of manufacturing technology, Grosskreutz et al. (2018) found no significant differences in the performance of the students between a classic lecture and one with the use of video material [9, 12]. Nevertheless, they were able to see a positive trend in the test results in the multi-year comparison. On average, students rated the use of videos as more advantageous. Expanding the range of learning opportunities with videos has also proven to be beneficial in the field of dentistry [9]. They found here that students who used the additional video material achieved a higher score in the final test or were better able to compensate for initial difficulties. However, the authors are critical of replacing the lecture completely by videos.

1.3 Virtual Reality Instructions

Virtual Reality (VR) is a learning tool that has not yet been able to establish itself on a broad scale, as the acquisition costs are a hurdle and it has to fit into existing lessons in a meaningful way [7]. There are also many technical variants, which are summarized under the term VR. Steuer (1992) writes that virtual reality is often defined by the technical component [19]. For him, this includes a computer, a head-mounted display and an operating option with the hands, referred to as "goggles 'n' gloves". This technical definition aptly describes the type of VR used in the study.

Since VR is said to have great potential [7], there are various studies that deal with their possible use in different areas. In the medical field alone, there are various approaches to this. Thus Gurusamy, K. Selvan et al. (2009) summarized 23 studies in a review for the field of laparoscopy alone, which compared either VR with video, VR with a classic laparoscopy trainer or VR with no training [20]. In this review, the authors concluded that training with VR achieves results that are at least as good as training with video trainers and recommend the use of VR as a supplement to classic laparoscopy trainers. Torkington et al. (2001), who compared the learning outcomes of VR trainers with the classic laparoscopy trainer, found no differences in performance between the two learning tools [21].

Lacko (2020) shows that a learning unit with VR can have positive effects on retaining the information presented in the area of safety training in companies [3]. The author shows that the participants of the VR condition answered more questions correctly in the final test (97% to 87% correct answers) compared to the classic presentation with video and lecture by the supervisor. In another test - one month later - an even clearer picture emerged (87% to 68% correct answers). This effect was also found in another study [22], in which a different VR technique (VR Power Wall) was used. In the subject of astrophysics, a case study from 2016 - conducted by Beijing Bluefocus E-Commerce Co., Ltd. And Beijing iBokan Wisdom Mobile Internet Technology Training Institutions - an advantage in learning concepts of astrophysics using VR over the previous teaching method (frontal teaching, videos) [23].

Checca and Bustillo (2020) found inconclusive results in their study [11]. They presented a virtual city tour either by video or by VR in the historic old town of Briviesca (Spain). In the subsequent knowledge test, the groups differed depending on the previous way of presenting the facts. Visually presented facts and the locations of historically significant buildings were, on average, better retained in the VR condition than in the video condition - while students in the video condition retained video information better on average than students in the VR condition. Overall, it shows that VR can be used effectively and purposefully in various areas. There is a lot of ongoing research on the usage of VR in training, especially in the medical field. The aim there is to replace expensive equipment as well as offering realistic trainings while excluding anyone getting harmed.

2 Research Questions and Hypotheses

It can be derived from Dale's (1946, quoted after Hasselhorn & Gold, 2013) information processing theory, known as the cone of experience, that the learning media paper, video and VR can have an influence on retention performance by addressing different sensory modalities [4]. In addition, previous comparative studies show that the choice of learning material can affect retention (also over time). The following questions arise from this:

1. Does the retention performance differ after one week, depending on the training tool used?
2. Does the transfer performance differ depending on the training tool used?
3. Does the assessment of task difficulty differ depending on the training tool?
4. Do the training tools differ in the assessment of usability?

The assumption that the transfer performance might differ between the groups cannot be derived theoretically due to the lack of studies and is therefore an exploratory question. The aim of this question is to find out whether, in addition to retention performance, transfer performance also benefits from the choice of learning material. If the performance data shows no differences between the learning materials, the choice of learning material can be based on the learner's preference. Therefore, usability and UX aspects are also collected. This results in the following hypotheses:

H1: Subjects in the virtual reality condition achieve higher or the same point values in retention performance on average than subjects in the paper and video condition.

H2: Subjects in the virtual reality condition achieve higher or the same point values in transfer performance on average than subjects in the paper and video condition.

H3: Subjects in the video condition achieve, on average, achieve higher scores in retention than subjects in the paper condition.

H4: Subjects in the video condition achieve, on average, higher point values in transfer performance than subjects in the paper condition.

H5: There are differences in the usability and UX evaluation between the learning tool groups.

3 Method

We collected data from our participants at two timestamps (one week apart from each other for each participant) and assigned the learning tools to the subjects in a pseudo-randomized manner according to gender at the first session. We recorded mental rotation as a covariate at the beginning of the first session and the questionnaires on task difficulty and usability at the end of both sessions. We asked the questions about the difficulty of the task related to the learning phase on the first session, and on the second relating to the learning achievement and the implementation of the transfer task. On both timestamps, the usability questionnaires (SEQ and UEQ) referred to the training tools used in the learning phase; one direct query of usability, one retrospective assessment of the learning tool. There were no repeated measurements for the variables of retention and transfer performance, since participants learned only during the first appointment and we used the query to determine the learning success. We collected the two dependent variables, retention and transfer benefit, during the second appointment. We describe the procedure in more detail in Sect. 3.4.

3.1 Pilot Studies

Before we started the experiment, we clarified what retention performance can be expected. We tested our design and expectation of a potential retention performance on one person using paper instructions. Furthermore, we tested the VR application with another person and checked whether the learning time did not exceed a tolerable level for the test persons.

Based on the results of the two preliminary tests, we decided from a methodological point of view not to implement any further learning unit in the second appointment, since we expected that some subjects would remember the sequence of steps completely and would therefore not need any further learning. Furthermore, for better comparability between the groups, we decided that the subjects in the paper and video condition get a real Rubik's cube (providing the advantage of the haptics of a real Rubik's cube), since VR offers the opportunity to interact with the cube, i.e. to practice, which is a privilege and thus a falsification of the results favorable to the VR. Although this reduces the derived advantage of VR from Dale's (quoted from Hasselhorn & Gold, 2013) information processing theory of the cone of experience, previous studies and the advantage of VR being able to display the instructions directly on the object itself still speaks for the hypotheses made.

3.2 Participants

We set a sample size of $N = 60$ (with $n = 20$), to calculate the preregistered ANOVA without limitations [24, 25]. We excluded participants with knowledge about solutions depending the Rubik's Cube and people with epilepsy a priori.

Within the first 60 participants, two were not able to take part in the second session due to illness. Another participant did not finish the first session. To reach the targeted sample size we recruited another three participants and matched them by gender to the participants that did not finish both sessions.

The final sample size was $N = 60$ (30 female; age $= 27.2$; $SD = 6.29$) consisting of employees of a research institution ($n = 32$) and students ($n = 28$). Colleagues did not get any compensation for participation, college students got credits points that they need in order to get their diploma. Groups are equal regarding gender distribution.

3.3 Materials

We used three different learning tools: paper instruction (see Fig. 1.), an instructional video (see Fig. 2) and a VR learning application (see Fig. 3 and Fig. 4). The paper instruction included a picture showing the eight steps and a written step-by-step instruction. The video included the same content – the step-by-step instruction in spoken words while each step was shown in the movie. We allowed participants to use the video in every way they wanted; including re-watching the video, pausing, fast forward and rewind, and jumping to certain steps directly.

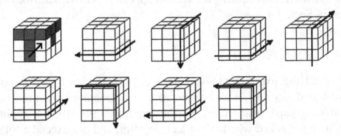

Fig. 1. Step sequence that was learned at the first appointment with the learning tool paper instruction. We used this illustration with additional text explaining the steps.

Fig. 2. Screenshot of the video instructions with navigation to the individual steps of the sequence of steps.

The VR application – realized with unity – contained a virtual Rubik's Cube with an overlay of slightly transparent arrows that indicated the next step. Additionally it was possible to deactivate the arrows and to reset the cube to the starting point. The VR application would also directly give feedback on the correctness of each step (see Fig. 4).

Fig. 3. Overview of the learning scenario in VR: Feedback bar (1), button to reset the cube (2), button to show and hide arrows (3), instructions provided by arrows directly on the cube (4).

To quantify mental rotation we used a digital version of a mental rotation test with tube figures [26]. Usability was measured with UEQ [27] and self-created questions based on a requirements catalogue for learning media [28], perceived task difficulty with SEQ [29] and Nasa TLX [30].

Fig. 4. VR learning scenario in the application with hidden arrows. Steps 4 and 6 were not carried out correctly

We used a computer with a monitor to present the questionnaires and the video and the Oculus Rift to present the VR application. Participants interacted with the virtual Rubik's Cube using controllers.

For testing the learning outcome at the first session and the retention performance as well as the transfer task during the follow up we used regular 3 × 3 Rubik's Cubes. We filmed both tasks during the follow up with a video camera for analysis.

3.4 Procedure

Session 1. After welcoming the participants, they filled out the informed consent and a questionnaire containing the exclusion criteria as well as demographic data. Mental rotation was measured with a digital version of a mental rotation test [26]. We assigned the learning tool to the participants pseudorandomized by gender. We did not inform the participants about the intended comparison between learning tools – we told them that we are interested in studying the assigned learning medium. The participants were instructed for the learning phase before they started learning with one of three learning media (paper, video or VR).

We allowed the participants in the VR group to practice the handling of a Rubik's Cube in VR and instructed them on how to rotate the cube in various directions, without including any hints on the upcoming task. We allowed them to interact freely with the blank Rubik's Cube as long as needed in order to feel confident in the handling.

The learning phase started when the participants signaled they were ready. We then presented the learning task to the participant in the assigned learning tool. In the video and paper instruction groups the participants were given a real Rubik's Cube to practice with. In the VR group the participants had the virtual Cube only.

The Learning phase consisted of two steps: Learning and a test to control for learning. Participants learned on their own with the selected learning medium until they assume to be able to reproduce the eight steps on a Rubik's Cube without help. When they stopped learning, they had to reproduce the eight steps five times correct to finish the learning phase. If a participant was not able to reproduce the eight steps s/he was allowed to learn again with the learning medium.

After completing the learning phase, participants filled out the SEQ [29], the NASA TLX [30] the UEQ [27] and the self-created questionnaire based on a requirements catalogue for learning media [28].

At the end, we instructed them to not learn anything regarding a Rubik's Cube and not to look up the steps again.

Session 2. Each participant had the second session exactly one week after the first session. The second session started with a retention task. Therefore, they got five prepared Rubik's Cube's in starting position, where they had to show the eight steps they learned seven days before. We filmed the participants' hands while adjusting the Rubik's Cubes for later analysis of correctness. Afterwards we got them another set of five prepared Rubik's Cube's to solve for the transfer task. We told the participants about the new target and that they would have to do – like in the retention task – eight steps to accomplish that target. We did not tell them which steps they had to do. Again, we filmed the performance for later analysis.

After finishing both tasks, we asked the participants to fill out the same questionnaires like in the first session. The questionnaires depending perceived task difficulty (SEQ and NASA TLX) referred to the retention and transfer task, the questionnaires depending usability referred to the learning phase in session one. We did this to compare the results of the evaluation of the learning tool directly after learning to the results a week after learning.

In the end, we explained the content and aim of the study to the participants and informed them about the other conditions (learning tools).

4 Analysis

First, we tested our hypotheses. Then we did further analysis, e.g. on the connection of the ability to rotate mentally and the transfer task score. The statistical evaluations were partly carried out with RStudio 1.2.5042 [31], R 3.6.1 [32] SPSS [33] and JASP [34].

4.1 Hypotheses Testing

In accordance with our preregistration, we first conducted an ANOVA between groups for differences in mental rotation measured with a mental rotation test [26]. There was no statistical significant difference between groups in the ability of mental rotation ($F_{(2, 57)} = 0.24, p = .79$). Therefore, we excluded mental rotation from following analyses. Next, we conducted an ANOVA for each dependent variable, since the transfer task is based on knowledge of the retention task. This confirms the high correlation between the two variables ($r = .63, p < .001$) [35].

We found no statistical significant difference between groups for either the retention task score ($F_{(2, 57)} = 0.22, p = .8, \eta2 = .007$) or the transfer task score ($F_{(2, 57)} = 0.19, p = .83, \eta2 = .007$). We show the means and the standard deviations of the scores in the retention and transfer task for each condition in Table 1. To test the informative value of the results regarding the null hypothesis (H1), we conducted a Bayes Factor Analysis. This analysis showed that our data is more likely – by factor 6 – under the null hypothesis concerning both variables (retention task: $BF_{10} = 0.159$; transfer task: $BF_{10} = 0.155$).

Table 1. Means and standard deviations of the two dependent variables (scores in retention and transfer task) by condition (paper, video and virtual reality).

	$M_{Retention}$	$SD_{Retention}$	$M_{Transfer}$	$SD_{Transfer}$
Paper	12.57	3.93	10.28	4.24
Video	13.31	3.32	10.96	3.87
Virtual Reality	12.8	3.47	10.31	3.74

Analysis of Usability. We measured the UEQ at both sessions during the experiment. In this section we will refer to the UEQ data from session 1 as "A1" and the UEQ data from session 2 as "A2". A Kolmogorov-Smirnov-test did not show a normal distribution for all UEQ data. An ANOVA should be robust to this violation with due to the chosen sample of 60 participants [24]. A Levene's Test was not significant.

An ANOVA found a significant effect for learning tool on AttractivesnessA1 ($F(2, 57) = 7.611$, p = .001), NoveltyA1 ($F(2, 57) = 19.376$, p < .001) StimulationA1 ($F(2, 57) = 10.352$, p < .001), but not for the dimension PerspicuityA1 ($F(2, 57) = .872$, p = .424), DependabilityA1 ($F(2,5 7) = .026$, p = .974) and EfficiancyA1 ($F(2, 57) = 1.748$, p = .183).

The ANOVA shows a significant effect for learning tool on the dimension AttractivesnessA2 ($F(2, 57) = 12.931$, p < .001), PerspicuityA2 ($F(2, 57) = 7.287$, p = .002), NoveltyA2 ($F(2, 57) = 21.253$, p < .000), StimulationA2 ($F(2, 57) = 18,386$, p < .001), and EfficiancyA2 ($F(2, 57) = 6,215$, p = .004) and a statistical trend for DependabilityA2 ($F(2, 57) = 2,828$, p = .067).

A Wilcoxon rang sum test was used to test for equality between the A1 and A2 dimensions of the UEQ. We found a significant result for the dimension attractiveness ($z = -3.137$, $p = .002$), but not for the dimensions Perspicuity ($z = -.675$, $p = .5$), Novelty ($z = -.867$, $p = .386$), Stimulation ($z = -1.227$, $p = .220$), Dependability ($z = -1.1462$, $p = .144$) and Efficiancy ($z = -1.505$, $p = .132$). Further analysis used the Delta (DimensionA2 – DimensionA1) of the UEQ dimensions. Main effects were found for learning tool on attractivenessdelta ($F(2, 57) = 4.3$, $p = .019$, $\eta^2 = .137$) and efficiencydelta ($F(2, 57) = 2.72$, $p = .029$, $\eta^2 = .201$). A Post Hoc Test Bonferroni corrected shows significant effects for Attractivenessdelta ($M_{dif} = -.489$, $SD = .198$, $p = .05$) and Effeciencydelta ($M_{dif} = -885$, $SD = .266$, $p = .005$) each between the learning media paper and video. There are significant main effects for the retention performance on Attractivenessdelta ($F = 8.58$, $p = .005$, $\eta^2 = .137$), Perspicuitydelta ($F = 6.09$, $p = .017$, $\eta^2 = .101$) and Stimulationdelta ($F = 4.32$, $p = .04$, $\eta^2 = .074$).

4.2 Further Analysis

To figure out which variables have an effect on the outcome of the retention and transfer task, we conducted further analysis. First, we took the excluded variable of mental rotation and calculated an ANCOVA. Here, we found a significant effect of the ability of mental rotation on the transfer task score ($p = .005$), but not on the retention task score. These results are underlined by the correlation between the task scores and the score of mental rotation test (retention task score * mental rotation test: $r = .2, p = .14$; transfer task score * mental rotation test: $r = .36, p = .005$).

Other analyses showed no significant impact of learning time and trials with the real cube during the first session on the retention score (learning time: $p = .8$; trials: $p = .99$) and the transfer task score (learning time: $p = .59$; trials: $p = .07$). Furthermore there were no significant effects for examiner (retention score: $p = .32$; trans-fer task score: $p = .68$), collection site (retention score: $p = .32$; transfer task score: $p = .6$) or gender (retention score: $p = .73$; transfer task score: $p = .91$).

The Kolmogorov-Smirnov test of goodness of fit does not show a normal distribution for the data of the SEQ. A rank correlation analysis finds a correlation between SEQ1 and SEQ2 ($rs = .320, p = .013, n = 60$) but no correlation between SEQ1 and learning resource ($rs = -.020, p = .879, n = 60$) or between SEQ2 and learning aids ($rs = .110, p = .401, n = 60$).

A Kolmogorov-Smirnov test shows a normal distribution for the values of the TLX 1 and the TLX 2. An ANOVA gave no significant results between the TLX1 and the learning tool ($F(2, 57) = .224, p = .8$). For TLX2 and learning materials, the ANOVA shows a statistical trend ($F(2, 57) = 3.101, p = .053$).

5 Discussion

The results show no evidence for a difference between the learning materials in terms of retention and transfer performance. The additional analysis with Bayesian statistics results in moderate evidence for the null hypothesis (hypothesis 1 and 2), which states that there is no difference in retention and transfer performance between the training agents.

There are no significant results for the NASA-TLX. This speaks for an equally high subjective stress on the test subjects from all three learning tools.

In the evaluation of the task difficulty (SEQ) there was no difference between the training materials in both dates. It turns out, however, that subjects who found the tasks on the first appointment difficult (learning the eight steps) also rated the task on the second appointment (retention and transfer performance) as more difficult. This suggests that the learning tool does not influence the evaluation of the difficulty of the task. The usability assessment varied from session 1 to session 2. Not all dimensions with significant results during the first session were significant during the second session and vice versa. One possible explanation is that the perception of some of the dimensions change over time, e.g. a new and original training tool seems to be less original after just one week. The assessment of these dimensions also seem to depend on the participants performance data. Future studies should investigate the influence of performance data and time on the assessment of usability more precisely.

5.1 Limitations

In order to carry out a fair comparison between the learning materials, all participants were learning with a cube (either real or virtual) in all groups. The addition of the real Rubik's Cube in the paper and video conditions added an acting component to both of them. As a result, the advantage of the integrated actions in the VR, which was derived from Dale's theory (1946, quoted after Hasselhorn & Gold, 2013) of the cone of experience, is no longer significant compared to the other two conditions. The difference between learning on the real cube (paper and video) and the virtual cube (VR) should be emphasized. From the results it can be deduced that virtual objects in VR can be equal to real objects in terms of learning. The results indicate that VR can be used to virtually represent interactions with objects.

Furthermore, subjects under all conditions had to carry out the steps at least five times on a real cube after the learning phase. This was identical in all groups, but could also include a learning effect that was not due to the learning material, but only to the interaction with the real cube. However, this can largely be ruled out, since the number of passes on the real cube after the learning phase in the explorative statistical analyzes did not show any significant influence on retention and transfer performance (retention: $p = .99$; transfer: $p = .07$). Nevertheless, subjects seem to benefit somewhat from the additional interaction with the real cube in relation to the transfer task.

The dependent variables consisted of the points achieved in the retention and transfer task. Since eight steps were carried out in both tasks, a maximum of 16 points could be achieved according to the developed coding scheme. Especially in the values of retention performance, it was shown that almost a third of the subjects (19) achieved the full 16 points on average, which may have prevented further variance due to a ceiling effect. More than 20 subjects had a mean between 15 and 16 points.In the transfer performance, a smaller proportion of subjects (4) achieved the full 16 points and only a fifth (12) of subjects achieved an average between 15 and 16 points. There does not seem to be a ceiling effect here. At least with regard to the transfer performance, it cannot be assumed that a possible ceiling effect meant that no significant difference could be found between the groups. Furthermore, the strict handling of omitted steps or the non-evaluation of only correct segments in the query of retention and transfer performance can influence the awarding of points, so that distortions can also be possible here. However, the strict assessment was justified with the avoidance of a ceiling effect, so that a lower level of strictness would have further favored it.

Criticism of Comparative Research on Learning Materials. At this point, the result of this study should first be set in relation to previous comparative studies. In contrast to this study, some studies have found a difference in the teaching of learning content between the learning materials used (Choi & Johnson, 2007; Lacko, 2020; Sacks et al., 2013). Others showed that different learning tools can partially complement each other (Al Madi & Khan, 2015; Checa & Bustillo, 2020; Kalludi et al., 2015; Rackaway, 2012), which cannot be derived from this study. Another proportion are studies which, in line with the present study, do not report a significant difference between the learning materials as a result (Grosskreutz et al., 2018; Gurusamy, K. Selvan et al., 2009; Torkington et al., 2001). Since Gurusamy, K. Selvan et al. (2009) and Torkington et al. (2001) refer to the learning of motor actions, these should be emphasized. The present study underscores the results that actions in VR can be learned in the same way as execution on real (training) objects.

Clark and Feldon's (2014) criticism of comparative learning material studies can be rejected in relation to this study, since according to their argumentation no difference was found between the learning materials. In addition, the study was designed in such a way that no learning material was disadvantaged by withholding relevant information. However, since they concede that some learning tools are better suited for certain areas, this can be related to the results of this study, specifically to VR. The difference in the learning materials is therefore not in the information available to the learner, but in the type of interaction object (real vs. virtual). Therefore, we can argue that VR is suitable for areas where interactions can be learned but cannot be performed on a real object for learning purposes.

5.2 Conclusion

The study shows moderate evidence that there are no differences between the learning materials when learning a sequential process. The recommendation can therefore be derived from the results that the choice of training material has no direct influence on retention and transfer performance. Depending on the subject and didactics, the right training material can be selected. Furthermore, this supports the use of VR in teaching and learning contexts to virtually represent interactions with objects, as the virtual representation of the object in this study did not result in any disadvantages compared to the physical object. The implementation of VR can make a decisive contribution to improving education, training and further education, especially in areas in which the learning objects are expensive to purchase or the interaction under real circumstances is associated with health or other risks. This is already shown by studies in the field of laparoscopy and safety training [3, 20]. The use of VR is already being evaluated for use in more complex areas, such as flight simulators [36]. However, more research is needed on the extent to determine whether more complex objects and therefore more complex interactions can also be represented equally well in VR.

The evaluation of the training materials by the subjects with regard to learning motivation, stimulation and future use also speaks in favor of orienting the choice of training materials primarily to the subject of learning and didactics.

5.3 Outlook

Due to the ever-changing technology of VR, this study is only a snapshot. Further research is needed on the implementation of training tools in this and other areas. Martín-Gutiérrez et al. (2017) see great potential in technology, but see an important point in researching didactics [7]. The didactics determine how the learning material can be effectively integrated into the existing learning situation and how it can be used in addition to previous learning materials. Due to the equivalence of the training tools in terms of retention and transfer performance, it is not the training tools that determine the learning success, but rather their didactic integration into the training. Therefore, future learning tool comparisons should focus more on didactics.

References

1. Craik, F.I., Lockhart, R.S.: Levels of processing. A framework for memory research. J. Verbal Learn. Verbal Behav. **11**, 671–684 (1972). https://doi.org/10.1016/S0022-5371(72)80001-X

2. Hyde, T.S., Jenkins, J.J.: Recall for words as a function of semantic, graphic, and syntactic orienting tasks. J. Verbal Learn. Verbal Behav. **12**, 471–480 (1973). https://doi.org/10.1016/S0022-5371(73)80027-1

3. Lacko, J.: Health safety training for industry in virtual reality. In: 2020 Cybernetics & Informatics (K&I), pp. 1–5. IEEE (2020). https://doi.org/10.1109/KI48306.2020.9039854

4. Hasselhorn, M., Gold, A.: Pädagogische Psychologie. Erfolgreiches Lernen und Lehren. Verlag W. Kohlhammer, Stuttgart (2013)

5. Al Madi, N.S., Khan, J.I.: Is learning by reading a book better than watching a movie? A computational analysis of semantic concept network growth during text and multimedia comprehension. In: 2015 International Joint Conference on Neural Networks (IJCNN), pp. 1–8. IEEE (2015). https://doi.org/10.1109/IJCNN.2015.7280761

6. Choi, H.J., Johnson, S.D.: The effect of problem-based video instruction on learner satisfaction, comprehension and retention in college courses. Br. J. Educ. Technol. **38**, 885–895 (2007). https://doi.org/10.1111/j.1467-8535.2006.00676.x

7. Martín-Gutiérrez, J., Mora, C.E., Añorbe-Díaz, B., González-Marrero, A.: Virtual technologies trends in education. EURASIA J. Math. Sci. Technol. Educ. **13** (2017). https://doi.org/10.12973/eurasia.2017.00626a

8. Dennis, K.A., Harris, D.: Computer-based simulation as an adjunct to Ab initio flight training. Int. J. Aviat. Psychol. **8**, 261–276 (1998). https://doi.org/10.1207/s15327108ijap0803_6

9. Kalludi, S., Punja, D., Rao, R., Dhar, M.: Is video podcast supplementation as a learning aid beneficial to dental students? J. Clin. Diagn. Res. JCDR **9**, CC04-7 (2015). https://doi.org/10.7860/JCDR/2015/14428.6944

10. Clark, R.E., Feldon, D.F.: Ten common but questionable principles of multimedia learning. In: Mayer, R. (ed.) The Cambridge Handbook of Multimedia Learning, pp. 151–173. Cambridge University Press, Cambridge (2014). https://doi.org/10.1017/CBO9781139547369.009

11. Checa, D., Bustillo, A.: Advantages and limits of virtual reality in learning processes: briviesca in the fifteenth century. Virtual Reality **24**(1), 151–161 (2019). https://doi.org/10.1007/s10055-019-00389-7

12. Grosskreutz, D., Logofatu, D., Schott, A.: The impact of video clips on teaching in technical study programs—learning faster or learning desaster? An approach from the perspective of a "manufacturing technology" module. In: 2018 IEEE Global Engineering Education Conference (EDUCON), pp. 95–99. IEEE (2018). https://doi.org/10.1109/EDUCON.2018.8363214

13. Mayer, R.E.: Multimedia Learning. Cambridge University Press, Cambridge (2005)

14. Statista: Anteil der Befragten, die der Nutzung der folgenden Anwendungen als Lernformen in Unternehmen in den kommenden drei Jahren eine zentrale Bedeutung beimisst, in der DACH-Region im Jahr 2019 (2020). https://de.statista.com/statistik/daten/studie/203748/umfrage/bedeutung-von-e-learning-anwendungen-in-unternehmen/

15. Weidenmann, B.: Lernen mit Medien. In: Krapp, A., Weidenmann, B. (eds.) Pädagogische Psychologie. Ein Lehrbuch. Anwendung Psychologie, pp. 423–476. Beltz PVU, Weinheim (2006)

16. Herzog, M.A., Sieck, J.: Mobiles lernen im education 3.0 kontext. In: Klimsa, P., Issing, L. (eds.) Online-Lernen. Handbuch für Wissenschaft und Praxis, pp. 283–296. Oldenbourg Wissenschaftsverlag GmbH, München (2011)

17. Choi, H., Johnson, D.S.: The effect of context-based video instruction on learning and motivation in online courses. Am. J. Dist. Educ. **19**, 215–227 (2005)

18. Choi, H.J., Johnson, S.D.: The effect of context-based video instruction on learning and motivation in online courses. Am. J. Dist. Educ. **19**, 215–227 (2005). https://doi.org/10.1207/s15389286ajde1904_3

19. Steuer, J.: Defining virtual reality. dimensions determining telepresence. J. Commun. **42**, 73–93 (1992). https://doi.org/10.1111/j.1460-2466.1992.tb00812.x

20. Gurusamy, K.S., Aggarwal, R., Palanivelu, L., Davidson, B.R.: Virtual reality training for surgical trainees in laparoscopic surgery. Cochrane Database Syst. Rev. CD006575 (2009). https://doi.org/10.1002/14651858.CD006575.pub2

21. Torkington, J., Smith, S.G.T., Rees, B.I., Darzi, A.: Skill transfer from virtual reality to a real laparoscopic task. Surg. Endosc. **15**(10), 1076–1079 (2001). https://doi.org/10.1007/s004640000233

22. Sacks, R., Perlman, A., Barak, R.: Construction safety training using immersive virtual reality. Constr. Manag. Econ. **31**, 1005–1017 (2013). https://doi.org/10.1080/01446193.2013.828844

23. Beijing Bluefocus E-Commerce Co., Ltd. and Beijing iBokan Wisdom Mobile Internet Technology Training Institutions: A Case Study. The Impact of VR on Academic Performance (2016). https://www.vive.com/cn/forum/forum.php?mod=attachment&aid=MzI1N3w5OTQxODc2NnwxNDgwMDc2NTQ1fDF8MjA5MA%3D%3D

24. Blanca, M.J., Alarcón, R., Arnau, J., Bono, R., Bendayan, R.: Non-normal data. Is ANOVA still a valid option? Psicothema **29**, 552–557 (2017). https://doi.org/10.7334/psicothema2016.383

25. Bortz, J., Schuster, C.: Statistik für Human- und Sozialwissenschaftler. Springer, Heidelberg (2010)

26. Stumpf, H., Fay, E.: Schlauchfiguren. Ein Test zur Beurteilung des räumlichen Vorstellungsvermögens. Verlag für Psychologie - Dr C. J. Hogrefe, Göttingen, Toronto, Zürich (1983)

27. Schrepp, M., Hinderks, A., Thomaschewski, J.: Applying the user experience questionnaire (UEQ) in different evaluation scenarios. In: Marcus, A. (ed.) DUXU 2014. LNCS, vol. 8517, pp. 383–392. Springer, Cham (2014). https://doi.org/10.1007/978-3-319-07668-3_37

28. Bayerisches Staatsministerium für Unterricht und Kultus, Wissenschaft und Kunst: Kriterien zur Begutachtung von Lernmitteln (2016). https://www.km.bayern.de/download/7432_allgemeiner_kriterienkatalog_stand_mai_2016.pdf

29. Sauro, J., Dumas, J.S.: Comparison of three one-question, post-task usability questionnaires. In: Olsen, D.R. (ed.) Proceedings of the SIGCHI Conference on Human Factors in Computing Systems. ACM Digital Library. ACM, New York (2009). https://doi.org/10.1145/1518701.1518946

30. Hart, S.G., Staveland, L.E.: Development of NASA-TLX (task load index): results of empirical and theoretical research. Adv. Psychol. **52**, 139–183 (1988)

31. RStudio Team: RStudio. Integrated Development Environment for R. Boston, MA (2020). http://www.rstudio.com/

32. R. Core Team: R. A Language and Environment for Statistical Computing. Vienna, Austria (2019). https://www.R-project.org/

33. IBM Corp.: IBM SPSS Statistics for Windows, Version 27.0. [Computer software]. IBM Corp, Armonk, NY (2020). https://www.ibm.com/de-de/analytics/spss-statistics-software

34. JASP Team: JASP (Version 0.9.2) [Computer software] (2020) https://jasp-stats.org/

35. Cohen, J.: Statistical Power Analysis for the Behavioral Sciences. Taylor and Francis, Hoboken (1988)

36. Dalladaku, Y., Kelley, J., Lacey, B., Mitchiner, J., Welsh, B., Beigh, M.: Assessing the effectiveness of virtual reality in the training of army aviators. In: Proceedings of the 2020 Annual General Donald R. Keith Memorial Capstone Conference, pp. 45–50 (2020)

Towards a Vision of Standardized Competency-Based Training and Assessment Implementation

Barbara Buck[1](✉), Elizabeth Biddle[2], Liz Gehr[1], and Kristi Eager[3]

[1] The Boeing Company, Saint Louis, MO, USA
{barbara.j.buck,liz.gehr}@boeing.com
[2] The Boeing Company, Orlando, FL, USA
elizabeth.m.biddle@boeing.com
[3] The Boeing Company, Seattle, WA, USA
kristi.r.eager@boeing.com

Abstract. In the past several years, the shift from traditional task-based training to competency-based training has gained traction within the training community. Rather than the traditional one-size-fits-all training solution, a Competency-Based Training and Assessment (CBTA) approach encourages tailoring the learning experiences to the learner and using evidence of learning to determine the student's competency for a variety of learning components. The challenge then is how best to assess student competency, and how to store this data and use it to adapt the training experience to the student's needs. In order to establish an effective CBTA methodology, we need to understand the requirements for clearly and consistently evaluating competencies both across students and learning opportunities, but also across multiple instructors who might be assessing different students. This paper seeks to develop a vision towards a standardized approach for CBTA data collection, grading, and assessment.

Keywords: Adaptive Instructional Systems · Intelligent Tutoring Authoring · Virtual Reality · Adaptive Simulation-Based Learning · Data Ecosystem

1 Introduction

1.1 Competency-Based Training and Assessment

The global growth in airlines is creating an unprecedented demand for new pilots to support ongoing airline operations [1, 2]. In the face of ever-changing and complex environments, today's commercial pilots must deal with increasingly sophisticated aircraft operating in fast-paced and often uncertain, challenging situations. In an effort to address the increasing demand in light of these complexities, Competency-Based Training and Assessment (CBTA) evolved as a methodology to capture training standards, combining skill, knowledge, attitudes and values required to perform flight operations tasks efficiently and safely. Defined formally, competency-based learning refers to "systems

R. A. Sottilare and J. Schwarz (Eds.): HCII 2023, LNCS 14044, pp. 206–218, 2023.
https://doi.org/10.1007/978-3-031-34735-1_15

of instruction, assessment, grading, and academic reporting that are based on students demonstrating that they have learned the knowledge and skills they are expected to learn as they progress through their education" [3].

Although the concept of CBTA originated quite some time ago [4], it has grown in popularity due to its demonstrated effectiveness in numerous industries—medicine, corporate training, and academia. Within the aviation domain, CBTA has its roots in the early the evidence-based training (EBT) approach to data collection and analysis developed by International Civil Aviation Organization (ICAO). Since that time, it has been implemented in various forms throughout the aviation training domain.

Figure 1 depicts the pilot competency framework as we have implemented it at Boeing [5]. It is a combination of aircraft technical skills (flight path management--manual and automation and application of procedures) and non-technical human factors skills such as workload management, communication and situation awareness. Application of Knowledge is a competency that underlies all the others, while Communication and Leadership & Teamwork are high-level competencies that are interwoven among all the others.

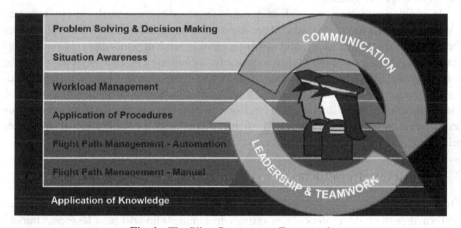

Fig. 1. The Pilot Competency Framework

1.2 Issues with Competency Assessment

Potential benefits of a CBTA approach to training include comprehensive assessment tightly coupled with the learning process in order to document continuous learning. Because competency-based approaches focus on knowledge, skill and attitude mastery, the learning experience can be personalized to accommodate each student's individual path to proficiency and competency demonstration. But that begs the question as to how do we implement competency-based assessment into current pilot training in a way that complies with regulatory requirements and learning strategies.

Current industry approaches require a mix of demonstrated knowledge and applied skills to meet aviation regulatory standards. Often times, this training footprint is a mix of classroom instruction followed up by knowledge validation exams and simulation-based instruction relying on subjective instructor assessment.

Within the domain of commercial pilot training, we have identified a number of challenges for simulation-based student grading and assessment from the instructors' perspective. It is often incumbent on an instructor to monitor performance over the course of a long training event, and then provide a single grade or even a grade on a number of competencies at the conclusion of the event.

Traditionally, subjective assessment on the part of flight instructors uses a 5-point grading scale, with 5 being exemplary performance and 1 being ineffective or unsatisfactory performance. Students must achieve a minimally acceptable ranking in order to pass that aspect of hands-on instruction. Instructors are encouraged to document specific aspects of the students' performance with detailed comments. However, due to issues of instructor workload and challenges with instructor grading tools, few comments are documented. For CBTA-based grading, instructors are asked to identify the observable behaviors and provide evidence to support their rating, in addition to the overall competency score. This approach can be fraught with high instructor workload, subjectivity, and labor intensive grading.

In addition to instructor workload, the subjective assessment methodology is potentially complicated by other issues. Many flight simulation-based lessons take place over the course of three-plus hours, and involve a team of student pilots carrying out a number of different tasks within a complex operational environment. How does an instructor summarize that down to a single rating on 2–3 focus competencies? How does an instructor choose from a handful of supporting observable behaviors to justify their ratings? More importantly, there is a potential confound of different instructors choosing to focus on different aspects of students' performance. This leads to confounds of inter-rater reliability. The following section describes the issues with instructor rater reliability.

2 Instructor Reliability

The aviation training industry relies heavily on instructors to assess the knowledge and performance of student pilots. Their ratings determine who will pass lessons, courses, and eventually fly an airplane. In the case of a course where there are multiple instructors interacting with a student on different days, the ratings give future instructors an idea of the capabilities of the students and allows the new instructor to more accurately tailor his instruction to each student. This reliance on instructors will only increase as we move to CBTA which will require instructors to assess not just the performance of a student pilot, but the student pilot's competence based on Observable Behaviors (OBs) or Knowledge, Skills and Abilities (KSAs). In addition, many airlines and training centers are moving to try to provide more personalized learning for the students. This will mean the instructor pilot's evaluation of a student's strengths and weaknesses may impact what material a student sees next, or how much further training is recommended for that particular student. However, if we cannot be sure of the accuracy and reliability of the instructor ratings, our decisions will be unreliable, and student pilots will not get accurate feedback about their preparedness to fly the aircraft.

The obvious importance of instructor ratings in student evaluations means we need to be sure those ratings reflect the underlying performance of the student. Although current instructor training may teach instructors how to rate students, and there may be grading rubrics provided for the instructors to use, we need to ensure that the instructors continue to rate against the established standards. If we can measure how valid and reliable the ratings are from our instructors are we will have a higher confidence in the student's abilities when they pass a course and begin flying. Baker & Dismukes [6] provide a good summary of the problem:

"Reliable and valid assessment of an aircrew cannot be made during LOE (or any other training and evaluation event) if pilot instructors do not agree on the types of crew behaviors observed and the level of performance these behaviors represent. When pilot instructors do not agree, performance ratings are a function of the particular instructor conducting the assessment as opposed to performance of the crew".

Baker & Dismukes cite several potential issues in obtaining accurate assessment of student pilots. Instructors may not have enough opportunities to observe pertinent behaviors during the given training scenario, as they are usually multi-tasking while they simultaneously running the simulator, role-playing air traffic control, as well as rating the student's performance. Also, organizational issues may provide undue pressure for what grades are acceptable to give, or provide hindrances to giving non-standard grades. They cite the issue of some organizations requiring comments if grades fall to an extreme, which incentivizes an instructor to only give ratings in the middle of the scale to avoid extra work. The third potential issue they cite is the varied level of background experience of the instructor pilots and lack of training many have of how to observe particular behaviors and assign correct grades.

The first need is an accurate measure of what level of instructor standardization currently exists. This is not a trivial step. Instructor pilots are often dispersed at many campuses observing diverse student populations. Measuring if they are all using the same standards to evaluate students requires the collection of additional data.

2.1 Inter-Rater Reliability (IRR)

IRR reflects how much different raters agree with each other after they observe the same scenario. This requires all raters to observe the same scenarios. This differs from Rater-Referent Reliability RRR (defined below) in that there is no ground truth for comparison, but the raters are compared to each other. This can measure if the raters agree with each other, but not if they agree with a standard. Thus, a high level of IRR could mean that all instructors agree on what the rating is, but it may not reflect the actual rating they should be giving if they all have the same bias. For example, all instructor pilots could rate a given scenario as 4 on the communication competency, but maybe they weren't trained to include eye contact in their grading, and this example had poor eye contact and should have been a 2. These pilots would exhibit high IRR, but their ratings would still be inaccurate.

The APA defines IRR as "the extent to which independent evaluators produce similar ratings in judging the same abilities or characteristics in the same target person or object. It often is expressed as a correlation coefficient [7]. If consistency is high, a researcher can be confident that similarly trained individuals would likely produce similar scores on targets of the same kind. If consistency is low, there is little confidence that the obtained scores could be reproduced with a different set of raters. Also called intercoder reliability; interjudge reliability; interobserver reliability; interscorer reliability".

Note that above definition says that similarly trained raters would produce the same score, not that the consistent score (reliability) they produce is the correct one (validity). IRR is also not a measure of sensitivity for it cannot tell if the raters are able to detect relevant differences and assign the correct grade.

Another issue that Holt et al. [8] point out with a measure like inter-rater reliability is the base rate issue. They describe it below:

"One thorny issue that arises in assessing evaluator reliability is the base-rate problem. The base-rate problem occurs when the frequency of some grades is very different from others. For example, on a 4-point grading scale where a "4" is excellent and a "3" is standard, it is possible for upwards of 90% of crew behaviors to be graded a "3". Of course, evaluators are cognizant of this fact and by simply selecting the modal grade can achieve relatively high agreement. Clearly these distributions can influence simple agreement measures such as percent agreement. However, such non-normal distributions could also make it difficult to interpret the real meaning of a correlation of say r = 0.80 between two evaluators".

Thus, evaluators could game the system by always assigning the most common score, thereby achieving a high, but meaningless, IRR score.

2.2 Rater-Referent Reliability (RRR)

RRR reflects how closely the evaluator is rating as compared to a standard rating for that exact scenario. In order to use this there must be a gold standard or ground truth available for the given scenario that establishes the referent score. An easy example would be altitude. If the pilot must maintain an altitude of 10,000 ft ± 500 ft to be correct, the accuracy of the assessor's assessment of the pilot's altitude maintenance can be compared to the actual altitude the pilot maintained. If there are established and objective criteria that differentiate the levels 1–5 on a grading scale, a script could be created and recorded that was designed to exhibit the behaviors of a specific level so that the assessor's grade could also be compared to this ground truth. However, without an external objective assessment of what the correct assessment is, RRR cannot be calculated.

High RRR will by default result in high IRR. One big advantage of RRR over IRR is that it does not perpetuate incorrect ratings. If new instructors, and instructors coming back for recurrent training, are measured against a standard rating for a scenario, rather than against their peers' ratings for that scenario, they will be able to get feedback and course correct any deviations from standard measurement that they have.

RRR "is a measure of sensitivity because it reflects the degree to which the evaluators' ratings co-vary with the true performance as defined by the referent rating" (Goldsmith and Johnson, [9]).

In an ideal world, instructor calibration would be achieved and measured by having all instructors trained and evaluated to a referent standard, and periodically re-assessed, and retrained, against standard ratings. RRR is the gold standard for this kind of measure. This would require the production and maintenance (including re-recording when necessary) of sufficiently large library of videos with a standard rating for the measure being evaluated. Although theoretically the best method, currently RRR may not be practical to implement. The greatest difficulty would be in assigning a standard rating for different metrics to the videos. Given the potential impact on training effectiveness and aviation safety, studies to evaluate training effectiveness of instructors with high RRR is recommended.

IRR is a good measure when RRR is not feasible. This would require the development of a library of videos for instructors to watch (ensuring it is sufficiently large so that an instructor does not watch the same video multiple times). However, by not having the RRR requirement of knowing what the score of the video should be, it will be easier to implement while still having different instructors watch the same videos.

Regulatory agencies also require measurement of IRR. European Union Aviation Safety Agency (EASA) documentation requires (note EASA calls IRR concordance):

- The operator shall establish an instructor concordance assurance programme.
- Relevant metrics must be used to support this programme.
- All instructors must be subject to this programme.
- Sufficient instructor concordance must be demonstrated.
- Concordance may not be inferred only from training data.

There are several ways to increase IRR. Initial training will ensure that all participants start with a common understanding of how to grade. Periodic recalibration will guard against standard drift and ensure instructors continue to accurately assess students. Introduction of a structured approach to the design of flight training lessons to ensure there are opportunities for the student pilots to demonstrate and for the instructor to assess the OBs of focus will also have a role to play in ensuring that instructors remain consistent. The Evidence Based Approach to Training (EBAT) methodology for constructing with trigger events specifically designed to elicit the training objectives for the lesson with associated performance measures, which was introduced by the United States Navy [10]. If instructors know that an event will occur during a training scenario, they can look out for it and have a higher likelihood of observing it even while they are busy with all the other tasks they are doing. EBAT will also hopefully reduce their workload which is another way it will ensure that performance measurement is accurate.

3 Initial Implementation

Figure 2 describes our initial approach to implementing a consistent, objective way to assess student performance within operational environments was the creation of our Intelligent Tutoring System (ITS) architecture [11]. This architecture involves three primary components: a Student Model, an Instructional Model, and an Expert Model. The student model maintains a profile of dynamic variables, each corresponding to one focus competency. These variables are evaluated over a number of observations as the student performs actions in the training scenario. As a result, changes due to learning are reflected across experiences, as the score increases due to correct performance (based on the expert model), or decreases as errors are made. The amount that scores are changed can be weighted according to the degree to which the action reflects mastery of the focus competency. The instructional model provides the appropriate lesson flow, including student feedback and help as needed, based on student actions. The lesson scoring is adjusted according to the degree of support (e.g., hints) the ITS provides to the student throughout the lesson.

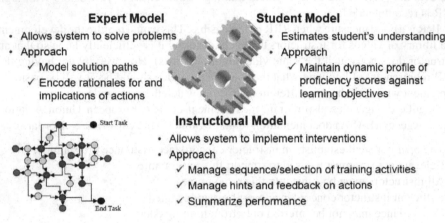

Expert Model
- Allows system to solve problems
- Approach
  - ✓ Model solution paths
  - ✓ Encode rationales for and implications of actions

Student Model
- Estimates student's understanding
- Approach
  - ✓ Maintain dynamic profile of proficiency scores against learning objectives

Start Task

End Task

Instructional Model
- Allows system to implement interventions
- Approach
  - ✓ Manage sequence/selection of training activities
  - ✓ Manage hints and feedback on actions
  - ✓ Summarize performance

Fig. 2. The Boeing ITS Architecture.

This initial capability, the Boeing ITS, uses discrete event scenarios in which the student's actions bring them through paths (using the instructional model) with varying degrees of optimality. This EBAT methodology [10] does not seek to assess the entire scenario, it makes use of focused, embedded events which are key to determining the KSAs that are critical to a competent pilot.

While the application of EBAT within the context of the ITS system is an initial step to evaluating competencies in an applied setting, it does not address how this approach can be expanded to the more complex full flight simulation environment with instructor pilots as subjective raters. The next section will address this more fully.

4   Advancing the State of the Art

Application of EBAT to lesson design and performance assessment coupled with data collection tools has the potential to standardize competency assessments during flight simulator training while reducing instructor workload. The development of quantitative, objective data based measurement methods enables the collection of detailed evidence to support competency assessment and grading and pave the way for self-learning experiences enabled by adaptive instructional systems (AISs). The following is a phased approach to integrating the EBAT scenario design and assessment methodology to commercial pilot training beginning with instructor-led simulator lessons and evolving towards AIS-supported immersive flight training experiences.

4.1 Instructor-Led CBTA Scenario Design and Assessment

EBAT has been applied to team and collective (team of teams) training in military [12] and health care [13]. In order to apply EBAT to a CBTA commercial pilot training curriculum, a library of elicitation events designed to trigger the performance of OBs needs to be created. This library should include multiple elicitation events designed to trigger the performance of each OB that underlies the pilot competencies. The instructional system designer (ISD) is then able to use the elicitation events as building blocks to develop the scenarios used in the flight simulator lessons – ensuring there are opportunities for the student to perform, and the instructor to observe, the desired aspects of the pilot competency (e.g., OBs or individual KSAs) the lesson addresses.

During training preparation and during the flight training lesson, the instructor has a timeline of the events to use for assessment. By providing the instructor the opportunity to plan when he or she needs to be observing a specific elicitation event, instructor workload is reduced from constantly being on the lookout for a number of different OBs to planned monitoring events for a specific OB. Additionally, the IRR issue described earlier is ameliorated by ensuring the instructors are using the same lesson events as the basis for their assessments.

If there is industry participation in the development of this library of elicitation events, standardized assessment across flight training organizations is possible, even with tailoring for an air carrier's flight route specific needs (e.g., location, weather conditions). Further, the elicitation event library and application of EBAT can be used to develop vignettes with master ratings for instructor assessment and grading calibration makes RRR possible within a flight campus. If the vignettes and master ratings are employed as an industry standard, there is potential for interoperability in CBTA assessment and grading throughout the commercial pilot training industry. Pilot competency performance can then be tracked across a pilot's career, enabling continual tailored instruction and professional development.

4.2 Instructor-Led CBTA with Subjective Assessment Tools

Observation tools to assist the instructor with making an initial assessment and comments that may be useful for diagnosing learning needs of the planned observable behaviors provide a means of further reducing workload and potential inaccuracies in recalling performance during the lesson. These tools can be tablet-based or built into a flight simulator's instructor operating station (IOS). Tablet-based assessment tools for instructors have long been used to support military team and collective training events, such as the Virtual Communications Assessment Tool used for instructors to assess fighter pilot collective performance [14] using an EBAT design training and performance assessment method. There are a number of commercial-off-the-shelf (COTS) tablet-based grading tools available for commercial pilot instructors, but the use of these tools is not standardized between training organizations and programs.

For use in a commercial pilot flight simulator environment, the application of hand-held tools needs to consider the instructor's interfaces to the flight training simulator and associated training materials (e.g., paper or tablet based instructor guides and flight manuals) to ensure the user interface is intuitive and enables the instructor to perform his or her other duties, such as controlling the simulator and role-playing scenario entities (e.g., air traffic control). Integration of the subjective assessment tool within the instructor operator station (IOS) is an option to consider as a means of potential overburdening the instructor with multiple interfaces while enabling seamless integration with simulator control interactions and supporting interfaces.

4.3 Instructor Assessment Tools with Objective Measurement Capabilities

Objective data assessments can be used to enhance the instructor assessments through use of simulator data for quantitative measurement of pilot performance linked to elicitation events, such as interactions with the flight deck or aircraft performance. Coupled with emerging technologies capable of analyzing voice communications [15] and physiological and behavioral data [16], there are opportunities for objective, automated assessments of the KSAs associated with most of the CBTA OBs. As with the subjective assessment tools, considerations of all of the instructors' tasks during a flight simulator lesson need to be considered in the interface design of such tools – including the decision to incorporate in a tablet-based solution or integration within the IOS. Milham, Laura & Pharmer, James & Fok, Audre demonstrated success of objective performance measures integrated with an IOS in a military training context [17].

The objective, automated assessments also have the potential to reduce instructor workload during debrief to support review of the lesson with the student [18]. In cases where the instructor and the pilot (student) disagree on what transpired during the lesson, the objective measures provide evidence to substantiate discussions during debrief. This evidence also provides a source of information for the instructor to reference when entering final grades for a lesson so that they are not solely reliant on memory and degradation in recall of events if there is a time lapse between the flight lesson and the opportunity document grades. The application of objective metrics to assist the instructor with team training has shown promise for increasing IRR in terms of assessments [19, 20].

This data provides evidence that can be used to tailor instruction to the student. When multiple instructors training are used throughout a flight training curriculum, this can help with sharing details regarding student performance to provide continuity to the instruction throughout the course. Similar to the instructor observation methods discussed earlier, the objective elicitation events and associated quantitative measures also enable a standardized approach to provide consistent within and between flight training organizations.

4.4 Standardized Methods for AIS-Based Flight Training

The commercial pilot flight training industry is exploring the adoption of high fidelity, low footprint simulations to provide more opportunities for pilots to develop procedural skills outside of a traditional flight campus. Standard, objective assessment of competencies will be needed to facilitate training with this capabilities due to necessity for remote or asynchronous instructor involvement. Similar to instructor-led training recommendations, the incorporation of EBAT to the design of flight training lessons is critical to guaranteeing the student pilot has the opportunity to demonstrate the OBs intended to be addressed. In cases where it is not possible to include an instructor in the loop, AIS based solutions require a structured approach to the design and assessment plan. An initial AIS, immersive pilot training prototype was described in [21] using a structured, EBAT approach to the design of ground-based procedures lesson.

The assessments can be used the AIS to diagnose learning issues and recommend remediation if there is a specific knowledge deficiency, or subsequent flight lessons designed to target the pilot's learning needs. An objective-based elicitation event library can be used to recommend a scenario for a subsequent lesson or for real-time instructional interventions implemented by an AIS for inserting events. Standard-based methods have been a research topic for many years. An initial investigation into tailored scenario generation [22] proposed a methodology for automated scenario recommendation for a military command and control task. Deployment of these capabilities requires an instructional design methodology as discussed in this section, as well as learning data interoperability standards.

5   CBTA Within the Learning Data Ecosystem

The learning ecosystem is the digital infrastructure required to support CBTA. It integrates different learning tools, platforms, and data to support personalized learning experiences that can span a single course or the entire career of a pilot. This ecosystem is responsible for managing data that is leveraged to provide actionable insights into the progress, performance, competency, and goals of an individual or team. This requires a variety of software systems to exchange, understand, and use data from across the industry [23].

This ecosystem provides several benefits for CBTA. It enables the standardization, capture, and storage of performance data, such as the completion of training modules, flight simulations, as well as the detailed results of assessments. This data can be used by the instructor and assessors to monitor the student pilot's progress, tailor the training journey, and provide guidance during debrief as discussed in the prior section. The results from training courses and operational performance can also support continuous improvement of the learning and assessment design by maintaining traceability from performance and observation to the course design footprint.

All of these features of a learning ecosystem require a wide variety of data. Some core data pillars include, but are not limited to [23]:

- Performance and observational data: This can include data about the pilot's performance during learning and operations, activities of flight simulation sessions, digital or written exams, evaluations and feedback provided by the pilot instructor(s), and flight events.
- Learner records data: This can include aggregated data about a pilot's learning history, such as course completions, and accreditations.
- Training and assessment context data: This can include metadata about the training course, such as the type of aircraft, learning objectives, competency frameworks, grading rubrics, libraries of elicitation events, the conditions in any given flight simulation, and the specific role the pilot is playing.

- Demographic data: This can include details about the pilot's background and demographics, such as age, gender, and prior career experience.

Some of this data can be considered highly sensitive, so privacy and governance are critical considerations. Effective data management enables the efficient storage, retrieval, and analysis of learning data, allowing organizations to make use of this data and remain in compliance with regional data protection regulations. The importance of data management in a learning ecosystem cannot be overstated. Effective data management builds trust between systems, individuals, and stakeholders that rely on data-driven insights.

The learning ecosystem for CBTA has the potential to revolutionize pilot training. Given the proper tools and data, overburdened instructors can focus on observing and assessing the pilot's competency, rather than data entry. Pilots can benefit from tailored training and support for career development. ISDs can use insights from performance data to continuously improve instruction and assessment design. Finally, airlines will be able to support growth and ensure pilots meet the highest standards for safety and competency.

6 Summary and Conclusions

As part of the increased safety focus in aviation training, we have implanted a CBTA approach to training and performance assessment. Instructors have an increased role in conducting personalized, facilitative learning focused on close observation and assessment of the student's progress with respect to competency requirements. This paper has identified some of the challenges associated with implementation of this approach, including potentially increasing instructor workload and issues of inter-rater and referent instructor reliability. In addition, this paper proposed a methodology and supporting tools that would help to manage these issues.

The Boeing-developed ITS is suitable for off-line, individual asynchronous learning and rehearsal of event-based scenarios. There are a number of additional tools under development to support this EBAT methodology going forward. Future efforts of our EBAT-enabled CBTA development will focus on identifying and creating the tools necessary to support instructor-based grading for simulation-based training exercises, as well as providing a similar capability to support CBTA-based learning in independent, immersive procedural or task-based environments. Finally, future development and expansion of the Learning Data Ecosystem provides the foundation for data collection and storage required to fully implement the CBTA approach and personalize pilot training. These advances will help to meet the increased demand in pilot training, and ensure that we are developing competent, safe, resilient pilots.

References

1. Wall, R., Tangel, A.: Facing a critical pilot shortage, airlines scramble to hire new pilots. Wall Street J. **1**, 1–3 (2018)
2. The Boeing Company (2020). http://www.boeing.com/commercial/market/pilot-technician-outlook. Accessed 29 Jan 2020

3. https://www.edglossary.org/competency-based-learning/
4. White, R.: Motivation reconsidered: the concept of competence. Psychol. Rev. **66**(5), 297–333 (1959). http://dx.doi.org/10.1037/h0040934
5. Caldwell, R.: Building resilience: A framework for pilot competency-based training and assessment (Rev. B). Boeing Internal Report 472-21-00018 (2022)
6. Baker, D.P., Dismukes, R.K.: A framework for understanding crew performance assessment issues. Int. J. Aviat. Psychol. **12**(3), 205–222 (2002)
7. https://dictionary.apa.org/interrater-reliability
8. Holt, R.W., Johnson, P.J., Goldsmith, T.E.: Application of psychometrics to the calibration of air carrier evaluators. In: Proceedings of the Human Factors and Ergonomics Society Annual Meeting, vol. 41, no. 2, pp. 916–920. SAGE Publications, Los Angeles (1997)
9. Goldsmith, T.E. Johnson, P.J.: Analysis of training of cognitive skills in a line-oriented flight training environment (2000). http://www.tc.faa.gov/logistics/grants/pdf/1994/94-g-013.pdf
10. Fowlkes, J., Dwyer, D.J., Oser, R.L., Salas, E.: Event-based approach to training (EBAT). Int. J. Aviat. Psychol. **8**(3), 209–221 (1998). https://doi.org/10.1207/s15327108ijap0803_3
11. Buck, B., Genova, M., Dargue, B., Biddle, E.: Adaptive learning capability: user-centered learning at the next level. In: Sottilare, R. (ed.) Intelligent Tutoring Systems Conference 2018 Industry Track Proceedings, pp. 3–11 (2018). http://ceur-ws.org/Vol-2121/Preface.pdf. Accessed 19 Feb 2019
12. Johnston, J.H., Sottilare, R.A., Kalaf, M., Goodwin, G.: Chapter 8 – Training for team effectiveness under stress. In: Sinatra, A.M., Graesser, A.C., Hu, X., Goldberg, B., Hampton, A.J., and Johnston, J.H. (eds.) Design Recommendations for Intelligent Tutoring Systems: Volume 9 - Competency-Based Scenario Design. US Army Combat Capabilities Development Command - Soldier Center, Orlando (2022). https://gifttutoring.org/documents/
13. Rosen, M.A., et al.: Tools for evaluating team performance in simulation-based training. J. Emerg. Trauma Shock. **3**(4), 353–359 (2010). https://doi.org/10.4103/0974-2700.70746. PMID: 21063558; PMCID: PMC2966568
14. Radtke, P., Johnston, J., Biddle, E., Carolan, T.: Integrating and presenting performance information in simulation-based air warfare scenarios. In: Proceedings of 2007 Interservice/Industry, Training, Simulation & Education Conference, Orlando, 26–29 November 2007 (2007)
15. Foltz, P., Melanie, M.: Automated communication analysis of teams. In: Team Effectiveness in Complex Organizations, Taylor & Francis Group, New York (2009)
16. Finseth, T., Dorneich, M., Keren, N., Franke, W., Vardeman, S.: Training for stressful operations using adaptive systems: conceptual approaches and applications. I/ITSEC 2021 (2021)
17. Milham, L., Pharmer, J., Fok, A.: Adaptive instructor operating systems: design to support instructor assessment of team performance. In: Proceedings of the Human Factors and Ergonomics Society Annual Meeting, vol. 59. pp. 1801–1805 (2015). https://doi.org/10.1177/1541931215591389
18. Fraser, K.L., Meguerdichian, M.J., Haws, J.T., et al.: Cognitive Load Theory for debriefing simulations: implications for faculty development. Adv. Simul. **3**, 28 (2018). https://doi.org/10.1186/s41077-018-0086-1
19. Adams, S., Basilico, J., Abbott, R., Gieseler, C., Forsythe, C.: Performance assessment to enhance training effectiveness. In: The 2010 Interservice/Industry, Training, Simulation and Education Conference Proceedings (2010). https://www.researchgate.net/publication/269872530_Performance_Assessment_to_Enhance_Training_Effectiveness/citation/download. Accessed 1 Feb 2023
20. Granåsen, D.: Towards automated assessment of team performance by mimicking expert observers' ratings. Cogn. Technol. Work **21**(2), 253–274 (2018). https://doi.org/10.1007/s10111-018-0499-6

21. Biddle, E., Buck, B.: Adaptive team training for one. In: Sottilare, R., Schwarz, J. (eds.) HCII 2019. LNCS, vol. 11597, pp. 15–27. Springer, Cham (2019). https://doi.org/10.1007/978-3-030-22341-0_2

22. Biddle, E., Perrin, B., Pike, W., Marvin, D.: Performance based advancement using SCORM 2004. In: Proceedings to 2004 Interservice/Industry, Training, Simulation and Education Conference (2004)

23. Smith, B., Schatz, S.: DoD learning enclave: realizing the defense-wide learning ecosystem (2022)

Identifying Individual Differences that Predict Usage of an Adaptive Training System in a United States Marine Corps Course

Nicholas W. Fraulini[1], Matthew D. Marraffino[2(✉)], and Allison E. Garibaldi[1]

[1] StraCon Services Group, LLC, Fort Worth, TX 76109, USA
{nicholas.w.fraulini.ctr,allison.e.garibaldi.ctr}@us.navy.mil
[2] Naval Air Warfare Center Training Systems Division, Orlando, FL 32826, USA
matthew.d.marraffino.civ@us.navy.mil

Abstract. The U.S. military is faced with expanding logistical challenges to train students effectively. Providing students with adaptive training (AT) systems during their courses can help address these challenges. It is unclear, however, what individual differences lead to students using AT systems as course aids. To answer this question, we conducted the current research to investigate usage of a flashcard-based AT system and its association with individual differences in U.S. Marine Corps students. We chose to examine self-regulated learning (SRL), intrinsic motivation (IM), and achievement goal orientation in relation to training system usage, as previous research has revealed associations between these variables and improved learning outcomes and positive learning behaviors. Students were provided an AT flashcard system on their military-issued laptops and told they could utilize it as a study aid as much or as little as they preferred during their course. Results revealed varying degrees of system usage overall. Additionally, we uncovered positive associations between achievement goals and IM as they related to AT system usage. We discuss implications for AT system usage in live classrooms, as well as provide suggestions for future AT system developers as they seek to improve system usage among students.

Keywords: Adaptive training · Flashcard training · Mastery learning · Individual differences

1 Introduction

Currently, instructors in United States Navy (USN) and United States Marine Corps (USMC) courses are faced with the challenge of modernizing instruction to provide Sailors and Marines individualized training at the point of need. It is becoming increasingly difficult to manage expanding training curricula and growing classroom sizes without the help of additional training days [1]. One potential solution to this issue could be the use of adaptive training (AT). AT has been defined as "training interventions whose content can be tailored to an individual learner's aptitudes, learning preferences, or styles prior to training and that can be adjusted, either in real time or at the end of a training

This is a U.S. government work and not under copyright protection in the U.S.; foreign copyright protection may apply 2023
R. A. Sottilare and J. Schwarz (Eds.): HCII 2023, LNCS 14044, pp. 219–235, 2023.
https://doi.org/10.1007/978-3-031-34735-1_16

session, to reflect the learner's on-task performance" [2]. Although AT systems have been shown to be effective at improving learning outcomes [3, 4], they typically are not implemented as required elements of curricula. Instead, these systems are provided to students as supplemental resources they can use for additional instruction on their own time. This places responsibility on the student to judge their own need for the AT system and use it sufficiently to address that need. Flashcards are a popular form of supplemental instruction used by students to study outside the classroom environment. To that end, we partnered with a USMC course to provide students with an adaptive flashcard system to identify factors that contribute to usage.

Flashcard-based adaptive training has been shown to be effective in many contexts, including geography [5], chemistry [6], species categorization [7], and word pairs [8]. In a pilot study, Whitmer and colleagues [9] developed the Flexible Adaptive Sequencing for Training (FAST) testbed to test whether using adaptive flashcards would be effective for learning outside the laboratory in a real-world classroom. The authors examined course outcomes by comparing the grade-point averages (GPA) and learning objective failures (i.e., failure to meet performance criteria for a particular course objective) among two cohorts of Marines enrolled in the USMC Automotive Maintenance Technician Basic Course (AMTBC). The AMTBC is a 52-day course divided into six sections that teach theories, troubleshooting, diagnosing, and maintenance of light, medium, and heavy automotive systems. Students begin the course by attending classroom-based lectures pertaining to automotive theory before progressing to hands-on sessions detailing the maintenance and repair of vehicles. Though students are provided lecture outlines and technical manuals relating to automotive maintenance, Whitmer and colleagues considered that students would benefit from a self-paced training system incorporating relevant course materials they could reference at the point of need. Additionally, use of the training system was completely voluntary and not required for the course. Results from their study found a 50% reduction in learning objective failures in the cohort that utilized FAST. Critically, the study also showed a high degree of variability of student engagement in terms of FAST usage.

The high variability in FAST usage observed by Whitmer and colleagues [9] is a potential barrier to the successful implementation of FAST in USMC and USN courses, and of AT systems in real-world learning contexts more broadly. Based on their findings, Whitmer and colleagues proposed future research aimed at linking usage rates among students to specific individual difference variables. These authors argued that understanding which traits are associated with system usage could help AT system designers develop systems aimed at increased engagement and, ultimately, improved learning outcomes. Previous AT research has emphasized the need to consider individual differences such as learner goals, motivation, and personality when designing adaptive approaches for instruction [10, 11]. Likewise, student engagement, or student involvement in educationally purposeful activities [12], has been linked with learners' achievement goals as well as positive outcomes such as graduation [13, 14]. Therefore, we designed the current study to examine individual differences in USMC students as predictors for usage of a flashcard AT system during students' course. The present study sought to explore the relationships between learning-related individual difference variables and FAST usage to investigate the reasons behind usage variability. Specifically, we chose to investigate associations between self-regulated learning (SRL), achievement goals, and intrinsic motivation (IM) and FAST usage, as these individual differences have been shown to predict both learning outcomes and study strategies [15–24].

1.1 Adaptive Training with Flashcards

AT is a training approach whereby training is tailored to individual trainees based on their current performance [2]. AT has been shown to be effective in a variety of contexts, including mathematics [25, 26], biology [27, 28] computer programming [29, 30], and medicine [31, 32]. The benefits of AT also extend to military domains involving multi-step functions such as problem solving and decision making [33–38]. An important development in AT research has been the incorporation of AT into flashcard-based learning procedures. These AT interventions typically use student performance to address when to retire flashcards and how to space them to take advantage of the *spacing effect*, which refers to the research finding that study sessions spaced over time facilitate long-term retention more effectively than sessions spaced close together [39].

Students have long used flashcards as a study method to test themselves on information and assess their current level of proficiency [40–43]. While using flashcards, students typically must make several decisions to assess their current progress. These decisions include determining when they have reached an acceptable level of proficiency for the domain, as well as understanding which flashcards require more study. Students often struggle, however, to make these decisions effectively [44]. This may result from students' inability to judge their own learning [45], or from their failure to identify effective learning strategies [41]. To address these shortcomings, researchers have fused AT and flashcard-based training approaches by developing systems that adapt the spacing between flashcard presentations [5, 46, and 6], the retirement criteria for individual flashcards [47], or both [6, 27, and 48]. Researchers adapting the spacing between flashcards develop algorithms that select flashcards for presentation based on several criteria, including accuracy, reaction times, and number of trials for previous presentations of a flashcard. Researchers adapting flashcard training based on retirement implement performance criteria for each flashcard that, when achieved, drops the flashcard from training. Prior research has shown that increasing retirement criteria for flashcard leads to greater learning efficiency [49, 50], though these findings do need to be considered in terms of their diminishing returns on long-term retention [51]. During their examination of USMC AMTBC students, Whitmer and colleagues [9] adapted both spacing and retirement to gain insights on how these interventions pair together to influence USMC course outcomes. For the purposes of the current study, however, we chose to only adapt retirement given the mixed findings of adaptive spacing presented by Whitmer and colleagues [9]. In the following sections, we describe the individual differences that may be important in predicting FAST usage.

1.2 Individual Differences in Learning

Self-regulated Learning. In considering individual differences that may predict FAST usage, self-regulated learning emerged as a potentially crucial predictor. SRL can be defined as the process by which learners monitor and direct their cognition, motivation, and behavior in pursuit of learning goals [52]. Self-regulating learners proactively monitor their progress toward their goals and adjust their methods of learning accordingly. Specifically, Zimmerman [53] outlined eight components of self-regulated learning: setting specific goals, using strategies to achieve those goals (e.g., self-directed practice), monitoring progress toward set goals, restructuring the physical and social context to be conducive to the achievement of goals (e.g., studying in a quiet environment), self-evaluating one's own learning methods, attributing causation to results, and adapting future learning methods. SRL has been associated with higher course grades [15], standardized achievement tests scores, [18], and scores on classroom assignments [20]. Experimental studies have corroborated these findings; an SRL mathematics intervention in which students were taught SRL strategies (e.g., self-evaluation, goal setting and planning) resulted in higher scores on a mathematics achievement test as compared to a group of students who did not receive the intervention [17].

Central to the current study, flashcard use can be considered a form of self-regulated learning, as it involves self-evaluation and is usually directed by the students themselves rather than by instructors [54]. Indeed, students have reported using self-testing as a means to monitor their learning [55], suggesting the use of flashcards is a self-regulated process. Thus, although students may vary in how effectively they use flashcards, self-regulated learners should be more likely to use a flashcard-based study system at all than students who are less effective at regulating their learning. However, it is important to note that post-secondary students often are not effective self-regulating learners and frequently use inefficient study strategies [44, 56].

Achievement Goals. Achievement Goal Theory has been a prominent area of research regarding individual differences in learning [57, 58]. Elliot and McGregor [59] defined achievement goals as the "purpose or cognitive-dynamic focus of competence-relevant behavior (p. 501)". In other words, achievement goals refer to the motivation behind learners' competence-related behavior, such as academic performance. Achievement goal theorists have established a 2×2 framework of achievement goals. The first dimension refers to the types of achievement goals one can have: either mastery or performance goals. Mastery goals are motivated by the development of competence (e.g., mastering a given task or concept), whereas performance goals are motivated by the demonstration of competence relative to others (e.g., performing well relative to classmates). The second dimension in the framework is the valence of achievement goals, which can be classified as either approach- or avoid-based goals. Approach goals are focused on achieving success, whereas avoid goals are focused on avoiding failure [60]. Together, the goal types and goal valences result in four achievement goal orientations: mastery-approach (MAP), mastery-avoid (MAV), performance-approach (PAP), and performance-avoid (PAV). At a high level, MAP-oriented individuals strive to achieve success relative to their own personal goals, whereas MAV-oriented individuals strive to avoid being less successful than their own personal standards [61]. On the other hand, PAP-oriented individuals strive to succeed in performing as well as or better than others, whereas PAV-oriented individuals strive to avoid not performing as well or better than others.

Although the distinction between approach and avoid goals may seem subtle, they have been shown to have differential effects on academic achievement. Specifically, approach goals are consistently better for achievement than avoid goals. For example, a meta-analysis by Baranik and colleagues [16] revealed that MAP and PAP were positively associated with academic performance (e.g., GPA, exam performance), whereas MAV and PAV were negatively correlated with performance. These results were corroborated by experimental studies, where encouraging approach-based goals was more beneficial for academic achievement than encouraging avoidance-based goals [24]. Additionally, experimentally inducing mastery-approach goals benefitted achievement more than inducing performance-approach goals, which corroborates the overall correlational finding that mastery goals are better for achievement than performance goals.

Beyond academic performance, achievement goals also predict studying behaviors. Elliot and colleagues [19] found mastery goals positively predicted the use of deep processing study strategies (e.g., thinking through topics and developing key points rather than simply re-reading course material), effort devoted to studying, and persistence in studying (e.g., allocating more time and effort to topics that were confusing rather than giving up). Though performance goals also positively predicted effort and persistence, they did not predict the use of deep processing study strategies; instead, they predicted the use of surface processing strategies (e.g., re-reading material repeatedly). Geller and colleagues [62] also observed that avoidance goals, regardless of goal type, were associated with increased use of cramming study strategies. More importantly for the present study, however, MAP goals were positively associated flashcard use and self-testing methods of studying, PAV goals were positively associated with use of self-testing strategies (but not flashcards specifically), and PAP and MAV goals were not associated with either method of study. Relatedly, Wallace and colleagues [63] found that mastery goals, regardless of valence, predicted increased use of retrieval practice for studying for an undergraduate course. Taken together, the results of these studies suggest that mastery-oriented students, and particularly mastery-approach oriented students, should be more likely to use the FAST testbed to study for the AMTBC.

Intrinsic Motivation. Intrinsic motivation (IM) is a psychological construct with a long history of empirical research as it pertains to well-being, performance, and engagement in various contexts. Intrinsic, as opposed to extrinsic, motivation refers to the completion of tasks out of inherent interest or enjoyment rather than for separate outcomes like rewards or punishments [64, 65]. Rather than a trait, IM can be thought of as a state, such that it can be either facilitated or hindered by the environment. For example, Deci and colleagues [66] found that using language that promotes a sense of autonomy rather than a sense of being controlled (e.g., 'you should' vs. 'you must') during an experiment resulted in higher self-reported IM. Thus, IM is task-specific; for example, a student may not be intrinsically motivated to study for a course, but they may be intrinsically motivated to play a video game.

In addition to its positive effect on psychological states, IM for learning has been reliably linked to learning outcomes [22]. In both a meta-analysis and a series of longitudinal studies, IM was positively associated with GPA for both high school and college students [23]. Intrinsically motivated students also tend to review course content more frequently, take the initiative to complete supplementary academic tasks, and evaluate their learning progress [21]. Thus, the current study is interested in students' IM for learning AMTBC material, as students high in IM factors may be more likely to use FAST to study for their course.

1.3 The Present Study

Given previously reported variability in FAST usage [9], the present study aimed to explore individual differences that predict usage of the AT system in a USMC course. Specifically, we were interested in the potential relationships between SRL, IM, achievement goals and FAST use, as these constructs have been shown to affect both academic achievement and use of learning strategies in laboratory and classroom environments. Furthermore, all three of these constructs have led to improved learning outcomes when manipulated experimentally, indicating that incorporating features into an AT system that promotes these constructs may result in both higher use and higher achievement. Thus, exploring whether SRL, IM, and achievement goals are related to FAST usage will provide evidence toward individual differences predicting use of AT instructional tools in a military setting, as well as provide insights to improve the ability of future AT systems to increase student learning outcomes. The data reported here are part of an ongoing experiment examining how to increase AT system usage rates by including performance-based feedback as part of the AT system.

2 Method

2.1 Participants

Participants were recruited from two separate AMTBC cohorts. The first cohort consisted of 36 students with a single student electing not to participate. The second cohort consisted of 46 students with a single student electing not to participate. Furthermore, three students' data were missing from either being re-classed midway through the course or from swapping out their computer. Overall, the sample included 77 participants (one female, $M_{Age} = 20.67$, $SD_{Age} = 2.30$).

2.2 Testbed

The Flexible Adaptive Sequencing for Training (FAST) system is a testbed that allows experimenters to manipulate the types of content and how flashcards are presented to students by varying the spacing, retirement criteria, feedback, and other settings for testing purposes. For this study, the FAST testbed was provided to students enrolled in AMTBC to allow them to study course material. FAST was installed by instructors on the course-issued laptops provided to students at the start of the course. Once opened, FAST allowed students to select a content area to study. Study sessions were structured such that training would last until all cards in the deck were correctly answered three out of the last four times they were presented. Otherwise, training would end after 30 min, or when 300 trials were completed if mastery of the deck was not achieved. Students could also opt to end early by closing a training session, which would bring them back to the content selection screen. During training, FAST presented content randomly and logged performance data for each trial presented to students. This data was aggregated to gather usage statistics.

Overall, 18 flashcard decks were available for students to study. The flashcard decks were created using content provided by AMTBC instructors and covered eight automotive systems, including electrical, compressed air, hydraulic, power plant, hydraulic and air-over-hydraulic brakes, and light and heavy suspension. Within the flashcard decks, students received three types of flashcards: identification, function, and location. Identification cards presented an image of a component and asked students to identify its name. Function cards presented an image of a component and its name and asked students to identify its function. Both identification and function cards required students to select the correct answer from four options. Feedback was provided such that if the student answered correctly, their selection would turn green. If the student answered incorrectly, their selection would turn red and the correct answer would turn green. Alternatively, location cards presented students with an image of an area of the automotive system and asked students to click the location in the image where a specific component was located. If the student selected the correct region of the screen, FAST would display "Correct" at the bottom of the screen and circle the component in the image. If the student selected an incorrect component, "Incorrect" would be displayed at the bottom of the screen and the correct component would be circled. Figure 1 provides examples of the three types of cards.

Fig. 1. Examples of location, function, and identification flashcards in FAST. (Color figure oinline)

2.3 Measures

Several surveys were administered to participants to measure potential individual difference predictors of FAST usage. The surveys included the Intrinsic Motivation Inventory [IMI; 67] to measure intrinsic motivation. The IMI includes 25 items and four scales: interest/enjoyment, perceived competence, effort/importance, and value/usefulness. Participants indicate how true a statement is by using a 7-point Likert scale with anchors that included: 1-not at all true, 4-somewhat true, and 7-very true. To measure self-regulated learning, the Self-Regulated Learning survey [SRL; 68] was administered. The SRL survey is a 30-item questionnaire with five scales: goal setting, help seeking, self-study strategies, managing physical environment, and effort regulation. Each item presents a statement (e.g., I contact someone to discuss my understanding) and participants rate their agreement on a five-point Likert-scale (1-strongly disagree, 2-disagree, 3-slightly agree, 4-agree, 5-strongly agree). Finally, the Achievement Goal Questionnaire – Revised (AGQ-R; [59] was used to identify the goal orientation of participants in the study.

The AGQ-R is a 12-item questionnaire with four scales: mastery-approach, mastery-avoidance, performance-approach, and performance-avoidance. Each item presents a statement (e.g., my aim is to perform well relative to other students) to which participants indicate their level of agreement on a five-point Likert-scale (1-strongly disagree, 5- strongly agree). Additionally, a general demographics questionnaire was given to participants to record age, rank, gender, and other demographic information.

2.4 Procedure

The study took place at the Marine Corps Combat Service Support School (MCCSSS) schoolhouse where the AMTBC is taught. Researchers administered the study procedures on two separate days: once prior to students beginning their coursework, and once towards the end of the course approximately 10 weeks later. On the first day, students were briefed on the experiment and informed that the content within FAST was developed by their instructors and could be a useful tool for ensuring their success in the course. They were also told that they could use FAST as much or as little as they wanted throughout the course. Afterwards, all instructors and course staff left the classroom so researchers could obtain consent from the students. Students were also informed that their instructors would have no way of knowing whether they chose to participate or not. Those who did not wish to participate in the research study were informed they would still have access to FAST, but their data would not be collected. After the consent process, researchers administered the pre-test, general demographics questionnaire, AGQ-R, and SRL. Next, researchers led students through a tutorial of FAST that included how to find the program, login, and select content for training. Once students were comfortable with this process, they were instructed to spend the next 30 min training with flashcards from the Electrical Theory deck. After the 30 min had expired, researchers told the students that FAST would be available for them to use as a study tool during the rest of their course and they could use it as little or as much as they preferred. Ten weeks later, researchers returned to the schoolhouse to administer a post-test along with the IMI. Afterwards, researchers conducted informal interviews with participants before they were debriefed and thanked for their participation in the study.

3   Results

3.1   Statistical Analysis

To assess whether our selected individual difference variables (i.e., SRL, AGQ-R, IMI) predicted FAST usage, we conducted exploratory Pearson product-moment correlations using each of the individual difference variables and FAST usage indicators (i.e., number of times participant used FAST, total trials completed, average number of trials completed, number of unique days trained in FAST, number of cards mastered, and number of unique decks the participant trained on). Given that we were interested in individual differences that related to usage, we excluded participants who did not use FAST after the initial training session from our analyses. Thus, our final sample included 36 participants. Of the included participants, one did not complete the AGQ-R; sample sizes for AGQ-R and usage correlations are therefore reduced to 35 participants. In the subsequent sections, we report the correlations between each individual difference variable and FAST usage.

3.2 Overall Usage

Consistent with Whitmer and colleagues [9], usage rates varied, with most students not using FAST beyond the initial introduction (see Table 1). As expected, those who used FAST multiple times tended to complete more trials (see Table 2). Interestingly, students who used FAST multiple times completed fewer cards during subsequent uses relative to the average number of trials completed by all students during their initial FAST tutorial on Day 1 of the study. Similarly, the number of mastered cards was generally low, indicating that students ended training prior to mastering all the cards in the deck.

Table 1. Descriptive statistics of FAST usage. Statistics in parentheses represent students who interacted with FAST beyond the initial introduction.

Metric	M	SD	Min	Max	Description
Number of FAST Uses	3.21 (5.55)	4.51 (5.69)	1 (2)	26 (26)	The number of times a student opened the system to complete at least one flashcard
Total Trials	142.72 (197.72)	120.59 (148.52)	21 (23)	689 (689)	The total number of flashcards completed across all training sessions
Average Number of Trials	66.16 (42.18)	37.70 (20.21)	11.5 (11.5)	135 (89.5)	The average number of flashcards completed during a training session
Number of Mastered Cards	18.91 (21.53)	15.44 (18.87)	0 (0)	69 (69)	The total number of flashcards mastered (I.e., answered correctly on 3 out 4 consecutive trials) across all training sessions
Unique Days Trained	2.08 (3.25)	1.81 (2.09)	1 (1)	9 (9)	The number of unique days on which the student completed at least one flashcard
Unique Decks Trained	2.38 (3.78)	2.17 (2.36)	1 (1)	12 (12)	The number of unique training decks in which the student completed at least one flashcard

Table 2. Correlations between FAST Usage Metrics for students who used FAST more than once.

Metric	1	2	3	4	5	6
1. Number of FAST Uses	–					
2. Total Trials	.803**	–				
3. Average Number of Trials	−.0327	.150	–			
4. Number of Mastered Cards	.222	.668**	.476**	–		
5. Unique Days Trained	.876**	.757**	−.312	.296	–	
6. Unique Decks Trained	.816**	.718**	−.273	.338*	.848**	–

3.3 Achievement Goals

Table 3 includes the correlation coefficients for the AGQ-R scales and FAST usage metrics. The MAP goal orientation was significantly and positively associated with the number of trials completed in FAST, whereas the MAV orientation was associated with a higher number of unique days trained in FAST. The PAV orientation was also positively correlated with the number of unique days trained, but the PAP orientation was not associated with any usage indicators.

Table 3. Correlations between Achievement Goals and FAST Usage.

AGQ-R	Number of FAST uses	Total Trials	Average Number of Trials	Number of mastered cards	Unique days trained	Unique decks trained
Mastery-Approach	.203	.353*	.307	.302	.283	.287
Mastery-avoid	.268	.250	−.052	.166	.363*	.274
Performance-approach	.028	.099	.201	.104	.108	.121
Performance-avoid	.171	.298	.001	.248	.336*	.290

Note. * Denotes a correlation significant at the .05 level, ** denotes a correlation significant at the .01 level.

3.4 Self-regulated Learning

None of the scores on the SRL scales significantly correlated with FAST usage (see Table 4).

Table 4. Correlations between Self-Regulated Learning and FAST Usage.

SRL scales	Number of FAST uses	Total Trials	Average Number of Trials	Number of mastered cards	Unique days trained	Unique decks trained
Goal Setting	−.101	−.121	−.025	.048	.137	.055
Help Seeking	−.059	.010	.059	.134	.142	.024
Self-study	−.016	.014	−.016	.067	.147	−.008
Physical Environment	−.029	.044	.072	.096	.020	−.125
Effort Regulation	−.004	.077	.178	.085	.116	−.060

Note. * Denotes a correlation significant at the .05 level, ** denotes a correlation significant at the .01 level.

3.5 Intrinsic Motivation

As seen in Table 5, scores on all four IMI scales were associated with a higher number of completed FAST trials. Perceived competence, effort/importance, and value/usefulness scales were associated both with a higher number of unique days and unique decks trained in FAST. Additionally, scores on the Effort/Importance and Value/Usefulness scales of the IMI were significantly and positively correlated with total number of FAST uses. Lastly, effort/importance was associated with a higher number of mastered cards.

Table 5. Correlations between IMI scales and FAST Usage.

IMI Subscales	Number of FAST uses	Total Trials	Average Number of Trials	Number of mastered cards	Unique days trained	Unique decks trained
Interest/Enjoyment	.288	.339*	.006	.230	.307	.175
Perceived competence	.317	.418*	.086	.308	.426**	.392*
Effort/Importance	.368*	.442**	.098	.404*	.377*	.348*
Value/Usefulness	.376*	.398*	−.037	.198	.399*	.386

Note. * Denotes a correlation significant at the .05 level, ** denotes a correlation significant at the .01 level.

4 Discussion

The present study explored how a flashcard-based AT system was used during a USMC course and whether there were associations between usage, SRL, IM, and achievement goals. To that end, the study presented correlations for each of these constructs in terms of several usage metrics in a real-world setting. Overall, usage rates varied considerably, with wide ranges of usage among each of the usage metrics (e.g., number of FAST uses, total number of trials completed, etc.). Additionally, only 36 of the 77 total participants used FAST after the initial training session. Based on interviews with students following the study, these results may be due to students forgetting FAST was available to them. Instructors did not require students to use FAST, and many students reported that they forgot FAST was installed on their laptops despite both the initial introduction by the instructor and researchers and the application being located directly on their desktop screen. Moreover, students who engaged with FAST after the initial training session mastered fewer cards relative to the average number of cards all students mastered during their Day 1 introduction to FAST. Interviews conducted with students after the study also revealed some students thought the content was not relevant for the course section with which they wanted supplemental training. The content provided within FAST was intended to cover function and identification of automotive components, which are primarily covered in the first two sections of the course. Later sections reinforce components' function; however, these sections focus heavily on hands-on maintenance actions and troubleshooting, which FAST content did not cover. Students also commented they thought the content was too easy and only did a handful of flashcards before closing FAST or moving on to a different content area. This behavior is in line with research suggesting learners tend to exercise poor judgement regarding when to stop studying a given flashcard [39, 54], which may have contributed to their ending training prior to reaching the mastery criteria.

Regarding individual differences and FAST usage, results indicated that achievement goals and IM, but not SRL, were positively associated with aspects of FAST usage. Although previous research has shown that SRL relates to positive learning activities, the current study did not find a significant relationship between SRL and FAST usage. As the current study focused on FAST usage and not other forms of positive learning activities (e.g., referencing technical manuals, course outlines, and other course-related materials asking for feedback from instructors), we may not have captured the effects of SRL in our outcome measures. That is not to say students with higher levels of SRL did not implement more successful strategies; these strategies may have simply manifested in other behaviors that were not measured during this study. Future studies examining AT system usage should consider how learning strategies are implemented and assessed when gauging how and why students interact with their system.

Regarding achievement goals, associations between goal orientations differed across usage metrics. Both avoid-orientations of the AGQ-R (MAV and PAV) were associated with a higher number of unique days trained in FAST, but neither were associated with any of the other usage metrics. MAP, however, was associated with a higher number of total trials completed. MAP and PAV have been associated with more use of self-testing [19], and mastery goals, regardless of valence, have been associated with more use of retrieval practice [63]. Higher levels of avoidance led to an increase in number of system uses; however, there is no evidence these goal orientations led to more trials completed within the training system. As previous research has discussed the association between avoidance goals and a decreased likelihood of establishing structured study routines [19, 62], designers of future AT systems may consider including features that provide structure during use to facilitate approach goals, which have been linked to improved performance [24]. Examples of such features include intermittent knowledge checks during study and feedback detailing training progress.

Results also revealed several correlations between IMI scales and flashcard system usage. All scales of the IMI correlated positively with total number of trials completed by students. This finding is consistent with previous research indicating higher levels of IM lead to behaviors that enhance learners' engagement in academic tasks on their own initiative [e.g., 21]. It is encouraging that students' reported understanding of the importance and value of the course material correlated with usage of the course's flash-card training system. Emphasizing these qualities of the course, as well as how the training system may facilitate students' feelings of competence in course topics, may lead to increased student usage of adaptive training systems in future courses. Future AT systems should consider implementing features to highlight the importance of criti-cal course information to facilitate intrinsic motivation and, ultimately, increased system usage. These features could take the form of summary notes at the conclusion of sections as well as information conveying practical applications of course content.

4.1 Limitations and Conclusion

Despite our efforts to extend the research conducted by Whitmer and colleagues [9], the current study was limited in some ways. For example, students were not required to use FAST during their course nor were instructors obligated to remind students the tool was available, as this could have potentially confounded the findings and introduced coercion. Though this may have reduced the overall usage of FAST and our sample size, it did allow us to identify relationships between individual differences and those who chose to use FAST on their own. Relatedly, we are unable to present individual difference findings that explain why students used FAST more than once throughout the course. As discussed previously, there are a multitude of factors that may have hindered students' engagement with FAST, including forgetting the system was available. Future research should investigate students' reasons for using and not using AT systems, as well as their preferences for system features. These limitations notwithstanding, the current study provides valuable insight into certain individual differences that relate to supplemental AT system usage in a USMC classroom. These results extend the research conducted by Whitmer and colleagues [9] by identifying individual differences that predict FAST usage. Overall, our study suggests that goal orientation and IM are related to FAST usage; however, no significant correlations were uncovered for our measure of SRL. Future research should consider these relationships when exploring ways to promote engagement with AT systems, as these systems have the capability to modernize learning approaches to USN and USMC courses.

Acknowledgments. We gratefully acknowledge Dr. Peter Squire and the Office of Naval Research for sponsoring this work (Funding Doc# N0001422WX00487). We would like to thank Dr. Cheryl

Johnson for her contributions developing, planning, and coordinating this research effort. We would also like to thank CWO Micah Soboleski and the instructors and students from the Automotive Maintenance Technician Basic Course (AMTBC) for their support, as well as Ms. Cherrise Ficke for her contributions developing and testing FAST. Presentation of this material does not constitute or imply its endorsement, recommendation, or favoring by the U.S. Navy or the Department of Defense (DoD). The opinions of the authors expressed herein do not necessarily state or reflect those of the U.S. Navy or DoD.

References

1. Barto, J., Daly, T., Lafleur, A., Steinhauser, N.: Adaptive blended learning experience (ABLE). In: Proceedings of the Interservice/Industry Training, Simulation & Education Conference (I/ITSEC). National Training Systems Association, Orlando (2020)
2. Landsberg, C.R., Van Buskirk, W.L., Astwood, R.S., Mercado, A.D., Aakre, A.J.: Adaptive training considerations for simulation-based training. (Special report 2010-001). Naval Air Warfare Center Training Systems Division, Orlando (2011)
3. Landsberg, C.R., Astwood, R.S., Jr., Van Buskirk, W.L., Townsend, L.N., Steinhauser, N.B., Mercado, A.D.: Review of adaptive training system techniques. Mil. Psychol. 24(2), 96–113 (2012)
4. Durlach, P.J., Ray, J.M.: Designing adaptive instructional environments: insights from empirical evidence. Technical report 1297. U.S. Army Research Institute for the Behavioral & Social Sciences, Arlington (2011)
5. Mettler, E., Massey, C.M., Kellman, P.J.: A comparison of adaptive and fixed schedules of practice. J. Exp. Psychol. Gen. 145(7), 897–917 (2016)
6. Mettler, E., Massey, C.M., El-Ashmawy, A.K., Kellman, P.J.: Adaptive vs. fixed spacing of learning items: evidence from studies of learning and transfer in chemistry education. In: Proceedings of the 42nd Annual Conference of the Cognitive Science Society (2020)
7. Mettler, E., Kellman, P.J.: Adaptive response-time-based category sequencing in perceptual learning. Vision. Res. 99, 111–123 (2014)
8. Fiechter, J.L., Benjamin, A.S.: Techniques for scaffolding retrieval practice: the costs and benefits of adaptive versus diminishing cues. Psychon. Bull. Rev. 26(5), 1666–1674 (2019). https://doi.org/10.3758/s13423-019-01617-6
9. Whitmer, D.E., Johnson, C.I., Marraffino, M.D., Hovorka, J.: Using adaptive flashcards for automotive maintenance training in the wild. In: Sottilare, R.A., Schwarz, J. (eds.) HCII 2021. LNCS, vol. 12792, pp. 466–480. Springer, Cham (2021). https://doi.org/10.1007/978-3-030-77857-6_33
10. Mödritscher, F., Garcia-Barrios, V.M., Gütl, C.: The past, the present and the future of adaptive e-learning. In: Proceedings of ICL 2004 (2004)
11. Shute, V.J., Towle, B.: Adaptive e-learning. Educ. Psychol. 38(2), 105–114 (2003)
12. Kuh, G.D.: The national survey of student engagement: conceptual and empirical foundations. New directions for Institutional Research (2009)
13. Miller, A.L., Fassett, K.T., Palmer, D.L.: Achievement goal orientation: a predictor of student engagement in higher education. Motiv. Emot. 45(3), 327–344 (2021). https://doi.org/10.1007/s11031-021-09881-7
14. Pascarella, E.T., Terenzini, P.T.: How College Affects Students: A Third Decade of Research, 1st edn. Jossey-Bass, San Francisco (2005)
15. Ali, A.D., Hanna, W.K.: Predicting students' achievement in a hybrid environment through self-regulated learning, log data, and course engagement: A data mining approach. J. Educ. Comput. Res. 60(4), 960–985 (2022)

16. Baranik, L.E., Stanley, L.J., Bynum, B.H., Lance, C.E.: Examining the construct validity of mastery-avoidance achievement goals: a meta-analysis. Hum. Perform. **23**(3), 265–282 (2010)
17. Camahalan, F.M.G.: Effects of self-regulated learning on mathematics achievement of selected Southeast Asian children. J. Instruct. Psychol. **33**(3) (2006)
18. Dent, A.L., Koenka, A.C.: The relation between self-regulated learning and academic achievement across childhood and adolescence: a meta-analysis. Educ. Psychol. Rev. **28**, 425–474 (2016)
19. Elliot, A.J., McGregor, H.A., Gable, S.: Achievement goals, study strategies, and exam performance: a mediational analysis. J. Educ. Psychol. **91**(3), 549 (1999)
20. Pintrich, P.R., De Groot, E.V.: Motivational and self-regulated learning components of classroom academic performance. J. Educ. Psychol. **82**(1), 33 (1990)
21. Lei, S.A.: Intrinsic and extrinsic motivation: evaluating benefits and drawbacks from college instructors' perspectives. J. Instruct. Psychol. **37**(2) (2010)
22. Ryan, R.M., Deci, E.L.: Intrinsic and extrinsic motivation from a self-determination theory perspective: definitions, theory, practices, and future directions. Contemp. Educ. Psychol. **61**, 101860 (2020)
23. Taylor, G., et al.: A self-determination theory approach to predicting school achievement over time: the unique role of intrinsic motivation. Contemp. Educ. Psychol. **39**(4), 342–358 (2014)
24. Van Yperen, N.W., Blaga, M., Postmes, T.: A meta-analysis of the impact of situationally induced achievement goals on task performance. Hum. Perform. **28**(2), 165–182 (2015)
25. Kalyuga, S.: Assessment of learners' organized knowledge structures in adaptive learning environments. Appl. Cogn. Psychol.: Off. J. Soc. Appl. Res. Mem. Cogn. **20**(3), 333–342 (2006)
26. Yang, E., Dorneich, M.C.: Affect-aware adaptive tutoring based on human–automation etiquette strategies. Hum. Factors **60**(4), 510–526 (2018)
27. Ahmad, T.R., Ashraf, D.C., Kellman, P.J., Krasne, S., Ramanathan, S.: Training visual pattern recognition in ophthalmology using a perceptual and adaptive learning module. [Pre-Print]. Research Square (2021). https://doi.org/10.21203/rs.3.rs-806381/v1
28. Van Seters, J.R., Wellink, J., Tramper, J., Goedhart, M.J., Ossevoort, M.A.: A web-based adaptive tutor to teach PCR primer design. Biochem. Mol. Biol. Educ. **40**(1), 8–13 (2012)
29. Davidovic, A., Warren, J., Trichina, E.: Learning benefits of structural example based adaptive tutoring systems. IEEE Trans. Educ. **46**(2), 241–251 (2003)
30. Lane, H.C., VanLehn, K.: Teaching the tacit knowledge of programming to novices with natural language tutoring. Comput. Sci. Educ. **15**(3), 183–201 (2005)
31. Romero, C., Ventura, S., Gibaja, E.L., Hervás, C., Romero, F.: Web-based adaptive training simulator system for cardiac life support. Artif. Intell. Med. **38**(1), 67–78 (2006)
32. Warner, D.O., et al.: Adaptive instruction and learner interactivity in online learning: a randomized trial. Adv. Health Sci. Educ. **25**, 95–109 (2020)
33. Billings, D.R.: Efficacy of adaptive feedback strategies in simulation-based training. Mil. Psychol. **24**(2), 114–133 (2012)
34. Marraffino, M.D., Johnson, C.I., Whitmer, D.E., Steinhauser, N.B., Clement, A.: Advise when ready for game plan: adaptive training for JTACs. In: Proceedings of the Interservice/Industry, Training, Simulation, and Education Conference (2019)
35. Marraffino, M.D., Schroeder, B.L., Fraulini, N.W., Van Buskirk, W.L., Johnson, C.I.: Adapting training in real time: an empirical test of adaptive difficulty schedules. Mil. Psychol. **33**(3), 136–151 (2021)
36. Serge, S.R., Priest, H.A., Durlach, P.J., Johnson, C.I.: The effects of static and adaptive performance feedback in game-based training. Comput. Hum. Behav. **29**(3), 1150–1158 (2013)

37. Van Buskirk, W.L., Johnson, C.I., Marraffino, M.D., Schroeder, B.L., Fraulini, N.W.: Adaptive training for submarine electronic warfare operators. Presented at the 20th Congress of the International Ergonomics Association, Florence, Italy (2018)
38. Whitmer, D.E., Johnson, C.I., Marraffino, M.D.: Examining two adaptive sequencing approaches for flashcard learning: the tradeoff between training efficiency and long-term retention. In: Sottilare, R.A., Schwarz, J. (eds.) HCII 2022. LNCS, vol. 13332, pp. 126–139. Springer, Cham (2022). https://doi.org/10.1007/978-3-031-05887-5_10
39. Kornell, N.: Optimising learning using flashcards: spacing is more effective than cramming. Appl. Cogn. Psychol.: Off. J. Soc. Appl. Res. Mem. Cogn. 23(9), 1297–1317 (2009)
40. Hartwig, M.K., Dunlosky, J.: Study strategies of college students: are self-testing and scheduling related to achievement? Psychon. Bull. Rev. 19, 126–134 (2012)
41. Karpicke, J.D., Butler, A.C., Roediger, H.L., III.: Metacognitive strategies in student learning: do students practise retrieval when they study on their own? Memory 17(4), 471–479 (2009)
42. Kornell, N., Bjork, R.A.: The promise and perils of self-regulated study. Psychon. Bull. Rev. 14(2), 219–224 (2007)
43. Wissman, K.T., Rawson, K.A., Pyc, M.A.: How and when do students use flashcards? Memory 20(6), 568–579 (2012)
44. Bjork, R.A., Dunlosky, J., Kornell, N.: Self-regulated learning: beliefs, techniques, and illusions. Annu. Rev. Psychol. 64, 417–444 (2013)
45. Pyc, M.A., Rawson, K.A., Aschenbrenner, A.J.: Metacognitive monitoring during criterion learning: when and why are judgments accurate? Mem. Cognit. 42(6), 886–897 (2014). https://doi.org/10.3758/s13421-014-0403-4
46. Metzler-Baddeley, C., Baddeley, R.J.: Does adaptive training work? Appl. Cogn. Psychol.: Off. J. Soc. Appl. Res. Mem. Cogn. 23(2), 254–266 (2009)
47. Whitmer, D.E., Johnson, C.I., Marraffino, M.D., Pharmer, R.L., Blalock, L.D.: A mastery approach to flashcard-based adaptive training. In: Sottilare, R.A., Schwarz, J. (eds.) HCII 2020. LNCS, vol. 12214, pp. 555–568. Springer, Cham (2020). https://doi.org/10.1007/978-3-030-50788-6_41
48. Mettler, E., Burke, T., Massey, C.M., Kellman, P.J.: Comparing adaptive and random spacing schedules during learning to mastery criteria. In: Proceedings of the 42nd Annual Conference of the Cognitive Science Society (2020)
49. Pyc, M.A., Rawson, K.A.: Testing the retrieval effort hypothesis: does greater difficulty correctly recalling information lead to higher levels of memory? J. Mem. Lang. 60(4), 437–447 (2009)
50. Vaughn, K.E., Rawson, K.A.: Diagnosing criterion-level effects on memory: what aspects of memory are enhanced by repeated retrieval? Psychol. Sci. 22(9), 1127–1131 (2011)
51. Pyc, M.A., Rawson, K.A.: Costs and benefits of dropout schedules of test–restudy practice: implications for student learning. Appl. Cogn. Psychol. 25(1), 87–95 (2011)
52. Pintrich, P.R.: Multiple goals, multiple pathways: the role of goal orientation in learning and achievement. J. Educ. Psychol. 92(3), 544 (2000)
53. Zimmerman, B.J.: Becoming a self-regulated learner: an overview. Theory into practice 41(2), 64–70 (2002)
54. Kornell, N., Bjork, R.A.: Optimising self-regulated study: the benefits—and costs—of dropping flashcards. Memory 16(2), 125–136 (2008)
55. Kornell, N., Son, L.K.: Learners' choices and beliefs about self-testing. Memory 17(5), 493–501 (2009)
56. Vosniadou, S.: Bridging secondary and higher education. The importance of self-regulated learning. Eur. Rev. 28(S1), S94–S103 (2020)
57. Dweck, C.S.: Motivational processes affecting learning. Am. Psychol. 41(10), 1040–1048 (1986)

58. Fisher, S.L., Ford, J.K.: Differential effects of learner effort and goal orientation on two learning outcomes. Pers. Psychol. **51**(2), 397–420 (1998)
59. Elliot, A.J., McGregor, H.A.: A 2 × 2 achievement goal framework. J. Pers. Soc. Psychol. **80**(3), 501 (2001)
60. Elliot, A.J., Murayama, K.: On the measurement of achievement goals: critique, illustration, and application. J. Educ. Psychol. **100**(3), 613 (2008)
61. Van Yperen, N.W., Elliot, A.J., Anseel, F.: The influence of mastery-avoidance goals on performance improvement. Eur. J. Soc. Psychol. **39**(6), 932–943 (2009)
62. Geller, J., et al.: Study strategies and beliefs about learning as a function of academic achievement and achievement goals. Memory **26**(5), 683–690 (2018)
63. Wallace, A.S., Elliot, A.J., Rogge, R.D.: Spontaneous use of retrieval and rereading: relation to achievement goals and exam performance. J. Educ. Psychol. **114**(6), 1412 (2022)
64. Deci, E.L., Ryan, R.M.: The "what" and "why" of goal pursuits: human needs and the self-determination of behavior. Psychol. Inq. **11**(4), 227–268 (2000)
65. Ryan, R.M., Deci, E.L.: Intrinsic and extrinsic motivations: classic definitions and new directions. Contemp. Educ. Psychol. **25**(1), 54–67 (2000)
66. Deci, E.L., Eghrari, H., Patrick, B.C., Leone, D.R.: Facilitating internalization: the self-determination theory perspective. J. Pers. **62**(1), 119–142 (1994)
67. Ryan, R.M.: Control and information in the intrapersonal sphere: an extension of cognitive evaluation theory. J. Pers. Soc. Psychol. **43**, 450–461 (1982)
68. Kocdar, S., Karadeniz, A., Bozkurt, A., Buyuk, K. Measuring self-regulation in self-paced open and distance learning environments. Int. Rev. Res. Open Distrib. Learn. **19**(1) (2018)

Which is Better Individualized Training for a Novel, Complex Task? Learner Control vs. Feedback Algorithms

Bradford L. Schroeder[1](✉), Wendi L. Van Buskirk[1], Michelle Aros[2], Jason E. Hochreiter[1], and Nicholas W. Fraulini[2]

[1] Naval Air Warfare Center Training Systems Division, Orlando, FL 32826, USA
{bradford.l.schroeder.civ,wendi.l.vanbuskirk.civ,
jason.e.hochreiter.civ}@us.navy.mil
[2] StraCon Services Group, Fort Worth, TX 76109, USA
{michelle.aros2.ctr,nicholas.w.fraulini.ctr}@us.navy.mil

Abstract. Providing feedback during training can help trainees address errors and deficiencies to improve performance. One method for presenting feedback is to implement adaptive training (AT) algorithms that assess trainees' performance and present feedback tailored to their current needs. Despite the precision with which adaptive feedback addresses trainees' needs, this algorithmic approach does not offer trainees agency during training. Providing trainees the opportunity to select their own instructional interventions may facilitate performance gains through increased motivation and improved self-regulatory strategies. Unfortunately, trainees inexperienced in a domain may struggle to choose appropriate feedback as a result of their naiveté. We conducted the present research to examine performance differences between trainees presented algorithm-controlled feedback and those who chose their instruction during an electronic warfare (EW) task. Based on the novel nature of the EW task, we hypothesized trainees receiving algorithm-controlled feedback would display improved performance at immediate (H1) and delayed retention (H2) compared to trainees who choose their feedback. Similarly, we hypothesized a differential effect across groups such that trainees who score higher at pretest would score higher at immediate posttest, but that this effect would be more pronounced for trainees' choosing their instructional interventions (H3). Our results revealed partial support for H1 and full support for H2 and H3. These results may reflect trainees' difficulty choosing appropriate feedback in a novel, complex task, as well as increased cognitive load associated with that choice.

Keywords: Adaptive Training · Feedback Algorithms · Learner Control · Electronic Warfare · Adaptive Instructional Systems

R. A. Sottilare and J. Schwarz (Eds.): HCII 2023, LNCS 14044, pp. 236–252, 2023.
https://doi.org/10.1007/978-3-031-34735-1_17

1 Introduction

1.1 Learning with Computer-Based Training

To train a complex task to an individual learner, tutors often rely on one-on-one instruction and multimedia methods for their trainees. Although one-on-one instruction is the ultimate instructional approach [1], computer-based training can capture some of the benefits of the one-on-one learning experience. Adaptive training (AT) systems that assess and adapt in real time closely approximate the benefits of one-on-one tutoring [2]. AT is tailored to learners' strengths and weaknesses [3], and adapts elements of the training experience to better support the learner's growth during training. Typically, AT systems adapt elements such as task difficulty [4], feedback content [5], or training material [6], and these adaptations may be informed by variables such as the learner's performance [7], ability [8], or individual differences [9]. Through these tailored adaptations, AT can mirror the instructional sensitivities of human tutors that are attuned to the dynamic needs of their learners. The present work focuses on the subject of feedback in an adaptive training system.

Feedback serves the purpose of directing a learner's attention to the correctness of their actions in order to result in a change in behavior (i.e., improving performance; [10]). Many factors influence under what circumstances different kinds of feedback are beneficial to the learner (see Landsberg et al. [11]), but for the present work, we focus on event-based immediate feedback, which is recommended for learning novel, complex tasks (e.g., [12, 13]; c.f. [14]). One technique to provide feedback is to offer learners agency with their learning experience. This idea is called "learner control," where learners can control their instructional content to some degree [15]. Learner control allows students to interact with their training and through this interaction can foster deeper understanding, better learning, and longer retention of the material [16, 17]. On the other hand, feedback has typically been provided in AT systems primarily through the use of algorithms hosted within the system. In an AT system, an algorithm will analyze many elements of a learner's performance which serve as a data source to adapt training to the individual. With this data source, adaptive training algorithms can pinpoint areas of weakness that may benefit from corrective feedback, or they could assess the learner's performance level to offer a more challenging training experience. These elements are but a few examples of ways to individualize a learning experience within AT systems. The goal of the present study is to compare instructional content delivered via feedback algorithm against the same instructional content selected by the learner.

1.2 Learner Control

As mentioned above, one way to present feedback within an AT system is to allow users to select the feedback they wish to receive. Learner control benefits learning by improving performance, attitude, and motivation. In a study by Ross and colleagues [18], undergraduate nursing and education majors were given the opportunity to choose the themes they wanted for the explanations and problems in their statistics instruction, and their performance improved when they had this choice [18]. Pascal [19] offered undergraduate students the opportunity to choose their choice of medium for their psychology lessons (lecture, lecture and discussion, and independent study). This yielded more positive student attitudes (but no difference in learning outcomes) towards their instruction than if students were restricted to a particular medium. Motivation may also be improved through learner control as found in a study where military trainees were allowed to choose training topics within computer adapted instruction in electronics [20]. The trainees developed more positive attitudes towards the instruction than when they were given topics that were based on their pretest scores. Other benefits of learner control include its ability to increase motivation [21, 22], encourage the use of self-regulation strategies [23], and assist learners to take charge of their personal learning process [24]. Learner control has been shown to benefit basketball throwing [25] and sequential timing tasks [26], but there is not extensive literature on its use in a complex cognitive training task.

However, learner control does have its drawbacks. According to Vandewaetere and Wauters [27], students may not always make good choices, and there are mixed results on its effects of student achievement. They suggested that learners may not have adequate metacognitive skills to discern when they need help and when they do not. Other research suggests that, when learners have full control over their learning content, they may not select what is most appropriate for their learning needs [28]. Others argue that some learners may wait to ask for hints or help and will hone-in on certain hints while ignoring higher priority feedback that could be more applicable to their errors [29]. These results are consistent with the Dunning-Kruger cognitive bias. The Dunning-Kruger effect asserts that those with low levels of expertise may have little insight into their own incompetence [30, 31]. This leads to poor performers being unable to recognize their mistakes which could result in poor performance. Likewise, cognitive overload could also be a limitation of learner control. Conklin [32] and Niederhauser and colleagues [33] suggest that learner control may cause overload due to the additional meta-cognitive resources required to assess one's own performance. Additionally, this added demand interferes with the attentional and cognitive processing needed to make strategic decisions about one's learning.

In summary, many of the limitations observed in learner control studies could be alleviated by an algorithmic approach to the delivery of instructional content. Instead of relying on a learner to have sufficient metacognitive skills to critique their own learning, a feedback algorithm could supplant this need for the learner. While some of the previously mentioned research touts benefits for learner control despite these limitations, we expect algorithm-based feedback to result in superior learning outcomes due to the novelty and complexity of the task in the present work.

1.3 Algorithm Control

Algorithm control is not a novel concept and has been used to adapt instruction successfully in Intelligent Tutoring Systems for decades. Indeed, Anderson's algebra and programming tutoring systems are well known for providing students with tailored feedback utilizing Bayesian algorithms and resulting in positive learning outcomes (for a review see Corbett, Koedinger, and Anderson [34]). When looking at feedback algorithms, specifically, as opposed to algorithms that adapt task difficulty, there is evidence to suggest that feedback algorithms may be beneficial for complex decision-making tasks. For instance, Buff and Campbell [35] compared tailored feedback derived by fuzzy logic algorithms to no feedback and outcome feedback. Participants in this study performed a military air defense warfare task. Results showed that diagnostic feedback created from algorithms led to posttest performance improvements while the no feedback and outcome feedback groups did not improve their performance. Landsberg and colleagues [3] compared an adaptive training system for Navy periscope operators to a non-adaptive training system that adapted the content of the feedback. These authors found a training efficiency for the adaptive group such that they made their calls faster than the non-adaptive counter parts. Additionally, the adaptive group was able to reach criterion performance faster and end training early as a result. Taken together, these research results suggest that algorithm control may be beneficial in an AT system for a complex task.

Feedback algorithms may also have limitations that vary with the design of the algorithm and the capability of the training system being used. A feedback algorithm can only deliver instructional content based on performance attributes that the system was designed to measure. Other factors, such as subjective states of the learner, the learner's mental models of the task, or learner individual differences may not always be considered when feedback algorithms are developed. In cases where performance is difficult to measure or abstract in nature, feedback may be more difficult to process through an algorithmic approach. These are general considerations for the judicious use of feedback algorithms, but in the present study, our Electronic Warfare (EW) task has a multitude of well-defined, objective performance elements. Therefore, we anticipate that an algorithm control approach should be effective for training EW skills.

Since EW is a novel task to the general population, one would logically expect good performance on an EW task to be based on how well task information is encoded during an instructional phase. For a general population, an error-sensitive feedback algorithm could be more beneficial during training, as the algorithm should deliver the most relevant instructional interventions to the user when it is needed. However, when considering previous literature on learner control and prior knowledge, it is possible there may be a different relationship when training with learner-chosen instructional interventions. Those who encode poorly during the instruction phase may not know what kind of instructional interventions they require to improve. On the other hand, those who encode well during the instruction phase may have a better idea of the instructional interventions they need. Further, those same learners may know better about what to expect for future performance, and may select instructional interventions that will better prepare them for future task elements. An error-sensitive algorithm would not be able to support this, as it cannot anticipate future errors or weak points like a human learner.

1.4   Present Study

In the present study, we examined an algorithm that adapted feedback presented to learners based on the importance and severity of their mistakes and compared this to learner-controlled instructional interventions. Based on previous literature that suggests that learner control may be more beneficial for those with higher skill, we believed that an algorithm may be better for a general sample of participants. As not everyone will possess equal encoding skills during instruction, the algorithmic feedback could be helpful in redirecting learners' attention to higher priority information. Learners were trained to perform an EW task with simulated tactical software, and also returned one week later to evaluate how well they retained their learning.

Therefore, we hypothesized that learners experiencing EW training with a feedback algorithm would show greater performance in posttest than learners who experienced EW training and chose their own instructional interventions (H1). Additionally, we hypothesized that the same pattern of results would emerge in delayed retention (H2). Lastly, we hypothesized that there would be a differential effect between both groups, where those in the learner control group would show greater learning gains in posttest when having higher levels of performance in pretest, assuming that pretest performance represents the quality of encoding during instruction (H3; relating to previously mentioned literature on the effect of expertise in learner control).

2   Method

2.1   Participants

The study took place over two sessions. In the first session, 38 undergraduate students participated in the study (17 in the algorithm group and 21 in the learner control group). For the second session, 34 participants returned (16 in the algorithm group and 18 in the learner control group). Participants were 23 females and 14 males (1 chose not to respond), and had an average age of 21.26 years (SD = 2.91 years).

2.2   Materials

Instructional Presentation. All participants received an instructional PowerPoint presentation containing information about radar theory, emitters and their signal properties (such as frequency, pulse repetition frequency, scan type, and scan time). Emitters are devices attached to radars that produce the radar's signals. After reviewing this background information, participants received details about their mission they were to perform, as well as the training and feedback they would receive. Participants were allowed to review this instructional material at their own pace.

Electronic Warfare (EW) Testbed. Participants performed the EW task using an electronic warfare tactical system emulator. This system displays data tables containing emitter parameters as well as visual data pertaining to emitters' waveforms. Alongside this tactical system emulator, participants had a computer-based reporting interface where they input information to classify and submit their emitter reports. These reports consisted of multiple elements (such as scan type, threat classification, and scan time), and these reports were expected to be submitted on-time based on rules specified in the instructional presentation. Upon submitting a report, participants' data would be scored for the accuracy of the report's contents (i.e., was each element of the report correct?), and the timeliness of the report submission. At the end of each scenario, participants would submit a final report and receive a score based on their performance over the entire scenario. Participants interacted with this system using a 17-inch gaming laptop connected with a computer mouse and secondary 22″ external monitor.

Instructional Videos. During training scenarios, participants were eligible to receive videos describing techniques for performing important parts of the mission (e.g., how to identify different scan types or how to take emitter measurements). If participants were in the algorithm feedback group, they received these videos periodically during training based on rules described in the next section. Those in the learner control group had access to all of the same instructional videos, but instead of having the videos selected for them via algorithm, they chose which instructional videos they wanted to see during training. Both groups had the same opportunities to see these videos (4 videos for each scenario; 12 videos in total). To ensure these videos were appropriate for our sample of undergraduate students, we checked each video script with the Flesch-Kincaid scale [36] to ensure the video content was at or below the 12th grade reading level. Video scripts averaged with a grade level score of 7.1 (maximum was 11.3). Additionally, the average duration of the videos was 30.05 s.

Feedback Algorithm and Learner Controlled Instructional Videos. For the algorithm feedback group, we created a series of feedback rules based on various performance aspects measured from submitted reports and other actions made by the learner. These performance aspects included participants' specific accuracy or timeliness scores, their time spent completing certain actions, or their prioritization of reports. Each feedback rule evaluated a specified threshold on a given performance aspect and represented a related error or deficiency; for example, submitting a certain report too late might be represented as "report delta >60 s." A narrated video designed to provide instruction addressing these errors was associated with each rule. We developed the rule algorithm based on all possible actions an operator could perform in the EW task. These actions were sorted into a rule list. The most important EW task elements were organized toward the top of this rule list, with the idea that delivering feedback relevant to the most critical errors that participants made would lead to improvements in performance. A task element's importance was based on its impact to the mission (e.g., identifying high-priority threats) or the possibility that it could have cascading effects. For example, misclassifying an emitter's scan type could cause a learner to incorrectly de-prioritize it, give it a lower threat classification, and/or take an incorrect measurement. Considering that some errors may produce second or third-order effects, the primary error must be addressed prior to any secondary or tertiary errors. During training, at designated feedback intervals, each rule was evaluated and the instructional videos associated with all rules that were violated based on the learner's actions were added to a list of candidate videos. The highest-priority candidate video that had not already been presented to the learner within a particular scenario was displayed during this feedback interval. Additionally, the scope of each rule varied in configuration to consider either the entire scenario up to the current feedback interval or only the portion of the scenario completed since the last instructional video was displayed. For example, some EW task elements are time-sensitive and are only appropriate to deliver at certain times (such as the timeliness of the learner's final report submission), but other elements are relevant throughout the duration of a scenario (such as the threat classification level of a report).

In the learner control group, a summary of the same set of instructional videos was presented to the learner at the same designated feedback intervals, allowing them to select a video to review. This summary was organized categorically independently of the algorithm feedback group's prioritization, with the order of the categories and the order of videos within each category shuffled each time it was presented to the learner. Each available instructional video had an associated button containing a short title describing its contents. At subsequent intervals, previously viewed videos would be indicated with a color change (see Fig. 1) and a tooltip to remind the learner that they had already watched them. However, learners were allowed to watch already-viewed videos again, if desired. Although this method of video selection was different from the algorithm, both groups had the same number of opportunities (4 per each training scenario) to view instructional videos.

2.3 Procedure

Instruction. The first session started with a PowerPoint presentation that described to participants their mission objectives and basic knowledge required to complete the mission. Participants were instructed which elements were most important to their mission. Once they completed the PowerPoint, participants completed a demonstration scenario in which they received live instruction on the EW task such as assessing, identifying, and reporting on emitter signals. This demonstration scenario was led by the instructor and allowed participants to witness the step-by-step procedure for analyzing and reporting emitter signals. Once all the concepts were covered by the instructor, the participant took control of the scenario for hands-on practice. They continued the scenario from where the instructor left off and finished what they could in the remaining 4–7 min. Participants were permitted to ask the instructor questions during this time. The demonstration was followed by a knowledge quiz in which the participant was asked questions about the content covered in the PowerPoint presentation and demonstration scenario. Upon completion of this quiz, the instructor reviewed any incorrect answers and explained why the answers were incorrect.

Training Scenarios. After completing the instruction phase, participants began the pretest scenario. Afterward, they were assigned randomly to the learner control or algorithm group and completed 3 ten-minute training scenarios in the respective group. During the training scenarios, feedback would periodically be presented as narrated instructional videos driven either by an algorithm (algorithm group) or by user choice (learner control group).

While feedback was displayed to the participant, whether automatically presented via the algorithm feedback group or chosen by the learner in the learner control group, the scenario timer was paused. After the training scenarios, participants completed a posttest scenario which was identical in difficulty to the pretest scenario.

Delayed Retention. Participants returned approximately one week later to complete a delayed measure of their learning. During this session, participants completed a short refresher scenario that consisted of a shortened version of the training scenarios. Participants were permitted to ask the experimenter questions during the refresher scenario. Once participants completed the refresher scenario, participants began the delayed

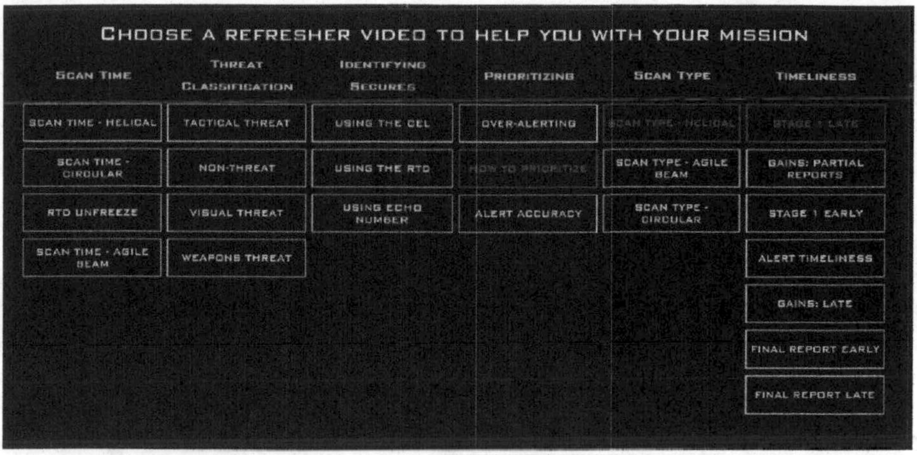

Fig. 1. Image of the Learner Control group's interface for selecting instructional videos to view. Previously-viewed videos have their buttons darkened with blue coloring. (Color figure online)

retention scenario. The retention scenario was similar to the first session scenarios, was ten-minutes long, and the instructor did not provide assistance. Participants were compensated $30 after each session for a total of $60 for the entire experiment.

3 Results

3.1 Comparing Performance at Posttest and Delayed Retention

To test our hypotheses, we compared our two groups using independent samples one-tailed t-tests at two timepoints: posttest, and delayed retention. These tests were selected for our directional hypotheses in favor of the feedback algorithm group. We examined timeliness and accuracy of reports, as well as the overall scenario score (which was a combination of accuracy and timeliness for all reports in the scenario). For posttest, those in the algorithm group were significantly more accurate with their reports than those in the learner control group, $t(36) = 1.81, p = .039$. Unexpectedly, they identified fewer targets on-time than the learner control group, $t(36) = 1.89, p = .033$, and made more late reports, $t(36) = 2.22, p = .016$. Lastly, those in the feedback algorithm group had a significantly higher overall scenario score than those in the learner control group, $t(36) = 2.07, p = .023$ (see Table 1 for descriptives). These results partially supported H1 (see Fig. 2 for a depiction of these results).

Examining the same comparisons in delayed retention, the algorithm group maintained their advantage over the learner control group in accuracy of reports, $t(32) = 2.04, p = .025$, and in overall scenario score $t(32) = 2.23, p = .017$. The differences for on-time and late reports in posttest did not re-emerge in delayed retention (see Table 1 for descriptives). These results supported H2 (see Fig. 3 for a depiction of these results).

Table 1. Descriptive statistics and t-test results for posttest and delayed retention performance

Posttest		M	SD	t(32)	d
Report Accuracy	A	79.83%	15.98%	1.81*	0.59
	LC	67.98%	22.75%		
On-Time Reports	A	27.73%	20.50%	−1.90*	−0.62
	LC	42.18%	25.35%		
Late Reports	A	63.87%	20.28%	2.22*	−0.57
	LC	48.30%	22.35%		
Overall Scenario Score	A	59.12%	16.14%	2.07*	0.68
	LC	46.71%	19.23%		
Delayed Retention					
Report Accuracy	A	85.59%	13.27%	2.04*	0.70
	LC	74.37%	18.13%		
On-Time Reports	A	39.29%	24.19%	−0.31	−0.11
	LC	42.06%	28.35%		
Late Reports	A	57.14%	25.02%	0.25	0.09
	LC	54.76%	29.09%		
Overall Scenario Score	A	61.19%	14.98%	2.23*	0.77
	LC	50.11%	14.02%		

Note. *$p < .05$, one-tailed, d = Cohen's d effect size. A = Algorithm group, LC = Learner Control group

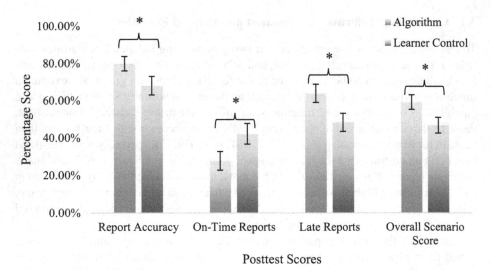

Fig. 2. (H1) Means for each group on posttest performance. Error bars are ±1 standard error of the mean. Significant differences between groups are indicated with asterisks where $p < .05$.

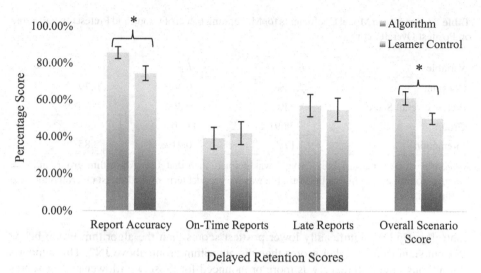

Fig. 3. (H2) Means for each group on delayed retention performance. Error bars are ±1 standard error of the mean. Significant differences between groups are indicated with asterisks where $p <$ .05.

3.2 Was Learner Control Better for Some but not Others?

To test our final hypothesis, we compared differences in posttest performance accounting for pretest scenario scores, with the assumption that a higher pretest scenario score would indicate better encoding of the instructional material. To analyze this research question, we constructed a moderation model using the Hayes [37] process macro version 4.1, where pretest scenario overall score was the predictor variable, posttest scenario score was the outcome variable, and group (algorithm or learner control) was the moderating variable. The overall model was significant, accounting for 49% of the variance in posttest performance, $F(3, 34) = 10.98$, $p < .001$, $R^2 = .49$, and the product term of pretest $\times$ group accounted for a significant 12% of the variance in this model, $F(1, 34) = 8.14$, $p = .007$, $R^2 = .12$. For the algorithm group, pretest score was a significant positive predictor of posttest performance ($B = 0.46$, $SE_B = 0.20$, $t = 2.42$, $p = .032$). The learner control group had a similar but stronger positive effect ($B = 1.63$, $SE_B = 0.36$, $t = 4.56$, $p = .0001$). In essence, higher scores in pretest predicted higher scores in posttest, and this was more pronounced for participants in the learner control group (regression coefficients provided in Table 2).

To understand the nature of this interaction and identify the regions of significance, we plotted the predicted slopes for each group in R studio and the interactions package [38–40], and computed Johnson-Neyman values as per Montoya [41] using OGRS 1.2 for SPSS. Computing the Johnson-Neyman values allows the comparison of both groups' slopes and identifies at which point(s) the slopes significantly differ at an alpha level of .05. As shown in Fig. 4, the slope line is relatively flat for the algorithm group, whereas the slope is much steeper for the learner control group. Based on the Johnson-Neyman values, the two groups were significantly different when pretest scores were below 25.02% (JN1), and when they were above 57.57% (JN2). As depicted, the learner

Table 2. Regression Model Coefficients for Moderating Effect of Group and Pretest Overall Score on Posttest Overall Score

Variable	B	SE_B	t
Constant	7.24%	9.20%	0.79
Pretest Overall Score	1.63%	0.36%	4.56**
Group	−38.91%	11.40%	3.41**
Interaction	1.17%	0.41%	2.85**

Note. **$p < .01$. The variable "Group" was defined such that $1 =$ Algorithm group and $0 =$ Learner Control group. Interaction variable was the product term of the Pretest Overall Score and Group variables.

control group had significantly lower posttest scores than the algorithm group below JN1 but significantly higher scores than the algorithm group above JN2. This supports H3, although the difference was more pronounced for those with lower pretest scores than for higher pretest scores.

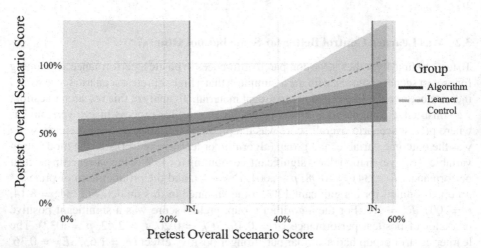

Fig. 4. (H3) Moderating effect of Pretest Overall Scenario Score on Group Predicting Posttest Overall Scenario Score. Plotted slopes are estimated based on the minimum (5%) and maximum (59%) scores observed in pretest overall scenario score. 95% confidence interval bands are displayed as shaded boundaries around each estimated slope. Johnson-Neyman regions of significance are depicted as green-shaded areas; $JN_1 = 25.02\%$, $JN_2 = 57.57\%$. Those in the Learner Control group performed more poorly on posttest than those in the Algorithm group when they had lower scores in pretest. However, they performed better in posttest than those in the Algorithm group when they had higher scores in pretest.

4   Discussion of Planned Analyses

We found partial support for H1 and supported H2 and H3. For H1, there appeared to be a speed-accuracy tradeoff, where those in the algorithm group favored accuracy at the cost of speed. Their reports were significantly more accurate than their counterparts in the learner control group, but they submitted fewer on-time reports and more late reports. During the instructional phase, participants were informed that speed and accuracy were equally important for their overall score. Based on the results, the algorithm group's poorer timeliness did not counteract their increased efforts for accuracy, as their overall scenario scores were higher than those in the learner control group.

Interestingly, when examining these performance variables in delayed retention for H2, the accuracy differences were similar and significant, but the timeliness differences were not statistically significant. After approximately one week between posttest and delayed retention, our results suggest that participants in the algorithm group retained the learning benefits of their training.

For H3, we posited that learner control would be more beneficial for those who encoded better during the instruction phase (with encoding quality assessed via pretest scenario overall score). Our analyses supported this linear relationship, but with evidence at the opposite end as well. Nearly half of our participants had pretest scores below the low-end JN value, and those participants had significantly lower posttest scores when they trained in the learner control group. Assuming that low posttest scores correspond with poorer encoding during the instructional phase, we questioned why the learner control group would have done more poorly in posttest than the algorithm group among participants with poorer pretest performance. It is possible that, because of their poorer initial encoding of instruction, they did not know the best instructional content to choose during training. Where the algorithm group would have received feedback relevant to the mistakes they had made, those in the learner control group may have chosen instructional content that was less relevant to their performance needs. In the next section, we describe follow-up analyses exploring the instructional content choices made by participants in the learner control group. In essence, we were concerned whether those in the learner control group chose instructional videos in a pattern similar to what the algorithm would have chosen for them, or whether the videos they chose were less relevant.

5   Exploratory Analyses: Why Did the Learner Control Group Perform More Poorly?

Within the learner control group, we conducted a follow-up analysis on which instructional videos participants selected. It is possible that the lower performance in this group was caused by participants selecting videos incongruent with what the feedback algorithm would have chosen (i.e., more relevant feedback based on the learner's errors). To quantify this, we examined which feedback rule was the highest-priority rule violated and compared it to which video the learner selected. There were 12 total opportunities throughout the 3 training scenarios to receive (or choose) instructional videos. For each of these 12 video opportunities, participants were given a score of 1 if their chosen video matched what the feedback algorithm would have selected, or a score of 0 if their chosen video did not match. Surprisingly, out of all 21 participants in the learner control group, there were only 14 discrete instances where a learner selected a video that was identical to what the feedback algorithm would have selected for them. This corresponded to a match rate of roughly 6%, which is not far from the rate of chance for selecting 1 out of 22 of the possible videos (4.5%). Unsurprisingly, these data were not significantly correlated with any measures of posttest performance (all $ps > .32$).

Since this strict measure of matching the algorithm was not predictive of performance, we sought a more generous measure to try to understand how "closely" these participants selected what the algorithm would have chosen. We considered that participants in the learner control group may have chosen instructional content that was relevant to a mistake that they made, but perhaps not the highest priority mistake that the algorithm would have chosen for them. To compute this score, we examined whether they chose any video that was relevant to mistakes that they made prior to that opportunity for video selection, scoring that choice from 0 to 100% based on how closely positioned it was to the highest priority feedback they would have received (i.e., what the algorithm would have chosen). This overall flexible algorithm match score was higher at 16.26% overall for the Learner Control group, but yielded similar correlation results as the stricter score (all $ps > .30$).

Finally, we examined a more general perspective of video selection. Instead of considering a comparison against what the algorithm would have chosen or what was relevant to the errors they had made up until that point, we scored the videos they selected based on their position in the feedback algorithm's rule list. For example, the most important rules are near the top of this list and correspond to the highest priority instructional topics. It is possible that the importance of the videos that learners selected (i.e., their rank position in the feedback algorithm) may be a better predictor for performance for those in the Learner Control group rather than if they had selected exactly what the algorithm would have selected. In addition, this score can be generated for both groups, allowing a fairer comparison in the importance of videos delivered by the feedback algorithm versus videos selected by participants. We conducted a two-tailed t-test to explore whether this score was different between groups. The algorithm group viewed significantly higher-ranked videos, $M = 7.85$, $SD = 1.48$, than the learner control group, $M = 11.78$, $SD = 2.01$, $t(36) = -.72$, $p < .001$, Cohen's $d = -2.19$ For context, the highest ranked rule was 1 and the lowest ranked rule was 22. This score was also significantly correlated with both report accuracy, $r(36) = -.42$, $p = .01$, and overall scenario score, $r(36) = -.44$, $p = .006$.

6 Discussion of Exploratory Analyses

These follow-up analyses revealed that those in the learner control group were not selecting the same instructional videos that the algorithm would have given them, nor were they selecting relevant instructional videos most of the time. When examining the relative importance of the videos that were viewed during training, those in the learner control group were selecting less important videos than what those in the algorithm group received. Since the importance of videos was correlated with posttest scenario performance, knowing which videos were important was key for performing well on the task. In essence, these analyses reveal three different ways that the learner control group was not selecting the instructional content they needed to know.

This could be understood through the lens of a Dunning-Kruger effect [31]. Those who encoded the instruction more poorly may have been less aware of their encoding deficiencies and chose instructional content that was less optimal for their learning needs. Our results also echo previous learner control research [27–29], which raised concerns about learners selecting appropriate content to help them perform better. For training programs including a learner control component, our results ultimately suggest that learner control is only beneficial when learners are aware of their deficiencies.

7   General Discussion and Limitations, and Recommendations

Revisiting the main question of this paper, our results suggest that feedback algorithms are better than learner control for learning a new, complex task. Not only are they better for learning in the short-term, but also for long-term retention of learning. However, this difference was observed within the context of a real-world, complex task, and some nuance in this comparison could be elucidated by future empirical research with simpler tasks. We contend that our results may generalize to other task domains where the task is complex and well-defined, but unfamiliar to the user; however, we must acknowledge several limitations of the present work.

Learners in the algorithm group sometimes saw repeated videos delivered to them (for mistakes they repeated in each scenario), whereas learners in the learner control group were more likely to select a new video at each opportunity. As mentioned in the method section, previously selected videos were indicated with a blue color. We cannot rule out that this blue coloring may have steered participants in this group away from repeating a video that they may have needed to see. However, this blue coloring was only a visual indication of previously viewed content. Learners were still able to select a previously selected video multiple times if they desired.

Those in the learner control group may have also experienced additional cognitive load or decision fatigue associated with the choices they needed to make. As a reminder, these videos were delivered periodically throughout training, causing a task interruption and requiring participants to reflect on their performance to select an appropriate video. This additional load could have been an independent factor that led to poorer general performance in the learner control group.

In a more general sense, algorithms may not always be the right choice for every type of training. Not only is learner control potentially more cost-effective to implement, but it may also be better suited for ill-defined or creative tasks. Performance is not always objectively measurable, so other educational contexts like creative writing, computer programming, or art may benefit better from learner controlled instruction. For example, a student experiencing writer's block might consider selecting content on writing techniques or narrative structuring to move past their impasse. If learner control is to be implemented for well-defined tasks, we recommend investing in up-front instruction to ensure learners encode well prior to further instruction or training.

7.1 Future Directions

The present study supports that error-sensitive feedback algorithms are generally superior to learner control for learning a novel, complex task such as electronic warfare. There were a few participants who did benefit from having control over their learning, and we suspect that this occurred because they had encoded the instruction well. Instructional designers may be interested in blending these techniques in training systems, depending on content complexity. Future research could investigate whether there is benefit to the adaptive implementation of these two approaches. For example, a training system could deliver feedback via algorithm when performance is relatively poor, and transition into a learner-controlled approach once performance improves. Future work should focus on understanding the factors that determine when to require system control of the learning experience and when to relax toward learner control.

Acknowledgments. We gratefully acknowledge Ms. Reganne Miller and Ms. Rebecca Pharmer for their assistance with instructional video development. We also acknowledge Mr. Chad Yagey for his assistance with data collection and testing the electronic warfare testbed. This work was funded under the Naval Innovative Science and Engineering program established by the National Defense Authorization Act, Section 219. Presentation of this material does not constitute or imply its endorsement, recommendation, or favoring by the U.S. Navy or the Department of Defense (DoD). The views expressed herein are those of the authors and do not necessarily reflect the official position of the Department of Defense or its components. NAWCTSD Public Release 23-ORL005 Distribution Statement A – Approved for public release; distribution is unlimited.

References

1. Bloom, B.S.: The 2 sigma problem: the search for methods of group instruction as effective as one-to-one tutoring. Educ. Res. **13**(6), 4–16 (1984)
2. Park, O.C., Lee, J.: Adaptive instructional systems. In: Handbook of Research on Educational Communications and Technology, pp. 647–680. Routledge, Oxfordshire (2013)
3. Landsberg, C.R., Mercado, A.D., Van Buskirk, W.L., Lineberry, M., Steinhauser, N.: Evaluation of an adaptive training system for submarine periscope operations. In: 56th Proceedings of the Human Factors and Ergonomics Society annual meeting, pp. 2422–2426. SAGE, Los Angeles (2012)
4. Marraffino, M.D., Schroeder, B.L., Fraulini, N.W., Van Buskirk, W.L., Johnson, C.I.: Adapting training in real time: an empirical test of adaptive difficulty schedules. Milit. Psychol. **33**(3), 136–151 (2021)
5. Billings, D.R.: Efficacy of adaptive feedback strategies in simulation-based training. Milit. Psychol. **24**(2), 114–133 (2012)
6. Shute, V., Towle, B.: Adaptive e-learning. Educ. Psychol. **38**(2), 105–114 (2003)
7. Van Buskirk, W.L., Fraulini, N.W., Schroeder, B.L., Johnson, C.I., Marraffino, M.D.: Application of theory to the development of an adaptive training system for a submarine electronic warfare task. In: Sottilaire, R., Schwartz, J. (eds.) HCII 2019. LNCS, vol. 11597, pp. 352–362. Springer, Heidelberg (2019). https://doi.org/10.1007/978-3-030-22341-0_28
8. Kalyuga, S.: Assessment of learners' organised knowledge structures in adaptive learning environments. Appl. Cogn. Psychol. **20**(3), 333–342 (2006)
9. Tseng, J.C., Chu, H.C., Hwang, G.J., Tsai, C.C.: Development of an adaptive learning system with two sources of personalization information. Comput. Educ. **51**(2), 776–786 (2008)

10. Kluger, A.N., DeNisi, A.: The effects of feedback interventions on performance: a historical review, a meta-analysis, and a preliminary feedback intervention theory. Psychol. Bull. **119**, 254–284 (1996)
11. Landsberg, C.R., Bailey, S., Van Buskirk, W.L., Gonzalez-Holland, E., Johnson, C.I.: Designing effective feedback in adaptive training systems. In: Interservice/Industry, Training, Simulation, and Education Conference, vol. 312, pp. 1–12. I/ITSEC, Orlando (2016)
12. Dihoff, R.E., Brosvic, G.M., Epstein, M.L., Cook, M.J.: Provision of feedback during preparation for academic testing: learning is enhanced by immediate but not delayed feedback. Psychol. Rec. **54**, 207–231 (2004)
13. Guadagnoli, M.A., Dornier, L.A., Tandy, R.D.: Optimal length for summary knowledge of results: the influence of task-related experience and complexity. Res. Q. Exerc. Sport **67**(2), 239–248 (1996)
14. Schooler, L.J., Anderson, J.R.: The disruptive potential of immediate feedback. In: 12th Annual Conference of the Cognitive Sciences Society, vol. 12, pp. 702–708. Psychology Press, Hove (1990)
15. Snow, R.E.: Aptitude, learner control, and adaptive instruction. Educ. Psychol. **15**(3), 151–158 (1980)
16. Bruner, J.: Going Beyond the Information Given. Norton, New York (1973)
17. Ebner, D.G.: Videodiscs can improve instructional efficiency. Instruct. Innov. **29**(6), 26–28 (1984)
18. Ross, S.M., McCormick, D., Krisak, N.: Adapting the thematic context of mathematical problems to student interests: Individual versus group-based strategies. J. Educ. Res. **79**, 245–252 (1986)
19. Pascal, C.E.: Instructional options, option preference, and course outcomes. Alberta J. Educ. Res. **17**(1), 1–11 (1971)
20. Hurlock, R.E., Lahey, G.E, McCann, P.H.: Student controlled versus program controlled CAI. American Educational Research Association (ERIC No. ED 089 68 1). Naval Personnel Research and Development Center, San Diego (1974)
21. Bandura, A.: Perceived self-efficacy in cognitive development and functioning. Educ. Psychol. **28**(2), 117–148 (1993)
22. Boekaerts, M.: Self-regulated learning at the junction of cognition and motivation. Eur. Psychol. **1**(2), 100–112 (1996)
23. Kirschenbaum, D.S.: Self-regulation and sport psychology: nurturing an emerging symbiosis. J. Sport Psychol. **6**(2) (1984)
24. Ferrari, M.: Observing the observer: Self-regulation in the observational learning of motor skills. Dev. Rev. **16**(2), 203–240 (1996)
25. Aiken, C.A., Fairbrother, J.T., Post, P.G.: The effects of self-controlled video feedback on the learning of the basketball set shot. Front. Psychol. **3**, 338 (2012)
26. Chiviacowsky, S., Wulf, G.: Self-controlled feedback: Does it enhance learning because performers get feedback when they need it? Res. Q. Exerc. Sport **73**(4), 408–415 (2002)
27. Vandewaetere, M., Wauters, K.: Learner control on feedback: a new extension to adaptive learning? In: 10th IEEE International Conference on Advanced Learning Technologies, pp. 406–408. IEEE, Piscataway (2010)
28. Admiraal, W., et al.: Personalizing learning with mobile technology in secondary education. In: 14th International Conference Mobile Learning, pp. 62–69. Curran Associates, New York (2018)
29. Aleven, V., Koedinger, K.R.: Limitations of student control: do students know when they need help? In: Gauthier, G., Frasson, C., VanLehn, K. (eds.) ITS 2000. LNCS, vol. 1839, pp. 292–303. Springer, Heidelberg (2000). https://doi.org/10.1007/3-540-45108-0_33
30. Dunning, D.: The dunning–kruger effect: on being ignorant of one's own ignorance. In: Advances in Experimental Social Psychology. Academic Press, Cambridge (2011)

31. Kruger, J., Dunning, D.: Unskilled and unaware of it: how difficulties in recognizing one's own incompetence lead to inflated self-assessments. J. Pers. Soc. Psychol. **77**(6), 1121 (1999)
32. Conklin, J.: Hypertext: an introduction and survey. In: IEEE Computer, vol. 20, pp. 17–41. IEEE, Piscataway (1987)
33. Niederhauser, D.S., Reynolds, R.E., Salmen, D.L., Skolmoski, P.: The influence of cognitive load on learning from hypertext. J. Educ. Comput. Res. **23**, 237–255 (2000)
34. Corbett, A.T., Koedinger, K.R., Anderson, J.R.: Intelligent tutoring systems (Chapter 37). In: Helander, M.G., Landauer, T.K., Prabhu, P. (eds.) Handbook of Human-Computer Interaction, 2nd edn. Elsevier Science, Amsterdam (1997)
35. Buff, W.L., Campbell, G.E.: What to do or what not to do?: identifying the content of effective feedback. In: 46th Proceedings of the Human Factors and Ergonomics Society Annual Meeting, pp. 2074–2078. SAGE, Los Angeles (2002)
36. Flesch, R.: A new readability yardstick. J. Appl. Psychol. **32**(3), 221 (1948)
37. Hayes, A.F.: Introduction to Mediation, Moderation, and Conditional Process Analysis: A Regression-Based Approach. Guilford Press, New York (2017)
38. Long, J.A.: Interactions: comperehensive, user-friendly toolkit for probing interactions. R package version 1.1.5 (2021). https://cran.r-project.org/package=interactions
39. RStudio Team: Rstudio: Integrated Development for R. Rstudio, PBC, Boston, MA (2020). https://www.rstudio.com
40. R Core Team: R: A language and environment for statistical computing. R Foundation for Statistical Computing, Vienna, Austria (2021). https://www.R-project.org/
41. Montoya, A. K.: Extending the Johnson-Neyman procedure to categorical independent variables: mathematical derivations and computational tools. Doctoral dissertation, The Ohio State University (2016)

Stress and Coping with Task Difficulty: Investigating the Utility of a Micro-adaptive Aptitude Treatment Interaction Approach

Wendi L. Van Buskirk[1]([⊠]), Bradford L. Schroeder[1], Michelle Aros[2], and Jason E. Hochreiter[1]

[1] Naval Air Warfare Center Training Systems Division, Orlando, FL 32826, USA
{wendi.l.vanbuskirk.civ,bradford.l.schroeder.civ, jason.e.hochreiter.civ}@us.navy.mil
[2] StraCon Services Group, Fort Worth, TX 76109, USA
michelle.aros2.ctr@us.navy.mil

Abstract. The goal of adaptive instructional systems (AISs) is to tailor instruction to meet an individual student's needs. The goal of the current research is to examine the feasibility of using a micro level Aptitude Treatment Interaction (ATI) approach to provide adaptive instruction. In other words, we are examining the utility of adapting instruction based on state measures of learner attributes during training. The aptitude variable of interest in this study is individual differences in stress coping techniques. There are three methods for coping strategies that include task-focused coping, emotion-focused coping, and avoidance coping. Task-focused coping (TFC) allows trainees to focus and strategize on how to develop solutions to their problems. Emotion-focused coping (EFC) is when trainees become overwhelmed and overcome by their own emotions and continuously blame themselves. Lastly, avoidance coping (AC) is when trainees avoid their problems altogether and refuse to address any possible solutions. Both EFC and AC are maladaptive as they cause learners to lose focus of important elements of their task. In the present study we will examine the relationship between maladaptive coping strategies and performance on a problem-solving task. Data collection is still underway but initial results suggest a relationship between maladaptive coping and problem-solving performance.

Keywords: adaptive instructional system · adaptive training · aptitude treatment interaction · individual differences

1 Introduction

1.1 Adaptive Instructional Systems and Aptitude Treatment Interaction Adaptations

The aim of Adaptive Instructional Systems (AISs) is to meet individual student trainee learning needs. Thus, AIS designers must consider how their training will adapt to best suit their student trainee's strengths, weakness, and/or other characteristics. Park

This is a U.S. government work and not under copyright protection in the U.S.; foreign copyright protection may apply 2023
R. A. Sottilare and J. Schwarz (Eds.): HCII 2023, LNCS 14044, pp. 253–264, 2023.
https://doi.org/10.1007/978-3-031-34735-1_18

and Lee [1] identified three different approaches to the development of AISs – macro-adaptation, micro-adaptation, and aptitude treatment interaction (ATI)-adaptation. As their name implies, macro-adaptations typically occur from high level assessments that occur prior to instruction. For example, Warner and colleagues [2] found that adapting instructional content presented to anesthesiology students based on their prior knowledge led to learning efficiency. On the other hand, micro-adaptations typically occur based on real-time assessments of task performance, and instructional changes occur more frequently due to this ongoing observation and assessment. For example, Marraffino and colleagues [3] adapted task difficulty within a 10-min scenario of a military radar detection task based on real-time assessment of a participant's performance.

While macro- and micro-adaptations have garnered most of the attention in the AIS domain, by comparison, relatively little research has gone into the use of ATIs. Aptitude (or Attribute) by Treatment Interactions have a long history in psychology, involving uniting experimental with differential or correlation psychology [4, 5]. Before ATI had earned its name, scientists were focused on understanding the performance of individuals in specific scenarios while accounting for biological factors of those individual, with the understanding that an individual's attributes can influence their behavior in different scenarios [4]. Indeed, Cronbach [4] argued "applied psychologists should deal with treatments and persons simultaneously. Treatments are characterized by many dimensions; so are persons (p.680)." This work resulted in a combination of experimental psychology techniques and correlation techniques in an effort to better understand human behavior. Over the next few decades, Cronbach [5] noted the growth of the ATI discipline, particularly in the domains of learning and motivation.

In recent decades, the idea of ATIs has been implemented in computer-based training, particularly within AISs. In these systems, the ATI approach to adaptation [1, 6] uses the assessment of a student trainee's aptitudes or traits to adapt the instructional intervention. While ATI is often discussed as a viable adaptive method, most researchers consider it from a pre-training (i.e., macro level approach) perspective [1, 7, 8]. Further, previous researchers [9–11] have noted that macro level ATI adaptations tend to be an ineffective method of improving learning and/or performance. Indeed, Park and Lee [1] noted that "abilities required by a treatment may shift as the task progresses so that the ability becomes more or less important (p. 659)" during the instructional session. Therefore, a potentially more effective implementation of the ATI approach would be to adapt instruction based on state (versus trait) measures of learner attributes during instruction (i.e., at the micro level). Indeed, research suggest that in-situ state measures more directly relate to task performance compared to pre-task measurements [12, 13].

1.2 Stress and Coping

One variable that has consistently been shown to affect task performance is stress [14–16]. Lazarus and Folkman [17] argued that individuals experience stress and cope with it in various ways as they interact with their environment. This interaction is iterative and constantly re-evaluated by the individual, who adjusts their appraisal of the environment in the context of their available resources. Depending on how the environment is appraised, individuals will cope in a variety of ways to "handle" the situation.

In AIS interactions, learners may experience stress and cope accordingly when the task is novel or unfamiliar, increases in difficulty, and/or changes in some way [18]. Matthews and Campbell [19] classified three different coping strategies based on stress research: Task-focused coping (TFC), emotion-focused coping (EFC), and avoidance coping (AC). TFC occurs when an individual focuses on the task and develops strategies to avoid mistakes and solve problems. EFC occurs when individuals become preoccupied with their own emotions, criticizing and blaming themselves when experiencing stressors. AC occurs when an individual decreases their effort or abandons the task. TFC is ideal for success in cognitive tasks, while EFC and AC are considered maladaptive coping strategies. These maladaptive strategies are ineffective for dealing with increased task demands [20] and cause task performance to decrease. In other words, maladaptive coping may limit the effectiveness of both macro and micro adaptive difficulty interventions.

In previous research, Schroeder and colleagues [13] demonstrated that EFC (via self-report) was associated with poor accuracy and slower report time in a complex military task. In this study, participants performed a task in which they had to detect, identify, and report contacts emitting radio frequencies within an AIS that adapted task difficulty. In addition to EFC being associated with poorer performance, these authors found that EFC was both predictive of future-task performance and reflective of post-task performance, such that those who had high EFC in early scenarios still exhibited poorer performance on later scenarios regardless of adaptive instructional technique presented. These results suggest that people who exhibit EFC may require a different type of instructional intervention. Matthews and Campbell [19] suggested that since EFC is maladaptive for performance on cognitive tasks, mitigating maladaptive coping should improve cognitive task performance. Therefore, if we can assess a student trainee's stress and coping during an instructional session, AIS designers could adapt the instructional intervention provided to minimize these maladaptive strategies with the goal of increasing performance for students who use EFC or AC strategies.

1.3 The Present Study

The goal of our research was to explore the use of micro-ATI adaptations of stress coping to improve learning and performance in a problem-solving task. However, in order to accomplish this, we wanted to ensure that we are inducing stress and stress coping. Therefore, in this exploratory study, we intended to examine individual differences in stress responses with problem-solving performance under time and performance pressure. Additionally, we benchmarked our experimental stimuli for difficulty in order to assess the suitability of the problems in a future AIS where we adapt difficulty. Specifically, we expected to see variation in problem difficulty in terms of both objective measures (i.e., ability to solve, time to solve, number of moves, etc.) and participants' perceptions of difficulty. Additionally, we wanted to confirm we were eliciting stress, temporal demand, and mental demand in order to trigger stress coping responses.

Additionally, we were interested in the state versus trait nature of stress coping and whether our chosen aptitude state measure would be viable in a micro-ATI AIS. Consistent with Lazarus and Folkman [17] mentioned above, we expected to see situational shifts in stress coping as participants reappraise and adjust their strategies to cope with the task, which may be influenced by dispositional coping tendencies. Furthermore, we also hoped to see that situational measures were more highly correlated (either positively or negatively) with performance than the dispositional measures as suggested by [9–11]. Lastly, we also expect to see a correlation between EFC and performance. Specifically, we anticipated that participants who self-report higher levels of EFC have lower success rates and higher perceived difficulty of the problems.

Finally, research from the areas of clinical and sport psychology has suggested that there are various stress mitigating techniques that can improve stress and coping skills. These techniques include cognitive reappraisal and expressive suppression [15]. Cognitive reappraisal is an overt emotion regulation technique that involves modifying one's cognition in order to keep control over emotional reactions [21], which should reduce the likelihood of using maladaptive coping strategies. Alternatively, expressive suppression occurs when one restrains emotionally expressive behavior in the face of emotional arousal [22]. Therefore, minimizing overt emotional reactions rather than targeting cognition is the main goal of the suppression strategy. As these strategies may affect stress coping, we are interested in examining them on an exploratory basis. Therefore, we also measured self-reported emotional regulation strategies and assess their effects (if any) on stress and performance.

2 Method

In order to examine the questions above, we are utilizing a within-subjects design where we will examine the individual differences in stress responses with performance under time pressure. Data collection is still underway. Therefore, partial data will be presented in this paper. However, the full results will be covered in the conference presentation.

2.1 Participants

To date, we have collected data from 13 participants (6 male, 7 female). Average age of participants was 29.38 years (SD = 10.06 years). Participants were recruited through online resources such as SONA systems and Reddit. Participants were paid $25 for 1.5 h for their time. Participants were also eligible to earn a bonus $25 payment if they performed well on the task. For this bonus, they were informed that the solution rates as well as the time to solve the problems were the two main factors for evaluating performance. All participants were instructed to try their best, even if they could not solve every problem. Participants were also informed that we did not anticipate that every participant would solve every problem.

2.2 Materials

River Crossing Problems. In the present research, we are investigating the use of stress coping feedback with river crossing problems. River crossing problems are attributed to the Northumbrian scholar, Alcuin of York, in the mid to late 700's. As an educational advisor to Charlemagne, Alcuin wrote several texts including *Propositiones ad Acuendos Juvenes* in which Alcuin's river crossing problems first appeared [23]. These problems were developed to teach problem-solving, and his original and most widely known problem – the "wolf, goat, and cabbages" – takes this form: "A man had to take a wolf, goat, and cabbages across a river. The only boat he could find could only take two of them at a time. But he had been ordered to transfer all of these to the other side in good condition. How could this be done? (translated by [23], p.112)." These puzzles have been circulated over time for thousands of years and can be found in oral and written histories in many different languages [24]. Indeed, in North Africa the problem was tailored to a goat herder who must cross a river with a jackal, a goat, and fig leaves.

We chose the river crossing problems for several reasons: they are cross-cultural, require a unique solution set, are suitable for online data collection, and can be used with a general audience that will not require task-specific training. Additionally, the level of difficulty can be changed based on the problem's rules and constraints. While we were interested primarily in the problem-solving aspect of the river crossing problems, many of the problems also contain a working memory demand. Further, we added a time component to the traditional presentation of these problems in order to create an additional temporal demand. For these reasons, we believe results from these problems may generalize to other complex problem-solving and decision-making tasks.

Questionnaires. We utilized several questionnaires in this study. First, the Emotion Regulation Questionnaire (ERQ) is a 10-item questionnaire developed by [25]. It was included to measure reappraisal and suppression regulation strategies. Participants respond to items such as "I control my emotions by changing the way I think about the situation I'm in" using a 7-point Likert scale from strongly disagree to strongly agree.

To measure coping strategies (i.e., TFC, EFC, and AC), we used the Coping Inventory for Task Stressors (CITS) first developed by Matthews and Campbell [19]. More specifically, we used the CITS-Dispositional (CITS-D) to measure a respondent's trait level coping strategies and the CITS-Situational (CITS-S) to measure state level coping strategies. Both the CITS-S and CITS-D are 21-item questionnaires where participants respond to items such as "I blame myself for not doing better" or "I work out a strategy for successful performance" using a 5-point Likert scale from Not at all to extremely [26].

The National Aeronautics and Space Administration-Task Load Index (NASA-TLX) developed by Hart and Staveland [27] served as a measure of subjective workload. While all participants completed all the sub-scales including physical demand, we were particularly interested in ensuring the river crossing problems elicited temporal and mental demand. Lastly, the demographics questionnaire was an 11-item questionnaire that included questions on age, major, education, etc. In addition to biographical information, we also included questions on average weekly game play and prior experience with different types of puzzles including river crossing puzzles.

2.3 Procedure

The river crossing problems and questionnaires were administered over Qualtrics. The experimental session was observed over a Teams meeting session where participants shared their desktop screen with the experimenter. This was done in order to ensure data quality and to troubleshoot any issues that may have come up during the session (i.e., screen resolution, poor internet connections, etc.). After informed consent was obtained, participants completed the ERQ and CITS-D.

Next, participants were given general instructions on river crossing problems. Then they were provided a variation of Alcuin's original wolf-goat-cabbages problem described above. In this practice problem, participants were instructed to get a farmer, fox, chicken, and corn across the river (see Fig. 1). This problem featured three constraints participants had to consider while solving, and participants were provided with feedback when they violated a rule or constraint (see Fig. 2). First, the farmer was able to row across the river with only up to one of the other items at a time. If the participant attempted to load more than two items onto the raft or row without the farmer present, they were presented a simple warning and allowed to continue. The remaining two constraints concerned unrecoverable errors: if the fox was left alone with the chicken, the fox would eat the chicken, and if the chicken was left alone with the corn, the chicken would eat the corn. Violating errors that would prevent the farmer from being able to move all items across the river led to a failure state. To increase the difficulty and time pressure of these river crossing problems, participants were required to restart the problem from the beginning upon reaching a failure state.

Fig. 1. River crossing problem (fox, grain, chicken) screenshot from Qualtrics survey.

After the practice problem, participants were randomly presented with a series of 12 river crossing problems that varied in difficulty. The more difficult problems featured more constraints, more complex constraints, or more items or people that needed to cross the river. For example, some problems included overall item weight capacities, time costs (separate from the puzzle timer) for each river traversal, and more complicated restrictions on the allowed arrangements of the items or people in the problem. To increase performance pressure on participants, all the problems including the practice had 6-min time limits. After each problem, participants rated the perceived difficulty of each river crossing problem using a 5-point Likert scale from very easy to very difficult. After a block of 4 problems, participants completed measures of their perceived workload via the NASA-TLX and their coping strategies via the CITS-S. At the end of the study, participants filled out the demographics questionnaire and then were debriefed on the purpose of the study.

A man has to get a fox, chicken, and corn across a river on a raft.

- The raft can only carry him and one other thing.
- If the fox and the chicken are left together, the fox will eat the chicken.
- If the chicken and the corn are left together, the chicken will eat the corn.

How does the man get everything across?

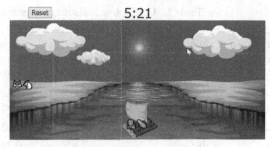

You lose! The fox ate the chicken.

Fig. 2. Example feedback provided when rule violation occurred.

3 Results

Consistent with our expectations, initial results indicate variance in our problem solution rates. As can be seen in Table 1, problem solution rates are ranging from 0%–100% and average perceived difficulty is ranging from 2.15 to 4.92. Also as expected, NASA-TLX scores for mental demand (M = 15.31, SD = 4.00) and temporal demand (M = 13.28, SD = 2.99) are above the midpoint of the scale (i.e., 10). Additionally, both the mental demand and "stress" subscale are correlated with solution rates ($r(37) = -.42, p < .01$ and $r(37) = -.50, p < .01$, respectively), indicating higher perceived demand and stress with lower solution rates. Interestingly, average time to solve and temporal demand are not currently correlated, $r(37) = .16$, n.s.

In addition, we examined preliminary results with the state level EFC, state level AC scores, behavioral data, and subjective difficulty ratings for each of the blocks of problems (see Tables 2 and 3, respectively). At present, there is only one statistically significant correlation coefficient for EFC scores and the problems in Block 2, where $r(11) = .60, p = .03$. However, we acknowledge with a small sample size that statistical power is low. We observed moderate correlation effect sizes for solution rate and time to solve, which is consistent with previous research suggesting that higher EFC results in poorer performance on cognitive tasks.

Examining state level AC scores reveals slightly more inconsistent results. Block 2 had strong correlation coefficients for number of errors, resets, and moves (all $rs > .70$, all $ps < .01$). It is possible that these are not completely independent results, as many errors can result in a reset, and every reset requires more moves to continue attempting to solve the problem. There was another significant result with number of errors in Block 1, $r(11) = .64, p = .018$, but otherwise, the patterns with AC were less clear. Most likely, there was a particularly challenging problem in Block 2 that may be responsible for these positive effects only occurring in that block.

As more data are collected, we plan to further explore the relationships among behavioral variables (such as error rates, error types, time between actions, and number of instances resetting the problem) as well as their interactions with individual differences in perceived workload, coping responses at the state and trait level, and emotion regulation techniques.

Table 1. Descriptive statistics of river crossing problem difficulty

Problem number	Solution Rate	Average time to Solve (seconds)	Average perceived difficulty	Average Number of Errors	Average Number of Resets	Average number of moves
1	92%	121	2.38	1.85	1.31	10.08
2	100%	132	2.15	1.23	1.31	13.69
3	100%	173	2.85	0.31	0.54	8.85
4	92%	215	2.69	1.31	1.31	18.62
5	77%	218	3.46	6.23	4.31	21.54
6	8%	352	4.77	5.15	7.08	34.07
7	38%	317	4.15	6.08	5.62	24.46
8	8%	349	4.46	6.38	6.54	23.46
9	69%	252	3.62	4.54	3.00	19.77
10	77%	230	3.46	3.85	3.07	16.46
11	0%	N/A	4.92	6.92	7.77	23.77
12	38%	340	4.31	7.69	6.46	26.92

Note. For average time to solve, 360 s (the problem time limit) was used for participants who failed to solve the problem; N/A reflects that no participants were able to solve Problem 11 within the time limit. Average perceived difficulty was rated 1 (extremely easy) to 5 (extremely difficult) on a Likert scale. Average number of moves refers to the number of times the boat was sent from one side to another while attempting the problem.

Table 2. Pearsons' r Correlation Coefficients for EFC (state) and Problem-solving Variables

Variable	Block1 EFC	Block2 EFC	Block3 EFC
Solution Rate	−.41	−.48	−.43
Time to Solve	.36	.60*	.52
Perceived Difficulty	.30	.42	.12
Number of Errors	.10	.12	.49
Number of Resets	.27	.20	.39
Number of Moves	−.23	−.05	.11

Note. * $p < .05$. Variables were averaged for 4 problems in each block. Total N = 13

Table 3. Pearsons' *r* Correlation Coefficients for AC (state) and Problem-solving Variables

Variable	Block1 AC	Block 2 AC	Block3 AC
Solution Rate	−.13	−.30	.20
Time to Solve	.10	.42	−.35
Perceived Difficulty	.11	.10	−.53
Number of Errors	.64*	.80**	.29
Number of Resets	.54	.71**	.18
Number of Moves	.37	.70**	.11

Note. * p < .05. Variables were averaged for 4 problems in each block. Total N = 13

4   Discussion and Future Research Direction

4.1   Interpretation of Preliminary Results

The early results we have presented are promising, showing effect sizes that are in the hypothesized direction. Interestingly, some correlation coefficients were lower than expected. The relationship between EFC (state) and number of errors and number of resets was inconsistent across blocks. Based on the literature, one might expect a relationship between error rates and EFC, such that those adopting higher levels of EFC might be more likely to make mistakes. However, there are a few considerations that must be made before interpreting the data with error rates. In our problem-solving testbed, error messages serve as valuable feedback, reminding participants of the constraints that they violated. Higher rates of errors may not necessarily reflect poorer performance, nor whether participants are more likely to fail to solve the problem. Similarly, number of resets may reflect a comparable effect. Some errors required the user to reset the problem (so some resets are linearly dependent on errors), but participants were able to reset at their leisure if they got stuck or wanted to start over. In these cases, an error message would not have been displayed.

We observed a few large effects with AC and the problems in Block 2. However, there was not a consistent pattern of results with solution rate or time to solve as we observed with EFC. Although these results were not statistically significant, we will be monitoring these moderate and large correlation coefficients as further data are collected.

Another limiting factor is that these problems were grouped in three 4-problem blocks, and so these correlations are not specific to any one problem. However, it is likely that they are driven by specific problems in each block. For this study, we were worried about inundating participants with questionnaires while also trying to benchmark every problem, but a goal of future research is to examine these relationships with greater precision.

Ultimately, these effects may change as more data are collected, and we offer our interpretation of these results with caution. Data collection is ongoing, and more detailed analyses will be provided when this research is presented.

4.2 Future Directions

The primary purpose of the present study is to explore coping responses in a generic, stressful task that requires minimal training. Our initial results are promising and may indicate that we can explore stress coping relationships with performance with river crossing problems. By examining a variety of problems with different levels of difficulty, we can form a basis for future studies examining how learners cope with adaptive training features, such as adaptive difficulty. Cox-Fuenzalida [18] suggested that some individuals can be sensitive to upward (or even downward) changes in difficulty, leading to maladaptive coping and poorer performance. This contrasts with the general finding that performance-based adaptive difficulty training improves learning outcomes (compared to non-adaptive training; e.g., [28]). These effects could contradict one another, such that adaptive difficulty may be less effective for those who tend to use maladaptive coping strategies such as EFC and AC. In essence, maladaptive coping patterns could signal that certain instructional interventions, like adaptive difficulty, may be less effective (or even detrimental) for that individual learner. Indeed, in other research, maladaptive coping patterns have been associated with poorer performance on cognitive tasks [26]. We have also observed this in applied Navy tasks [13], and in future research, we intend to empirically examine methods to counteract or mitigate the consequences of maladaptive coping on performance.

The scientific literature involving stress and the coping techniques mentioned previously have not come to consensus on the possible countermeasures to prevent maladaptive coping such as EFC or AC in cognitive tasks. Some information regarding stress countermeasures can be found in sports psychology and clinical research. This field suggests possible countermeasures as psychology consultancy sessions, stress inoculation therapy, simulation interventions, and emotion regulation interventions [29]. However, these methods require long-term sessions with trained psychologists or other medical personnel [30] which is not practical for many Navy training domains. Thus, there is a gap in the literature to examine whether it is possible to counteract maladaptive coping in a shorter-term human performance/cognitive context. In our future research, we plan to compare experimental countermeasures (such as expressive suppression, cognitive reappraisal, and goal-congruent feedback) and their efficacy in changing coping patterns.

As Cronbach [4] argued, the students we are instructing are just as complex as the AIS we are developing. The main advantage of AISs is the capability to tailor instruction to the needs of the learner. Thus, if we ignore characteristics of the trainee (such as EFC or AC) that cause them to falter under typical instructional interventions, we are doing them and ourselves a disservice.

Acknowledgments. This work was funded by the Office of Naval Research (N0001422WX01634) under Ms. Natalie Steinhauser under the Office of Naval Research. Presentation of this material does not constitute or imply its endorsement, recommendation, or favoring by the U.S. Navy or the Department of Defense (DoD). The opinions of the authors expressed herein do not necessarily state or reflect those of the U.S. Navy of DoD. This paper was approved for public release under NAWCTSD Public Release 23-ORL006.

References

1. Park, O., Lee, J.: Adaptive instructional systems. In: Jonassen, D.H. (ed.) Handbook of Research for Educational Communications and Technology, pp. 651–685. Lawrence Erlbaum, Mahwah (2004)
2. Warner, D.O., Nolan, M., Garcia-Macinkiewicz, A.: Adaptive instruction and learner interactivity in online learning: a randomized trial. Adv. Health Sci. Educ. **25**(1), 95–109 (2019). https://doi.org/10.1007/s10459-019-09907-3
3. Marraffino, M.D., Schroeder, B.S., Fraulini, N.W., Van Buskirk, W.L., Johnson, C.I.: Adapting training in real time: an empirical test of adaptive difficulty schedules. Mil. Psych. **33**, 136–151 (2020). https://doi.org/10.1080/08995605.2021.1897451
4. Cronbach, L.J.: The two disciplines of scientific psychology. Am. Psych. **12**(11), 671–684 (1957)
5. Cronbach, L.J.: Beyond the two disciplines of scientific psychology. Am. Psych. **30**(2), 116 (1975)
6. Shute, V., Towle, B.: Adaptive e-learning. Educ. Psych. 105–114 (2018)
7. Krause, U., Stark, R., Mandl, H.: The effects of cooperative learning and feedback on e-learning in statistics. Learn. Instruc. **19**(2), 158–170 (2009). https://doi.org/10.1016/j.learnstruc.2008.03.003
8. McGregor, M.U., Schunn, C.D., Saner, L.D.: Expertise as effective strategy use: testing the adaptive strategies model in the ill-structured domain of leadership. Technical report 1204, US Army Research Institute for the Behavioral and Social Sciences (2007)
9. Nancekivell, S.E., Sun, X., Gelman, S.A., Shah, P.: A slippery myth: how learning style beliefs shape reasoning about multimodal instruction and related scientific evidence. Cog. Sci. **45** (2021). https://doi.org/10.1111/cogs.13047
10. Pashler, H., McDaniel, M., Rohrer, D., Bjork, R.: Learning styles: concepts and evidence. Psych. Sci. Pub. Int. **9**(3), 105–119 (2009)
11. Van Buskirk, W.L., Steinhauser, N.B., Mercado, A.D., Landsberg, C.R., Astwood, R.S.: A comparison of the micro-adaptive and hybrid approaches to adaptive training. In: Proceedings of the Human Factors and Ergonomics Society Annual Meeting, pp. 1159–1163. Sage Publications, Los Angeles (2014)
12. Matthews, G., et al.: Fundamental dimensions of subjective state in performance settings: task engagement, distress, and worry. Emotion **2**(4) (2002)
13. Schroeder, B.L., Fraulini, N.W., Marraffino, M.D., Van Buskirk, W.L., Johnson, C.I.: Individual differences in adaptive training: distress, workload, and coping with changes in difficulty. In: Proceedings of the Human Factors and Ergonomics Society Annual Meeting, pp. 2154–2155. Sage Publications, Los Angeles (2019)
14. Driskell, J.E., Johnston, J.H., Salas, E.: Does stress training generalize to novel settings? Hum. Factors **43**(1), 99–110 (2001). https://doi.org/10.1518/001872001775992471
15. Szalma, J., Hancock, P., Hancock, G.: Task loading and stress in human–computer interaction: theoretical frameworks and mitigation strategies. In: Jacko, J.A. (ed.) Human Computer Interaction Handbook: Fundamentals, Evolving Technologies, and Emerging Applications, 3rd edn. Taylor & Francis Group (2012)
16. Wickens, C.D.: Designing for stress. In: Driskell, J.E., Salas, E. (eds.) Stress and Human Performance, pp. 279–295. Lawrence Erlbaum (1996)
17. Lazarus, R.S., Folkman, S.: Stress, Appraisal, and Coping. Springer, Heidelberg (1984)
18. Cox-Fuenzalida, L.-E.: Effect of workload history on task performance. Hum. Factors **49**(2), 277–291 (2007). https://doi.org/10.1518/001872007X312496
19. Matthews, G., Campbell, S.E.: Task-induced stress and individual differences in coping. In: Proceedings of the Human Factors and Ergonomics Society Annual Meeting, pp. 821–825. Sage Publications, Los Angeles (1998)

20. Matthews, G., Joyner, L., Gilliland, K., Campbell, S., Falconer, S., Huggins, J.: Validation of a comprehensive stress state questionnaire: towards a state big three. Person. Psych. in Eur. 7, 335–350 (1999)
21. Speisman, J.C., Lazarus, R.S., Mordkoff, A., Davison, L.: Experimental reduction of stress based on ego-defense theory. J. Abnorm. Soc. Psychol. 68(4), 367–380 (1964). https://doi.org/10.1037/h0048936
22. Gross, J.J., Levenson, R.W.: Emotional suppression: physiology, self-report, and expressive behavior. J. Pers. Soc. Psych. 64(6), 970–986 (1993). https://doi.org/10.1037/0022-3514.64.6.970
23. Hadley, J., Singmaster, D.: Problems to sharpen the young. Math. Gaz. 76(475), 102–126 (1992)
24. Ascher, M.: A river-crossing problem in cross-cultural perspective. Math. Mag. 63, 26–29 (1990). https://doi.org/10.1080/0025570X.1990.11977478
25. Gross, J.J., John, O.P.: Individual differences in two emotion regulation processes: Implications for affect, relationships, and well-being. J. Person. Soc. Psych. 85(2), 348–362 (2003). https://doi.org/10.1037/0022-3514.85.2.348
26. Matthews, G., Hillyard, E.J., Campbell, S.E.: Metacognition and maladaptive coping as components of test anxiety. Clin. Psychol. Psychother.: Int. J. Theory Pract. 6(2), 111–125 (1999)
27. Hart, S.G., Staveland, L.E.: Development of NASA-TLX (Task Load Index): results of empirical and theoretical research. Adv. Psych. 52, 139–183 (1988)
28. Wickens, C.D., Hutchins, S., Carolan, T., Cumming, J.: Effectiveness of part-task training and increasing-difficulty training strategies: a meta-analysis approach. Hum. Factors 55(2), 461–470 (2013)
29. Kent, S., Devonport, T.J., Lane, A.M., Nicholls, W., Friesen, A.P.: The Effects of coping interventions on ability to perform under pressure. J. Sports Sci. Med. 17(1), 40–55 (2018)
30. Rand Corporation. Enhancing performance under stress: Stress inoculation training for battlefield airmen. Technical Report, DTIC Publication No. ADA605157 (2014). https://apps.dtic.mil/sti/pdfs/ADA605157.pdf

Exploring the Individual Differences in Multidimensional Evolution of Knowledge States of Learners

Liang Zhang[1,2(✉)], Philip I. Pavlik Jr.[1,3], Xiangen Hu[1,2,3,4],
Jody L. Cockroft[1,3], Lijia Wang[1,2], and Genghu Shi[5]

[1] Institute for Intelligent Systems, University of Memphis, Memphis, TN 38152, USA
{lzhang13,ppavlik,xhu,lwang3}@memphis.edu
[2] Department of Electrical and Computer Engineering, University of Memphis,
Memphis, TN 38152, USA
[3] Department of Psychology, University of Memphis, Memphis, TN 38152, USA
[4] School of Psychology, Central China Normal University,
Wuhan 430079, Hubei, China
[5] Department of Psychology, Guangxi Normal University,
Guilin 541000, Guangxi, China

Abstract. The key to the effectiveness of Intelligent Tutoring Systems (ITSs) is to fit the uncertainty of each learner's performance in performing different learning tasks. Throughout the tutoring and learning process, the uncertainty of learners' performance can reflect their varying knowledge states, which can arise from individual differences in learning characteristics and capacities. In this investigation, we proposed a multidimensional representation of the evolution of knowledge states of learners to better understand individual differences among them. This assumption about this representation is verified using the Tensor Factorization (TF) based method, a modern state-of-the-art model for knowledge tracing. The accuracy of the Tensor-based method is evaluated by comparing it to other knowledge-tracing methods, to gain a deeper insight into individual differences among learners and their learning of diverse contents. The experimental data under focus in our investigation is derived from the AutoTutor lessons that were developed for the Center for the Study of Adult Literacy (CSAL), which employs a trialogue design comprising of a virtual tutor, a virtual companion and a human learner. A broader merit of our proposed approach lies in its capability to capture individual differences more accurately, without requiring any changes in the real-world implementation of ITSs.

Keywords: Intelligent tutoring systems · Knowledge tracing ·
Knowledge states of learners · Individual differences · Tensor-based
method · Tutoring · Learning process

1 Introduction

Intelligent Tutoring System (ITSs) are deemed as intelligent due to their capabilities to capture various uncertainties of learners and ensure flexible and adaptive interactions tailored to each individual needs [1–4]. The sources of uncertainties can arise both explicitly and implicitly from various dimensions, such as the learner's background, skills, diverse experience in the learning domain, learning characteristics, learning styles, and other psychological characteristics that cause individual differences in the learning process, learning ability or performance of learners [1,5–7]. Generally, modeling that relies on learning data can be a powerful and commonly used way to quantify sources of uncertainties in both academic and industry settings. The fluctuations of parameters obtained in such models to some extend reflect the physical sense of individual differences among learners, and can potentially serve as a reference for the real-world implementation of ITSs. However, such modeling work remains a challenging task due to the complexity of human learning nature (involves acquiring knowledge under the effects of task difficulties, memory, time, practice, sequence, etc.), the particularities for different domain knowledge, the existing uncertainties from the environment and learners, as well as instructional interventions [8–10].

Sensing and capturing the individual differences of each learner in modeling is crucial for achieving adaptiveness in ITSs. AI tools and techniques (based on the machine learning within our research scope) can contribute to the modeling work (may focus on certain or specific aspects of learning) by providing mathematical descriptions of the knowledge learning states of learners, as well as reasoning and problems-solving mechanisms along the tutoring/learning progress [5]. This can typically be achieved through the use of knowledge tracing approaches that allow the system to trace changes in the learner's knowledge state during learning, to implement probability estimates of the learner's performance, and guide pedagogical decisions based on mastery learning principles [11–14]. The knowledge tracing approaches basically assume that the learner' prior performance can help in predicting the performance of the learner on subsequent tasks. For example, the sequence of prior performance on practicing items for each learner is utilized for estimating the probability of answering each subsequent item correctly [15]. Usually, many researchers use elementary fragments of domain knowledge, like the concepts or concept-like elements, the Knowledge Units (KUs), Knowledge Components (KCs), or other question-related knowledge items if KCs are not specified, to generically constitute the implication relations or internal links among those items in domain knowledge [15–17]. They will serve as the knowledge of how to apply learning proficiency to estimate the probability of success when the learner responds to practice items in knowledge tracing. At the same time, the intelligent tutor can present adaptive instructions based on the probability prediction of the learner's performance, and aims to reach the goal of bolstering the learner's evolving knowledge state to converge to the wholly master states (or some pre-specified criterion, e.g. mastery criterion of probability of 0.95 [11,18]) in the targeted domain.

The state-of-the-art models for knowledge tracing can be generally categorized as factor analysis models and Bayesian Knowledge Tracing (BKT) [19]. The models within the family of factor analysis can be traced back to the development of Item Theory Response (IRT) [15,20]. The core idea of IRT is to estimate the probability of student success on the test items based on various factors of that item, typically using a logistic function. Usually, the skills, concepts, knowledge, or cognitive operations that are considered necessary for answering the item correctly are represented in the form of Q-matrices [15,21]. Some prototypes of the factor analysis models are the Additive Factor Model (AFM) [22] and Performance Factor Analysis (PFA) [23]. The BKT is theoretically supported by the hidden Markov model and Bayesian Belief Network. BKT estimates the learner's mastery of a skill and predicts the probability of the learner's success with a binary knowledge state (the learned state and unlearned state) [11]. Many BKT variants may include Individualized BKT [24], Dynamic BKT Model [25], and so on.

Moreover, some advanced methods for knowledge tracing are recently proposed, like the SPARse Factor Analysis (SPARFA) [26] and Tensor Factorization (TF) based method [27]. The SPARFA uses the quantized matrix completion to predict student performance in knowledge tracing. Specifically, the SPARFA represents the probability of answering a question successfully in terms of three factors: 1) the learner's knowledge of a set of latent or underlying concepts, 2) the connections between the question and concepts, and 3) the intrinsic difficulty of each question [26]. The TF based method refers to structurally represent student knowledge in three-dimensional space by taking into account the critical factors (e.g. learners, problems, and attempts) that significantly influence the learning progress. It implements probability estimates on student performance via tensor factorization mathematically. Some of TF variants in knowledge tracing are three-dimensional Bayesian Probability Tensor Factorization (3D-BPTF) [28], Feedback-Driven Tensor Factorization (FDTF) [27], Rank-Based Tensor Factorization (RBTF) [29].

The TF-based method is highlighted in this study. In an ITS learning environment, the learners' performance data can be captured, collected and reorganized in multiple ways to express their learning state and track their learning progress over time, which can be then utilized for modeling or other statistical analyses. In the TF-based method, one 3-dimensional tensor factorization framework can be built by involving the most critical factors of learners, attempts, and questions, for deeply exploring and exploiting their ensemble effects in the learning process. Some reasons for this choice include: 1) the capability of this method to handle the multiple dimensionalities of the factors (from learners, attempts or time, and questions) that critically affect the performance, 2) the scalability in the "elastic" size of these dimensions, 3) its generality in exploring and exploiting the learning model accurately (will be verified by the results) [30]. Additionally, the tensor-based construction is capable to avoid the "distortion" of effects from the sequence in modeling. Therefore, this proposed approach lay the foundation for us to explore the individual differences on the basis of accurate modeling, fidelity and multidimensionality.

Lastly, it is worth noting that the modeling work heavily relies on the experimental data from real scenarios as it can provide us lots of information about the learners' performance. The modeling work involves evaluating multiple candidate models, and the model that best fits the pattern of knowledge learning observed in existing experimental data is selected for further research.

2 A Brief Review of Study Case: CSAL AutoTutor

In this investigation, the Center for the Study of Adult Literacy (CSAL) Auto-Tutor, one example expectation-misconception-tailed (EMT) dialogue ITS, is under focus. The CSAl AutoTutor employs the trialogues design, which includes two computer agents (virtual tutor and virtual learner) and one human learner [31]. Figure 1(a) shows a screenshot of the interface for CSAL AutoTutor from the lesson on the topic of "Cause and Effect". The actions of learner while interacting with CSAL AutoTutor can involve a range of physical actions such as clicking, scrolling, dragging, and dropping on the exchange surface, and the system tracks the learner's performance based on the selected menu alternative at each turn in the conversation when a response is expected (this belongs to the categorical responses) [3,31–33].

The diagram for calling questions queue by hierarchical task difficulty levels (including intermediate, easy and hard, which are computed by the Coh-Metrix system [31,34,35]) in the system is shown in Fig. 3(b). After the human learner completes reading the entire text in the specific CSAL reading comprehension lesson, the questions will be displayed. The question at the intermediate difficulty level, denoted as $(Q_{Inter\_1}, Q_{Inter\_2}, Q_{Inter\_3}, \dots)$, will be retrieved first from the question queue and presented the human learner. The human learner will then respond to the question within the context of the text, and provide categorical answers by clicking the relevant selection buttons provided. The human learner's performance on the questions can be assessed by comparing their answers with the expected ones, and their score will calculated sequentially. Once the intermediate queue is completed, there will be a switch to another one. If the match scores meet to or exceed the threshold of expectation (upgrade), the call is directed to the hard level queue $(Q_{Hard\_1}, Q_{Hard\_2}, Q_{Hard\_3}, \dots)$. Otherwise, the call will be directed to the easy level question queue $(Q_{Easy\_1}, Q_{Easy\_2}, Q_{Easy\_3}, \dots)$ for a downgrade. The response sequence of each individual human learner's performance (usually consisting of categorical responses such as correct or incorrect in CSAL AutuTutor) is generated sequentially as the question queue runs. This is the diagram commonly used to illustrate the process of calling different task difficulty levels of question queues for most CSAL lessons.

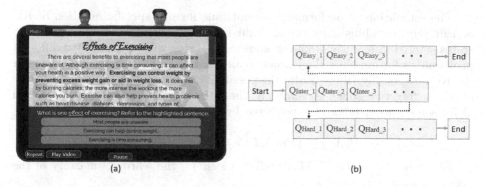

Fig. 1. CSAL AutoTutor: (a) screenshoot of interface, (b) diagram for calling different difficulty levels of questions queue

3   Multidimensional Evolution of Knowledge States of Learners for CSAL AutoTutor

As mentioned previously, the TF-based method introduces a multidimensional perspective to describe human learning. The similar perspective was originally from the book edited by Newell and Simon five decades ago [36]. It seeks to decode human learning as three-dimensional space, which includes the task dimension (different classes of task environments), performance-learning-development dimension (activities related to performing, learning, and developing are correlated with time scale), and the individual-difference dimension (various populations with a varying difference) in an evolutionary sense. In this study, we adopt this idea as a starting point and extract implementable concepts to instantiate a three dimensional space based on the dimensions of learners, questions, and attempts in real learning scenarios of ITS. And we aim to present a structural and systematical framework that incorporates modern development of knowledge tracing methodologies to enable deeper and more extensive study of human learning (mainly focus on the individual differences in this paper).

As discussed earlier, in the CSAL AutoTutor system, the generation of a sequence of the learner's responses (performances in EMT-based ITSs) follows the running of the questions queue progressively. The elementary fragments of domain knowledge, like concepts or concept-like elements, KUs, KCs, or question-related items if the KCs are not specified, constitute the knowledge domain, which can be represented as [16, 17]:

$$\Delta = \{\delta_1, \delta_2, \delta_3, ..., \delta_n\} \tag{3.1}$$

where the Δ specifies the knowledge domain and the δ refers to the KC or KU (if labeled, else question item). Note that KCs can be identified or refined by the "manual" approaches by the domain expert, some automated methods, or semi-automated methods; there are many examples of research on the identification of the KCs in different domains [37–39], but it is beyond the scope of this investigation to make these efforts.

The estimation of performance or outcome for one specific question or KC is definitely probabilistic by the individual difference of the learner's knowledge states. Stated differently, different knowledge states will contribute to different probabilities for enabling the learner to answer the question correctly or master the KC successfully (there is also the possibility of failure in performing because of slip or forget reasons). Accordingly, the estimation of mastery of the domain Δ for some learner (e.g. l_1) is predicted by probability as:

$$P(\Lambda_{l_1}^t) = \{P(\delta_1), P(\delta_2), P(\delta_3), ..., P(\delta_n)\} \tag{3.2}$$

For example, in the CSAL AutoTutor system, the learner's mastery of the domain can be estimated as:

$$\Lambda_{l_1}^t = \{0.52, 0.63, 0.85, 0.91, 0.92, ..., 0.93, 0.95\} \tag{3.3}$$

By encoding the actual performance of a learner sequentially as an array of binary values (1 for correct and 0 for incorrect), we can represent the learner's knowledge state as:

$$\Lambda_{l_1}^t = \{1, 1, 0, 1, 1, ..., 0, 1\} \tag{3.4}$$

The evolving knowledge state of each learner, encompassing all moments and questions, for each learner can be defined as a matrix frame:

$$\Lambda_{l_1} = [P_{i,j}]_{n \times m} = \begin{Bmatrix} Y_1 \\ Y_2 \\ Y_3 \\ \vdots \\ Y_i \\ \vdots \\ Y_n \end{Bmatrix} = \begin{pmatrix} P_{11} & P_{12} & P_{13} & \cdots & P_{1m} \\ P_{21} & P_{22} & P_{23} & \cdots & P_{2m} \\ P_{31} & P_{32} & P_{33} & \cdots & P_{3m} \\ \vdots & \vdots & \vdots & \ddots & \vdots \\ P_{n1} & P_{n2} & P_{n3} & \cdots & P_{nm} \end{pmatrix} \tag{3.5}$$

where the P_{ij} is determined by predictions of the observed probability of the individual learner for mastering the ith question (or associated KCs) at the jth moment or attempt. The row vectors $\{Y_1, Y_2, Y_3, \cdots, Y_i, \cdots, Y_n\}^T$, also the observation vectors of Λ_{l_1}, demonstrate the learner's performance in the dimension of questions or KCs by some sequential order.

Taking the multiple learners into account, we can extend the two-dimensional matrix mentioned in (3.6) into three-dimensional tensor (including dimensions of learners, questions or KCs, and time or attempts).

If the domain of learners L (including total u learners) can be represented as:

$$L = \{l_1, l_2, l_3, \cdots, l_u\} \tag{3.6}$$

And accordingly, the tensor-based knowledge states of learners T for the learners' domain L is:

$$T = [\Lambda_{l_1}, \Lambda_{l_2}, \Lambda_{l_3}, \cdots, \Lambda_{l_u}] \tag{3.7}$$

4   Exploration of Models Based on Knowledge Tracing

To regularize the modeling work and improve the interpretability of all entries in modeling, two fundamental restricting assumptions are given:

- Non-negativity: Negative impact of the learner's knowledge on the probability of successfully answering present questions is not allowed. In other words, the entries about the quantized performance data (probability values) are non-negative.
- Sparsity: Data sparsity inevitably exists in the experimental dataset for modeling. For example, there may be some zero entries in modeling when students are incomplete or miss performance in answering questions.

4.1   About the Approaches

Four typical knowledge tracing models are to be explored in this study: 1) TF-based method, 2) PFA, 3) BKT, 4) SPARFA-Lite (one variant of the SPARFA).

(1) TF-based method: The-TF based method relies on the 3-dimensional tensor to represent students performance. Given a 3-dimensional tensor $T \in R^{I \times S \times J}$, the three dimensions donate the total number of learners (I), the total number of attempts (S), and the total number of questions (J) separately. Each cell τ_{isj} of T represents the performance variable of student l_i on question q_j at attempt a_s, e.g. $\tau_{isj} = \{0, 1\}$ with 1 representing a correct answer and 0 an incorrect answer in the CSAL AutoTutor case.

To obtain the third order $\hat{T}$, we define a vector U and a matrix V (as shown in Figure 7) [27],

$$\hat{T} \sim U \otimes V \tag{4.1}$$

where $U \in R^{I \times S \times C}$ and $V \in R^{C \times J}$. In this decomposition (Tucker Decomposition), the tensor U represents the knowledge of learners on the latent KCs at each attempt on questions, the matrix V represents the latent KCs required for solving each question, and the obtained $\hat{T}$ is the approximation of the T constructed by real data (its accuracy is evaluated by best-fit computing mathematically). Here we use vector $u_{is:}$ of U to represent the KCs required for the student l_i to answer questions at the attempt a_s, and the vector $v_{:j}$ to represent the latent KCs vector on the question q_j.

If we take into account bias from these factors of learner's ability, question difficulty, or student cohort strength, we add the learner, question, and attempt biases (b_l, b_a, b_q) in addition to an overall cohort bias (μ) to our above mentioned model, so the estimated $\hat{\tau}_{isj}$ is [29]:

$$\hat{\tau}_{isj} \approx u_{is:} \cdot v_{:j} + b_l + b_a + b_q + \mu \tag{4.2}$$

The objective function can be minimized as [29]:

$$\xi_1 = \sum_{isj}(\hat{\tau}_{isj} - \tau_{isj})^2 + \lambda(b_l^2 + b_a^2 + b_q^2) + \lambda_1 \parallel u_{is:} \parallel^2 + \lambda_2 \parallel v_{:j} \parallel^2 \qquad (4.3)$$

We assign the cohort bias μ as $\mu = \frac{\sum_{isj}\tau_{isj}}{\sum_{isj}\Gamma(isj)}$, where $\Gamma(i,s,j)$ is an indicator function returning 1 if the tuple (i,s,j) is in our training set; otherwise 0 [29]. This is the regular type of TF-based method.

(2) PFA: PFA is a logistic regression model that predicts the probability of a learner's answer response on a question as a function of the learner's learning ability, KC-related features (e.g. difficulty), and previous success and failures [15, 23, 40–42]. One variant of PFA is given [15, 42]:

$$logit(p_{ikj}) = \theta_i + \theta_j + \gamma_{ik}S_{ikj} + \rho_{ik}F_{ikj} \qquad (4.4)$$

where i, j, and k represent the learner, attempts and KC separately. The θ_i is the coefficient for the learner i (about learning proficiency) and the θ_j the coefficient for KC k (about difficulty). The S_{ikj} refers to the number of prior successes the learner i has had on the KC k. The F_{ikj} refers to the number of prior failures the learner i has had on the KC k. The γ_{ik} the coefficient for the benefit of previous success on the KC k for the learner i. The ρ_{ik} becomes the coefficient for the benefit of previous failures on the KC k for the learner i. And the $logit(p_{ikj})$: is usually obtained by $ln(\frac{p_{ikj}}{1-p_{ikj}})$.

(3) BKT: BKT estimates the learner's master level on a skill and predicts the probability of a learner's binary response (correct or incorrect) in a binary state (the learned state or the unlearned state) [11]. It uses the Bayesian network to make the learner's performance up to one point linked by four parameters probabilistically [11, 13, 43–46]. Four important notations in BKT are given:

- $P(L_0)$: the initial or prior probability of mastering the skill for the learner.
- $P(T)$: the probability of acquiring or learning knowledge the learner by transforming from the unmastered state on one skill to the master state.
- $P(S)$: the probability of making an incorrect answer response by slipping in the mastered state on a skill for the learner.
- $P(G)$: the probability of making a correct answer response by guessing in an unmastered state on a skill for the learner.

Note that we define $P(L_l)$ as the probability of mastering the skill for a learner at attempt l. In CSAL AutoTutor case, we use $P(L_l \mid O_l)$ as the probability of learning a skill for the learner based on the learner's previous response, where $O_l \in \{0, 1\}$. The O_l is 1 if the answer response is correct and 0 if incorrect. So the $P(L_l \mid O_l)$ can be calculated through following equation [43–46]:

$$P(L_{l-1} = 1 \mid O_l = 0) = \frac{P(L_{l-1} = 1) * (1 - P(S))}{P(L_{l-1} = 1) * (1 - P(S)) + (1 - P(L_{l-1} = 1)) * P(G)} \qquad (4.5)$$

$$P(L_{l-1} = 1 \mid O_l = 1) = \frac{P(L_{l-1} = 1) * P(S)}{P(L_{l-1} = 1) * P(S) + (1 - P(L_{l-1} = 1)) * (1 - P(G))}$$
$$(4.6)$$
$$P(L_{l-1} = 1 \mid O_l) = P(L_{l-1} = 1 \mid O_l) + (1 - P(L_{l-1} = 1 \mid O_l)) * P(T) \quad (4.7)$$

(4) SPARFA-Lite: The SPARFA-Lite is the variant of the SPARse Factor Analysis (SPARFA). The SPARFA-Lite leverages matrix completion to analyze the quantized graded learner responses, and automatically identify the required number of KCs [47]. The "Lite" means low computational complexity as compared to the conventional SPARFA [47]. The prediction of learners' performance is driven by the exploration of the number of KCs in SPARFA-Lite.

Suppose that the unknown and low-rank matrix Z represents the learners' responses to questions. Since it's a two-dimensional level, the entries of Z can represent overall quantized measurements by taking into account all responses through all attempts for the specified question.

Let $Y_{ij} \in \mathcal{O}$, where $\mathcal{O} = \{1, \cdots, P\}$ is a set of P ordered labels. Inspired by [47,48], we use the following model for the observed response $Y_{i,j}$:

$$Y_{i,j} = \mathcal{Q}(Z_{ij} + \epsilon_{ij}), \text{ and } \epsilon_{ij} \sim Logistic(0, 1) \quad (4.8)$$

where $\{\omega_0, \cdots, \omega_P\}$ is a set of quantization bin boundaries, with $\omega_0 \leq \omega_1 \leq \cdots \leq \omega_{P-1} \leq \omega_P$. The quantization bin boundaries $\{\omega_0, \cdots, \omega_P\}$ is assumed to known a priori.

In terms of the likelihood of the observed graded leaner response Y_{ij}, the model in (1) can be written equivalently as

$$p(Y_{ij} = p \mid Z_{ij}) = \Phi(w_p - Z_{ij}) - \Phi(w_{p-1} - Z_{ij}) \quad (4.9)$$

where $\Phi(x) = \frac{1}{1+e^{-x}}$ corresponds to the inverse link function.

In order to recover the low-rank matrix Z, we try to minimize the negative log-likelihood of the observed graded measurement of learner response $Y_{i,j} \in \Omega_{obs}$. The optimization problem can be described as following:

$$\begin{cases} minimize \ f(Z) = -\sum_{ij:(i,j)\in\Omega_{obs}} \log p(Y_{ij} \mid Z_{ij}) \\ subject \ to \ \|Z\| \leq \lambda \end{cases} \quad (4.10)$$

This optimization can be solved efficiently via the FISTA framework [49]. Here, the constant $\|Z\| \leq \lambda$ is used to promote the low-rank solution Z and the parameter $\lambda > 0$ is used to control its rank. In practice, the nuclear norm constant $\|Z\|_* \leq \lambda$ is applied here.

The gradient step is given by $\hat{Z}^{l+1} \leftarrow Z^l - s_l \nabla f$, where the s_l is the step-size at iteration l. For simplicity, s_l is the step-size $s_l = 1/L$, where the L is the Lipschitz constant, which is given by $L_{log} = 1/4$ for the inverse logit link.

The gradient of the objective function $f(Z)$ with respect to Z is given by:

$$[\nabla f]_{ij} = \begin{cases} \frac{\Phi'(L_{ij}-Z_{ij}) - \Phi'(U_{ij}-Z_{ij})}{\Phi(U_{ij}-Z_{ij}) - \Phi(L_{ij}-Z_{ij})}, & if \ (i,j) \in \Omega_{obs} \\ 0, & otherwise \end{cases} \quad (4.11)$$

where the derivative of the inverse logit link function corresponds to $\Phi'(x) = \frac{1}{2+e^{-x}+e^x}$. The $Q \times N$ matrices U and L contain the upper and lower bin boundaries corresponding to the measurements Y_{ij}, i.e. we have $\omega_{Y_{ij}}$ and $L_{ij} = \omega_{Y_{ij}-1}$.

The projection step imposes low-rankness on Z. It's also the regularization preventing overfitting. The nuclear norm constant case $\|Z\|_* \leq \lambda$, this step requires a projection onto the nuclear norm ball with radius λ, which can be performed by first computing the SVD of Z followed by projecting the vector of singular values onto an l_1-norm ball with radius λ [50].

$$Z^{l+1} \leftarrow \tilde{U}diag(s)\tilde{V}^T, with \ s = P_\lambda(diag(S)) \tag{4.12}$$

where the $\tilde{U}diag(s)\tilde{V}^T$ denotes the SVD of the $\hat{Z}^{l+1}$. The operator $P_\lambda(\cdot)$ denotes the projection of a vector onto l_1-norm ball with radius λ, which can be computed at low complexity. In our study, the biased matrices that implicitly contain the intrinsic question difficulty and KCs are considered for Eq. 4.10.

If we define the $Q \times N$ matrix A with $A_{ij} = \Phi(Z_{ij}) \in [0,1]$, which is the denoised and completed version of the (partially observed) graded leaner response matrix Y. The correctness is computed using the model's prediction (rounded toward 0 or 1 using 0.5 as the threshold) and the actual correctness of the student step in the data.

4.2   Evaluation Metrics

How can we measure what is "good" modeling? All reported results are the average 5-fold cross-validation (or run 5 times). Three measures of quality, Mean Absolute Error (MAE), Root Mean Square Error (RMSE), and Area Under the Curve (AUC) Score, are used to evaluate the performance of these models in modeling knowledge tracing for CSAL AutoTutor lessons case data.

$$MAE = \frac{1}{n} \sum | y_{pred} - y_{obs} | \tag{4.13}$$

$$RMSE = \sqrt{\frac{1}{n}(y_{pred} - y_{obs})^2} \tag{4.14}$$

where the y_{obs} refers to the observations while the y_{pred} represents the predictions by the corresponding model. The lower the value of these MAE and RMSE metrics, the better (the higher accuracy) the corresponding model is. And the AUC is computed by obtaining all y_{pred} values, and then using them to form the Receiver Operator Characteristic (ROC) curve in one orthogonal plane coordinate system (x-axis is true positives rate, and the y-axis is false negative rate). The AUC score refers to the area under that ROC curve. The model with a higher AUC score is better at modeling knowledge tracing.

5   About the Dataset

The prior dataset used for this study is collected from the CSAL AutoTutor lessons [51–53]. We select four lessons in the series of topics on stories and texts,

which consist of Lesson 1 "Evaluating Information in Persuasive Text" (for finding the main arguments and support), Lesson 2 "Cause and Effect" (for finding
causes and consequences in texts), Lesson 3 "Problems and Solutions" (for identifying problems and how to solve them), and Lesson 4 "Inferences from Texts"
(for making inferences in informational texts). Each lesson has between 10 and
30 categorized-responses-based questions for assessing their performance about
their literacy skill. The questions in each lesson are classified into three categories according to levels of task difficulties, which are intermediate (M), easy
(E), and hard (H). Table 1 shows the simple statistics of this dataset.

Table 1. Statistics of dataset from CSAL AutoTutor lessons

Dataset	#learners	#questions	Max. attempts
Lesson 1	107	8(M)+8(E)+11(H)	9
Lesson 2	118	9(M)+10(E)+10(H)	9
Lesson 3	140	11(M)+8(H)	5
Lesson 4	46	10(M)+9(E)+10(H)	7

* Note: (1) Throughout the table, the number of questions is not
evenly distributed among the different levels of task difficulties.
For example, some easy-level questions in some lessons are rarely
called in real experiments, e.g. only 2 learners in Lesson 1, and
0 learners in Lesson 3. (2) The number of learners differs in
different levels of task difficulties for each lesson. The learners
that finished the intermediate difficulty level of questions can be
split into two parts (upgraded hard level and downgraded easy
level) based on their performance at the intermediate level.

6   Results and Discussion

The results of evaluating four types of knowledge tracing models (BKT, PFA,
SPARFA-Lite, and TF-based method) are shown in Table 2. As mentioned above,
the M, E, and H refer to the intermediate, easy, and hard level of task difficulties
of questions separately. And both PFA and BKT are evaluated under single-KC-
fits-all mode (marked as "Single KC") and one-KC-one-question mode (marked
as "Unique KC").

In order to get the best fit, the tuning parameters of these models need to
be adjusted in optimization. For the current BKT used in our study, the initial values for the initial learning rate $P(L_0)$, slip parameter $P(S)$, and guess
parameter $P(G)$ are randomly selected within the range of 0.05 to 0.95. The
setting of these initial parameters' values in BKT are individualized for individual questions or skill items, and then they are used for the implementation
of individualized knowledge tracing for each learner. During the BKT process,
the values of the parameters are allowed to be adjusted by EM. This allows the

model to converge towards the optimal values of these parameters and more accurately estimate the learning performance of the learner. The values of the tuning parameters obtained through BKT for different KCs are likely to be different depending on the specific KC. Some example BKT tuples that correspond to the KC items (or questions) from the intermediate level of Lesson 1 under the "Unique KC" mode are given in Eq. 6.1. Different values of all adjusted parameters $(P(L_0), (P(T), P(G), P(S))$ for different KCs $(KC1, KC2, KC3, \cdots, KC8)$ demonstrate unique characteristics or individual differences of each KC and the individualization for learner when learning each KC item.

$$BKT\ Tuples \begin{cases} [0.95, 0.45, 0.45, 0.10] \Rightarrow [P(L_0), (P(T), P(G), P(S)]_{KC1} \\ [0.95, 0.95, 0.45, 0.05] \Rightarrow [P(L_0), (P(T), P(G), P(S)]_{KC2} \\ [0.75, 0.80, 0.05, 0.45] \Rightarrow [P(L_0), (P(T), P(G), P(S)]_{KC3} \\ \qquad\qquad\qquad \vdots \\ [0.05, 0.05, 0.45, 0.45] \Rightarrow [P(L_0), (P(T), P(G), P(S)]_{KC8} \end{cases} \quad (6.1)$$

The estimation of PFA using the generalized linear mixed model with individual learners as random effects for each KC (under "Unique KC" mode) emphasizes the consideration of individual differences among different learners and their related skills for acquiring KCs in learning process [15, 40]. Different estimates of intercepts and coefficients in a CSAL AutoTutor lesson indicate that it is possible to implement different learner models for the same lesson.

The function of averaging the overall performance across multiple attempts was used for getting the original matrix Z in the SPARFA-Lite. However, this definitely can mask individual variations in learning progress, and the factors that influence it, such as memory, time, and practice [10, 54].

The RBTF type of TF method was applied in this study. The tuning parameters of RBTF can be different for different CSAL AutoTutor lessons, which mainly include λ, λ_1, λ_2, ω, the number of KCs C, and learning rate for this model lr.

As we can see from Table 2, the TF-based method beats the other three approaches based on the three metrics obtained by these four modeling, overall (although there may be some instances where the performance of RBTF is slightly worse than that of some other methods). It presents that across all these ten lessons, both the MAE values and RMSE values for seven lessons are lower than those of the other three models, and all AUC score values are larger than those of the other three models. It seems that for the instances where the performance is slightly worse, the values of MAE or RMSE are still close to the lowest value reported among the models. For example, the RMSE value of Lesson 1 (H) is 0.4019, which is only slightly higher than the RMSE value of 0.4011 for the BKT (Unique KC). And another example is the MAE value of Lesson 2 (E), which is 0.2758. This value is close to the lowest value of 0.2503 for the SPARFA-Lite model. The difference between these two values is relatively small. Therefore, our overall results suggested TF model performs better than the other three models.

Table 2. Comparisons of different knowledge tracing models on the CSAL AutoTutor dataset

Dataset	Metrics	BKT (Single KC)	BKT (Unique KC)	PFA (Single KC)	PFA (Unique KC)	SPARFA-Lite	TF-based method
Lesson 1 (M)	MAE	0.4623	0.3777	0.4500	0.4071	0.3954	**0.3706**
	RMSE	0.4790	0.4351	0.4733	0.4550	0.6287	**0.4301**
	AUC	0.5632	0.7571	0.5809	0.6703	0.5010	**0.7712**
Lesson 1 (H)	MAE	0.3535	0.3347	0.3340	0.3350	**0.2387**	0.2763
	RMSE	0.4178	**0.4001**	0.4315	0.4152	0.4850	0.4019
	AUC	0.5320	0.7067	0.5363	0.5929	0.4998	**0.7425**
Lesson 2 (M)	MAE	0.4252	0.3257	0.4150	0.3806	0.3245	**0.2982**
	RMSE	0.4575	**0.3957**	0.4557	0.4390	0.5691	0.3964
	AUC	0.5526	0.8119	0.5534	0.6744	0.5146	**0.8223**
Lesson 2 (H)	MAE	0.4184	0.3141	0.4003	0.3595	0.2979	**0.2871**
	RMSE	0.4512	**0.3851**	0.4490	0.4358	0.5449	0.3907
	AUC	0.5465	0.7955	0.5639	0.6584	0.5101	**0.8111**
Lesson 2 (E)	MAE	0.3731	0.3461	0.3666	0.3507	**0.2503**	0.2758
	RMSE	0.4261	0.4113	0.4415	0.4389	0.4969	**0.4072**
	AUC	0.5797	0.7156	0.4606	0.5269	0.5014	**0.7759**
Lesson 3 (M)	MAE	0.3330	0.3155	0.3293	0.3256	**0.2158**	0.2958
	RMSE	0.4077	0.3936	0.4227	0.4098	0.4644	**0.3884**
	AUC	0.4912	0.6970	0.5158	0.5308	0.4993	**0.7133**
Lesson 3 (H)	MAE	0.4588	0.3275	0.4446	0.4380	0.3400	**0.3015**
	RMSE	0.4768	0.4074	0.4782	0.4704	0.5826	**0.3950**
	AUC	0.4850	0.8226	0.5423	0.5432	0.5059	**0.8362**
Lesson 4 (M)	MAE	0.4598	0.4156	0.4437	0.4487	0.3625	**0.3424**
	RMSE	0.4766	0.4553	0.4775	0.4799	0.6008	**0.4544**
	AUC	0.5584	0.6583	0.5401	0.5308	0.5014	**0.7371**
Lesson 4 (H)	MAE	0.4945	0.3968	0.4914	0.4815	0.4287	**0.3838**
	RMSE	0.4968	0.4655	0.5154	0.5027	0.6544	**0.4567**
	AUC	0.4772	0.7255	0.5823	0.5312	0.5063	**0.7461**
Lesson 4 (E)	MAE	0.4819	0.4354	0.4789	0.4806	0.3583	**0.3490**
	RMSE	0.4929	0.4750	0.4989	0.4939	0.5789	**0.4674**
	AUC	0.5429	0.6585	0.4687	0.5000	0.5455	**0.8368**

* Because the easy-level questions in Lesson 1 and Lesson 3 are rarely called, their corresponding modeling results are missing in this table. The metric values may exhibit slight variations depending on the tuning parameters.

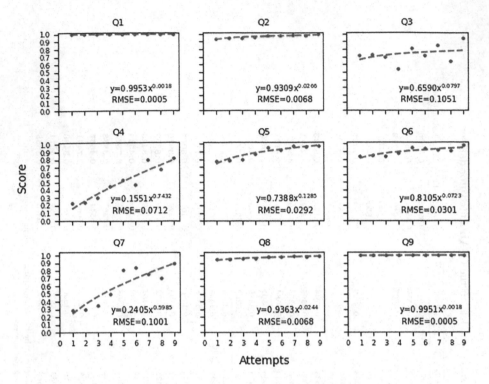

Fig. 2. The distribution of learner's performance for one learner in Lesson 2 (M). Note that the data is modeled by power-law functions and the RMSE is used as goodness-of-fit measure for the regression.

The tensor framework $(\hat{T})$ computed from TF can be regarded as the state space representation described in Session 3. In this sense, the $(\hat{T})$ provides intensive representation of the knowledge learning information that captures underlying structure and relationships between its elements, which overcomes the sparsity of original tensor by tensor factorization mathematically. This lays a foundation for helping us analyze, interpret and store the information more efficiently, more interpretable and easier.

Next, we investigated the individual differences derived from the tensor framework obtained from the TF method. The Lesson 2 (M) is taken as the example here.

Figure 2 shows the distribution of learner's performance for one learner from Lesson 2 (M). We make the following observations: 1) the score converges to 1 driven by attempts (a score of 1 represents the wholly master state), and 2) all distributions were well modeled by the same form of the power-law function:

$$Y = aX^b \tag{6.2}$$

where the Y represents the performance (probability for gaining correct answers), and X is the number of opportunities to practice a skill or attempts. a and b are the regression coefficients. In our research, a can represent a measurement of the student's starting level or ability in a given KC-related skill or knowledge. And b could be used to represent the learning rate of the learner, specifically in relation to knowledge acquired through practice. This finding confirms the well-known "power law learning curve" in educational or training contexts [55,56], which opens up another opportunity for further investigation when combined with the TF-based method.

In the CSAL AutoTutor lesson that includes the series of questions $[Q_1, Q_2, Q_3, Q_4, Q_5, Q_6, Q_7, Q_8, Q_9]$, the fluctuations of these two parameters can represent differences between learners in their learning of different skills (mainly in aspects of their learning styles, abilities, and progress). By exploring the boundaries of the model parameters, we can obtain the ranges of the values that the parameters can take.

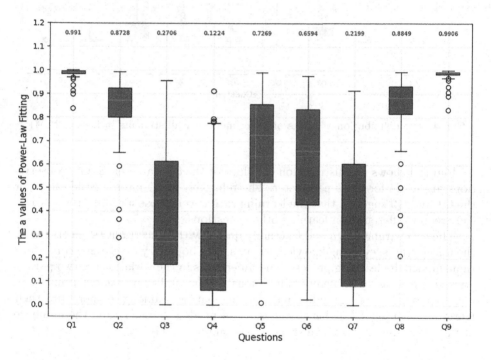

Fig. 3. The distribution of values of a parameter for all students in Lesson 2 (M)

Figure 3 shows the distribution of values of the a parameter. The interquartile range for the Q1 and Q9 are relatively shorter, which indicates that the initial learning features (starting level or ability) of the learners are very similar to each other. On the other hand, for the other questions, the difference is relatively larger, which suggests that there is more diversity in the initial abilities of the learners.

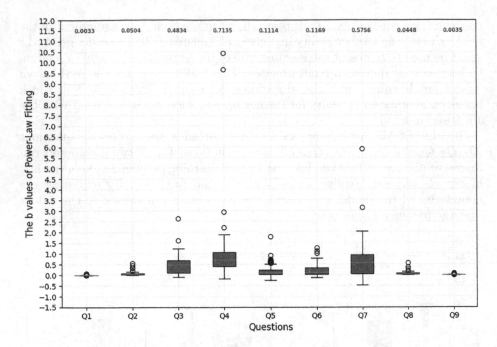

Fig. 4. The distribution of values of b parameter for all students in Lesson 2 (M)

Figure 4 shows the distribution of values of the b parameter. Similar observations are made for the b parameter. The relatively short interquartile range for the Q1 and Q9 suggests that the learning rate is very close for all learners, while the greater differences in learning other questions.

The two parameters a and b actually quantify the uncertainties generated by the initial states, evolving knowledge states, and boundary or extreme conditions that impact the learning process. The differences in the variations of two parameters a and b across different dimensions in the multidimensional framework, can be indicative of the individual learning patterns among learners and their learning of contents. Further research is still needed to understand the influence of these parameters on learning outcomes quantitatively.

7   Conclusion

To summarize, based on the results of the analysis, it appears that the tensor-based framework (TF-based) generates the best-fitting model for modeling the learning process (knowledge-level) for AutoTutor CSAL lessons. The findings suggest that the TF-based method can provide a relatively accurate way of capturing and predicting the learner's performance for real-world implementation of ITSs. This conclusion is based on the comparison of the model's performance measures (e.g., MAE, RMSE, and AUC) with those of other models. Observing that the distribution of parameters used in the model of an ITS fits a power-law function can provide valuable insights into the individual differences among learners, especially when considering multiple dimensions. By capturing the individual differences among learners, the ITS can provide more personalized and effective instruction, leading to improved learning outcomes.

The advantages of TF-based method (RBTF) over BKT, PFA, and SPARFA-Lite are: 1) the capability of this method to handle the multiple dimensionalities of the factors (from learners, attempts, or time, and questions) that critically affect the performance, 2) the scalability in the "elastic" size of these dimensions, 3) its generality in exploring and exploiting the learning model accurately, 4) its practical potential that more accurately capture the individual differences among learners without requiring any changes in the real-world implementation of ITSs.

Also, it is the potential to combine the use of TF-based method, BKT, and PFA (or just two of them) in order to model human learning more accurately in the future. By incorporating multiple methods, it may be possible to capture different aspects of the learning process and account for memory, time, practice, and sequence, as well as interactions between these factors.

This work is still progress, more deeper and extensive results will be presented in other paper.

Acknowledgements. This research was supported by the National Science Foundation Learner Data Institute (NSF #1934745).

References

1. Granić, A., Adams, R.: User sensitive research in e-learning: exploring the role of individual user characteristics. Univ. Access Inf. Soc. **10**(3), 307–318 (2011)
2. O'Shea, T., et al.: Tools for creating intelligent computer tutors. In: Proceedings of the International NATO Symposium on Artificial and Human Intelligence, pp. 181–199 (1984)
3. Graesser, A.C., et al.: Assessment with computer agents that engage in conversational dialogues and trialogues with learners. Comput. Hum. Behav. **76**, 607–616 (2017)
4. Mousavinasab, E., et al.: Intelligent tutoring systems: a systematic review of characteristics, applications, and evaluation methods. Interact. Learn. Environ. **29**(1), 142–163 (2021)
5. Woolf, B.P.: Building Intelligent Interactive Tutors: Student-Centered Strategies for Revolutionizing e-Learning. Morgan Kaufmann, Burlington (2010)
6. Egan, D.E.: Individual differences in human-computer interaction. In: Handbook of Human-Computer Interaction, pp. 543–568. Elsevier (1988)
7. Kuurstra, J.: Individual differences in human-computer interaction: a review of empirical studies (2015)
8. Landriscina, F.: Simulation and Learning. Springer, Heidelberg (2013)
9. MacLellan, C.J.: Computational models of human learning: applications for tutor development, behavior prediction, and theory testing. Ph.D. thesis. Carnegie Mellon University (2017)
10. Illeris, K: A comprehensive understanding of human learning. In: Contemporary Theories of Learning, pp. 1–14. Routledge (2018)

11. Corbett, A.T., Anderson, J.R.: Knowledge tracing: modeling the acquisition of procedural knowledge. User Model. User-adapted Interact. **4**(4), 253–278 (1994)
12. Block, J.H., Burns, R.B.: Mastery learning. Review Res. Educ. **4**, 3–49 (1976)
13. Pardos, Z.A., Heffernan, N.T.: Modeling individualization in a Bayesian networks implementation of knowledge tracing. In: De Bra, P., Kobsa, A., Chin, D. (eds.) UMAP 2010. LNCS, vol. 6075, pp. 255–266. Springer, Heidelberg (2010). https://doi.org/10.1007/978-3-642-13470-8_24
14. Trifa, A., Hedhili, A., Chaari, W.L.: Knowledge tracing with an intelligent agent, in an e-learning platform. Educ. Inf. Technol. **24**(1), 711–741 (2019)
15. Pavlik, P.I., Eglington, L.G., Harrell-Williams, L.M.: Logistic knowledge tracing: a constrained framework for learner modeling. IEEE Trans. Learn. Technol. **14**(5), 624–639 (2021)
16. Essa, A.: A possible future for next generation adaptive learning systems. Smart Learn. Environ. **3**(1), 1–24 (2016)
17. Brusilovsky, P.: Adaptive hypermedia for education and training. Adapt. Technol. Training Educ. **46**, 46–68 (2012)
18. Corbett, A.T., Anderson, J.R.: Student modeling and mastery learning in a computer-based programming tutor. In: Frasson, C., Gauthier, G., McCalla, G.I. (eds.) ITS 1992. LNCS, vol. 608, pp. 413–420. Springer, Heidelberg (1992). https://doi.org/10.1007/3-540-55606-0_49
19. Abdelrahman, G., Wang, Q., Nunes, B.P.: Knowledge tracing: a survey. ACM Comput. Surv. **55**, 1–37 (2022)
20. Embretson, S.E., Reise, S.P.: Item Response Theory. Psychology Press (2013)
21. Barnes, T.: The Q-matrix method: mining student response data for knowledge. In: American Association for Artificial Intelligence 2005 Educational Data Mining Workshop, Pittsburgh, PA, USA, pp. 1–8. AAAI Press (2005)
22. Cen, H., Koedinger, K., Junker, B.: Comparing two IRT models for conjunctive skills. In: Woolf, B.P., Aïmeur, E., Nkambou, R., Lajoie, S. (eds.) ITS 2008. LNCS, vol. 5091, pp. 796–798. Springer, Heidelberg (2008). https://doi.org/10.1007/978-3-540-69132-7_111
23. Pavlik, P.I., Jr., Cen, H., Koedinger, K.R.: Performance factors analysis–a new alternative to knowledge tracing. Online Submission (2009)
24. Yudelson, M.V., Koedinger, K.R., Gordon, G.J.: Individualized Bayesian knowledge tracing models. In: Lane, H.C., Yacef, K., Mostow, J., Pavlik, P. (eds.) AIED 2013. LNCS (LNAI), vol. 7926, pp. 171–180. Springer, Heidelberg (2013). https://doi.org/10.1007/978-3-642-39112-5_18
25. Käser, T., et al.: Dynamic Bayesian networks for student modeling. IEEE Trans. Learn. Technol. **10**(4), 450–462 (2017)
26. Lan, A.S., et al.: Sparse factor analysis for learning and content analytics. arXiv preprint arXiv:1303.5685 (2013)
27. Sahebi, S., Lin, Y.-R., Brusilovsky, P.: Tensor factorization for student modeling and performance prediction in unstructured domain. In: International Educational Data Mining Society (2016)
28. Sahebi, S., Huang, Y., Brusilovsky, P.: Parameterized exercises in Java programming: using knowledge structure for performance prediction. In: The Second Workshop on AI-Supported Education for Computer Science (AIEDCS), University of Pittsburgh, pp. 61–70 (2014)
29. Doan, T.-N., Sahebi, S.: Rank-based tensor factorization for student performance prediction. In: 12th International Conference on Educational Data Mining (EDM) (2019)

30. Karatzoglou, A., et al.: Multiverse recommendation: N-dimensional tensor factorization for context-aware collaborative filtering. In: Proceedings of the Fourth ACM Conference on Recommender Systems, pp. 79–86 (2010)
31. Graesser, A.C., et al.: Reading comprehension lessons in AutoTutor for the Center for the Study of Adult Literacy. In: Adaptive Educational Technologies for Literacy Instruction, pp. 288–293. Routledge (2016)
32. Graesser, A.C., Li, H., Forsyth, C.: Learning by communicating in natural language with conversational agents. Curr. Dir. Psychol. Sci. **23**(5), 374–380 (2014)
33. Fang, Y., Lippert, A., Cai, Z., Hu, X., Graesser, A.C.: A conversation-based intelligent tutoring system benefits adult readers with low literacy skills. In: Sottilare, R.A., Schwarz, J. (eds.) HCII 2019. LNCS, vol. 11597, pp. 604–614. Springer, Cham (2019). https://doi.org/10.1007/978-3-030-22341-0_47
34. Graesser, A.C., et al.: Coh-Metrix measures text characteristics at multiple levels of language and discourse. Elementary Sch. J. **115**(2), 210–229 (2014)
35. McNamara, D.S., et al.: Automated Evaluation of Text and Discourse with Coh-Metrix. Cambridge University Press, Cambridge (2014)
36. Newell, A., Simon, H.A., et al.: Human Problem Solving, vol. 104. 9. Prentice-Hall, Englewood Cliffs (1972)
37. Cen, H., Koedinger, K., Junker, B.: Learning factors analysis–a general method for cognitive model evaluation and improvement. In: Ikeda, M., Ashley, K.D., Chan, T.-W. (eds.) ITS 2006. LNCS, vol. 4053, pp. 164–175. Springer, Heidelberg (2006). https://doi.org/10.1007/11774303_17
38. Koedinger, K.R., Corbett, A.T., Perfetti, C.: The knowledge-learning-instruction framework: bridging the science-practice chasm to enhance robust student learning. Cogn. Sci. **36**(5), 757–798 (2012)
39. Aleven, V., Koedinger, K.R.: Knowledge component (KC) approaches to learner modeling. Des. Recommendations Intell. Tutoring Syst. **1**, 165–182 (2013)
40. Yudelson, M., Pavlik, P.I., Koedinger, K.R.: User modeling–a notoriously black art. In: Konstan, J.A., Conejo, R., Marzo, J.L., Oliver, N. (eds.) UMAP 2011. LNCS, vol. 6787, pp. 317–328. Springer, Heidelberg (2011). https://doi.org/10.1007/978-3-642-22362-4_27
41. Chi, M., et al.: Instructional factors analysis: a cognitive model for multiple instructional interventions. In: EDM 2011, pp. 61–70 (2011)
42. Eglington, L.G., Pavlik, P.I., Jr.: How to optimize student learning using student models that adapt rapidly to individual differences. Int. J. Artif. Intell. Educ. 1–22 (2022)
43. Baker, R.S.J., Corbett, A.T., Aleven, V.: More accurate student modeling through contextual estimation of slip and guess probabilities in Bayesian knowledge tracing. In: Woolf, B.P., Aïmeur, E., Nkambou, R., Lajoie, S. (eds.) ITS 2008. LNCS, vol. 5091, pp. 406–415. Springer, Heidelberg (2008). https://doi.org/10.1007/978-3-540-69132-7_44
44. Baker, R.S.J., Corbett, A.T., Aleven, V.: Improving contextual models of guessing and slipping with a truncated training set (2008)
45. van De Sande, B.: Properties of the Bayesian knowledge tracing model. J. Educ. Data Min. **5**(2), 1–10 (2013)
46. Wang, D., et al.: Traditional knowledge tracing models for clustered students (2021)
47. Lan, A.S., Studer, C., Baraniuk, R.G.: Quantized matrix completion for personalized learning. arXiv preprint arXiv:1412.5968 (2014)
48. Lan, A.S., Studer, C., Baraniuk, R.G.: Matrix recovery from quantized and corrupted measurements. In: 2014 IEEE International Conference on Acoustics, Speech and Signal Processing (ICASSP), pp. 4973–4977. IEEE (2014)

49. Beck, A., Teboulle, M.: A fast iterative shrinkage-thresholding algorithm for linear inverse problems. SIAM J. Imaging Sci. **2**(1), 183–202 (2009)
50. Cai, J.-F., Candès, E.J., Shen, Z.: A singular value thresholding algorithm for matrix completion. SIAM J. Optim. **20**(4), 1956–1982 (2010)
51. Shi, G., Pavlik, P., Jr., Graesser, A.: Using an additive factor model and performance factor analysis to assess learning gains in a tutoring system to help adults with reading difficulties. In: Grantee Submission (2017)
52. Shi, G., et al.: Diagnostic assessment of adults' reading deficiencies in an intelligent tutoring system. In: ITS Workshops, pp. 105–112 (2018)
53. Shi, G., et al.: Exploring an intelligent tutoring system as a conversation-based assessment tool for reading comprehension. Behaviormetrika **45**(2), 615–633 (2018). https://doi.org/10.1007/s41237-018-0065-9
54. Wickelgren, W.A.: Human learning and memory. Ann. Rev. Psychol. **32**(1), 21–52 (1981)
55. Newell, A., Rosenbloom, P.S.: Mechanisms of skill acquisition and the law of practice. Technical report. Carnegie-Mellon University, Pittsburgh, PA, Department of Computer Science (1980)
56. DeKeyser, R.: Skill acquisition theory. In: Theories in Second Language Acquisition, pp. 83–104. Routledge (2020)

Applications of Adaptive Instructional Systems

Ibigkas! Math 2.0: An Intelligent Computer-Supported Collaborative Learning Application for Grade 5 Mathematics

Rex P. Bringula[1,2]([✉])

[1] Ateneo de Manila University, Quezon City, Philippines
rexbringula@gmail.com
[2] University of the East, Manila, Philippines

Abstract. This paper reports the design and development of an intelligent mobile computer-supported collaborative learning (mCSCL) application in mathematics for Grade 5 elementary students named *Ibigkas! Math*. In the first experiment, we deployed the non-adaptive version of *Ibigkas! Math*. This software is a collaborative mobile-based game application where a team of students answers basic arithmetic problems. The player has to read aloud the arithmetic problems and answer multiple-choice items. The correct answer appears on one of the team members' devices. A team consists of three students with varying mathematical competencies and personality types. Thirty-seven Grade 5 students (male = 25, female = 12, average age = 10.5 years old) participated in the initial experiment. The initial results of the study revealed that the students always chose problems involving addition with the same level of difficulty throughout the game sessions. It was also observed that students exhibited "button-smashing" – a gaming behavior where students guess a game answer. These game behaviors lead to higher game scores. However, the game scores could not reflect the mathematical competencies of the students. A collaborative-intelligent math CSCL was developed to make the software adaptive to these behaviors. Aggregated model of constraint-based collaborative filtering algorithm (CBCF), Rasch model (RM), and computational fluency (CF) (e.g., trials-to-criterion approach) were integrated into the software. The revised version will then be deployed in the same setting to test its impact on students' learning and gaming behavior.

Keywords: adaptive game · algorithm · collaborative learning · collaboration

1 Introduction

Mathematics is widely regarded as one of the most difficult subjects to master [1, 32]. Some students dislike the subject and have developed negative attitudes and feelings toward it [19, 30]. Collaborative learning is one method for reducing the difficulty of a subject [18]. Collaborative learning is a learning strategy in which students pool their resources and talents to achieve a common goal (for example, solving a math problem)

© The Author(s), under exclusive license to Springer Nature Switzerland AG 2023
R. A. Sottilare and J. Schwarz (Eds.): HCII 2023, LNCS 14044, pp. 287–297, 2023.
https://doi.org/10.1007/978-3-031-34735-1_20

[3]. Researchers in educational technology use computers or mobile devices to support collaborative learning. Computer-supported collaborative learning (CSCL) refers to collaborative learning implemented on computers, whereas mobile CSCL (mCSCL) refers to collaborative learning implemented on mobile devices [29]. The field of mathematics takes advantage of the benefits of mCSCL, resulting in a new area of interest known as math mCSCL [3].

It has been found that math mCSCL creates a friendly and fun learning environment [9, 23]. It also has a positive impact on the attitudes and socialization skills of the students [3]. Moreover, the student's motivation to learn the subject increased through the use of math mCSCL. However, despite these advantages of math mCSCL, very little software was developed, and only a handful of studies were conducted in this field [3]. Furthermore, a scoping review of math mCSCL showed that adaptive technologies are not yet being employed to detect certain behaviors in this learning environment. The current status of the math mCSCL research not only leaves a fertile ground for research, but also a gap in the literature on maximizing the potential of mobile devices for collaborative learning. This study intends to address this gap in the literature. Specifically, this study reports the design and development of *Ibigkas! Math 2.0* – a web-based mCSCL for Grade 5 mathematics. This paper will also provide a background on the previous version of *Ibigkas! Math* and its limitations. Then, it will discuss the design of the updated version of the software and the plan for deploying it. The conclusion section is the last part of this paper.

2   The Previous *Ibigkas! Math* Version and Its Limitations

Ibigkas! Math is a mobile-based learning application for students in Grades 1 through 6. It is a collaborative game that deals with arithmetic problems (addition, subtraction, multiplication, and division of whole numbers and fractions). The application generates arithmetic problems, which are displayed on the mobile devices of one of the team members (see Fig. 1; [4, 5]). The player must read aloud the arithmetic problems. The answers are presented as multiple-choice questions. The correct answer will be displayed on the device of one of the team members.

Our initial experiment found two behaviors related to the use of the software [4]. Thirty-seven Grade 5 students (M = 10.5 years old; 25 male and 12 female students) participated in the initial experiment. The first behavior is that the students tend to solve problems that they are comfortable with. They did not attempt to solve more difficult problems. As a result, they only demonstrated the skill that they already possess, and the software may not contribute to the improvement of their mathematical skills. Second, students tend to guess the answers. They rapidly press the buttons, thereby exhibiting "gaming the system" behavior. There are also logistics constraints in the implementation of a mobile-based math mCSCL because of the COVID-19 pandemic [5]. Students could not meet face-to-face to use the game. Thus, there is a need to change the platform of the game.

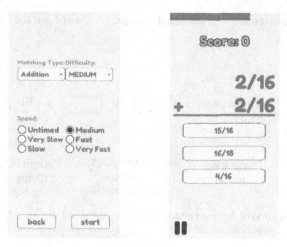

Fig. 1. The First Version of *Ibigkas! Math*

3   Design of *Ibigkas! Math 2.0* – An Adaptive Math mCSCL

The second version of the software intends to address the limitations of the previous version. The second version used different algorithms to make it adaptive to the educational needs and detect the gaming behavior of the students. The adaptive version of the game intends to intervene in two ways. First, the software will suggest problems to be solved. To carry out this goal, collaborative intelligence will be applied. Specifically, the game will be developed based on the aggregated model of a content-based filtering algorithm for a group. The second intervention is to detect the gaming behavior of the students. Feedback will be provided, informing the students that they are gaming the system and reminding them to refrain from this behavior. The platform has also been altered. Instead of a mobile app, *Ibigkas! Math 2.0* is developed as a web-based system.

3.1   Constraint-Based Collaborative Filtering

Constraint-based collaborative filtering is an algorithm for building recommender systems (Fig. 2). It based its suggestions on user requirements, rules, or constraints. The algorithm aggregates the requirements of the group and provides recommendations based on these group requirements. There is a growing body of research that employs this algorithm based on group preference (e.g., [24 [27]. For example, the study of Yanhui et al. [35] implemented content-based and collaborative filtering algorithms in massive online open courses (MOOCs) to recommend suitable courses for online learners. The researchers disclosed that 87% of online learners are satisfied with the system.

CBCF algorithm is suitable for *Ibigkas! Math* because this software is intended for group activity. Using this algorithm, an aggregated model of a content-based filtering algorithm for a group is given in Definition 1. As shown in Fig. 2, the selected problems of the individual user (u_i) will comprise their user profile (*up*). A user profile is composed of problems solved (s_n) by an individual user. These user profiles are then combined using the aggregate model. The collected user profiles will form the aggregated profile (gp).

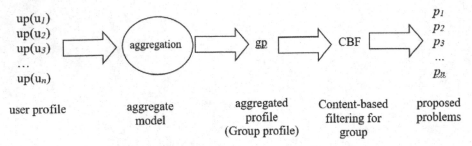

up(u_1)								p_1
up(u_2)								p_2
up(u_3)	⟹	aggregation	⟹	gp	⟹	CBF	⟹	p_3
...								...
up(u_n)								p_n

| user profile | aggregate model | aggregated profile (Group profile) | Content-based filtering for group | proposed problems |

Fig. 2. Implementation of Aggregate Model of Content-based Filtering Algorithm for Group

The CBCF for a group is then applied to the group profile to generate a recommendation (that is, the problems to be solved by the group). Instead of recommending the highest similarity of problems solved, the game will recommend the least solved. The formal definition of the CBCF algorithm for a group is defined as follows:

Definition 1: Aggregated Model of Content-based Filtering Algorithm for Group.
   The recommendation task R for groups in a CBCF algorithm is a three-tuple.
   R = (U, S, P) where
   R = recommendation task.
   U = {u_1, u_2, u_3, ..., u_i} is a set of users.
   S = {s_1, s_2, s_3, ..., s_n} is a set of problems solved, a subset of P.
   P = {p_1, p_2, p_3, ..., p_n} represents set of recommended problems to solve.
   The recommended problem P is a finite set of game settings. There are 4 arithmetic operations, 5 difficulty levels, and 5 speed settings. Thus, problem P has 100 possible game settings. In other words, there are 100 possible recommended problems. To generate the recommended problem P (or the game setting), it will be based on the prior problems solved (s_n) by the individual users up(u_n). The recommended problem P is solved using the dice coefficient (Eq. 1), where gp represents the group profile and p_n is the game setting. The dice coefficient can have a value from 0 to 1 (Eq. 1; [10]). The smallest similarity value between gp and p_n will be recommended since this means that it is the least problem solved by the user profiles *up*.

$$similarity(gp, p_n) = \frac{2 * |categogies(gp) \cap categories(p_n)|}{|categories(gp)| + |categories(p_n)|} \tag{1}$$

3.2 Item Response Theory/Rasch Model

Item response theory (IRT) or the Rasch Model (RM) is a statistical approach that provides a probabilistic model that attempts to explain the response of a person to an item [7, 11]. The Rasch model has been widely applied in many fields, such as psychological testing, educational measurement, item banking, cognitive psychology, marketing, sports sciences, and patient-reported outcome measurement [33]. For example, the Rasch model is used to construct valid and reliable educational test items (e.g., [2, 6, 16]).

Another capability of this model (and of the IRT in general) is that it can detect misfits. Misfit occurs when a student's ability does not match the difficulty of the item. If the student's ability is less than the difficulty of the item and yet that student correctly answers the item, this is considered a misfit [8]. This type of test behavior is interpreted as guessing [28].

3.3 Computational Fluency

A student may be highly skilled in computing arithmetic problems. A highly skilled student may solve the problem quickly, and, therefore, this should not be construed as guessing. This skill is called computational fluency. Computational fluency (CF) is an indicator of mathematics mastery. It is defined as the "connection between conceptual understanding and computation proficiency" [[20], p. 152] and characterized by accurate, efficient, and flexible use of computation for multiple purposes. Mental math (i.e., calculating problems completely mentally) and complex computation (i.e., increasing difficulty levels) are the two domains of computational fluency [14]. Computational fluency is an important performance metric of students' mathematics mastery and achievement. It is a personal measure of student achievement and mastery. This is an important consideration in the development of the adaptive version of Ibigkas! Math because a quick response to a question could be interpreted as a demonstration of mastery rather than guessing. Thus, it is important to consider computation fluency when improving *Ibigkas! Math*. CF is included in the design of the software so that feedback and interventions can be provided appropriately.

Various studies attempted to determine computation fluency using various metrics. Podell et al. [25] used trials-to-criterion to determine the effects of computer-assisted instruction (CAI) and a traditional paper and pencil test in promoting the automatization of basic skills in addition and subtraction. Trials-to-criterion is the number of trials or practices needed to reach a predetermined performance criterion [13]. Podell et al. [25] used average response time and accuracy as measures of trials-to-criterion. Response time is measured within 100 s while answering a 20-item test. The authors used 90% accuracy as the standard threshold. This threshold is also reported in the study of Miller and Heward [17].

Miller and Heward [17] defined accuracy as the correctness of an academic performance. Korn [14] also used this variable to measure computational fluency. However, as pointed out by Miller and Heward [17], accuracy could not determine the progress of the students. Speed is another important indicator of computational fluency. Speed is the accuracy of the performance concerning the amount of time. It can be noted that response time and speed are the same concepts.

3.4 Guessing Detector and Scoring System

The algorithm and the models discussed above served as the basis for the development of the guessing detector for *Ibigkas! Math 2.0*. The capabilities of the RM are suitable to detect guessing [2, 6]. Hence, RM is also utilized in the development of the second version of the *Ibigkas! Math*. The guessing behavior of a student s (Gs) is a dichotomous classification based on the results of the IRT, the response time (RT), and accuracy (Acc) (Definition 2). Response time (RT) and accuracy (ACC) are indicators of computation fluency [15, 34]. RT and Acc are based on the trials-to-criterion approach and the threshold values for these criteria are based on the initial results of the study [4]. RT is based on the Time Spent Answering a Problem (in seconds) and Acc is based on Accuracy. The threshold values for RT and ACC are based on the values of the z-scores. RT and Acc will have a value of 1 when their z-scores exceed the threshold values.

Definition 2: A guessing behavior of a student s (HBs) is a dichotomous classification and is a function of guessing (RM), the response time (RT), and accuracy (ACC) of computational fluency.

$$G_s = \begin{cases} \text{guessing} & \text{,RM} \wedge \text{RT} \wedge \text{Acc} = 1 \\ \text{not guessing} & \text{,otherwise} \end{cases}$$

RM has also a dichotomous value (1 = guessing, 0 = not guessing) based on the threshold value of the average RM. The average RM (ARM) is the number of guessed items divided by the total problems solved. The ARM will have a range of values from [0, 1]. If ARM > 0.50, this means that a student correctly guessed more than 50% of the items. If ARM exceeds the threshold value of 0.50, RM will have a value of 1. The 50% threshold value is based on the correction of guessing strategies discussed in the literature [31]. Therefore, Gs = 1 (i.e., guessing) when a student guessed more than 50% of the total items, and their computational fluency exhibits artificial mathematics performance.

If at least one of the students exhibits GTS, individual textual feedback informs the student that the game has detected that he/she is guessing the answers. It will also remind the student to refrain from the said behavior because of its possible negative impact on mathematics competencies [26]. Individualized textual feedback is selected to avoid student embarrassment and shame [21, 22]. Individual and group scores will be awarded to students. Individual scores will be based on the different gaming behaviors of the students. Specifically, Table 1 shows the different guessing scenarios, their corresponding game interventions, and the scoring system.

Table 1. Guessing Scenarios, Mathematics Competency Behavior, Game Intervention Decision, and Game Score

Scenarios	Exhibiting Mathematics Competency Behavior?	Game Intervention Decision	Game Score
Case 1. None of the students are button-smashing	They might be exhibiting mathematics competency both at the individual and group levels	No intervention is needed	Both individual and group points will be given
Case 2. The group exhibits button-smashing	They might not be exhibiting mathematics competency both at the individual and group levels	Intervention is needed	No points will be given to the individual and the group
Case 3. A member or two is/are button-smashing/GTS	The members who are button-smashing do not exhibit mathematics competency	The intervention will be applied to the students who button-smashed	Points will be given to the individual student that did not exhibit GTS. However, no points will be given to the group

4   The *Ibigkas! Math 2.0* and Future Works

Ibigkas! Math 2.0 is the improved version of *Ibigkas! Math*. The former can now be accessed in a web browser. The most recent version incorporated various algorithms to make it adaptive to students' learning needs and usage behaviors. A series of initial tests of the software shows that it can detect guessing (Fig. 3). Furthermore, the software is capable of providing game-setting recommendations for the least selected mathematics problems (Fig. 4).

To determine the impact of the latest version, an experiment will be conducted. Grade 5 students from a private university in Manila will be grouped in teams of three members. Teams of students of different mathematical competencies (struggling/low-, average-, and high-performing) and personality types will be formed. The mathematics teacher of the students will be requested to select students based on these categories. The Big Five personality types (OCEAN) [12] will be used in this study because of their relevance to the study (i.e., the test is intended for children).

Students will use the game for 15 min without any interventions from the software and facilitators. Each team member will have an equal chance to host the game. The host of the game chose the game settings. The game settings include the type of problem-solving (addition, subtraction, multiplication, and division), difficulty levels (very easy, easy, medium, hard, and very hard), and speed (very slow, slow, medium, fast, and

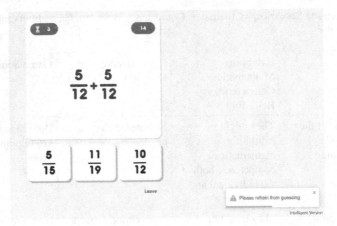

Fig. 3. *Ibigkas! Math 2.0* detects a guessing behavior.

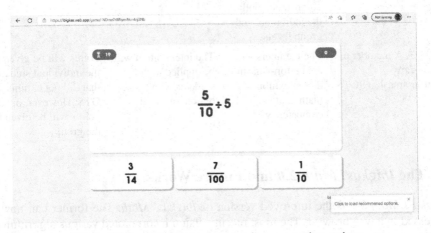

Fig. 4. Ibigkas! Math 2.0 recommends game-setting options

very fast). The game scores are based on the speed setting. The untimed speed has no equivalent points. The points for the other settings are as follows: a very slow time setting corresponds to 2 points, slow for 5 points, medium for 10 points, fast for 15 points, and very fast for 15 points. All students will be given a token of participation, and the three groups with the highest game scores will receive prizes. During this process, interactions with the applications will be tracked and automatically recorded in the system.

A pretest will be administered before the start of the game, and the posttest will be given after the game [4]. The tests consist of 12 items (three questions on each of the four arithmetic operations on fractions). The interaction log files will be collected from the system. The dataset will contain interaction logs with eight features (i.e., game host, difficulty level, speed, type of problem solved, time start, time end, number of attempts, and correct attempts). The game host indicates the game ID of the student who chose the game setting. A student who will host the game will be coded as 1 and

0, otherwise. Correct attempts refer to whether the response is correct or not. Difficulty level, type of problem to be solved, and correct attempts are nominal data. Time spent is a derived feature that indicates the time used in answering problems. Time spent will be calculated by subtracting time end from time start. The number of attempts is the total number of responses provided by learners in answering a given problem. Accuracy will be computed by taking the ratio between correct attempts and the number of attempts. These data will be subjected to statistical analysis to determine if the system has an impact on students' learning.

5 Conclusions

This paper presents the design and development of an adaptive game for Grade 5 students called *Ibigkas! Math* 2.0. The limitations of the previous version of the *Ibigkas! Math* prompted the researcher to enhance its functionalities. A constraint-based collaborative filtering algorithm was employed to develop a recommender system for the system, while RM and CF were used to detect the guessing behavior of the student. The algorithms employed in the study show promising results in detecting the guessing behavior of the students as well as recommending problems to be solved.

A set of participants will use the adaptive version to determine whether it can prevent guessing and whether it has a pedagogical impact. The results of this future research may then be utilized to further improve the software.

Acknowledgment. This paper is funded by the Department of Science and Technology-Engineering Research and Development for Technology and by the affiliation of the author.

References

1. Acharya, B.R.: Factors affecting difficulties in learning mathematics by mathematics learners. Int. J. Elementary Educ. **6**(2), 8–15 (2017)
2. Bin Khairani, A.Z., Bin Abd Razak, N.: Modeling a multiple choice mathematics test with the Rasch Model. Indian J. Sci. Technol. **8**(12), 1–6 (2015)
3. Bringula, R., Atienza, F.A.L.: Mobile computer-supported collaborative learning for mathematics: a scoping review. Educ. Inf. Technol. **28**, 4893–4918 (2022). https://doi.org/10.1007/s10639-022-11395-9
4. Bringula, R., Rodrigo, M.M.: Can "stag-and-hare hunt" behavior be modeled using interaction data from a mobile-supported collaborative learning application? In: Chang, M., So, H.-J., Wong, L.-H., Shih, J.-L., Yu, F.-Y. (Eds.), Proceedings of the 27th International Conference on Computers in Education, vol. 2, pp. 770–773. Asia-Pacific Society for Computers in Education, Taiwan (2019). http://ilt.nutn.edu.tw/icce2019/04_Proceedings.html
5. Bringula, R., Rodrigo, M.M.: Predicting stag and hare hunting behaviors using hidden Markov model. In: So, H.-J., Rodrigo, M.M., Mason, J., Mitrovic, A. (Eds.), 28th International Conference on Computers in Education Conference Proceedings, vol. I, pp. 403–405. Asia-Pacific Society for Computers in Education (APSCE), Taiwan (2020). https://apsce.net/upfile/icce2020/ICCE%202020%20Proceedings%20-%20Volume%20I%20v4.pdf

6. Clements, D.H., Sarama, J.H., Liu, X.H.: Development of a measure of early mathematics achievement using the Rasch model: the research-based early maths assessment. Educ. Psychol. **28**(4), 457–482 (2008)

7. Culligan, B.: Item response theory, reliability and standard error (2011). https://www.worden gine.jp/research/pdf/IRT_reliability_and_standard_error.pdf. Accessed 10 Oct 2019

8. Edwards, A.: Alcock, L: Using Rasch analysis to identify uncharacteristic responses to undergraduate assessments. Teach. Math. Appl. Int. J. IMA **29**(4), 165–175 (2010)

9. Dlab, M.H., Botički, I., Hoic-Bozic, N., Looi, C.K.: Exploring group interactions in synchronous mobile computer-supported learning activities. Comput. Educ. **146**, 103735 (2020)

10. Felfernig, A., Boratto, L., Stettinger, M., Tkalčič, M.: Group Recommender Systems: An Introduction. Springer, Cham (2018). https://doi.org/10.1007/978-3-319-75067-5

11. Hambleton, R.K., Swaminathan, H., Rogers, H.J.: Fundamentals of Item Response Theory. Sage, Newbury Park (1991)

12. John, O.P., Srivastava, S.: The Big Five Trait Taxonomy: History, measurement, and theoretical perspectives. In: Pervin, L.A., John, O.P. (eds.) Handbook of Personality: Theory and Research, 2nd edn., pp. 102–138. Guilford Press, New York (1999)

13. Kansas Technical Assistance System Network (TASN): Guidelines for using trials to criterion (2015). https://www.ksdetasn.org/resources/1939. Accessed 19 Oct 10 2019

14. Korn, A.: Building calculation fluency. School specialty–literacy and intervention (2011). https://eps.schoolspecialty.com/EPS/media/Site-Resources/Downloads/products/aca demy-math/research_math_fluency.pdf?ext=.pdf. Accessed 1Oct 1 2019

15. Lee, Y.-H., Jia, Y.: Using response time to investigate students' test-taking behaviors in a NAEP computer-based study. Large-Scale Assessments Educ. **2**(1), 1–24 (2014). https://doi.org/10.1186/s40536-014-0008-1

16. Long, C., Bansilal, S., Debba, R.: An investigation of mathematical literacy assessment supported by an application of Rasch measurement. Pythagoras **35**(1), 1–17 (2014)

17. Miller, A.D., Heward, W.L.: Do your students really know their math facts? Using daily time trials to build fluency. Interv. Sch. Clin. **28**(2), 98–104 (1992)

18. Mullins, D., Rummel, N., Spada, H.: Are two heads always better than one? Differential effects of collaboration on students' computer-supported learning in mathematics. Int. J. Comput.-Support. Collab. Learn. **6**(3), 421–443 (2011)

19. Namkung, J.M., Peng, P., Lin, X.: The relation between mathematics anxiety and mathematics performance among school-aged students: a meta-analysis. Rev. Educ. Res. **89**(3), 459–496 (2019)

20. National Council of Teachers of Mathematics: Principles and standards for school mathematics: NCTM, Reston, VA (2000)

21. Ordonez, R.V., Gandeza, N.: Integrating traditional beliefs and modern medicine: Filipino nurses' health beliefs, behaviors, and practices. Home Health Care Manage. Pract. **17**(1), 22–27 (2004). https://doi.org/10.1177/1084822304268152

22. Page, R.M., Zarco, E.P.: Shyness, physical activity, and sports team participation among Philippine high school students. Child Study J. **31**(3), 193–204 (2001)

23. Papadakis, S., Kalogiannakis, M., Zaranis, N.: Comparing tablets and pcs in teaching mathematics: an attempt to improve mathematics competence in early childhood education learning history through location-based games view project support distance learning program in mathematics view project. Preschool Primary Educ. **4**(2), 241–253 (2016). https://doi.org/10.12681/ppej.8779

24. Paschen, J., Wilson, M., Ferreira, J.J.: Collaborative intelligence: how human and artificial intelligence create value along the B2B sales funnel. Bus. Horiz. **63**(3), 403–414 (2020)

25. Podell, D.M., Tournaki-Rein, N., Lin, A.: Automatization of mathematics skills via computer-assisted instruction among students with mild mental handicaps. Educ. Train. Ment. Retard. **27**(3), 200–206 (1992)
26. Roll, I., Aleven, V., McLaren, B.M., Koedinger, K.R.: Can help seeking be tutored? searching for the secret sauce of metacognitive tutoring. In: AIED, vol. 2007, pp. 203–210. IOS Press, Netherlands (2007)
27. Skopik, F.: Collaborative Cyber Threat Intelligence: Detecting and Responding to Advanced Cyber-Attacks on National Level. CRC Press, USA (2018)
28. Sumintono, B.: Rasch model measurements as tools in assessment for learning. In: 1st International Conference on Education Innovation (ICEI 2017). Atlantis Press, USA (2018)
29. Suthers, D.D., Seel, N. M.: Computer-supported collaborative learning. In: Seel, N.M. (Ed.), Encyclopedia of the sciences of learning, pp. 719–722. Springer, Netherlands (2012). https://doi.org/10.1007/978-1-4419-1428-6_389
30. Ukobizaba, F., Ndihokubwayo, K., Mukuka, A., Uwamahoro, J.: From what makes students dislike mathematics towards its effective teaching practices. Bolema: Boletim de Educação Matemática, **35**, 1200–1216 (2021)
31. University of Antwerp, How to cope with student guessing on multiple-choice tests. https://www.uantwerpen.be/en/centres/centre-expertise-higher-education/didactic-information/teaching-tips-english/assessing-students/guessing-mc-tests/ Accessed 1 Oct 2019
32. Vitasari, P., Herawan, T., Wahab, M.N.A., Othman, A., Sinnadurai, S.K.: Exploring mathematics anxiety among engineering students. Procedia Soc. Behav. Sci. **8**, 482–489 (2010)
33. Von Davier, M.: Rasch analysis. In: Michalos A.C. (eds) Encyclopedia of Quality of Life and Well-Being Research. Springer, Dordrecht (2014). https://doi.org/10.1007/978-94-007-0753-5_2411
34. Wise, S.L., Kong, X.: Response time effort: a new measure of examinee motivation in computer-based tests. Appl. Measur. Educ. **18**, 163–183 (2005). https://doi.org/10.1207/s15324818ame1802_2
35. Yanhui, D., Dequan, W., Yongxin, Z., Lin, L.: A group recommender system for online course study. In: 2015 7th International Conference on Information Technology in Medicine and Education (ITME), pp. 318–320. IEEE, China (2015)

Teaching Diffusion of Innovations Involving Technology Startups Using Agent-Based Simulation Modeling: Architecture and Design Considerations

Joseph Benjamin Ilagan(✉) and Jose Ramon Ilagan

Ateneo de Manila University, Quezon City, Philippines
{jbilagan,jrilagan}@ateneo.edu
https://www.ateneo.edu

Abstract. Entrepreneurship education has traditionally been based on business management education, which has been ineffective in teaching the complex, dynamic, and non-linear nature of entrepreneurship. Recent attempts at entrepreneurship education have involved using computer simulations to reduce time and cost. One type of computer simulation, agent-based modeling and simulation (ABMS), takes into account the behaviors, reactions, and interactions of individual agents and has the potential to capture the behavior of a complex system, such as a market, more accurately than traditional approaches. This study proposes the use of ABMS in a technology entrepreneurship program to teach students about the theory of diffusion of innovations and how to implement various technology strategies, such as pursuing technology leadership or behaving as an early adopter. The simulation will involve a minimal model implemented using NetLogo and students will be able to explore different strategies and experience the advantages and drawbacks of each. The learning experience will be designed based on entrepreneurial process theories, learning by trying/emergence, learning from failure, bounded rationality, effectuation, entrepreneurial cognition, and entrepreneurial management and growth. The goal of the simulation is to provide students with an experiential and adaptive learning environment that allows them to understand as entrepreneurs how consumers adopt new innovations and receive feedback on their decisions. The user interface will show an animation of the model's results and output, some of which include: the adoption curve, adopter profiles, and the social network.

Keywords: Agent-based modeling · Agent-based simulation modeling · Computer simulation · Entrepreneurship education · Diffusion of innovations

1 Introduction

1.1 Context: Entrepreneurship Education

Entrepreneurship involves continuously pursuing novel or better products and business models amidst constraints, uncertainty, and constant change among

R. A. Sottilare and J. Schwarz (Eds.): HCII 2023, LNCS 14044, pp. 298–311, 2023.
https://doi.org/10.1007/978-3-031-34735-1_21

participants (or "agents") in the ecosystem [7]. It is a complex, dynamic, and non-linear activity [23]. Entrepreneurship education needs to be flexible and adaptive, but studies show that higher education does not have the necessary flexibility [22]. Traditional teaching approaches to entrepreneurship have been based on business management education, which is inflexible and ineffective [8]. Entrepreneurship research and study concern questions on attaining success through open-ended possible effects based on pre-existing means and avoiding failure in the market [30]. Aside from starting and running a business while enrolled in university, recent entrepreneurship education and entrepreneurial experiential learning attempts involve the use of computer simulations to compress learning cycles, reduce time and cost [1] and to model and illustrate how agent behaviors and interactions in a complex environment involving entrepreneurial ecosystems.

This paper is a part of a larger set of studies using agent-based modeling and simulation for entrepreneurship education [12].

1.2 Agent-Based Modeling and Simulation as a Tool to Understand the Entrepreneurship-Related Theory of the Diffusion of Innovations

Agent-based modeling and simulation (ABMS), one type of computer simulation [25], covers interactions among independent agents [19] and the analysis of emergent outcomes from the behaviors and interactions of these agents [10]. ABMS is useful in developing and testing entrepreneurship theory and helps entrepreneurs understand, predict, and explain the potential consequences of their decisions [30]. ABMS takes into account the individuals' behaviors, reactions, and interactions. It has the potential to capture the behavior of a complex system, such as a market, more accurately than is possible in traditional approaches [28].

One theory illustrating the complexity and emergent outcomes brought about by agent attributes, behaviors, and interactions with other agents is the theory of diffusion of innovations. Rogers' [26] theory of the diffusion of innovations is a model that explains how, why, and at what rate ideas and technologies spread [13]. In the context of a social system, it reflects adoption timing and decisions made by individual consumers [27]. The following classification scheme is based on the timing of adoption of the innovation by various groups: (1) innovators, (2) early adopters, (3) early majority, (4) later majority, and (5) laggards [26]. The theory of diffusion of innovations has been a common application of agent-based modeling to date [5, 10, 13, 15, 18, 27].

1.3 Objective

This study describes the methodology, architecture, and design of an agent-based simulation model and focuses on the theory of diffusion of innovations for teaching and educational purposes. Existing work [10, 28] using agent-based models for the diffusion of innovations describes the fidelity, verification, and validation considerations involved. The output is a minimal model [16] plausible enough for use in education and illustration of the concept of diffusion of innovations.

1.4 Research Questions

This study is part of a larger study on using ABMS for teaching and learning technology entrepreneurship. The aim of the larger study is to cover the viability of using an agent-based model computer for this purpose by building a simulation model for a specific scenario (diffusion of innovations in this case). Meanwhile, this study aims to complement the parent study by focusing on aspects of the human interface adaptability of an agent-based modeling simulator for diffusion of innovations as a teaching tool.

RQ1: What human interface and adaptability features must be present in the agent-based simulation system to teach the concept of diffusion of innovations?

RQ2: What software building blocks are needed to develop an agent-based modeling system as an adaptive teaching tool?

2 Related Work

The design of the learning experience follows concepts related to entrepreneurial process theories, learning by trying/emergence, learning from failure, bounded rationality, effectuation, entrepreneurial cognition, and entrepreneurial management and growth [8].

With the diffusion of innovations as the simulation scenario, students may experiment with various technology strategies-from pursuing technology leadership as an innovator to behaving as an early adopter or a fast follower-and they can experience the respective advantages and drawbacks of these strategies [28]. Garcia [10] offers possible research issues involving the diffusion of innovations that the use of ABMs may tackle: *effects of network externalities, word-of-mouth networks, modeling tipping points,* and *social networks and viral marketing.* Specific skills imparted by the simulation environment related to diffusion of innovations, as inspired by [28], are market entry, global product launch strategies, pricing strategies, product life-cycle and portfolio management, and technology strategy.

There has been little work discussing using ABMS as a tool for teaching and learning, especially in business and entrepreneurship. Social simulation in business has not been very successful so far, because the emphasis has been on using it as a predictive tool rather than as a learning tool [5]. Related to this, In spite of several studies already having featured diffusion of innovations implemented in ABMS, none have been explicitly tied to teaching or learning entrepreneurship. This study, as well as the larger study it supports, aims to contribute the aspect of contextualizing this tool to be useful for entrepreneurship education.

Specific skills imparted by the simulation environment, as inspired by [28], are market entry, global product launch strategies, pricing strategies, product life-cycle and portfolio management, and technology strategy. Garcia [10] offers possible research issues involving the diffusion of innovations that the use of ABMs may tackle: *effects of network externalities, word-of-mouth networks, modeling tipping points,* and *social networks and viral marketing.*

Agent-based models visually convey the behavior of the model clearly and quickly. However, designing an effective visualization can be challenging for model authors as most of them do not have visual design training. Work establishing principles for designing cognitively efficient, aesthetic, and communicative visualizations [17] can help modelers improve the visual design with ABM toolkits. This paper will use concepts in [17] to frame discussions on the User Interface elements of the simulation.

3   Approach

The process of modeling and design is usually ad-hoc, driven by the modeler's creativity and natural attitudes toward modeling [14]. While there have been attempts to design the model based on well-established frameworks, there will be gaps left to the discretion of the researchers. This study will use the existing methods described, particularly prototyping, model architecture design, agent and agent rule design, agent and environment design, implementation, and verification. There are limitations of existing work related to the use of ABMS in learning environments and in particular, entrepreneurship education. The study aims to facilitate learning through the assessment of simulation outcomes per iteration based on parameters set by the students. The outcome of each run is logged, analyzed, and presents to the students as meaningful feedback [6] and a set of suggestions for supplementary learning from an LMS in preparation for succeeding simulation iterations. Students also get to reflect on their performance and plans after each simulation iteration.

A process presented in [20] for ABMS development consists of the following general steps. *prototyping, model architecture design, agent and agent rule design, agent and environment design, implementation,* and *verification.*

Following the steps outlined in [10], the simulation environment and elements comprise the prototype in this study.

1. Theory operationalization through a cognitive map creation
2. Agent specification
3. Environmental specification
4. Rules establishment
5. Measurement/Data Recording
6. Run-time Specification

4   Design

4.1   Considerations

Previous models can be extended to enable the investigation of a wide range of questions and scenarios related to the spread of innovations within a population.

Existing work [10,28]using agent-based models for the diffusion of innovations describes the fidelity, verification, and validation considerations involved.

Fidelity is the amount of realism in a model [9]. A simulation model of the diffusion of innovations will exhibit fidelity if it accurately and realistically represents the system or phenomenon being studied. In the context of agent-based modeling for the diffusion of innovations, agents can have different demographic attributes (e.g. age, gender, income, etc.), personal preferences (e.g., individual preferences for certain product attributes and individual communication behavior [28]), and social connections.

Validation aims to ensure that the simulation is designed to correctly model the processes that exist in reality with a satisfactory range of accuracy matching the simulated model against what is in the real world [9,16]. A valid model produces results that align closely with real-world data on the diffusion of an innovation. There are several ways a simulation model of the diffusion of innovations can exhibit validity. For example, the model might capture the overall rate, and patterns of adoption within the population, such as the Sshaped curve that is often observed in the diffusion of innovations [11]. The model might also capture the effects of various factors on the diffusion process, such as the influence of early adopters or different communication strategies on the spread of innovation [2]. For this research, the practical approach is *face validity*, that is, processes and outcomes are reasonable and plausible within the frame of theoretic basis and implicit knowledge of system experts [16].

Verification establishes whether the simulated model captures the real-world model scenarios and variables as intended and checks for errors, inconsistencies, or other issues affecting model accuracy and reliability [11].

4.2   Parameterization and Calibration

Calibration is the process of tuning a model to fit detailed empirically supported data. During calibration, parameters and initial conditions are tested and tweaked so that the behaviors of individual agents in the model are consistent with the empirical characteristics of the modeled agents [11]. When working with simulation (particularly ABSM), parameterization and calibration are important due to the models' multi-level structure, and often parameter-rich nature [14]. These will involve both *Fixed* (given or exogenous) parameters that can be estimated from available data or gleaned from the literature (as deterministic values, stochastic distributions, or dynamic functions), and *free* (experimental or variable) parameters that are unknown due to lack of relevant data or model specifications [14]. The appropriate numbers of parameters and variables depend on the goal of the model, and the degree of realism and accuracy needed.

4.3   Applying the Process Framework

The process applied in this section shall be based on the steps discussed at the end of Sect. 3 of this paper.

Theory Operationalization Through a Cognitive Map Creation. Table 1 illustrates the distribution which will serve as the basis of the number of agents initialized per simulation run. These distribution percentages are fixed at this point, and they are applied to the prescribed population (which is variable).

Table 1. Distribution of innovation adoption timings.

Consumer Agent	Type	Pct. of Population
Innovator	innovator (not influenced)	2.5%
Early Adopter	imitator	13.5%
Early Majority	imitator	34%
Late Majority	imitator	34%
Laggard	imitator	16%

For this simulator, agents adapt only to what happens during runtime, which is their only source of data. The agents' behavior is based on predefined rules acting on states rather than additional sources of external data.

Agent Specification. Based on [21], the agents in the model have the following characteristics: modularity, autonomy, sociality, and conditionality. Similar to [15], the number of agents chosen for each type is large enough to allow for a realistic dispersion of agents (Table 2).

Table 2. Provider agents and their initial quantities

Agent	Description	Quantity
Consumer	Entity (person or organization) adopting the innovation	5000
Provider Startup	Main entity offering the innovative product or service	1
Provider Competitor	Entity offering a competing product or service	1

The parameters of the agent model representing sensitivity influencing adoption of the innovation are loosely based on the work presented in [27], which refers to each parameter as an index. The *Feature Sensitivity Index* represents the impact of the product's features on the adoption decision. It represents the combination of the product's features and the consumer agent's sensitivity to the features. This study treats this number as an arbitrary number aligned to the adoption timing characteristics of the group of agents. Unlike in [15] with detailed features, this study will treat feature sensitivity in aggregate and generic. The

Price Sensitivity Index represents the impact of price on the adoption decision and is calculated by multiplying the consumer agent's sensitivity to price by one minus the product provider agent's price value; this calculation incorporates the positive adoption response to a lower price. The *Promotion Sensitivity Index* represents the product provider's promotional intensity efforts on influencing a consumer's decision to adopt the innovation. The Index is calculated by first multiplying consumer agent sensitivity to promotional activity by the brand agent's promotion intensity. The result is then multiplied by a value representing the previous interactions that have occurred between a given brand and consumer agent pair. The *Social Influence Sensitivity Index* represents the effect of the social influence on the consumer's decision to adopt the innovation. This index is derived by multiplying the consumer's sensitivity to social influence by the total proportion of consumer agents that have adopted the brand.

Agent Relationships. Literature on ABMS uses edges or the number of edges or spatial links to denote network density, which in turn is expected to have a large impact on adoption and market share development because information spreads faster in more densely structured networks [15]. The current version of this simulation will not have physical edges for now, but relationships will be indirectly formed through proximity between agent nodes. This simulator will adopt the simple rule for consumer agents to query its eight neighbors about their individual preferences for a product and then make an informed decision about whether to adopt the same innovation [10].

Environment Specification. Agent behavior is largely influenced by predefined rules specified in the next section and the proximity between two agents. Except for possible competitors of the main provider, nothing else in the environment will influence the behavior of the agents in this simulator.

Rules Establishment. As the innovation gets more adoption over time, the product's unit price tends to drop [3]. The pseudocode below shows a simple implementation of that rule. The new price is a factor of the previous price and the percentage of the population already converted. The parameter β is an arbitrary number.

function CALCNEWPRICE(*oldprice, population, converted, β*)
    return *oldprice* $\times \left[1 - \beta \times \left(\frac{converted}{population}\right)\right]$
end function

The consumer adoption threshold (CAT) is defined as a function of features, price, promotion, social influence, etc. [27]. This simulation will use a simplified version: given the pre-determined sensitivity for feature, price, promotion, and influence for timing categories, for each converted consumer, try to convert each unconverted physical neighbor (as a substitute for some stronger link for now).

Each unconverted agent will be assigned a random number for each sensitivity attribute. If all the random numbers generated pass the threshold, then the neighbor agent gets converted into an adopter. The pseudocode below illustrates the decision on when to convert an agent to an adopter of the innovation.

$feature \leftarrow random(0, 100)$
$price \leftarrow random(0, 100)$
$promotion \leftarrow random(0, 100)$
$influence \leftarrow random(0, 100)$
assign threshold values based on the agent's innovation timing category
if $feature > featurethreshold$ &
   $price > pricethreshold$ &
   $promotion > promotionthreshold$ &
   $influence > influencethreshold$ **then**
   mark agent as converted
   color agent as green
end if

Measurement and Data Recording. For each iteration by the student, the simulator generates log files containing 1) the set of sensitivity parameters and 2) the periodic as well as beginning and ending values of adoption rates, market share, and unit price. A set of log files are associated with a specific student user of the simulation.

Runtime Specification. NetLogo [29] is an open-source programming language and modeling environment specifically designed for agent-based modeling. NetLogo has been used as a platform for modeling the diffusion of innovations.

Integration with a Learning Management System (LMS) can be done either through file transfer of NetLogo logs or through network/API callouts for content from LMS (through NetLogo's Python Extension). The outcome of each simulation run is logged, analyzed, and presented to the students as meaningful feedback and suggestions for supplementary learning from the LMS in preparation for succeeding simulation iterations.

4.4 User Experience Design Considerations for Agent-Based Models

While ABM visualization guidelines may be challenging due to the broad nature of the models, an attempt to define visualization guidelines [17] will serve as the basis for the user interface of this study's model. In this diffusion of innovations model, the finite states a consumer agent can follow the *cellular automata* category prescription of mapping an agent to a specific color.

Figure 1 shows the state of the simulator before the run. The layout of the agents follows the colors specified in Table 3 and the distribution resembles the curve based on the distribution in Table 1.

Table 3. Consumer agent state and color mappings.

Consumer Agent State	Color
Innovator	Yellow
Early Adopter	Orange
Early Majority	Blue
Late Majority	White
Laggard	Gray
Converted/Adaptor	Green
Adaptor/Captured by Competitor	Red

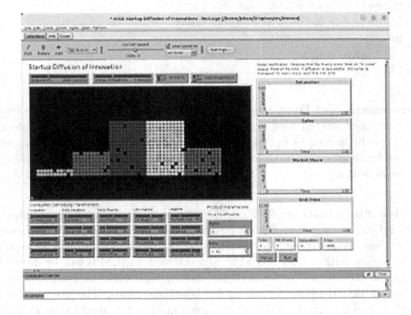

Fig. 1. Simulator state before the run.

The *Mobile* switch allows agents to move around the screen to allow close with other agents and get the chance to influence their neighbors at a particular moment to adopt the new technology. Since one of the limitations of this simulation model is that there are no explicit relationships between agents, nearness or location proximity will be the basis for agents to influence others. If the mobile switch is turned off, the agents laid out in the bell curve will only be able to influence others in a static location. This simplifies simulation runs, but one drawback of this setup is that agents can only directly influence others of specific timing characteristics (which is not what happens in the real world).

Aligned with *face validation*, support for animation must be on the appropriate level of detail and display all relevant dynamic aspects of the elements in a way that they are easily detectable by a human [16].

For this simulator, the expected theoretical S-curves [11] and diminishing prices [4] shall be reflected graphically and animated over time (or ticks in NetLogo). The animation will also show the adoption by consumer agents over time through the changes in states as represented by the colors defined in Table 3.

An animated chart showing overall market revenue over time.

The agents' behavior rules are partly deterministic based on literature and partially stochastic based on ranges of theoretical thresholds to address the model's validity. Even when the student adjusts specific parameters in the model, the agents will continue to behave autonomously based on the programmed rules and behaviors governing the propensity of each agent to adopt the innovations based on the parameters.

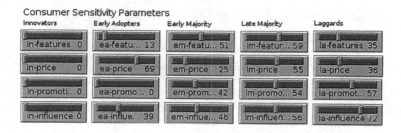

Fig. 2. Sliders for consumer sensitivity.

Figure 3 shows the simulator's state after the run. The main animation area in the middle of the screen shows the physical dispersion of agents after they are made to move in random directions. With all agents colored green, this indicates a full saturation state. While this may not fit well with the model's overall validity, the simplicity is still within acceptable levels of detail [9] and lends well to discussions of saturation from a teaching perspective.

A chart on the right shows an S-curve for the adaption of the innovations, with all green indicating full saturation. Another chart shows revenue per period, indicating tapering off revenues as the innovation matures and eventually declines.

The characteristics of the revenues chart are generally the same, but the curve is not as right-skewed as [3], where the peak happens in the early stages of the product or innovation life cycle. This is mainly due to the simplification of the price decline formula.

The decline in market share is expected since the simulator introduced a simple scenario with two competitors emerging shortly after the presence of early adopters.

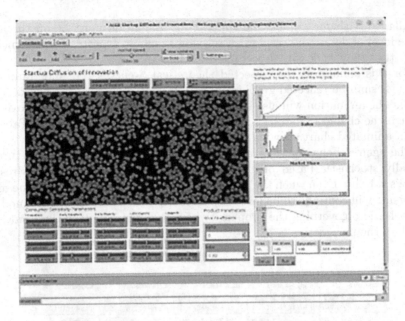

Fig. 3. Simulator state after the run.

5   Limitations

This initial version of the model shall consider only one product to be introduced to the market.

Many mobile agents can display complex spatial or color patterns, but very little visual interaction (if any) with the environment. As such, the background color of the simulator can be left as **black**.

While Netlogo has limitations regarding user interface design options, this study takes the stance that students may be overwhelmed by too many interface elements, so avoiding too much complexity allows students to grasp the intended learning objectives more easily [28]. As the simulator transitions to more empirical data for rules governing the behaviors of agents, future versions of the simulation may incorporate additional user interface and simulator elements.

6   Discussions and Conclusions

Through this study, we demonstrated that the simulator interface can be aligned to concepts involving diffusion of innovations where students can readily visualize the configuration, layout, and animation of agents behaving based on students' manipulation of parameters. User interface design aligns well with goals of fidelity and validity of the underlying simulation model. Each simulation allows agents to adapt to various thresholds set by the students. These address RQ1 involving human interface and adaptability features in the ABMS platform.

Aside from the simulation interface, the ABMS environment also allows for capturing logs per simulation run which can be transferred to an LMS. The resulting charts show validity consistent with expected theoretical and empirical outcomes (ex., adoption saturation S-curve). These address RQ2 involving the software building blocks needed by the simulator as an adaptive teaching tool for diffusion of innovations.

While aiming for high validity is conceivably beneficial, limitations on the model were deliberately factored in from a teaching and learning perspective because too much detail may be detrimental [9]. One limitation of this simulation model is that there are no direct and explicit relationships between agents through links, but rather only through proximity to one another. Future versions of this simulation will allow direct relationships and will not be constrained to proximity as the basis for being able to influence others.

Another limitation of the model is that the rules, based on formulas, have been greatly simplified. In the future, β machine learning (ML) and AI techniques, in turn, will enhance the behavior and capabilities of agents in [24] in future versions of this simulator. Switching to ML-based techniques will enable future versions of the simulation to incorporate additional user interface and AI-based simulator elements.

Finally, another shortcoming of this simulation is that the behavior of competitors is fixed and lacking. With the introduction of ML and AI techniques, adaptive competitor behavior will make the simulator more interesting to the technology entrepreneurship students as they will see consumer and producer (competitor) behavior.

Acknowledgements. I wish to thank Maria Mercedes T. Rodrigo, Ph.D., my adviser, for the support and encouragement given to me since the beginning of this journey.

References

1. Almeida, F., Simões, J.: Serious games in entrepreneurship education. In: Encyclopedia of Information Science and Technology, 4th edn., pp. 800–808. IGI Global (2018)
2. Bass, F.M.: A new product growth for model consumer durables. Manage. Sci. **15**(5), 215–227 (1969)
3. Bass, F.M.: The relationship between diffusion rates, experience curves, and demand elasticities for consumer durable technological innovations. J. Bus. S51–S67 (1980)
4. Bass, F.M.: A new product growth for model consumer durables. Manage. Sci. **50**(12_supplement), 1825–1832 (2004)
5. Bonabeau, E.: Agent-based modeling: methods and techniques for simulating human systems. Proc. Nat. Acad. Sci. **99**(suppl_3), 7280–7287 (2002)
6. Cadotte, E.: The use of simulations in entrepreneurship education: opportunities, challenges and outcomes. Ann. Entrepreneurship Educ. Pedag. **2014**, 280–302 (2014)
7. Eisenmann, T.R.: Entrepreneurship: a working definition. Harv. Bus. Rev. **10**, 2013 (2013)

8. Fayolle, A., Gailly, B.: From craft to science: teaching models and learning processes in entrepreneurship education. J. Eur. Industr. Train. **32**(7), 569–593 (2008). https://doi.org/10.1108/03090590810899838

9. Fox, J., Pittaway, L., Uzuegbunam, I.: Simulations in entrepreneurship education: serious games and learning through play. Entrepreneurship Educ. Pedag. **1**(1), 61–89 (2018). https://doi.org/10.1177/2515127417737285

10. Garcia, R.: Uses of agent-based modeling in innovation/new product development research. J. Prod. Innov. Manage. **22**(5), 380–398 (2005)

11. Garcia, R., Rummel, P., Hauser, J.: Validating agent-based marketing models through conjoint analysis. J. Bus. Res. **60**(8), 848–857 (2007). https://doi.org/10.1016/j.jbusres.2007.02.007, https://www.sciencedirect.com/science/article/pii/S0148296307000410

12. Ilagan, J.B.: The design and use of agent-based modeling computer simulation for teaching technology entrepreneurship. In: Proceedings of the 30th International Conference on Computers in Education, vol. 2, pp. 719–723. Asia-Pacific Society for Computers in Education (2022)

13. Johanning, S., Scheller, F., Abitz, D., Wehner, C., Bruckner, T.: A modular multi-agent framework for innovation diffusion in changing business environments: conceptualization, formalization and implementation. Complex Adapt. Syst. Model. **8**(1), 1–32 (2020)

14. Kasaie, P., Kelton, W.D.: Guidelines for design and analysis in agent-based simulation studies. In: 2015 Winter Simulation Conference (WSC), pp. 183–193. IEEE (2015)

15. Kiesling, E.: Planning the market introduction of new products: an agent-based simulation of innovation diffusion. na (2011)

16. Klügl, F.: A validation methodology for agent-based simulations. In: Proceedings of the 2008 ACM Symposium on Applied Computing, SAC 2008, pp. 39–43. Association for Computing Machinery, New York (2008). https://doi.org/10.1145/1363686.1363696

17. Kornhauser, D., Wilensky, U., Rand, W.: Design guidelines for agent based model visualization. J. Artif. Soc. Soc. Simul. **12**(2), 1 (2009). https://www.jasss.org/12/2/1.html

18. Kotthoff, F., Hamacher, T.: Calibrating agent-based models of innovation diffusion with gradients. J. Artif. Soc. Soc. Simul. **25**(3), 4 (2022). https://doi.org/10.18564/jasss.4861, http://jasss.soc.surrey.ac.uk/25/3/4.html

19. Macal, C.M., North, M.J.: Agent-based modeling and simulation: ABMS examples. In: Proceedings - Winter Simulation Conference, pp. 101–112 (2008). https://doi.org/10.1109/wsc.2008.4736060, https://www.scopus.com/inward/inward/record.uri?eid=2-s2.0-60849084592&doi=10.1109%2fWSC.2008.4736060&partnerID=40&md5=b5d6f62b004bdba79921f0260a5c67ae

20. Macal, C.M., North, M.J.: Introductory tutorial: agent-based modeling and simulation. In: Proceedings - Winter Simulation Conference, pp. 1451–1464 (2011). https://doi.org/10.1109/wsc.2011.6147864, https://www.scopus.com/inward/record.uri?eid=2-s2.0-84858040377&doi=10.1109%2fWSC.2011.6147864&partnerID=40&md5=adda3f2e26a085b79a4b12b3f9b61998

21. Macal, C.M., North, M.J.: Introductory tutorial: agent-based modeling and simulation. In: Proceedings of the 2013 Winter Simulation Conference - Simulation: Making Decisions in a Complex World, WSC 2013, pp. 362–376 (2013). https://doi.org/10.1109/wsc.2013.6721434, https://www.scopus.com/inward/record.uri?eid=2-s2.0-84894175204&doi=10.1109%2fWSC.2013.6721434&partnerID=40&md5=b710071077ea15a4abb24109c07bab2e

22. Matlay, H., Mitra, J.: Entrepreneurship and learning: the double act in the triple helix. Int. J. Entrepreneurship Innov. **3**(1), 7–16 (2002)
23. Neck, H.M., Greene, P.G.: Entrepreneurship education: known worlds and new frontiers. J. Small Bus. Manage. **49**(1), 55–70 (2011). https://doi.org/10.1111/j.1540-627x.2010.00314.x
24. Rand, W.: Machine learning meets agent-based modeling: when not to go to a bar. In: Conference on Social Agents: Results and Prospects (2006)
25. Roberts, S.D.: Tutorial on the simulation of healthcare systems. In: Proceedings - Winter Simulation Conference, pp. 1403–1414 (2011). https://doi.org/10.1109/wsc.2011.6147860, https://www.scopus.com/inward/record.uri?eid=2-s2.0-84858040457&doi=10.1109%2fWSC.2011.6147860&partnerID=40&md5=88056a4fcd94bc02163f0c7020ef35b0
26. Rogers, E.M.: Diffusion of innovations (1983)
27. Schramm, M.E., Trainor, K.J., Shanker, M., Hu, M.Y.: An agent-based diffusion model with consumer and brand agents. Decis. Support Syst. **50**(1), 234–242 (2010)
28. Stummer, C., Kiesling, E.: An agent-based market simulation for enriching innovation management education. Cent. Eur. J. Oper. Res. **29**(1), 143–161 (2021)
29. Tisue, S., Wilensky, U.: Netlogo: A simple environment for modeling complexity. In: International Conference on Complex Systems, Boston, MA, vol. 21, pp. 16–21 (2004)
30. Yang, S.J.S., Chandra, Y.: Growing artificial entrepreneurs: advancing entrepreneurship research using agent-based simulation approach. Int. J. Entrepreneurial Behav. Res. **19**, 210–237 (2013)

Iterative Improvement of Automatically Generated Practice with the Content Improvement Service

Bill Jerome⬤, Rachel Van Campenhout(✉) ⬤, Jeffrey S. Dittel⬤, Rich Benton, and Benny G. Johnson⬤

VitalSource Technologies, Pittsburgh, PA 15218, USA
{bill.jerome,rachel.vancampenhout}@vitalsource.com

Abstract. The Content Improvement Service (CIS) is a platform-level adaptive system that monitors millions of automatically generated formative practice questions that are available to students as a study feature in thousands of textbooks. The CIS was designed to do what was not possible by humans—use real-time data to monitor question performance at enormous scale and determine if a change is required. The CIS was designed to use multiple types of data and analyses to make its decisions, including question difficulty (mean score) and student feedback (ratings). In this paper, we outline the decisions made by the CIS for both methods. We also show how human investigation of these analyses can identify trends and insights useful to automatic question generation systems.

Keywords: Content Improvement Service · formative practice · automatic question generation · iterative improvement · adaptive system

1 Introduction

Artificial intelligence has been employed to solve many different educational challenges. One such application is automatic question generation to create large volumes of formative practice questions. By adding formative practice questions to textbook expository content, students can become engaged in a learning by doing method that is highly effective for learning [1–3]. Yet the generation of millions of practice questions across thousands of textbooks creates a new challenge—how to ensure all questions are of the highest quality. It is not possible to use human review at this scale, so an automated system is needed. The Content Improvement Service (CIS) is a platform-level adaptive system that monitors real-time data for millions of automatically generated (AG) formative practice questions and makes decisions on whether each question will remain in the learning environment [4].

As an adaptive system, the CIS does not adapt questions per individual student, but rather, adapts the content across the entire platform. Vandewaetere et al. [5] developed a classification framework for adaptive systems that describes the source of adaptation (what determines adaptation), target of adaptation (what is being adapted), and pathway

R. A. Sottilare and J. Schwarz (Eds.): HCII 2023, LNCS 14044, pp. 312–324, 2023.
https://doi.org/10.1007/978-3-031-34735-1_22

of adaptation (how it is adapted). In this case, the AG questions in the platform are both the source and target of adaptation and the CIS is the pathway of adaptation. The CIS adapts at the individual question level, while doing so at the platform level across thousands of textbooks.

The practical need for the CIS is to monitor and take action on questions since the scale of the AG questions is too large for human review. However, the CIS is also an automated system that fulfills a key part of learning technology development: iterative improvement cycles. The automatic question generation (AQG) system and formative practice delivered to students as a study tool were developed using learning engineering as a practice and process. Learning engineering, first imagined by Herb Simon at Carnegie Mellon University [6], has been formalized as "a practice and process that uses human-centered engineering design and data-informed decision making to support learners" [7]. Iterative improvement is a necessary step of the learning engineering process, in which data from the learning environment is analyzed to determine what improvements could be made in a next iteration of the process. This data analysis phase is critical yet is often undertaken with great human effort and only periodically, such as the end of a school year or semester once all student data is collected for a course (e.g., [8]). The CIS accomplishes this same analysis, but in a continuous manner—achieving a continuous loop of iterative improvement cycles at the individual question level.

When considering how to decide if a question should be removed, the CIS has a guiding philosophy of recall over precision [4]. A recall approach is removing all low-performing questions, even if that also means mistakenly removing some good questions. A precision approach means a goal of only removing questions that are certainly bad and never removing good questions. Precision and recall are generally at odds with each other and are considered to exist in a trade-off continuum; the balance between the two is determined by the problem at hand. In this educational context, it is better to have a recall philosophy where questions are removed and (if possible) replaced at the first indication of a problem, even if that means some good questions are also removed. This recall philosophy is easily supported in this context, as more questions are generated than used so new questions can easily replace those selected for removal.

The CIS uses several tools to evaluate questions from different types of student data. One type of data is question difficulty data, i.e., how often students get that question correct. A second type of data is direct student feedback; when students answer a question they are able to rate it with a thumbs up or down button. The questions flagged for removal by the CIS can be analyzed in multiple different contexts. First, of all the questions removed, how were they distributed between student feedback and question difficulty? For each reason for question removal, there are also details to investigate further, e.g., were some question types more frequently removed than others?

There are many insights that the CIS can reveal besides the strict question removal data on a question-by-question basis. Human oversight of this adaptive system can investigate patterns and trends the CIS is not designed to take action on. For instance, questions flagged for removal may reveal a pattern of questions generated that may not be suitable for learning. This information can be used to improve the AI question generation process itself. Or, a large number of questions removed in a single textbook may indicate an issue with that particular title that should be investigated further. By including humans as part of the adaptive system, the entire CIS becomes a more effective tool to improve the student learning experience.

In this paper, we analyze data collected from over six thousand textbooks as students naturally engaged with the automatically generated questions included as a study tool. Our primary research questions are:

- How did the automatically generated questions perform according to the parameters of the CIS?
- What are features of questions that have low performance according to the CIS?
- What insights are revealed using human review of the CIS data?

2 Methods

The AQG system applied in this paper uses the textbook as the corpus for natural language processing and machine learning processing to identify important sentences and terms, and transforms them into questions [9]. Kurdi et al. [10] developed a classification system that describes the level(s) of understanding and procedure(s) of transformation. In this AQG system, both syntactic and semantic information from the textbook are used for the levels of understanding, and an expert-developed rule-based approach is used for the procedure of transformation. There are several question types created through this process, including matching, multiple choice (MC), pulldown, fill-in-the-blank (FITB), self-graded submit and compare (SGSC), and free response. Some question types also trigger a follow-up question or series of questions in a tutorial activity. These questions are formative in nature, so students can get immediate scaffolding feedback, spelling assistance if needed, and can retry until they get the question correct. As seen in Fig. 1, the questions open in a panel next to the textbook content, allowing students to refer back to the content while they answer if needed.

As students answer questions, the clickstream data for each interaction is captured. This type of microdata gathered by the technology platform accumulates large quantities of data that can be applied to answer questions on learning previously not possible to investigate [11]. The student data in this analysis is an aggregation of all students who interacted with the questions across all textbooks, as the goal of this paper is not to evaluate indicators of student learning, but rather to investigate question quality and features as determined by the CIS. A set of questions is delivered with a textbook, and all students who used that textbook and chose to answer questions are included in the data set. This means that students who may have noticed the questions and tried only a few of them and students who may have been using the questions as a homework feature of their course are both included. This variation reflects the same data the CIS is using to make decisions, but it is notable that this aggregation of data from varying uses could impact question performance data (compared to classroom-based datasets).

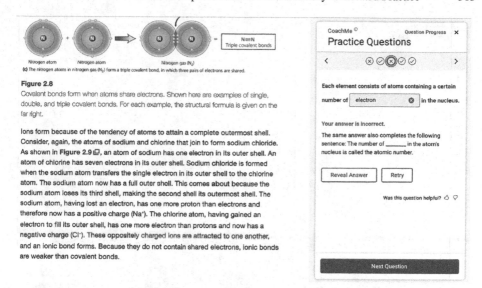

Figure 2.8

Covalent bonds form when atoms share electrons. Shown here are examples of single, double, and triple covalent bonds. For each example, the structural formula is given on the far right.

Ions form because of the tendency of atoms to attain a complete outermost shell. Consider, again, the atoms of sodium and chlorine that join to form sodium chloride. As shown in **Figure 2.9** 🖭, an atom of sodium has one electron in its outer shell. An atom of chlorine has seven electrons in its outer shell. Sodium chloride is formed when the sodium atom transfers the single electron in its outer shell to the chlorine atom. The sodium atom now has a full outer shell. This comes about because the sodium atom loses its third shell, making the second shell its outermost shell. The sodium atom, having lost an electron, has one more proton than electrons and therefore now has a positive charge (Na⁺). The chlorine atom, having gained an electron to fill its outer shell, has one more electron than protons and now has a negative charge (Cl⁻). These oppositely charged ions are attracted to one another, and an ionic bond forms. Because they do not contain shared electrons, ionic bonds are weaker than covalent bonds.

Fig. 1. An example fill-in-the-blank question showing scaffolding feedback, reveal answer and retry buttons, and the student rating option.

The CIS is designed to be an automated system that can monitor live data and make decisions on question quality using a variety of individual tools that can be updated, added, or removed over time. There are two primary tools that the CIS uses (that will be analyzed in detail in the following section). The first is Bayesian analysis of student-question data that removes questions with a mean score that is highly likely to be below a minimum acceptable threshold (for more details, see [4]). A question is removed when it is determined to be likely that its mean score is below the threshold, because it is observed that when a question has a very low mean score, there is a higher likelihood something is wrong with it, and so removing questions with the lowest mean scores likely removes bad questions. Not all questions with a low mean score are necessarily bad, but this decision is a recall approach rather than a precision approach [4]. The Bayesian analysis requires three things: a prior distribution for the mean score, a minimum threshold mean score, and a confidence level for deciding when to remove the question. The first two are derived empirically, using a separate prior and threshold for each question type because the question types have different score distributions. The prior distribution is obtained by fitting a beta function to a dataset of mean scores of actual questions, and the threshold is obtained as a percentile of those scores. For example, the FITB prior distribution is Beta(2.04, 1.54) and the score threshold is 0.351 (20th percentile), whereas the matching prior distribution is Beta(3.31, 0.84) and the score threshold is 0.538 (10th percentile) (Fig. 2). A confidence level of 90% is used to trigger question removal.

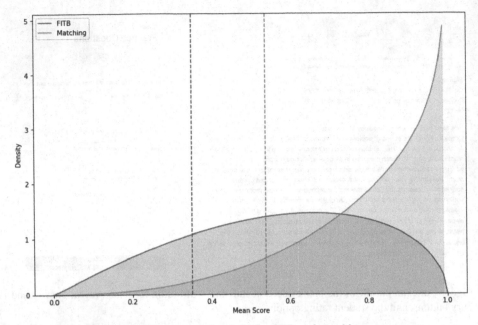

Fig. 2. Prior distribution and threshold for FITB and matching mean score.

Another method the CIS uses to evaluate questions is student feedback. Once a student has attempted a practice question, a feedback mechanism becomes available. As seen in Fig. 1, students can rate the question thumbs up or down. A single rating is not necessarily an indicator of question quality either way, as we know students are more likely to rate questions down if they are incorrect on the first attempt—as well as knowing that even expert inter-rater reliability is often low. The CIS is set to remove questions with more than one thumbs down rating within the first 100 answers.

3 Results

For this analysis, the dataset was compiled using only data from the 2022 calendar year for simplicity. This timeframe also coincides with the first year that the automatically generated questions were made available to students, making this dataset the first analysis of the original set of questions delivered. The dataset was also restricted to the inline formative questions, excluding the end-of-chapter practice quizzes only available in a subset of textbooks. The question types included in this analysis are matching, multiple choice (MC), self-graded submit and compare (SGSC), and fill-in-the-blank (FITB). Two question types were excluded from analysis: pulldown questions were generated infrequently and had very little data, and free response questions were not scored. Given these criteria, the dataset includes a total of 3,594,408 question attempts. There were 6,215 textbooks, 239,965 students, and 752,467 AG questions in the dataset. Table 1 shows more detail on the data by question type, including first attempt mean score.

Table 1. The dataset segmented by question type.

Question Type	Question Attempts	Questions	Students	Mean Score
FITB	2,357,037	493,323	204,362	0.540
Matching	1,100,320	226,508	184,131	0.791
SGSC	76,572	19,417	26,768	0.803
MC	60,479	13,219	26,412	0.727

3.1 Mean Score

One method the CIS uses to determine if questions should be removed is if its mean score is highly likely to be below a minimum difficulty threshold. From this dataset, a total of 4,527 questions, or 0.6%, were removed. This overall percentage is very low, but also is impacted by the proportion of questions that did not yet have enough student data to make a decision. Table 2 shows questions the CIS flagged for removal grouped by question type. The FITB are the most common question type that also had the lowest mean first attempt score, which makes it reasonable to expect this question type had the largest number and percentage of questions removed. Comparatively, matching questions had less than half of the percentage of questions removed. The MC questions are similar to matching in that they are a recognition type question, and interestingly had a similar percentage of questions removed as matching. The SGSC had the fewest questions removed, which is a logical result given that they are self-graded by students.

Table 2. Questions removed according to mean score.

Question Type	Questions	Removed Questions	Mean Score
FITB	493,323	3,777	0.090
Matching	226,508	687	0.202
SGSC	19,417	12	0.226
MC	13,219	12	0.132

Examples of rejected questions help illustrate the decisions of the CIS. Matching, one of the easiest recognition question types, does have some questions that act as outliers to this general observation. One such question was answered incorrectly by all nine students who attempted it: "The {scarcity} {dependence} relationship can further be seen in the power situation of {employment}." While this statement may read like a reasonable sentence with key terms selected, no students selected the correct order for terms. The closest student swapped the first two terms, but no one was correct on the first attempt. Given the confusion for students on the first attempt, the question was rejected by the CIS after nine consecutive incorrect responses. This matching question shows that sometimes a question that may seem reasonable to a human reviewer is actually more challenging for students, and only the data revealed to what extent.

The SGSC questions make for interesting examples because students are self-reporting whether the answer they typed is correct when compared with the answer provided. While this question type had the highest (self-reported) mean score, a SGSC question was removed because only four of 21 students reported getting it correct (mean score = 0.190). The question was: "Write a definition for 'low-density lipoprotein'." Interestingly, while this question was flagged for removal, it did receive a single thumbs up rating (no thumbs down), which may be cause to consider the removal criteria for self-graded questions.

3.2 Student Ratings

Another method the CIS uses to determine if a question should be rejected is student feedback data from the rating feature. Each question answered creates a rating opportunity. Of the 239,965 students, 10,564 (4.40%) used the rating feature, giving a total of 18,940 ratings: 11,969 thumbs up and 6,971 thumbs down. Of the 752,467 questions, 16,540 (2.20%) were rated (either thumbs up or thumbs down). The overall thumbs down rate was 6,971 out of 3,594,408 rating opportunities (0.194%). Of the 16,540 rated questions, 403 (2.44%) received more than one thumbs down and were flagged for removal.

As noted in Table 3, FITB had the largest number of removed questions from ratings with matching following and MC and SGSC with fewer than 10 each. Notably, the mean score for the removed questions is much higher than what was seen previously. This shows that students were not only thumbing down questions they found especially difficult. Simply put, the mean difficulty and student rating data approaches are not necessarily targeting the same questions for removal.

Table 3. Questions removed by student ratings.

Question Type	Questions	Removed Questions	Mean Score
FITB	493,323	335	0.408
Matching	226,508	51	0.696
SGSC	19,417	9	0.629
MC	13,219	8	0.478

An example of a question that most students answered correctly yet was flagged for removal from thumbs down ratings is a matching question: "There are various surgical options for dealing with patients with obstructing splenic {flexure} {colon} {cancer}." Seven students answered with a mean score of 0.857. While only one student got it incorrect on the first attempt, it still got two thumbs down. When considering the question, it could be that students did not find the sentence substantive and meaningful for studying, so rated it down quickly.

Another interesting example of a question rated negatively is a multiple choice question that resulted from a rare generation error. The generated question stem consisted only of a pronunciation and a reference to another term ("Hă-ver′zhen see osteon"). Because of this, the multiple choice correct response ("Haversian system") became apparent simply from the pronunciation presented and 12 of 13 students selected the correct response. The two thumbs down ratings were from students who got the question correct, showing that the student feedback is critical for identifying errors in questions that may have high first attempt accuracy.

4 Human Review of the CIS Analyses

The CIS is a necessary system to do what humans simply cannot: monitor millions of AG questions and make decisions about their quality using data in real time. However, the value of this system increases when we consider the advantages of combining human and computer analyses. While the CIS alone is responsible for day-to-day automated decision-making at the question level, a human review of CIS data can reveal insights and patterns the CIS alone could not uncover. This partially automated human-computer review approach (affectionately referred to as "cyborg mode") has thus far identified two categories of new insights: trends in features of removed questions and patterns of down-rated question formats and books.

4.1 Features of Removed Questions

Given the large quantity of AG questions with student data available to the CIS, we have a unique opportunity to investigate features of the removed questions. Studying the removed questions can help us understand how questions flagged for removal differ from other questions. If features can be discovered that distinguish rejected questions, this could lead to development of predictive models that improve the quality of questions released, or simply modification of the AQG process to avoid questions with features correlating with higher rejection rates. Here we present some initial exploratory data analyses toward that goal, using FITB questions since this question type has the most data.

Removal by Mean Score. The largest group of questions removed was due to the Bayesian analysis of mean score. Table 4 shows the five most common answer part-of-speech (POS) tags (which account for more than 99% of questions) and compares their proportions among rejected and not rejected questions (that had a minimum of 20 responses). Both noun and adjective proportions are similar, with not rejected being slightly higher. The proportion of proper noun answers in questions not rejected was relatively higher than for the other parts of speech. Verbs and adverbs, however, were rejected at a higher proportion than not rejected. A chi-square goodness of fit test found the proportions differ by answer POS, $\chi^2(4, 3719) = 88.48$, $p < .001$.

Removal by Student Ratings. As previously seen, student ratings target a different set of questions than those with low mean score, so this student-selected set of rejected questions may provide interesting insights into features of questions that students do

Table 4. Mean score of rejected and not rejected questions grouped by POS.

POS	Rejected		Not Rejected	
	N	Proportion	N	Proportion
NOUN	2,254	0.606	9,978	0.607
ADJ	1,021	0.275	4,651	0.283
VERB	292	0.079	848	0.052
PROPN	90	0.024	726	0.044
ADV	62	0.017	232	0.014

not care for. In this analysis, we compare questions flagged for removal by receiving at least two thumbs down to questions receiving no ratings with a minimum of 20 students answering. As seen in Table 5, the most frequent POS for the FITB questions is noun, which has a higher proportion of not rejected to rejected questions. By comparison, verbs and adverbs were about three times more likely to be rejected than not rejected. A chi-square goodness of fit test was performed to evaluate whether the proportion of answer POS was equal between the two groups of questions. The proportions did differ by answer POS, $\chi^2(4, 320) = 102.97, p < .001$.

Table 5. Student rated rejected and not rejected questions grouped by POS.

POS	Rejected		Not Rejected	
	N	Proportion	N	Proportion
NOUN	184	0.575	8,743	0.609
ADJ	55	0.172	4,081	0.284
VERB	48	0.150	737	0.051
PROPN	18	0.056	601	0.042
ADV	15	0.047	196	0.014

Answer Position. Another feature of the FITB questions is the position of the answer word in the sentence. The blank for students to fill in could occur anywhere from the first word to the last word of the sentence. To see if there were any meaningful insights for the answer position, the rejected and not rejected questions were plotted according to the answer position (with a cutoff on sentence length for clarity). Figures 3 and 4 show bar graphs of answer position for mean score and student ratings, respectively. In both cases, the red rejected bar is visibly taller for several early sentence positions. For mean score, the second, third, fourth, and seventh answer positions have more rejected questions. For student ratings, the first, second, third, and sixth answer positions have more rejected questions.

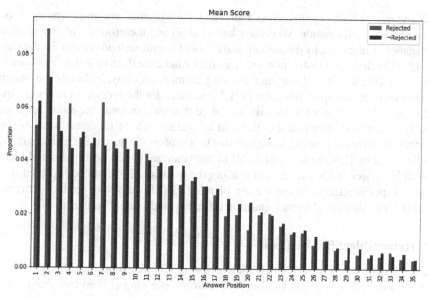

Fig. 3. Answer position for mean score rejected and not rejected questions.

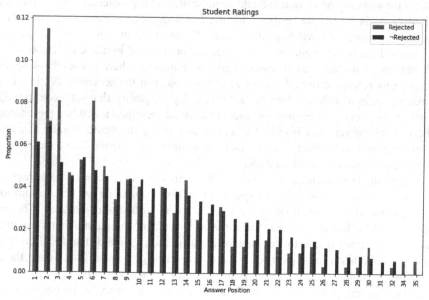

Fig. 4. Answer position for student rated rejected and not rejected questions.

This was a somewhat surprising finding that will require additional investigation. It seemed unlikely *a priori* that early answer blanks are less suitable for making questions, yet both mean score and student rating flagged disproportionately more early blanks for removal. One hypothesis for this finding is that it may be less of a question quality issue and more about cognitive load. Humans have a limited working memory capacity for storing new information (secondary knowledge) and therefore the ability to process information is impacted by the amount and types of cognitive load present for the learner [12, 13]. The design of instruction and activities can be ineffective if they involve extraneous cognitive activities that reduce working memory capacity, including the design of learning content that splits attention [12]. If we consider the process of reading a question wherein the first word is a blank, we notice that we must read the entire sentence to identify the context, then return to the start to evaluate what the correct word might be now that we have the context. Compare this to a sentence wherein the blank is near the middle or the end; we have the first half of the sentence for context and could identify a possible answer on the first pass of reading the question. It should be explored further through experimentation to see if early blanks in FITB questions produce extraneous cognitive load that could impact question difficulty and student satisfaction.

4.2 Human-Identified Patterns

The first example of a pattern that human review of CIS decisions identified comes from student-rated questions. The number of questions receiving at least two thumbs down was sufficiently small that reviewing them manually was practical. Reviewing this group of questions was also of particular interest in this first year of the AG question usage to monitor for ways the AQG system could be improved. One problematic pattern revealed in this review is illustrated by the following FITB question: "Figure 1.1 {illustrates} how the three areas of development interact." Three of the first nine students gave this question a thumbs down and so it was flagged for removal by the CIS. Upon review, multiple questions removed followed a common pattern wherein a textbook-specific named entity reference (e.g., Figure 1.1) is the subject of the sentence. While a figure reference within a sentence does not automatically disqualify that sentence for AQG, the review of questions removed by student ratings determined that when the reference is the subject, the sentence is often focused on describing the figure (similar to a figure caption) rather than declaring a useful fact about the subject matter. These sentences are thus not good source content for AQG.

As a result of this finding, two actions were taken. First, the database of all previously generated questions was searched for questions following the same pattern. An additional 6,709 questions (~1.3 per book at the time) were identified and removed. The great majority of these had not yet been encountered by students at all, and therefore, would never be encountered due to this pattern identification. Second, the AQG code was updated so that this type of question would no longer be generated. In this case, the CIS served as a feedback loop into the question generation process itself.

Human review of the CIS data can also quickly identify problematic books, not just individual questions. If an entire textbook has a thumbs down rate much higher than the average, it may indicate a systematic problem with AQG on the book's content. Therefore, the thumbs down rate was also calculated for each book and books with the highest rates were then examined. For example, one textbook had 8 total thumbs down ratings in the first 141 rating opportunities—a 5.67% thumbs down rate for the book— which is much higher than the baseline thumbs down rate of 0.194%. The title of the book was "Discovering Statistics Using IBM SPSS Statistics." Mathematical subject areas are not appropriate for our AQG algorithm and, as a rule, not included as candidates for the AQG application. However, metadata that identified this title as a mathematical text was missing and the title was not flagged by human review. At the time this was discovered by human review of the CIS analysis, only 14 students had used the automatically generated questions in this book, and they were turned off with minimal exposure to students.

5 Conclusion

The Content Improvement Service was developed to solve a new problem: how to monitor millions of questions generated with artificial intelligence as students interact with them. This platform-level adaptive system can use aggregated data from all students who use these formative questions in a textbook, no matter what institution or course those learners are in. The methods used by the CIS can identify a low-performing question in typically less than 20 students and remove that question immediately, which would simply not be possible by human effort. Between question difficulty and student ratings, only 0.6% of the 752,467 questions in the data set from 2022 were removed.

   While human review of millions of automatically generated questions would not be reasonable, reviewing the results of the data analyses from the CIS is easily done. Investigating decisions made from both question difficulty and student ratings revealed new insights into features of questions that performed less well than others. For example, fill-in-the-blank questions with a verb as the blank were removed more often than other parts of speech for both the difficulty and rating data. Also, questions with the answer blanks early in the sentence were removed more often than those with the answer blank at the middle or end. The CIS data facilitated these observations that may benefit question generation methods in the future. Furthermore, human review of student rating data identified a grammar pattern that was unsuitable for questions, and all questions of that pattern were identified and removed. The modular and extensible nature of the CIS allows us to automatically monitor more and more measures of question quality over time. While the CIS will continue to make decisions on questions in real-time, expert review of this data will continue to help advance question generation approaches and the student experience.

References

1. Koedinger, K., McLaughlin, E., Jia, J., Bier, N.: Is the doer effect a causal relationship? How can we tell and why it's important. In: Learning Analytics and Knowledge. Edinburgh, United Kingdom (2016). https://doi.org/10.1145/2883851.2883957
2. Van Campenhout, R., Johnson, B.G., Olsen, J.A.: The doer effect: replication and comparison of correlational and causal analyses of learning. Int. J. Adv. Syst. Meas. **15**(1&2) (2022). http://www.iariajournals.org/systems_and_measurements/tocv15n12.html
3. Van Campenhout, R., Jerome, B., Johnson, B.G.: The doer effect at scale: investigating correlation and causation across seven courses. In: 13th International Learning Analytics and Knowledge Conference (LAK 2023) (2023). https://doi.org/10.1145/3576050.3576103
4. Jerome, B., Van Campenhout, R., Dittel, J.S., Benton, R., Greenberg, S., Johnson, B.G.: The content improvement service: an adaptive system for continuous improvement at scale. In: Meiselwitz, G., et al. (eds.) Interaction in New Media, Learning and Games (HCII 2022).

LNCS, vol. 13517, pp. 286–296. Springer, Cham (2022). https://doi.org/10.1007/978-3-031-22131-6_22

5. Vandewaetere, M., Desmet, P., Clarebout, G.: The contribution of learner characteristics in the development of computer-based adaptive learning environments. Comput. Human Behav. **27**(1), 118–130 (2011). https://doi.org/10.1016/j.chb.2010.07.038

6. Simon, H.A.: The job of a college president. Educ. Rec. **48**, 68–78 (1967)

7. Goodell, J.: What is learning engineering? In: Goodell, J., Kolodner, J. (eds.) Learning Engineering Toolkit: Evidence-Based Practices from the Learning Sciences, Instructional Design, and Beyond. Routledge, New York (2022)

8. Campenhout, R.: Learning engineering as an ethical framework. In: Sottilare, R.A., Schwarz, J. (eds.) HCII 2021. LNCS, vol. 12792, pp. 105–119. Springer, Cham (2021). https://doi.org/10.1007/978-3-030-77857-6_7

9. Van Campenhout, R., Dittel, J.S., Jerome, B., Johnson, B.G.: Transforming textbooks into learning by doing environments: an evaluation of textbook-based automatic question generation. In: Third Workshop on Intelligent Textbooks at the 22nd International Conference on Artificial Intelligence in Education. CEUR Workshop Proceedings, pp. 60–73 (2021). http://ceur-ws.org/Vol-2895/paper06.pdf

10. Kurdi, G., Leo, J., Parsia, B., Sattler, U., Al-Emari, S.: A systematic review of automatic question generation for educational purposes. Int. J. Artif. Intell. Educ. **30**(1), 121–204 (2019). https://doi.org/10.1007/s40593-019-00186-y

11. Fischer, C., et al.: Mining big data in education: affordances and challenges. Rev. Res. Educ. **44**(1), 130–160 (2020). https://doi.org/10.3102/0091732X20903304

12. Chandler, P., Sweller, J.: Cognitive load theory and the format of instruction. Cogn. Instr. **8**(4), 293–332 (1991)

13. Sweller, J.: Cognitive load theory and educational technology. Educ. Tech. Res. Dev. **68**(1), 1–16 (2019). https://doi.org/10.1007/s11423-019-09701-3

Merging Human and Non-human (System) Data to Describe Students' Adaptive Learning Experience in Postsecondary Gateway Math Courses

James R. Paradiso(✉) 📵, Tammy Muhs📵, and Baiyun Chen📵

University of Central Florida, Orlando, FL 32816, USA
james.paradiso@ucf.edu

Abstract. Due to the historically high DFW (D-F-Withdraw) rates of College Algebra students at the University of Central Florida (UCF), adaptive instructional systems (AISs) have become an integral instructional component for the faculty who teach this course, with one strong impetus driving this shift: Prior to incorporating AISs into College Algebra, DFW rates averaged 31% (fall 2011–summer 2015); however, since integrating AISs into the curriculum (c. 2015), this course has seen an approximately 58% decline in DFW rates from 31% to 13% (fall 2015–summer 2022). One particular AIS, Realizeit, has been utilized consistently over the years to help close the learning gaps for students and support their academic success. To evaluate the extent to which Realizeit has impacted student achievement in College Algebra, results from a student-facing survey—aligned with a set of Realizeit data reports—were collected to tell both human and non-human (system) sides of the student journey, exposing how a combination of qualitative and quantitative data can be used to improve teaching and learning outcomes in future iterations of this course.

Keywords: Adaptive Instructional Systems · Educational Technology · Personalized Learning · College Algebra · Student Experience

1 Introduction

Adaptive Instructional Systems (AISs) have been leveraged for educational purposes for many years [1]; however, the results have varied in terms of the impact AISs have had on student achievement, engagement, and overall experience [2]. Within higher education, AISs have been strategically deployed to help improve learning outcomes in the most persistently dropped/failed (DFW) courses [3]. College Algebra, in particular, has been an object of attention, as this course has one of the highest postsecondary DFW rates [4] and possesses considerable upside for at-risk students—making it a prime candidate for teaching and learning interventions with AISs [5, 6].

At the University of Central Florida (UCF), for instance, the personalized adaptive learning (PAL) team and teaching faculty associated with the PAL initiative aim to provide appropriate learning content to the 'right students' at the 'right time' to maximize their potential for success. AISs, such as Realizeit, are utilized to support this effort, as they are designed to offer students a heightened level of agency/choice via system recommendations—allowing students to engage in meaningful metacognition around their learning goals.

Realizeit is a content agnostic AIS that requires course developers and/or subject-matter-experts (SMEs) to create or use existing educational content, arrange (granularize) that content into a pre-requisite sequence (Fig. 1), and configure the course-level settings in a way that leverages the AIS algorithms to furnish content pathways that optimize the student experience and result in learning mastery.

For UCF's adaptive version of College Algebra, the course instructor authored original content directly into Realizeit to provide opportunity for the most flexible, personalized student experience.

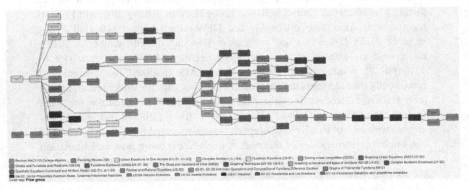

Fig. 1. Realizeit Prerequisite Map (course developer view): [10] (Weeks 1–14).

The content creation process in Realizeit generally begins at the 'node' (lesson) level, which represents a single learning concept. Multiple nodes are then collected into what is referred to as an 'objective.' An objective is a collection of nodes which are time-based, interconnected (or related) subsets of the course content. Lastly, a collection of the objectives constitutes the academic course. Each node in the College Algebra curriculum has multiple sections including an Introduction, Learning, Worked Examples, Examples, Summary, Try It, and Check of Understanding. Five of the seven section types adapt to the learner (Table 1).

Table 1. Individual section names, characteristics, and adaptive/personalized features

Section Name	Section Characteristics	Section Adaptivity and Personalization
Introduction	The motivation for the node and applicable learning objective(s)	None
Learning	Algorithmic learning content presented in multiple formats including passive reading, video, pencast, interactive reading, or mixed format	Learning sections are formatted based on learning performance and learning characteristics. Learners are also given the option to request additional learning content from a menu
Worked Examples	Algorithmic examples with each step explained in detail. No mathematical steps are assumed; hence, all calculations are included and explained. Interactive examples are included to check the learners' understanding of the worked examples	Preset conditions are used to deliver Worked Examples to the struggling learner. If the learner demonstrates poor understanding of the interactive examples, the AIS redirects the learner back to the Worked Examples section
Examples	Algorithmic examples with all the trivial steps removed leaving only the key steps and associated explanations. Interactive examples are included to check the learners' understanding of these streamlined examples	Preset conditions are used to deliver streamlined Examples to high-performing learners. If the learner demonstrates poor understanding of the interactive examples, the AIS redirects the learner to the Worked Examples section
Summary	The key concepts from the learning material	None
Try It	A question bank (store) of algorithmic practice exercises. Some of the exercises include locations, events, and programs specific to UCF and the name banks used in examples and exercises are proportionally representative of UCF's student demographics and gender	Application problems (word problems) included in practice exercises (Try It) and assessments (Check of Understanding) are personalized to the individual student's program of study to address concerns of course relevance
Check of Understanding	A short formative assessment of knowledge	This section determines the next step for the learner: to advance or complete additional work

At the start of each assignment, Realizeit recommends that the learner complete a set of targeted questions (Determine Knowledge, DK) taken from the objective-based lessons (nodes) contained in the assignment (Fig. 2).

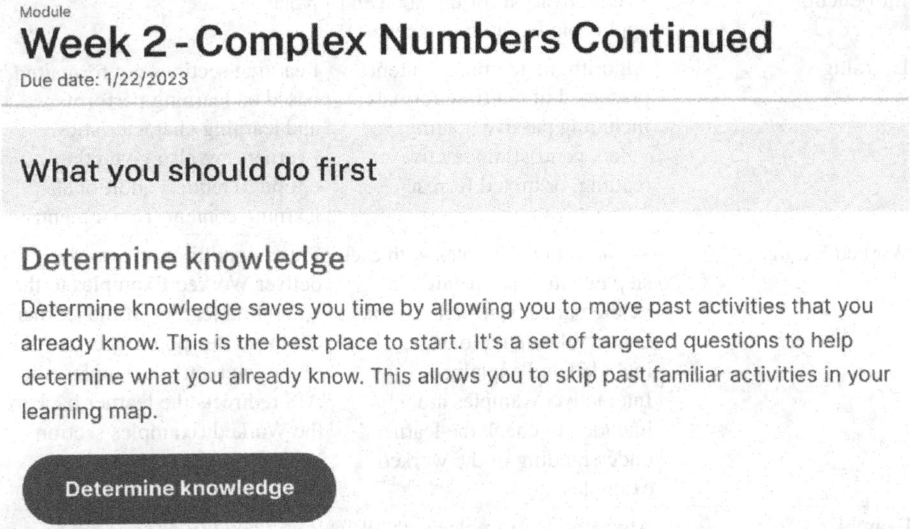

Module
Week 2 - Complex Numbers Continued
Due date: 1/22/2023
What you should do first
Determine knowledge
Determine knowledge saves you time by allowing you to move past activities that you already know. This is the best place to start. It's a set of targeted questions to help determine what you already know. This allows you to skip past familiar activities in your learning map.
Determine knowledge

Fig. 2. Realizeit starting recommendation (i.e., no prior knowledge recorded): Week 2 – Complex Numbers Continued [10].

Upon first entry (prior to completing DK), students encounter a collection of nodes that can be navigated in any number of ways—depending on their DK score (Fig. 3).

Multiplying Complex Numbers
Powers of i
Dividing Complex Numbers
Finding the Conjugate

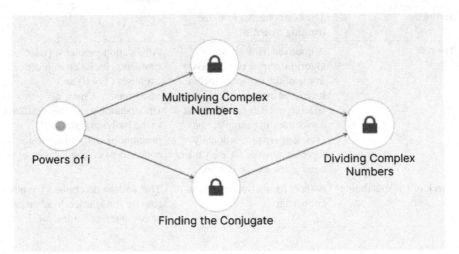

Fig. 3. Realizeit Learning Map prior to completing DK: Week 2 – Complex Numbers Continued [10].

After students complete DK and show a basic level of content proficiency (e.g., 60% or above), the system unlocks one or more lesson nodes, and the AIS begins to recommend alternative pathways for students to improve their content knowledge.

Multiplying Complex Numbers
Powers of i
Dividing Complex Numbers
Finding the Conjugate

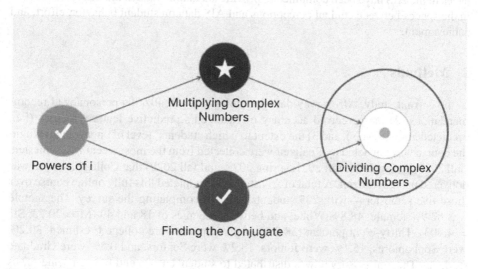

Fig. 4. Realizeit Learning Map after completing DK: Week 2 – Complex Numbers Continued [10].

What you should do next
Learn
Dividing Complex Numbers
This is the only available activity that you have yet to complete. It will take you about 20 minutes to learn.
Learn
Practice module
This is a great way to improve and build on your existing knowledge before working on the last activity.

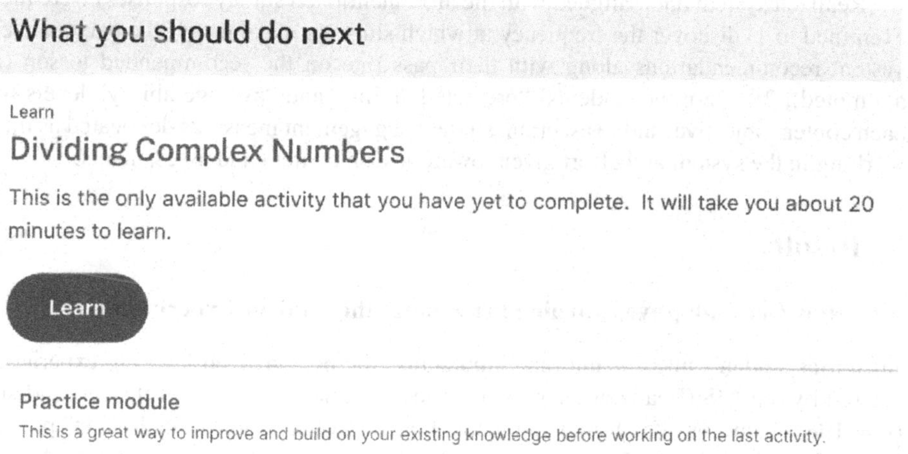

Fig. 5. Realizeit content recommendation(s) after completing DK: Week 2 – Complex Numbers Continued [10].

This personalization is based on students predicted ability on each node and is adjusted continuously as students interact with interconnected material in the course (cf. Fig. 1). This information along with student perceptions of their learning experiences in the AIS have been combined to provide a dynamic look at the nuances that exist in the spaces between student perceptions and AIS data on student behavior, effort, and achievement.

2   Methods

In the current study, AIS survey data pertaining to 1) Realizeit's personalized recommendations, 2) the perceived accuracy of Realizeit's predictive features/metrics (i.e., predicted ability levels), and 3) the extent to which students' level of engagement within the course was impacted by Realizeit were collected from the most recent five semesters (fall 2020, spring 2021, fall 2021, spring 2022, and fall 2022) that College Algebra was delivered using Realizeit. A total of 254 students completed this fully online course over those five semesters—with 205 students (80.7%) completing the survey. The sample was 62.9% female, 48.8% White, and between the ages of 18 and 49 (M = 20.72, SD = 4.303). Thirty-eight percent (38.0%) of participants were college Freshmen, 30.2% were Sophomores, 15.1% were Juniors, 13.2% were Seniors, and 0.5% were Graduate students. This online survey was distributed to students at the end of each semester as a graded survey inside the learning management system (Canvas). Note: Respondents were able to skip any question during the survey; thus, the percentages reported in the study do not account for skipped questions.

Realizeit system data (aligned with the aforementioned survey responses) were then examined to 1) discover the frequency at which students make use of the personalized system recommendations along with their pass rate on the recommended lesson (if attempted), 2) determine students' "predicted ability" and "average ability" levels for each content objective, and 3) ascertain student engagement measures delineated as time working in the system and effort given toward lesson content and assessments.

3   Results

3.1   How Does Adaptive Learning Personalize the Student Experience?

Insofar as students maximizing (and embracing) the personalized learning experience offered by the AIS (Realizeit), survey analyses indicate that 52.9% of the respondents (n = 108) always or often follow the recommended "What you should do next" path in Realizeit, and another 25.5% sometimes follow the recommendation (n = 52) (Table 2).

Table 2. How often did you follow the suggested "What you should do next" path in Realizeit?

Rating	Frequency	Percent
Never	9	4.4%
Rarely	32	15.7%
Sometimes	52	25.5%
Quite Often	51	25.0%
Always	57	27.9%
I'm not sure	3	1.5%
Total	204	100%

Realizeit system data, on the other hand, revealed that 89% of students followed the AIS's primary "What you should do next" path and that 63% of the students who did so earned a passing score on their first attempt at the lesson. Ultimately, 42.4% of survey respondents (n = 87) strongly agreed or agreed that the system became personalized to them over time (Table 3).

Table 3. The Realizeit system became personalized to me over time.

Rating	Frequency	Percent
Strongly Disagree	7	3.4%
Disagree	52	25.6%
Neither Agree nor Disagree	53	26.1%
Agree	71	35.0%
Strongly Agree	15	7.4%
I'm not sure	5	2.5%
Total	202	100%

3.2 How Does Adaptive Learning Affect Student Content Mastery?

In terms of how students perceived their Realizeit determined 'ability levels' (which are based on a weighted mean of multiple accuracy and engagement measures), 52.9% of survey respondents (n = 107) either strongly agreed or agreed that the ability levels reported by Realizeit were accurate (Table 4), and 51.5% of respondents (n = 104) either strongly agreed or agreed that the Realizeit assessments were effective in measuring their learning (Table 5).

Table 4. The ability levels reported by Realizeit were accurate.

Rating	Frequency	Percent
Strongly Disagree	9	4.5%
Disagree	35	17.3%
Neither Agree nor Disagree	47	23.3%
Agree	94	46.5%
Strongly Agree	13	6.4%
I'm not sure	4	2.0%
Total	202	100%

Table 5. Realizeit's assessment exercises were effective in measuring my learning.

Rating	Frequency	Percent
Never	13	6.4%
Disagree	34	16.8%
Neither Agree nor Disagree	49	24.3%
Agree	89	44.1%
Strongly Agree	15	7.4%
I'm not sure	2	1.0%
Total	202	100%

In Realizeit, students' "predicted ability" (i.e., Knowledge State/Mastery) is the final value derived from their scoring "history" and represented in the form of "effect" change. The "effect" fluctuates each time a student attempts a question related to a designated learning "objective"—whether the question is being asked 1) in a lesson or 2) on an assessment that lives extraneous to the lesson.

While over 50% of student reported that Realizeit predicted ability levels were accurate, one noteworthy component to these results is that many of the final 'predicted ability' levels in the AIS were not factored into the final grade of an assignment, as only improved scores were sent back to the Canvas gradebook after the due date. In fact, system analytics show that many of the students' predicted ability levels actually lowered after the assignment due date. The lowered level is on account of questions from the lessons being repurposed on quizzes and tests and answered incorrectly by the students and/or students randomly entering erroneous answers on questions while searching for specific questions to study for an assessment.

3.3   How Does Adaptive Learning Impact Student Engagement?

Regarding student engagement, 66.8% of respondents (n = 137) stated that they spent much more or more time learning content in their class using Realizeit than in a math class without Realizeit (Table 6), and 55.7% of them (n = 112) strongly agreed or agreed that Realizeit increased their engagement with the content (Table 7).

Table 6. How much time did you spend in Realizeit compared to a traditional math class without Realizeit?

Rating	Frequency	Percent
Much Less	6	2.9%
Less	23	11.2%
The Same	30	14.6%
More	63	30.7%
Much More	74	36.1%
I'm not sure	9	4.4%
Total	205	100%

Table 7. Realizeit increased my engagement with the course content.

Rating	Frequency	Percent
Strongly Disagree	21	10.4%
Disagree	33	16.4%
Neither Agree nor Disagree	34	16.9%
Agree	87	43.3%
Strongly Agree	25	12.4%
I'm not sure	1	0.5%
Total	201	100%

The Realizeit system analytics also showed that students were highly engaged in the learning activities. The average learning hours (h) (active time spent on task) per student ranged from 60 to 85 h per semester—averaging 70 h across the five targeted semesters. Fitting into a 14-week semester, that is about 5 h per student per week excluding the first and last exam week of the semester. Students also completed (on average) 1,860 questions, ranging from 1,802 on the low side to 1,923 at the peak (cf. Table 8).

4 Discussion

4.1 How Does Adaptive Learning Personalize the Student Experience?

While a large majority of students took advantage of Realizeit's recommendations when engaging with the learning materials, what was unable to be determined from the survey and system data was why students chose "What you should do next" over manually selecting an alternative pathway through the content.

Table 8. Realizeit learner engagement.

Variable	2020 Fall	2021 Spring	2021 Fall	2022 Spring	2022 Fall
Class Size	39	36	36	47	96
Average Learning Hours Per Student	68.501	84.938	63.141	59.515	73.024
Average Questions Per Student Completed	1,857.69	1,883.11	1,883.17	1,802.11	1,923.20

Two motivations may be at work: 1) The visual (and cognitive) convenience of the recommendation and/or 2) the perceived trustworthiness of the recommendation based on the visual agreement between the learning map and recommendation (cf. Fig. 4 and Fig. 5)—making the recommended 'next' step hard (or seemingly foolish) to ignore.

While 89% of students attempted the "What you should do next" lesson, only 63% of them passed that recommended lesson—bringing into question the validity of the recommendation(s). In Fig. 5, for example, the system may have done better to recommend additional practice on "Powers of i" and/or "Finding the Conjugate" rather than the final 'unattempted' lesson "Dividing Complex Numbers" since both of those nodes indicate moderate (orange) to low (red) level of understanding (cf. Fig. 6).

Mastery bands

Beginning	Improving	Competent	Experienced	Master
0% to 40%	40% to 70%	70% to 80%	80% to 90%	90% to 100%

Fig. 6. Students' predicted ability level designations in Realizeit [10]. (Color figure online)

Untimely or ineffective recommendations may have also contributed to the nearly even spread between students who believed or did not believe the system became personalized to them over time with approximately 29.0% disagreeing or strongly disagreeing, 26.1% neither agreeing nor disagreeing, and 42.4% agreeing or strongly agreeing (cf. Table 3).

To be fair, the above assertion (regarding potentially unideal recommendations) is only one possibility for explaining the low pass rate of the recommended lessons. Other scenarios include students not passing due to having to exit a lesson abruptly or making an inadvertent data entry issue, such as leaving the "i" under the radical, which would later be designated as correct by the instructor (changing the student lesson outcome from failing to passing).

4.2 How Does Adaptive Learning Affect Student Content Mastery?

Approximately 53% of the students stated the ability levels reported by Realizeit were accurate and 52% reported that the assessments were effective—leaving slightly less than 50% in both expressing a clear disagreement or neutral response (neither agreeing nor disagreeing with the above statements).These two survey questions (cf. Table 4 and Table 5) showed nearly identical statistics across the Likert-type scale, which may indicate the closeness in which students interpreted the meaning of both statements.

While students may rightly equate ability with their assessment scores, one is not directly proportionate to the other. For instance, getting 8 out of 10 correct on a question set represents an 80%, yet students' 'ability' is an algorithmically derived number which takes many other factors (aside from raw score) into account, including effort and timing (e.g., more recent scores carry more weight). Therefore, the jump from 4% to 18% in ability (as shown in Fig. 7) is not an increase students will ever be able to determine from adding and dividing numbers they can see in Realizeit, as there are many calculations happening beyond the users' line of sight. (This may also help explain the 50/50 split in student perceptions.)

My understanding of your ability has increased from 4% to 18%. My understanding of your knowledge state for this module (Week 1 - Linear Equations in One Variable) has increased from 36% to 43%.

Fig. 7. Realizeit on-screen message regarding student ability after completing a lesson. Week 1 – Linear Equations in One Variable [10].

According to Realizeit, predicted 'ability' is generated by the AI of the system and considers the prerequisite network and a learner's performance, particularly on previous attempts. The average of each lesson ability is then accumulated and manifested as "knowledge state" at the objective level (which is combined with student completion of lessons to arrive at the final/composite score that gets sent to the learning management system gradebook).

4.3 How Does Adaptive Learning Impact Student Engagement?

Over two-thirds of students felt they spent more time engaged with Realizeit than in classes without it. This increased engagement partially occurred due to the AIS's dynamic approach to gathering student evidence toward content mastery, which rewards students for putting forth extra effort and prompts them via system recommendations to practice and revise their work.

Whether this increased engagement resulted in an improved final score in the course is not addressed in this paper; however, a correlation between student engagement and student achievement has been made by numerous studies in the past [7–9]. Therefore, further investigation is warranted to determine the relationship between engagement and learning, particularly when using an AIS.

5 Conclusion (and Future Work)

In an academic climate where educational technology is more heavily invested in than ever before, this study posits that looking precisely at the student experiences and technical affordances (e.g., recommender systems) of an AIS (Realizeit, in this case) could have considerable upside potential for historically challenging gateway math courses, such as College Algebra.

A deeper look into how matters of personalization, predicted abilities, and student engagement impact course outcomes (e.g., student grades) would provide an additional layer to the basic observations discussed in this paper and may be a logical next step for investigating how adaptive learning can improve academic outcomes for students.

References

1. Xie, H., Chu, H.C., Hwang, G.J., Wang, C.C.: Trends and development in technology-enhanced adaptive/personalized learning: a systematic review of journal publications from 2007 to 2017. Comput. Educ. **140**, 103599 (2019). https://doi.org/10.1016/j.compedu.2019.103599
2. Dziuban, C., et al.: Adaptive analytics: it's about time. Curr. Issues Emerg. eLearn. **7**(1), 4 (2020). https://scholarworks.umb.edu/ciee/vol7/iss1/4
3. Brown, C.L., Grussendorf, J., Shea, M.D., DeMas, C.J.: Changing the paradigm? Creating an adaptive course to improve student engagement and outcomes in introductory political science classes. J. Political Sci. Educ. **18**, 301–326 (2022). https://doi.org/10.1080/15512169.2022.2069573
4. Saxe, K., Braddy, L.: A common vision for undergraduate mathematical sciences programs in 2025. Mathematical Association of America (2015)
5. Quinton, S.: Georgia State improved its graduation rate by 22 points in 10 years. The Atlantic 23 (2013)
6. Komar, J.A., Troka, T.: Improving performance in College Algebra using technology. In: 2015 ASEE Annual Conference and Exposition, pp. 26–923. Seattle (2015)
7. Finn, J.D., Zimmer, K.S.: Student engagement: what is it? Why does it matter? In: Handbook of Research on Student Engagement, pp. 97–131 (2012)
8. Christenson, S., Reschly, A.L., Wylie, C.: Handbook of Research on Student Engagement, vol. 840. Springer, New York (2012). https://doi.org/10.1007/978-1-4614-2018-7
9. Raza, S.A., Qazi, W., Umer, B.: Examining the impact of case-based learning on student engagement, learning motivation and learning performance among university students. J. Appl. Res. High. Educ. **12**(3), 517–533 (2019). https://doi.org/10.1108/JARHE-05-2019-0105
10. Muhs, T.: MAC1105C-23Spring 0W60 – College Algebra [Online course]. Realizeit (2023). https://ucf.realizeithome.com

Towards Application of Adaptive Instructional Systems in Simulation-Based Lifeboat Training Using Bayesian Networks

Reza Zeinali-Torbati[1]([✉]) [iD], Jennifer Smith[2] [iD], Randy Billard[3] [iD], Bruno Emond[4] [iD], Joshua Barnes[4] [iD], and Brian Veitch[1] [iD]

[1] Memorial University of Newfoundland, St. John's, Canada
{r.zeinalitorbati,bveitch}@mun.ca
[2] Marine Institute, St. John's, Canada
jennifer.smith@mi.mun.ca
[3] Virtual Marine, Paradise, Canada
randy.billard@virtualmarine.ca
[4] National Research Council Canada, Ottawa, Canada
{bruno.emond,joshua.barnes}@nrc-cnrc.gc.ca

Abstract. Lifeboat coxswains need to be trained and assessed regularly on their performance in plausible emergencies. The ability to do this frequently is limited by the safety risks and logistics of practicing in harsh offshore conditions. Simulation-based lifeboat training provides a means for coxswains to practice typical offshore emergency scenarios, which are usually performed under the supervision of an instructor with occasional interventions. This research serves as a pilot study for automating the role of a human instructor and providing a customized training experience for learners by developing an adaptive instructional system (AIS) for simulation-based lifeboat training. To inform the learner model of the AIS, probabilistic models of learners' behaviors were developed using Bayesian networks for launching, navigation, and slow-speed maneuvering tasks of a typical lifeboat training exercise. The model is able to evaluate learners' actions and behaviors to diagnose their skill levels, strengths, and weaknesses, based on the evidence collected while the learners perform a variety of tasks during a training scenario. A case study is presented to demonstrate how the learner model can be trained with simulation-based assessment data and applied to inform a pedagogical model of an AIS to tailor instructional pace, training scenarios, and feedback to the learners' needs. The results of this study provide an important step towards applying AISs in simulation-based lifeboat training and other maritime safety simulation-based training environments, which are expected to improve learners' skill acquisition and speed their time to competence.

Keywords: Adaptive instructional systems · Bayesian networks · learner model · simulation-based lifeboat training · marine operations

R. A. Sottilare and J. Schwarz (Eds.): HCII 2023, LNCS 14044, pp. 337–352, 2023.
https://doi.org/10.1007/978-3-031-34735-1_24

1 Introduction

In recent years, applications of artificial intelligence (AI) have become popular in many domains, such as medicine and finance. Research in the application of AI to education has been underway for decades [14, 17]. AI has enabled the education field to incorporate intelligent and adaptive systems to enhance instructional strategies and provide a more efficient learning process for learners [12]. While most instructional systems can provide benefits such as improved performance, feedback support, and effective learner-instructor collaboration, they focus mainly on the technical learning objectives and often ignore the pedagogical aspects of the instructional systems [13]. Learners acquire new skills in different ways and paces, so an adaptive pedagogy that can address these differences and provide a tailored experience for learners can enhance the learning process [10]. This study aims to provide a model for identifying the differences between learners' competencies, which can be used for development of an adaptive pedagogy in simulation-based lifeboat training.

2 Adaptive Instructional Systems

Adaptive instructional systems (AISs) are the most popular applications of AI in education [8] and consist of a range of technologies, including intelligent tutoring systems, adaptive multimedia, and training content recommenders [9]. AISs are artificially intelligent computer-assisted learning technologies that are tailored to the goals, preferences, needs, and cognitive states of an individual or a team in the context of learning goals [26]. Unlike conventional approaches where a human instructor is heavily involved in decision-making, AISs have the ability to simulate instruction capable of adapting to learners' learning strategies by automating the interactions of the instructor [25]. Most learning environments are non-adaptive and use the same training content for every learner. An example of this is simulation-based training that usually use the same instructions and scenarios for virtual training, independent of learners' competencies and skill levels, with occasional interventions from a human instructor. Application of AISs in simulation-based training can reduce the work load on the instructors and improve learners' skills and performance through predicting learners' needs and providing optimized learning materials, corrective feedback, and tailored practice scenarios [16]. A recent empirical study in the maritime training domain has shown evidence that AISs and automated instructors can also score complex tasks more consistently compared to live instructors [5].

While AISs have been well discussed in the literature and described as effective in providing tailored instructions, there have been few real-world examples and practices for the implementation of these systems in educational settings [28]. One reason for the sparse use of the AISs in real educational settings is likely the significant effort required for the development of adaptive systems [20], as well as the lack of interoperability [20, 27]. However, the recent COVID-19 pandemic advanced the use of intelligent and AI-driven systems such as AISs in the education field [18]. Similarly, there are limited applications of AISs in simulation-based training, which have been found to be effective ways to provide tailored instructions for improving learners' outcomes [6]. While there have been some examples of AISs implementation for training purposes in the military, aviation, and medicine domains (e.g., [1, 21, 29]), there has been no application of AISs in the marine field to train seafarers for navigation under typical offshore emergency scenarios. This pilot research is a part of a larger study [7] and provides a step towards the integration of AISs in simulation-based lifeboat training, which aims automate instructors' interventions, reduce instructors' workload, improve training efficiency, and enhance learners' performance by providing tailored feedback, instructions, and practice scenarios.

AISs have four major components (Fig. 1), which includes the domain model, the learner (or student) model, the pedagogical (or tutoring or instructional) model, and the user (or student-tutor) interface model [23]. The domain model includes the set of skills, knowledge, tactics (or actions), and strategies (or action plans) of the instructed topic, as well as the ideal knowledge from experts. It could also include information on the learner's typical misconceptions and contain the entire possible learner states in the domain [19, 24]. The learner model is usually considered as a subset of the domain model that changes over the instructional course, which contains various states (e.g., cognitive, affective, and motivational) that arise during the learning course. The required data for prediction and classification of these psychological states are typically obtained using sensors, inputs and assessment data from learners, as well as historical records, which are used to make pedagogical decisions [19, 27]. The pedagogical model uses learning theories, as well as the information from the domain and learner models to offer recommendations for selecting appropriate tactics and strategies to guide the learner to a more optimal performance [19]. The user interface model takes the information from the learner via typing, speech, or clicking to interpret their contributions and then presents the outputs in various media such as texts, diagrams, animations, or agents [19]. The user interface model also controls the interaction between learner and the instructional contents and uses the associated learner's behaviors to optimize learning outcomes while updating the learner states and environmental conditions [27]. This research primarily focuses on developing a learner model of AIS that can investigate learners' behaviors to diagnose their needs, weaknesses, and strengths and identify their competence levels.

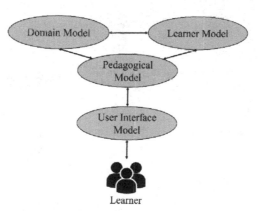

Fig. 1. Components of AIS model structure [11].

3   Methodology

Deployment of AISs in simulation-based training can be done through Bayesian networks (BNs), which is one of the most popular artificially intelligent approaches used in AISs [16]. BNs can provide adaptive instructions, assess the learner's performance, and revise the learner model accordingly [16]. This study uses BNs to analyze learners' competence levels through adding intelligence to the learner model of simulation-based lifeboat training. Simulation-based training programs commonly use an Evidence-Centered Design approach [15] to assess skills and model competence. Performance measures taken from simulator exercises provide observable evidence to quantify the learner's ability to complete tasks, or competence in a task type. Competency is modelled using scoring rubrics and evidence rules based on the skill being measured (scoring rules and rubrics). Statistical models, including BNs, link observational data to the competency models, and can be continually updated with new data. BN approach has been previously employed in [3] to create a lifeboat coxswain competence model for slow-speed maneuvering (SSM) using both expert and simulator data. While a task modeling approach was used in [3], here a more advanced modeling approach was used to investigate the behaviors that learners represent when completing the tasks in a typical lifeboat drill simulation. The task modeling approach in [3] focused on the learner's ability to complete the task, which was the primary measure of performance. Extending the model to behaviors allows for analysis of the actions and that affect the ability to complete tasks. This model can provide insights on the behaviors that are associated with having or not having the competence, or being a novice or expert.

A typical offshore emergency scenario involves a series of tasks and subtasks, where learners are evaluated on their launching, navigation, and SSM. For example, the scenario shown in Fig. 2 represents a plausible lifeboat launch emergency scenario that involves a simple maneuvering exercise. The BN models were developed in GeNIe Modeler and can be used as diagnostic tools to analyze learners' competence and identify their strengths and weaknesses based on evidence gathered in training. The BN states for learners' competencies are inferred from their interaction with the learning system and how they

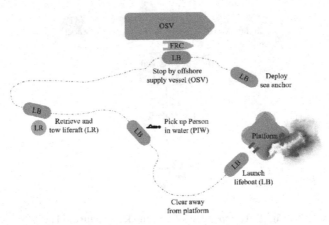

Fig. 2. An illustration of the tasks in a plausible lifeboat launch emergency scenario.

perform each task in the simulated scenario. For each competence, a BN was developed. While launching includes mainly procedural nodes, SSM includes psychomotor tasks that require hands on practice to master [2]. A detailed description of the launching, navigation, and SSM tasks in the scenario can be found in [2] and [4].

Figure 3 and Fig. 4 show the BNs for all the tasks in the given scenario (Fig. 2), where the relationships and interactions among competence and different tasks are presented by arrows. The BNs in Figs. 3 and Fig. 4 show extended dynamic models that account for learners' progression through multiple attempts of the same tasks or scenarios, which is very common in a simulation setup. As learners perform a given scenario, evidence of their performance and behaviors for completing the launching, navigation, and SSM tasks are collected. For example, while performing the SSM tasks, learners' behavioral measures such as speed on approach, approach angle relative to wind, proximity to target, stopping time duration, stopping speed, and stopping angle relative to wind are captured in a simulator's log file for various subtasks in the scenario, including picking up a person in water (PIW), retrieving a life raft (LR), stopping by an offshore supply vessel (OSV), and deploying the sea anchor (DSA). The speed on approach and approach angle are measured in four different zones (as depicted in Fig. 5) when approaching the object of interest (PIW, LR, or OSV). Based on a set of defined thresholds, the captured data are classified into BN states and used to inform the BNs for inferring the states of learners' competencies. The thresholds used for discretizing continuous variables (e.g., headings, speed evaluation radii, speed limits, etc.) are selected using a scoring rubric that was developed based on expert advice and the training standards from the International Convention on Standards of Training, Certification and Watchkeeping for Seafarers (STCW).

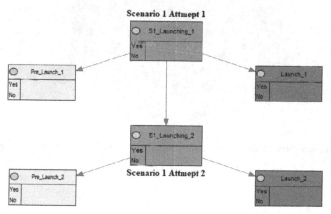

Fig. 3. Bayesian network for the launching tasks of the given simulation-based lifeboat training scenario. The Pre_launch task has two child nodes; Critical_Errors_Count and Non_Critical_Errors_Count. The Launch Node has 11 child nodes; Permission_To_Launch, Inform_Crew_Before_Launch, Start_Engine, Lower_Without_Stopping, Activate_Air_And_Deluge, Hook_Release_Time, Throttle_Engagement_Time, Contact_With_Platform, Clear_Away_Direction, Clear_Distance_from_Platform, and Tasks_Done_In_Order. A description of all these tasks can be found in [4].

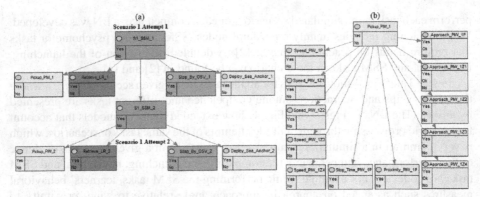

Fig. 4. Bayesian network for a) all the SSM tasks and b) an expanded node of the given simulation-based lifeboat training scenario. The *Pickup_PIW* task has 12 child nodes; *Speed_PIW_P*, *Speed_PIW_Z1*, *Speed_PIW_Z2*, *Speed_PIW_Z3*, *Speed_PIW_Z4*, *Approach_PIW_P*, *Approach_PIW_Z1*, *Approach_PIW_Z2*, *Approach_PIW_Z3*, *Approach_PIW_Z4*, *Stop_Time_PIW_P*, and *Proximity_PIW_P*. Similarly, the *Retriev_LR* and *Stop_By_OSV* tasks have 12 child nodes, but with different measurement criteria. The *Deploy_Sea_Anchor* node has three child nodes; *Speed_DSA*, *Heading_DSA*, and *Stop_Time_DSA*.

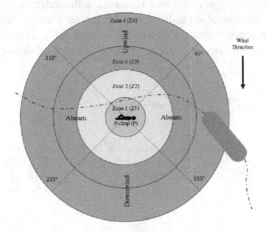

Fig. 5. A representation of the zones and approach for the lifeboat simulation task involving picking up a PIW.

4   Model Training - Case Study

This research serves as a pilot study for applying AISs in simulation-based lifeboat training, which requires a large sample of data to train and validate the developed Bayesian models. However, to show how the model should be trained, a small set of representative data (five trial runs of the scenario presented in Fig. 2) were collected using a lifeboat training simulator at Virtual Marine. The simulator log files associated with the five trials were imported into a Python script to extract the information needed for the classification of the variable states for the BNs presented in Fig. 3 and Fig. 4. The extracted data were compared against the sample defined criteria (Table 1) to identify the BN states (Tables 2 and 3) for all variables of the BN models in Fig. 3 and Fig. 4. The identified states presented in Tables 2 and Tables 3 were used as inputs to the developed BN models in GeNIe Modeler to train the models. The probability values were generated by running the trained BN models to represent the competence probabilities for the tasks in the scenario based on the evidence gathered for model training, which serves as a basis for predicting a new learner's competency. The evidence collected during the first attempt of a new learner's performance are entered into the BN models in Fig. 3 and Fig. 4 to generate probability estimations for the learner's competence in completing the tasks for a second attempt. For example, a probability of 25% indicates a low probability for the learner being able to complete the task, therefore the learner likely does not have the competence or proficiency in the task. On the contrary, a probability of 80% indicates the learner likely does have the competence. The probabilities generated through BNs can be used to assess the predictive accuracy of the developed models based on data that is collected, and diagnose the skill (or competence) of learners to inform a pedagogical model for providing adaptive training.

Table 1. The sample criteria used for the classification of the BN states for all variables in the launching and SSM BN models. The last three columns indicate the classification of the BN states, where Yes, Ok, and No, represent the desired, satisfactory, and undesired levels of the variables, respectively. The variables were classified into two or three states (e.g., low, high, short, long, correct, acceptable, and incorrect) based on a set of thresholds extracted from a scoring rubric. A description of the launching variables can be found in [4], and the SSM variables were detailed in Sect. 3 of this paper.

Subtasks	Variables	Classification of the BN States		
		YES	OK	NO
Pre-Launch	Critical_Errors_Count	Low	-	High
	Non_Critical_Errors_Count	Low	-	High
Launch	Permission_to_Launch	Done	-	Failed
	Inform_Crew_Before_Launch	Done	-	Failed
	Start_Engine	Done	-	Failed
	Lower_Without_Stopping	Done	-	Failed
	Activate_Air_and_Deluge	Done	-	Failed
	Hook_Release_Time	Short	-	Long
	Throttle_Engagement_Time	Short		Long
	Contact_with_Platform_Count	Low	-	High
	Clear_Away_Direction	Correct	-	Incorrect
	Clear_Distance_from_Platform	Long	-	Short

(*continued*)

Table 1. (*continued*)

Subtasks	Variables	YES	OK	NO
		Classification of the BN States		
	Tasks_Done_In_Order	Done	-	Failed
Pick-up PIW	Speed_PIW_P	Low	-	High
	Speed_PIW_Z1	Low	-	High
	Speed_PIW_Z2	Low	-	High
	Speed_PIW_Z3	Low	-	High
	Speed_PIW_Z4	Low	-	High
	Approach_PIW_P	Correct	Acceptable	Incorrect
	Approach_PIW_Z1	Correct	Acceptable	Incorrect
	Approach_PIW_Z2	Correct	Acceptable	Incorrect
	Approach_PIW_Z3	Correct	Acceptable	Incorrect
	Approach_PIW_Z4	Correct	Acceptable	Incorrect
	Stop_Time_PIW_P	Long	-	Short
	Proximity_PIW_P	Short	-	Long
Retrieve LR	Speed_LR_R	Low	-	High
	Speed_LR_Z1	Low	-	High
	Speed_LR_Z2	Low	-	High
	Speed_LR_Z3	Low	-	High
	Speed_LR_Z4	Low	-	High
	Approach_LR_R	Correct	Acceptable	Incorrect
	Approach_LR_Z1	Correct	Acceptable	Incorrect
	Approach_LR_Z2	Correct	Acceptable	Incorrect
	Approach_LR_Z3	Correct	Acceptable	Incorrect
	Approach_LR_Z4	Correct	Acceptable	Incorrect
	Stop_Time_LR_R	Long	-	Short
	Proximity_LR_R	Short	-	Long
Stop by OSV	Speed_OSV_C	Low	-	High
	Speed_OSV_Z1	Low	-	High
	Speed_OSV_Z2	Low	-	High

(*continued*)

Table 1. (*continued*)

Subtasks	Variables	Classification of the BN States		
		YES	OK	NO
	Speed_OSV_Z3	Low	-	High
	Speed_OSV_Z4	Low	-	High
	Approach_OSV_C	Correct	Acceptable	Incorrect
	Approach_OSV_Z1	Correct	Acceptable	Incorrect
	Approach_OSV_Z2	Correct	Acceptable	Incorrect
	Approach_OSV_Z3	Correct	Acceptable	Incorrect
	Approach_OSV_Z4	Correct	Acceptable	Incorrect
	Stop_Time_OSV_C	Long	-	Short
	Proximity_OSV_C	Short	-	Long
Deploy Sea Anchor	Speed_DSA	Low	-	High
	Heading_DSA	Correct	Acceptable	Incorrect
	Stop_Time_DSA	Short	-	Long

Table 2. The BN states of the variables in the launching BN model for five trial runs of the given scenario. The BN states Yes, Ok, and No were identified based on the defined criteria in Table 1 and represent the desired, satisfactory, and undesired levels of the variable, respectively. A description of the launching variables can be found in [4].

Variables	Trial 1	Trial 2	Trial 3	Trial 4	Trial 5
Critical_Errors_Count_1	Yes	Yes	Yes	Yes	Yes
Non_Critical_Errors_Count_1	Yes	Yes	Yes	Yes	Yes
Permission_to_Launch_1	Yes	Yes	Yes	Yes	Yes
Inform_Crew_Before_Launch_1	Yes	Yes	Yes	Yes	Yes
Start_Engine_1	Yes	Yes	Yes	Yes	Yes
Lower_Without_Stopping_1	No	Yes	No	Yes	No
Activate_Air_and_Deluge_1	Yes	Yes	No	Yes	Yes
Hook_Release_Time_1	No	Yes	-	Yes	No
Throttle_Engagement_Time_1	No	Yes	-	Yes	No
Contact_with_Platform_Count_1	Yes	No	-	Yes	Yes
Clear_Away_Direction_1	No	-	-	Yes	No
Clear_Distance_from_Platform_1	Yes	-	-	Yes	No

(*continued*)

Table 2. (*continued*)

Variables	Trial 1	Trial 2	Trial 3	Trial 4	Trial 5
Tasks_Done_In_Order_1	Yes	Yes	-	No	Yes
Critical_Errors_Count_2	Yes	Yes	Yes	Yes	Yes
Non_Critical_Errors_Count_2	Yes	Yes	Yes	Yes	Yes
Permission_to_Launch_2	Yes	Yes	Yes	Yes	Yes
Inform_Crew_Before_Launch_2	Yes	Yes	Yes	Yes	Yes
Start_Engine_2	Yes	Yes	Yes	Yes	Yes
Lower_Without_Stopping_2	Yes	Yes	Yes	Yes	Yes
Activate_Air_and_Deluge_2	Yes	Yes	Yes	Yes	Yes
Hook_Release_Time_2	Yes	No	No	Yes	No
Throttle_Engagement_Time_2	Yes	No	No	Yes	No
Contact_with_Platform_Count_2	Yes	Yes	No	Yes	Yes
Clear_Away_Direction_2	Yes	No	-	Yes	Yes
Clear_Distance_from_Platform_2	Yes	Yes	-	Yes	No
Tasks_Done_In_Order_2	Yes	Yes	Yes	Yes	No

Table 3. The BN states of the variables in the SSM BN model for five trial runs of the given scenario. The BN states Yes, Ok, and No were identified based on the defined criteria in Table 1 and represent the desired, satisfactory, and undesired levels of the variable, respectively. A description of the launching variables can be found in Sect. 3.

Variables	Trial 1	Trial 2	Trial 3	Trial 4	Trial 5
Speed_PIW_1P	Yes	Yes	No	Yes	Yes
Speed_PIW_1Z1	Yes	No	Yes	Yes	Yes
Speed_PIW_1Z2	Yes	No	Yes	No	Yes
Speed_PIW_1Z3	Yes	No	No	Yes	Yes
Speed_PIW_1Z4	Yes	No	No	Yes	No
Approach_PIW_1P	Yes	Ok	Ok	Yes	No
Approach_PIW_1Z1	Yes	No	Ok	Yes	Yes
Approach_PIW_1Z2	Yes	No	Ok	No	No
Approach_PIW_1Z3	Yes	Ok	No	Ok	No
Approach_PIW_1Z4	Ok	No	No	Ok	No
Stop_time_PIW_1P	Yes	Yes	Yes	No	Yes
Proximity_PIW_1P	Yes	Yes	Yes	Yes	Yes

(*continued*)

Table 3. (*continued*)

Variables	Trial 1	Trial 2	Trial 3	Trial 4	Trial 5
Speed_LR_1R	Yes	Yes	Yes	Yes	Yes
Speed_LR_1Z1	Yes	Yes	Yes	Yes	No
Speed_LR_1Z2	No	Yes	Yes	Yes	No
Speed_LR_1Z3	No	Yes	Yes	No	No
Speed_LR_1Z4	No	No	Yes	Yes	No
Approach_LR_1R	Yes	Yes	No	Ok	No
Approach_LR_1Z1	Yes	No	Yes	Ok	No
Approach_LR_1Z2	Yes	No	No	Ok	Yes
Approach_LR_1Z3	No	Ok	No	No	Yes
Approach_LR_1Z4	No	Ok	No	No	No
Stop_Time_LR_1R	Yes	Yes	Yes	No	Yes
Proximity_LR_1R	Yes	Yes	Yes	No	Yes
Speed_OSV_1C	Yes	Yes	No	Yes	No
Speed_OSV_1Z1	No	Yes	No	Yes	No
Speed_OSV_1Z2	Yes	Yes	No	Yes	No
Speed_OSV_1Z3	Yes	Yes	No	No	No
Speed_OSV_1Z4	No	Yes	Yes	No	No
Approach_OSV_1C	Yes	Ok	Ok	Yes	Ok
Approach_OSV_1Z1	Yes	Yes	Ok	Yes	Yes
Approach_OSV_1Z2	Yes	Ok	Ok	Yes	Yes
Approach_OSV_1Z3	Ok	Ok	Yes	Yes	Ok
Approach_OSV_1Z4	Yes	Yes	Ok	Ok	Ok
Stop_Time_OSV_1C	Yes	Yes	Yes	No	Yes
Proximity_OSV_1C	Yes	Yes	No	No	Yes
Speed_DSA_1	Yes	Yes	No	Yes	Yes
Heading_DSA_1	Yes	No	No	No	Yes
Stop_Time_DSA_1	Yes	Yes	No	Yes	Yes
Speed_PIW_2P	Yes	Yes	Yes	Yes	Yes
Speed_PIW_2Z1	Yes	Yes	Yes	Yes	Yes
Speed_PIW_2Z2	Yes	Yes	Yes	No	Yes
Speed_PIW_2Z3	Yes	No	No	No	Yes
Speed_PIW_2Z4	Yes	No	No	No	No

(*continued*)

Table 3. (*continued*)

Variables	Trial 1	Trial 2	Trial 3	Trial 4	Trial 5
Approach_PIW_2P	Yes	Ok	Yes	Yes	Ok
Approach_PIW_2Z1	Yes	No	Yes	Yes	Yes
Approach_PIW_2Z2	Yes	No	Ok	Ok	Yes
Approach_PIW_2Z3	Yes	Ok	Ok	Ok	No
Approach_PIW_2Z4	Yes	No	Ok	Ok	No
Stop_time_PIW_2P	Yes	Yes	Yes	Yes	Yes
Proximity_PIW_2P	Yes	Yes	Yes	Yes	Yes
Speed_LR_2R	Yes	Yes	Yes	Yes	Yes
Speed_LR_2Z1	Yes	Yes	Yes	Yes	Yes
Speed_LR_2Z2	No	Yes	Yes	Yes	Yes
Speed_LR_2Z3	Yes	Yes	No	No	No
Speed_LR_2Z4	No	Yes	Yes	No	No
Approach_LR_2R	Yes	Yes	No	Yes	Ok
Approach_LR_2Z1	Yes	Ok	Yes	Ok	No
Approach_LR_2Z2	Yes	Ok	Yes	Ok	Yes
Approach_LR_2Z3	No	Ok	Ok	No	Yes
Approach_LR_2Z4	No	Ok	No	No	Ok
Stop_Time_LR_2R	Yes	Yes	Yes	Yes	Yes
Proximity_LR_2R	Yes	Yes	Yes	Yes	Yes
Speed_OSV_2C	Yes	Yes	Yes	Yes	No
Speed_OSV_2Z1	Yes	Yes	No	Yes	Yes
Speed_OSV_2Z2	Yes	Yes	Yes	Yes	No
Speed_OSV_2Z3	Yes	Yes	Yes	No	No
Speed_OSV_2Z4	No	Yes	Yes	Yes	No
Approach_OSV_2C	Yes	Ok	Ok	Yes	Yes
Approach_OSV_2Z1	Yes	Yes	Yes	Yes	Yes
Approach_OSV_2Z2	Yes	Ok	Ok	Yes	Ok
Approach_OSV_2Z3	Ok	Ok	Yes	Yes	Yes
Approach_OSV_2Z4	Yes	Yes	Ok	Ok	Yes
Stop_Time_OSV_2C	Yes	Yes	Yes	Yes	Yes
Proximity_OSV_2C	Yes	Yes	Yes	Yes	Yes

(*continued*)

Table 3. (*continued*)

Variables	Trial 1	Trial 2	Trial 3	Trial 4	Trial 5
Speed_DSA_2	Yes	Yes	Yes	Yes	Yes
Heading_DSA_2	Yes	No	Yes	No	Yes
Stop_Time_DSA_2	Yes	Yes	Yes	Yes	Yes

5 Conclusions

This study aimed to provide a BN approach to a learner model that can be used to apply AISs to simulation-based lifeboat training. The BN models developed in this study allow for transparent measurement of the learners' behaviors at different granularity levels and have the ability to identify the set of behaviors and skills that lead to the highest likelihood of successfully completing the tasks during simulation-based lifeboat training. The presented learner model can capture behavioral evidence that indicates whether the learner has the competence. The learner model presented here forms a detailed model of competence for lifeboat operators based on evidence-based task measures. As more data from simulation-based assessments becomes available, this learner model can be used to build statistical models of performance. The learner model can be applied to diagnose competence in learners, which can be used to inform a pedagogical model that can tailor instructions and adapt training accordingly. The results of the probabilistic BN models presented here can be integrated with machine learning algorithms (e.g., decision trees) and instructor feedback [22] to develop AISs that can customize training to the learners' needs during simulation-based lifeboat training. This study provides an important step towards automating instructor guidance, assessment and feedback for simulation-based lifeboat training. The successful employment of an AIS in simulation-based lifeboat training enables empirical testing of the hypothesis that using the optimized scenarios and tailored instructions from an AIS increase learner skill acquisition related to lifeboat operations, as well as the training efficiency. Such benefits have the potential to increase seafarers' competence, speed the time to competence, reduce the cognitive load on instructors, and result in a cost reduction of training scenario development.

5.1 Future Work

Future studies will analyze the developed BN models to structure learner models of novice and expert performance that can be linked into an AIS for simulation-based lifeboat training. Future work will implement, validate, and improve the learner model based on experimental studies and data from simulation-based assessments. This research is part of a larger study that aims to build on the learner model presented in this paper to develop a pedagogical model that takes inputs from the developed learner model and suggests the appropriate course of action based on skill levels identified by the learner model. The addition of an intelligent pedagogical model to simulation-based lifeboat training can provide an AIS that can adjust instructional pace, provide corrective (or packaged) feedback, and tailor practice scenarios to the learners' skill levels (Fig. 6).

The AIS will iteratively evaluate learners' competencies for providing tailored instructions and feedback until they represent skill mastery (Fig. 6). The approach presented in this study can also be used towards building adaptive instructional systems for other maritime safety simulation-based training environments, which could provide intelligent and more efficient systems for simulation-based training of seafarers.

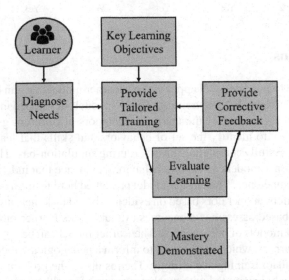

Fig. 6. Adaptive training flowchart for simulation-based lifeboat training.

Acknowledgement. This project was supported in part by collaborative research funding from the National Research Council of Canada's Artificial Intelligence for Logistics Program.

References

1. Bell, B., Bennett, W.W., Nye, B., Kelsey, E.: Helping instructor pilots detect and respond to engagement lapses in simulations. In: Sottilare, R.A., Schwarz, J. (eds.) HCII 2021. LNCS, vol. 12793, pp. 3–14. Springer, Cham (2021). https://doi.org/10.1007/978-3-030-77873-6_1
2. Billard, R., Musharraf, M., Veitch, B., Smith, J.: Using Bayesian methods and simulator data to model lifeboat coxswain performance. WMU J. Marit. Aff. **19**(3), 295–312 (2020). https://doi.org/10.1007/s13437-020-00204-0
3. Billard, R., Smith, J., Masharraf, M., Veitch, B.: Using Bayesian networks to model competence of lifeboat coxswains. TransNav Int. J. Mar. Navig. Saf. Sea Transp. **14**, 585–594 (2020)
4. Billard, R., Smith, J., Veitch, B.: Assessing lifeboat coxswain training alternatives using a simulator. J. Navig. **73**(2), 455–470 (2019)
5. Billard, R., Smith, J.: Using simulation to assess performance in emergency lifeboat launches. In: Proceedings of Interservice/Industry Training, Simulation, and Education Conference, Paper No. 18179. Orlando, FL, United States (2018)

6. Dunagan, L., Larson, D.A.: Alignment of competency-based learning and assessment to adaptive instructional systems. In: Sottilare, R.A., Schwarz, J. (eds.) HCII 2021. LNCS, vol. 12792, pp. 537–549. Springer, Cham (2021). https://doi.org/10.1007/978-3-030-77857-6_38

7. Emond, B., et al.: Development of AIS using simulated learners, Bayesian networks and knowledge elicitation methods. In: Sottilare, R.A., Schwarz, J. (eds.) Adaptive Instructional Systems (HCII 2022). LNCS, pp. 143–158. Springer, Cham (2022). https://doi.org/10.1007/978-3-031-05887-5_11

8. Emond, B.: Formal methods in human-computer interaction and adaptive instructional systems. In: Sottilare, R.A., Schwarz, J. (eds.) HCII 2021. LNCS, vol. 12792, pp. 183–198. Springer, Cham (2021). https://doi.org/10.1007/978-3-030-77857-6_12

9. Emond, B.: Learning traces, measurement and assessment templates for AIS interoperability. In: Sottilare, R.A., Schwarz, J. (eds.) HCII 2020. LNCS, vol. 12214, pp. 71–87. Springer, Cham (2020). https://doi.org/10.1007/978-3-030-50788-6_6

10. Ghadirli, H.M., Rastgarpour, M.: A web-based adaptive and intelligent tutor by expert systems. In: Meghanathan, N., Nagamalai, D., Chaki, N. (eds.) Advances in Computing and Information Technology. AISC, vol. 177, pp. 87–95. Springer, Heidelberg (2013). https://doi.org/10.1007/978-3-642-31552-7_10

11. Goenka, N., Choudhury, T., Ahuja, N.J.: Enhancing number sense of dyscalculia learners by pedagogical agents: a review. Emerg. Technol. Data Min. Inf. Secur. **1286**, 827–839 (2021)

12. Guo, L., Wang, D., Gu, F., Li, Y., Wang, Y., Zhou, R.: Evolution and trends in intelligent tutoring systems research: a multidisciplinary and scientometric view. Asia Pac. Educ. Rev. **22**(3), 441–461 (2021). https://doi.org/10.1007/s12564-021-09697-7

13. Kabudi, T., Pappas, I., Olsen, D.H.: AI-enabled adaptive learning systems: a systematic mapping of the literature. Comput. Educ. Artif. Intell. **2**, 1–12 (2021)

14. Luckin, R., Holmes, W., Griffiths, M., Forcier, L.B.: Intelligence Unleashed: An Argument for AI in Education. Pearson Education, London (2016)

15. Mislevy, R.J., Almond, R.G., Lukas, J.F.: A brief introduction to evidence-centered design. CSE Report 632, US Department of Education (2004)

16. Mousavinasab, E., Zarifsanaiey, N.R., Niakan Kalhori, S., Rakhshan, M., Keikha, L., Ghazi Saeedi, M.: Intelligent tutoring systems: a systematic review of characteristics, applications, and evaluation methods. Interact. Learn. Environ. **29**(1), 142–163 (2018)

17. Pan, J., Wang, L., Shubeck, K., Hu, X.: A generic CbITS authoring tool using xAPI. In: Sottilare, R.A., Schwarz, J. (eds.) HCII 2021. LNCS, vol. 12792, pp. 243–253. Springer, Cham (2021). https://doi.org/10.1007/978-3-030-77857-6_16

18. Pantelimon, F.V., Bologa, R., Toma, A., Posedaru, B.S.: The evolution of AI-driven educational systems during the Covid-19 pandemic. Sustainability **13**(23), 13501 (2021)

19. Pavlik, P., Brawner, K., Olney, A., Mitrovic, A.: A review of learner models used in intelligent tutoring systems. In: Design Recommendations for Intelligent Tutoring Systems - Learner Modeling, vol. 1, pp. 39–68. Orlando, FL, United States (2013)

20. Santos, G.S., Jorge, J.: Interoperable intelligent tutoring systems as open educational resources. IEEE Trans. Learn. Technol. **6**(3), 271–282 (2013)

21. Siu, K.C., Best, B.J., Kim, J.W., Oleynikov, D., Ritter, F.E.: Adaptive virtual reality training to optimize military medical skills acquisition and retention. Mil. Med. **181**(5), 214–220 (2016)

22. Smith, J., Zeinali-Torbati, R., Billard, R., Emond, B., Veitch, B.: Developing an adaptive instructional system for simulation-based lifeboat training using instructor feedback. In: 14th International Conference on Applied Human Factors and Ergonomics (AHFE). San Francisco, CA, USA (2023)

23. Sottilare, R.A., Graesser, A.C., Hu, X., Sinatra, A.M.: Introduction to team tutoring and GIFT. Des. Recom. Intell. Tutor. Syst. **6**, 1–15 (2018)

24. Sottilare, R.A.: A comprehensive review of design goals and emerging solutions for adaptive instructional systems. Technol. Instr. Cogn. Learn. **11**(1), 5–38 (2018)

25. Sottilare, R.A.: Applying adaptive instruction to enhance learning in non-adaptive virtual training environments. In: Bagnara, S., Tartaglia, R., Albolino, S., Alexander, T., Fujita, Y. (eds.) IEA 2018. AISC, vol. 822, pp. 155–162. Springer, Cham (2019). https://doi.org/10.1007/978-3-319-96077-7_16

26. Sottilare, R., Brawner, K.: Exploring standardization opportunities by examining interaction between common adaptive instructional system components. In: Proceedings of the 1st Adaptive Instructional Systems (AIS) Standards Workshop, US Army Research Laboratory, Orlando, FL, United States (2018)

27. Sottilare, R.: Exploring methods to promote interoperability in adaptive instructional systems. In: Sottilare, R.A., Schwarz, J. (eds.) HCII 2019. LNCS, vol. 11597, pp. 227–238. Springer, Cham (2019). https://doi.org/10.1007/978-3-030-22341-0_19

28. Verdú, E., et al.: Intelligent tutoring interface for technology enhanced learning in a course of computer network design. In: 2014 IEEE Frontiers in Education Conference Proceedings, pp. 1–7. IEEE, Madrid, Spain (2014)

29. Witte, T.E.F., Schmettow, M., Groenier, M.: Diagnostic requirements for efficient, adaptive robotic surgery training. In: Sottilare, R.A., Schwarz, J. (eds.) HCII 2019. LNCS, vol. 11597, pp. 469–481. Springer, Cham (2019). https://doi.org/10.1007/978-3-030-22341-0_37

Author Index

R. A. Sottilare and J. Schwarz (Eds.): HCII 2023, LNCS 14044, pp. 353–354, 2023.
https://doi.org/10.1007/978-3-031-34735-1

Printed in the United States
by Baker & Taylor Publisher Services